Love Me,
Love Me Not

10

IO SAKISAKA

Contents

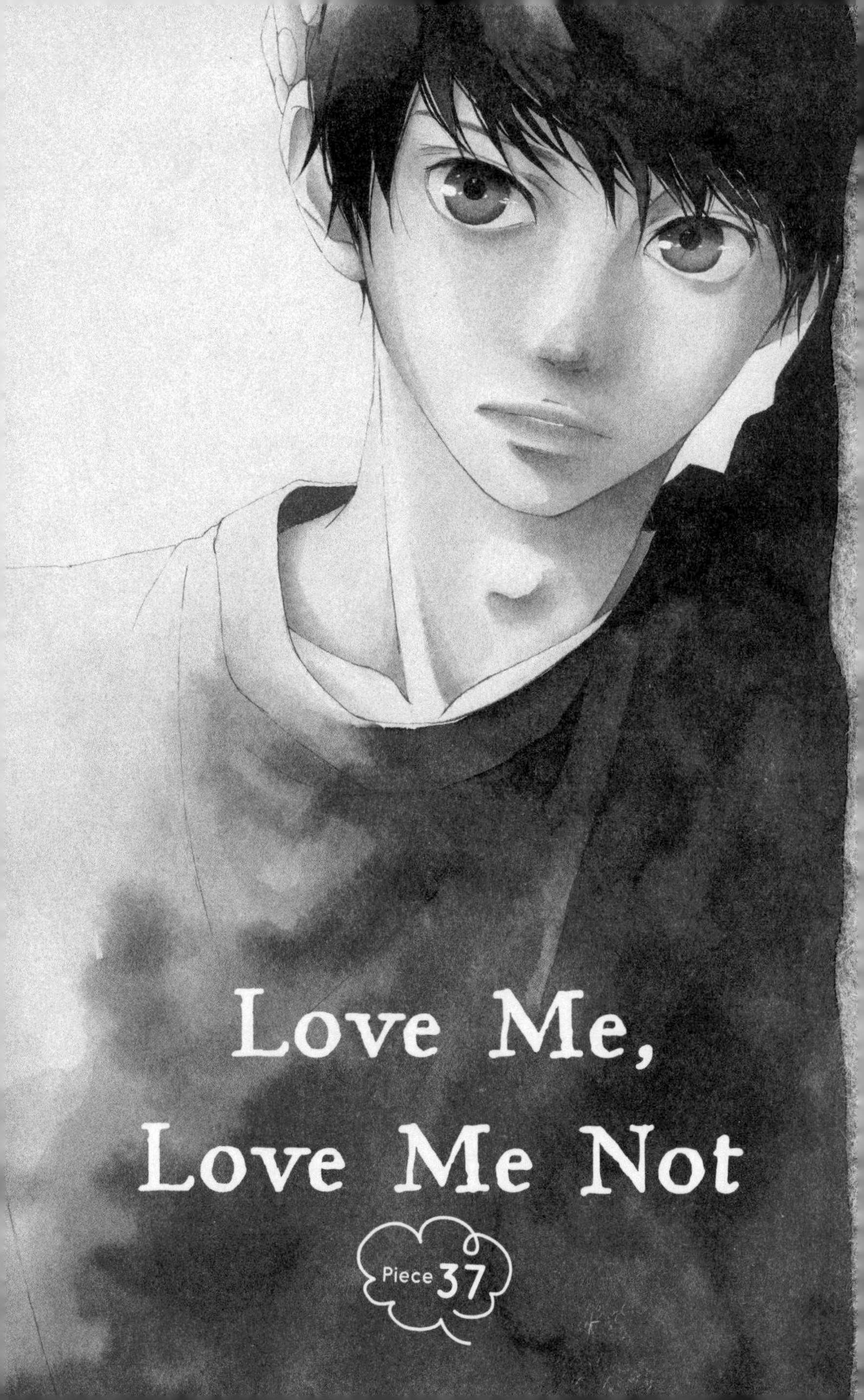
Love Me,
Love Me Not
Piece 37

GREETINGS

Hello, I'm Io Sakisaka. Thank you very much for picking up volume 10 of *Love Me, Love Me Not*.

Thanks to you, *Love Me, Love Me Not* has made it to volume 10! I've had a hard time keeping to a certain number of pages for each chapter because I have so many things I want to share, and I want to carefully portray the emotions of all the characters. Somehow I manage to crystallize my ideas on to the pages every month, and these crystals stack up and turn into volumes. To think that these crystals have become ten volumes is very moving. And it is all thanks to people like you who collect them. Thank you so much for discovering this series. I plan to continue writing carefully crafted stories that will stay with you. I look forward to your support. Please stay with me through the end of *Love Me, Love Me Not* volume 10.

Io Sakisaka

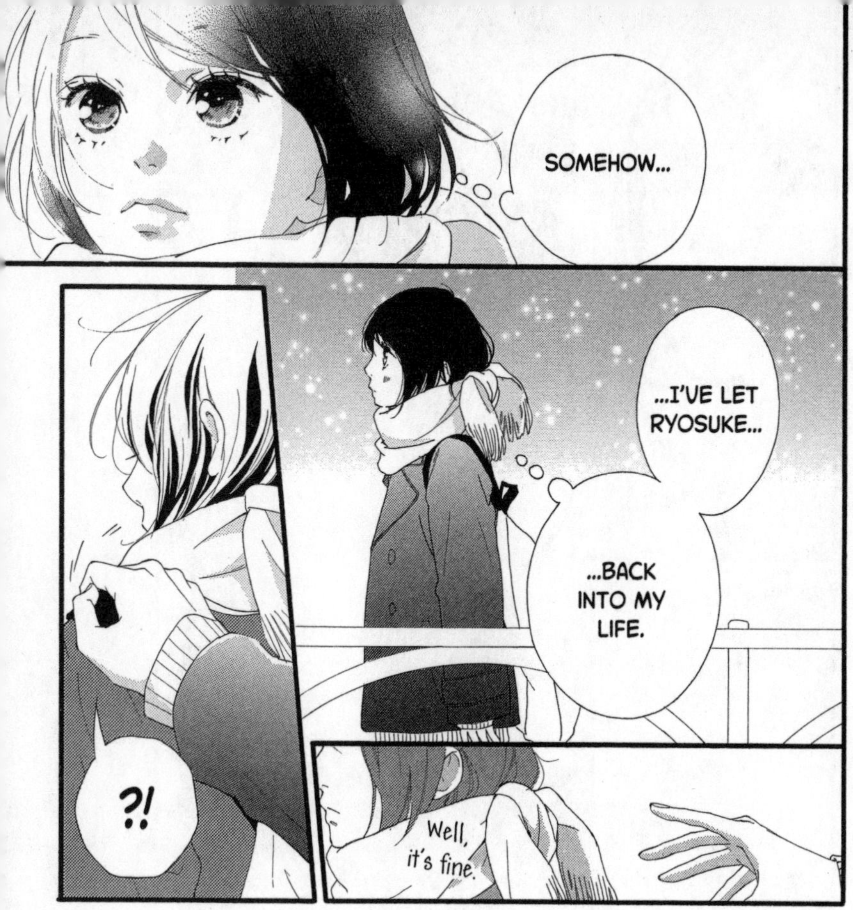
SOMEHOW...
...I'VE LET RYOSUKE...
...BACK INTO MY LIFE.
Well, it's fine.
?!

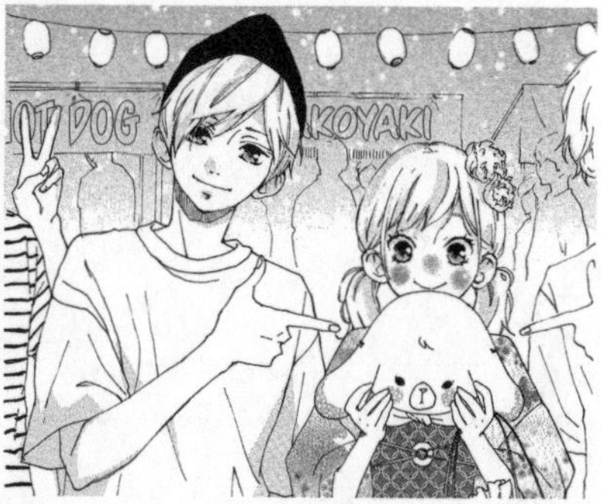

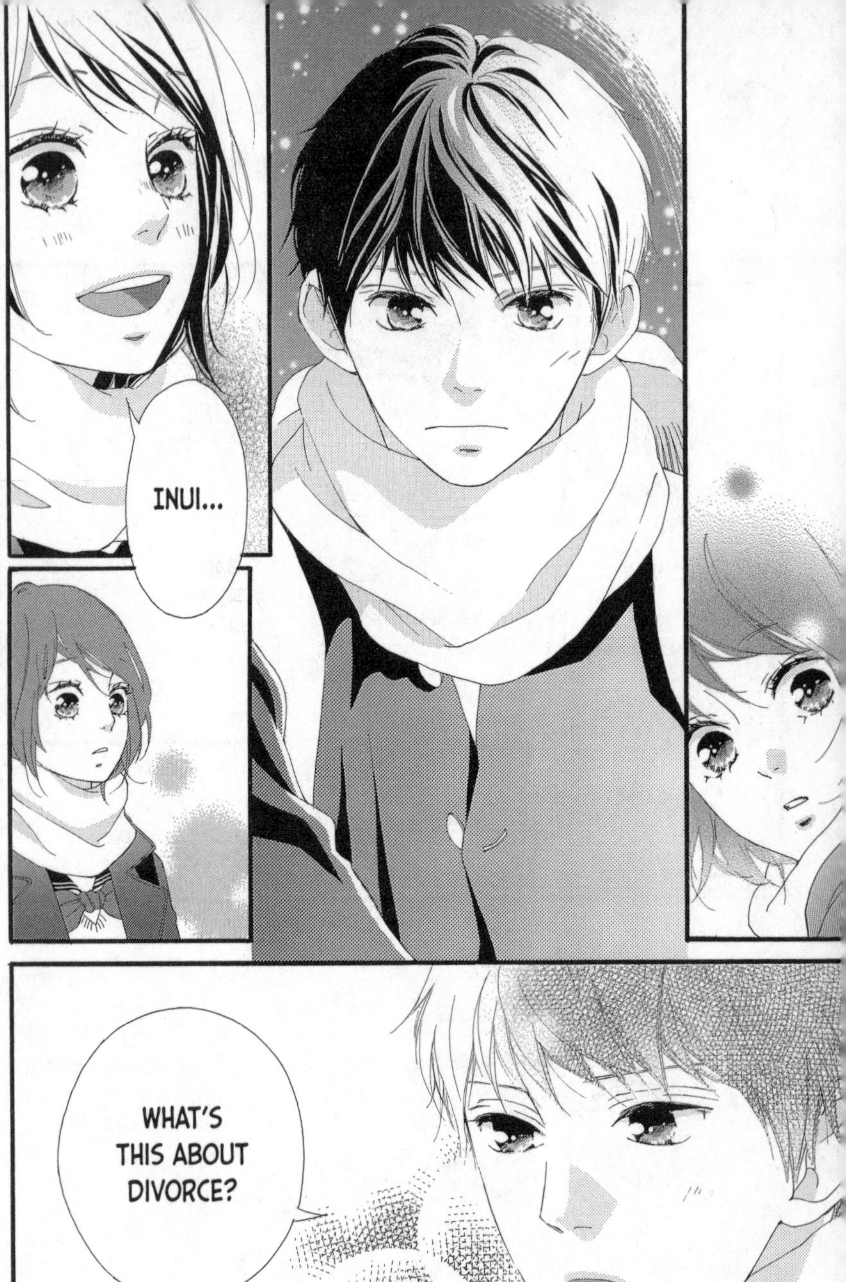
INUI...
WHAT'S THIS ABOUT DIVORCE?

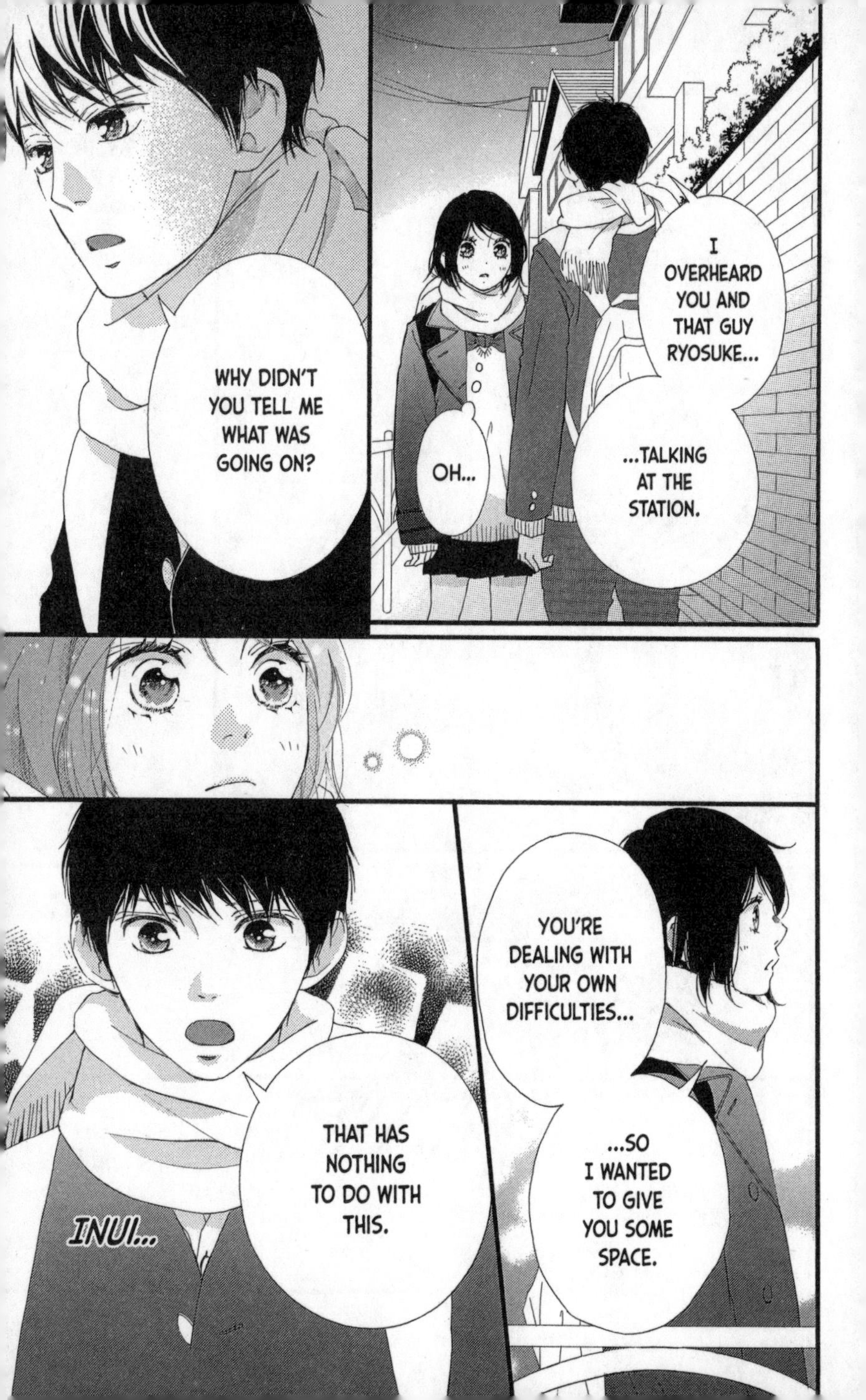
I OVERHEARD YOU AND THAT GUY RYOSUKE...
...TALKING AT THE STATION.
OH...
WHY DIDN'T YOU TELL ME WHAT WAS GOING ON?
YOU'RE DEALING WITH YOUR OWN DIFFICULTIES...
...SO I WANTED TO GIVE YOU SOME SPACE.
THAT HAS NOTHING TO DO WITH THIS.
INUI...

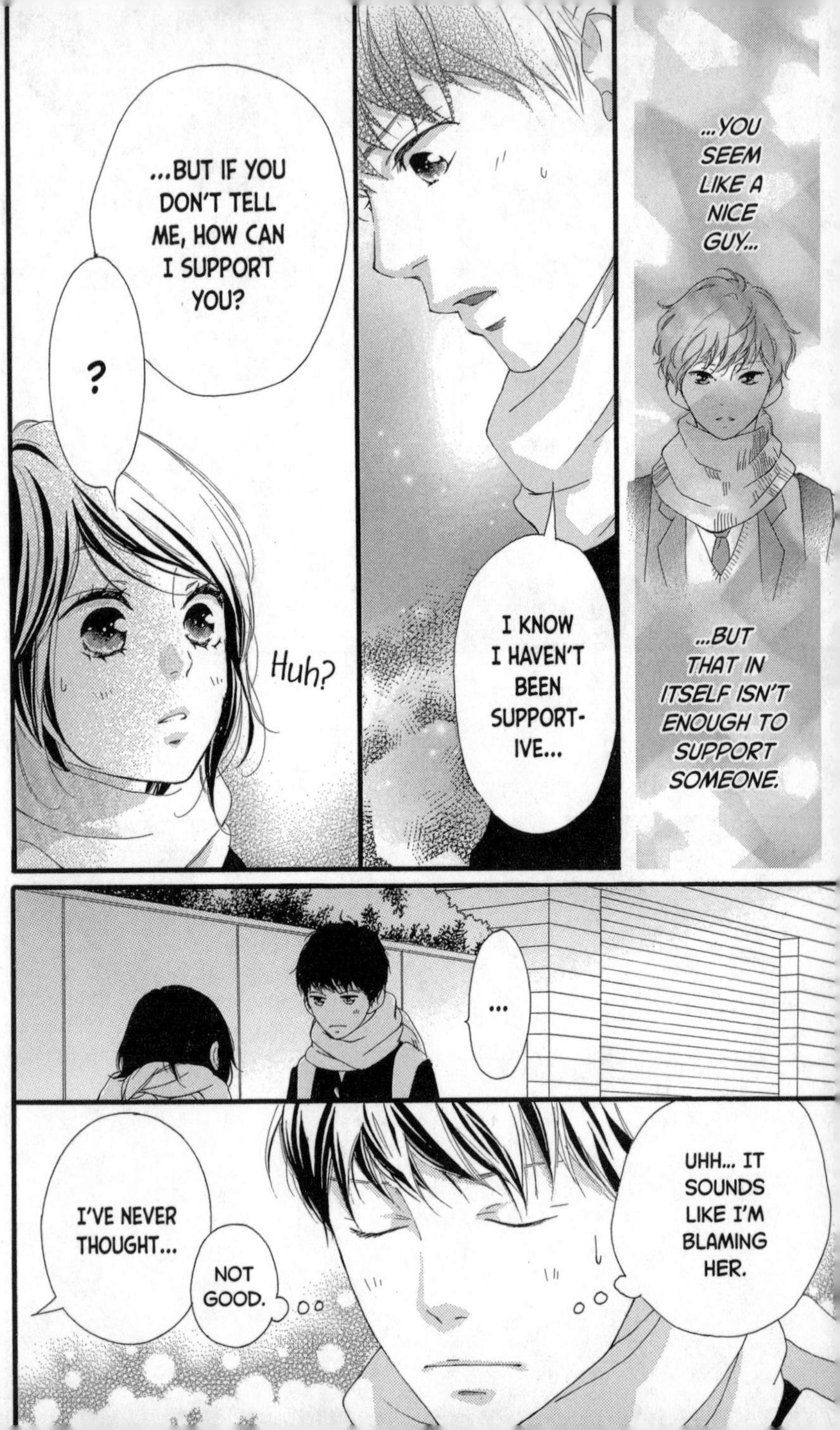
...YOU SEEM LIKE A NICE GUY...
...BUT THAT IN ITSELF ISN'T ENOUGH TO SUPPORT SOMEONE.
I KNOW I HAVEN'T BEEN SUPPORT-IVE...
...BUT IF YOU DON'T TELL ME, HOW CAN I SUPPORT YOU?
?
Huh?
...
UHH... IT SOUNDS LIKE I'M BLAMING HER.
NOT GOOD.
I'VE NEVER THOUGHT...

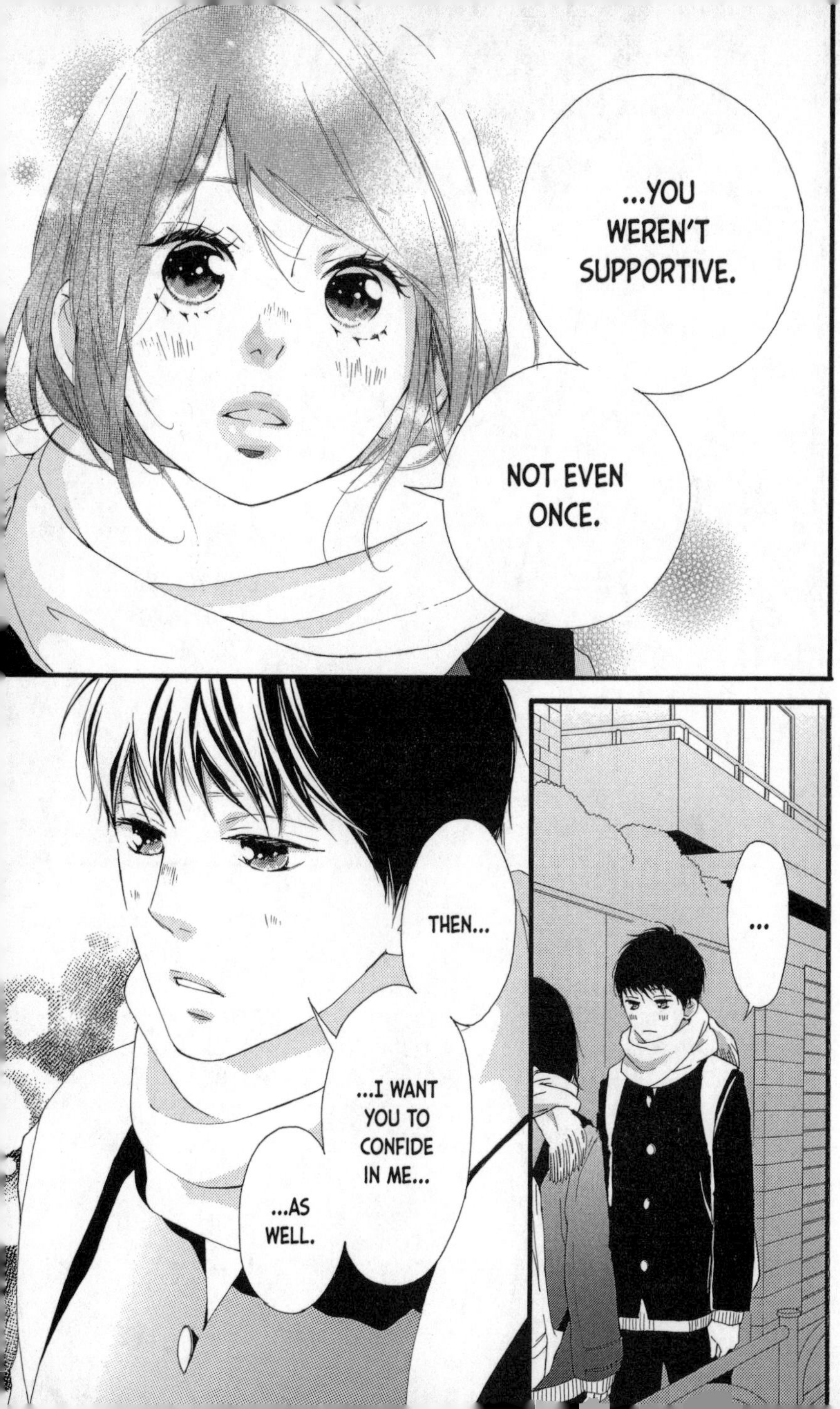
...YOU WEREN'T SUPPORTIVE.
NOT EVEN ONCE.
...
THEN...
...I WANT YOU TO CONFIDE IN ME...
...AS WELL.

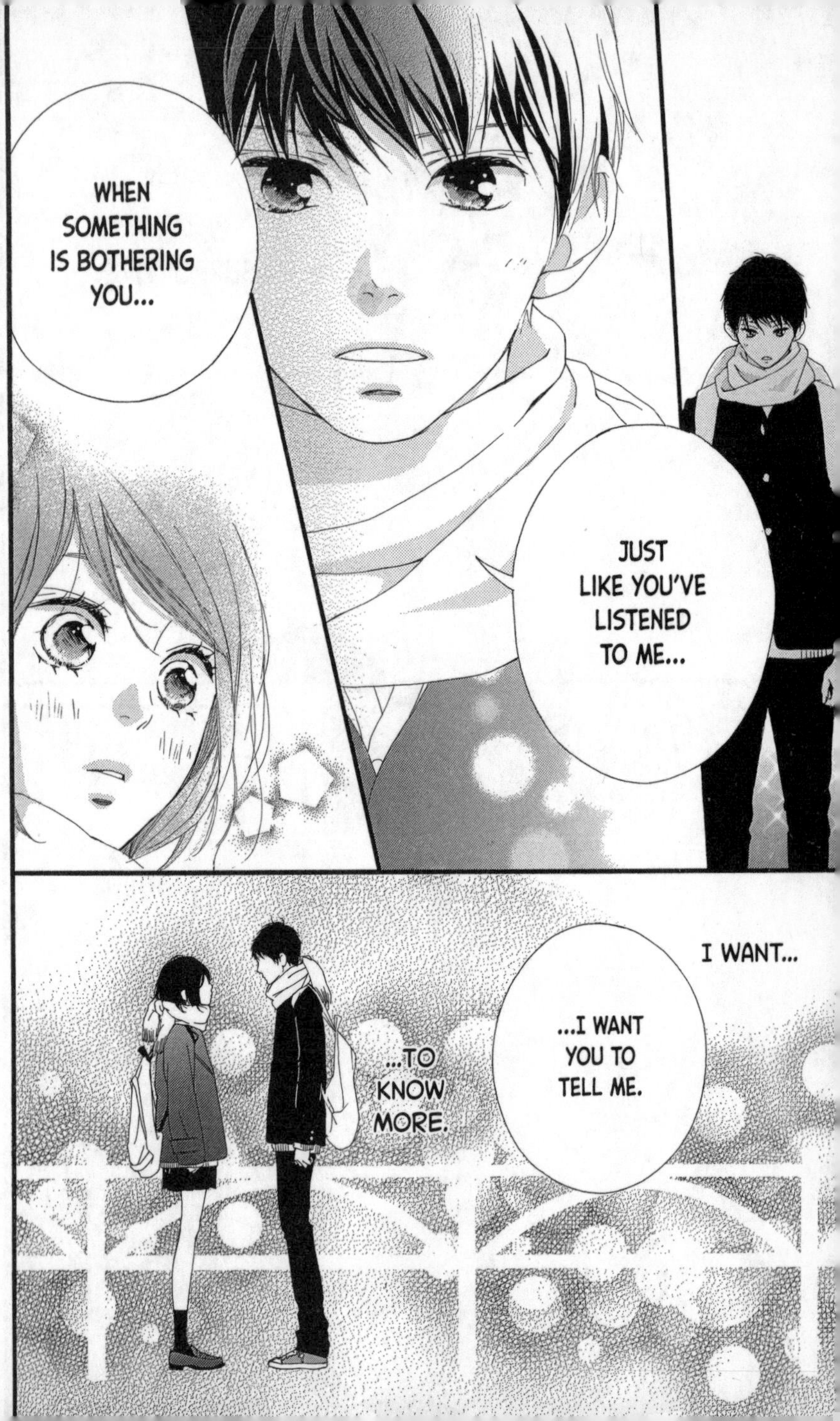
JUST LIKE YOU'VE LISTENED TO ME...
WHEN SOMETHING IS BOTHERING YOU...
I WANT...
...I WANT YOU TO TELL ME.
...TO KNOW MORE.

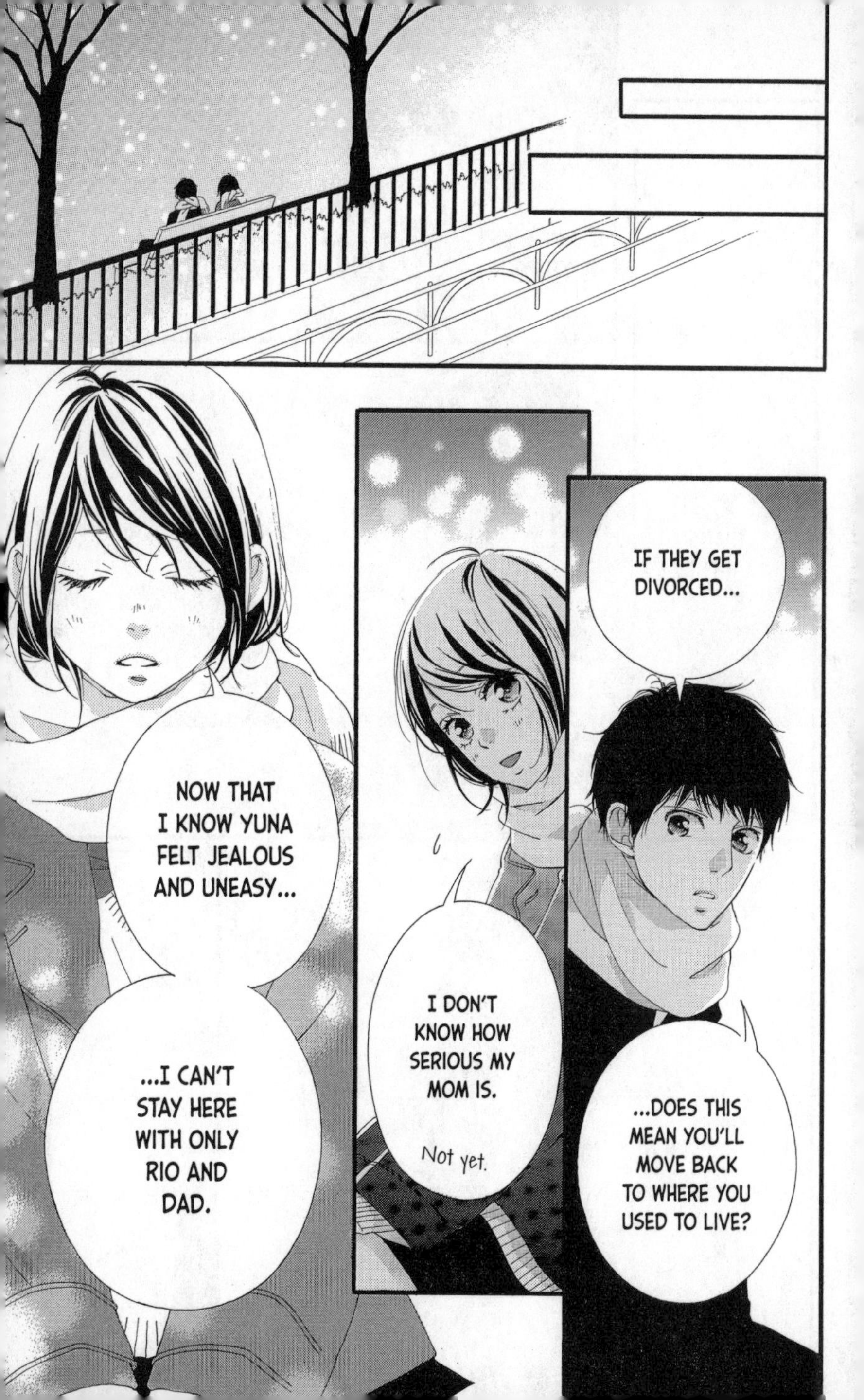
IF THEY GET DIVORCED...
...DOES THIS MEAN YOU'LL MOVE BACK TO WHERE YOU USED TO LIVE?
I DON'T KNOW HOW SERIOUS MY MOM IS.
Not yet.
NOW THAT I KNOW YUNA FELT JEALOUS AND UNEASY...
...I CAN'T STAY HERE WITH ONLY RIO AND DAD.

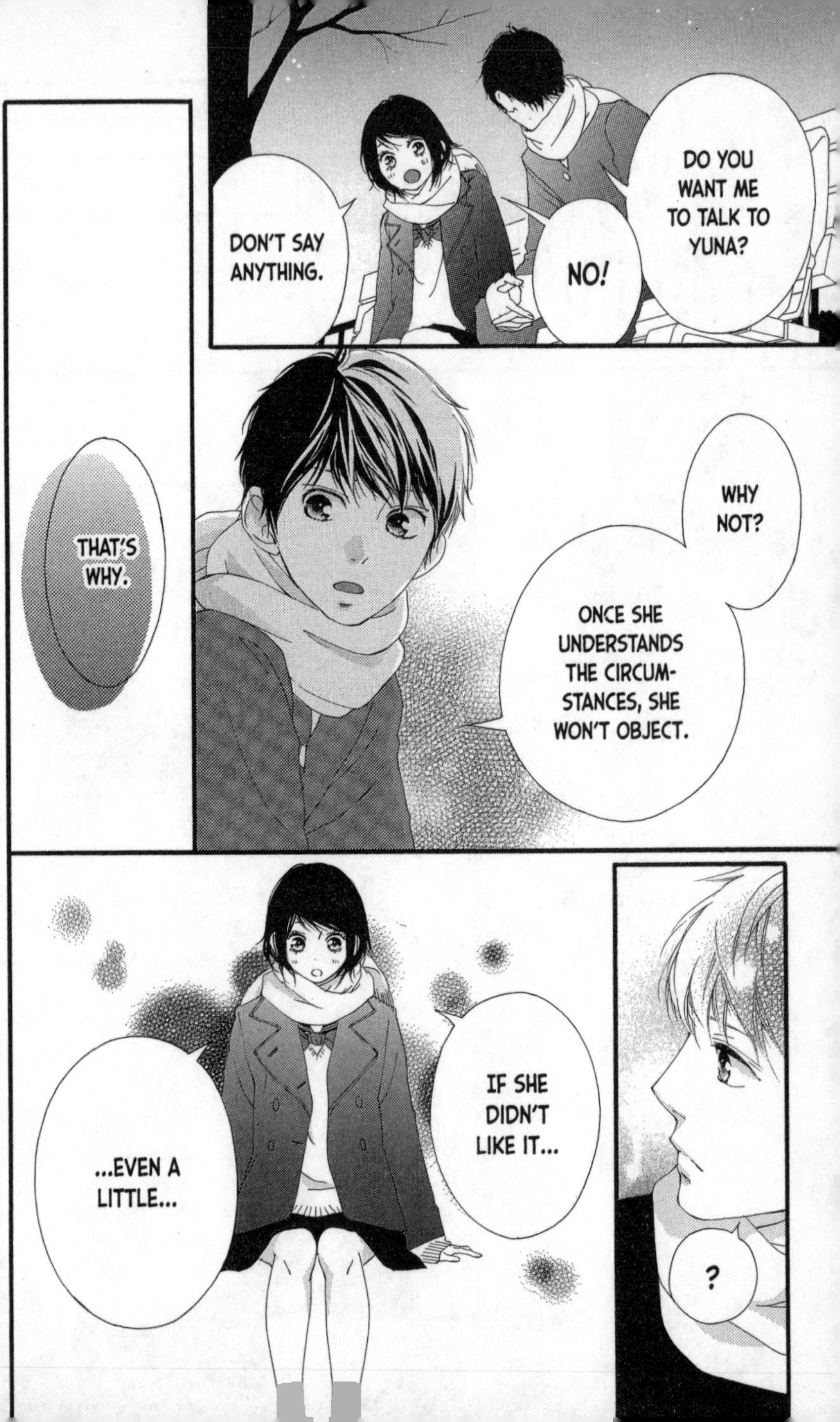
DO YOU WANT ME TO TALK TO YUNA?
NO!
DON'T SAY ANYTHING.
WHY NOT?
ONCE SHE UNDERSTANDS THE CIRCUM-STANCES, SHE WON'T OBJECT.
THAT'S WHY.
?
IF SHE DIDN'T LIKE IT...
...EVEN A LITTLE...

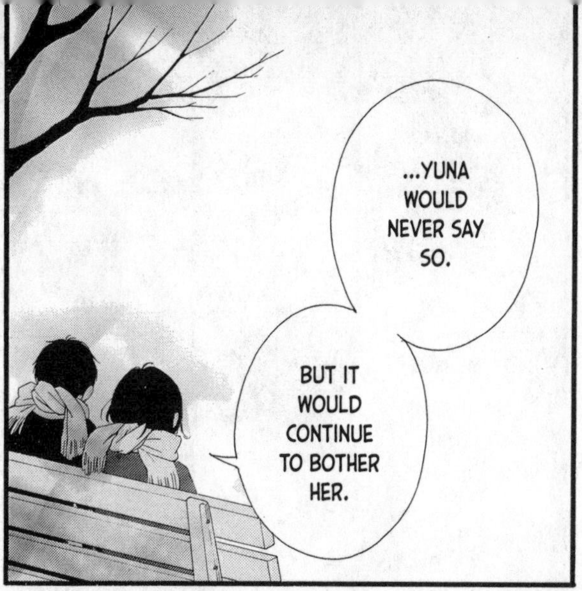
...YUNA WOULD NEVER SAY SO.
BUT IT WOULD CONTINUE TO BOTHER HER.

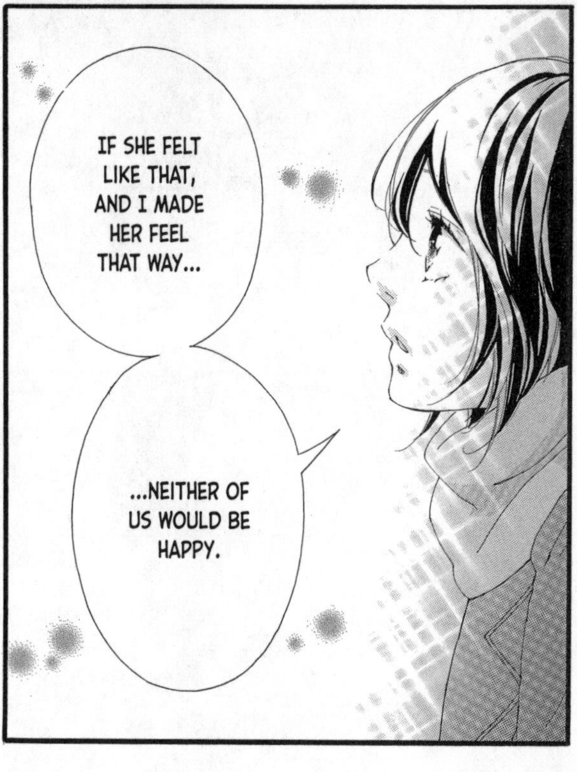
IF SHE FELT LIKE THAT, AND I MADE HER FEEL THAT WAY...
...NEITHER OF US WOULD BE HAPPY.

When I draw color pages, I usually use color ink. I wash my brushes in plastic cups that were gelatin containers. I've used them since I was first asked for color pages and went to buy supplies. I don't remember if I forgot to buy the brush cleaner, but I've been using those plastic cups from the very beginning. There was a point when I thought they looked a little sad, so I went out and purchased a brush cleaner. I used it once, but the gelatin cups were so much easier to wash that I immediately went back to them. But, when they did a photo shoot about me creating color pages, I was embarrassed about the plastic cups, so I used something else. I upgraded them to glass jam jars.

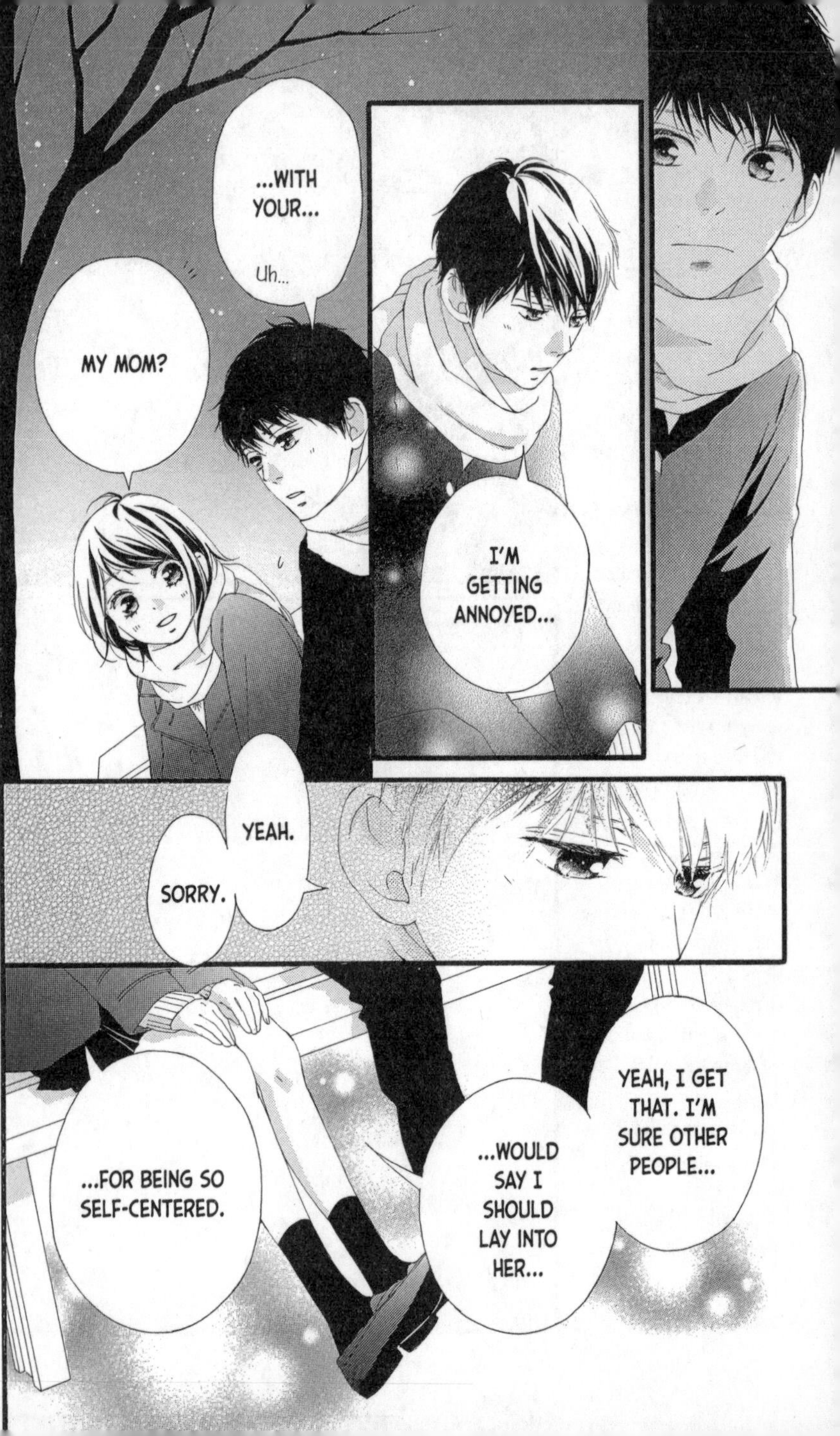
I'M GETTING ANNOYED...
...WITH YOUR...
Uh...
MY MOM?
YEAH.
SORRY.
YEAH, I GET THAT. I'M SURE OTHER PEOPLE...
...WOULD SAY I SHOULD LAY INTO HER...
...FOR BEING SO SELF-CENTERED.

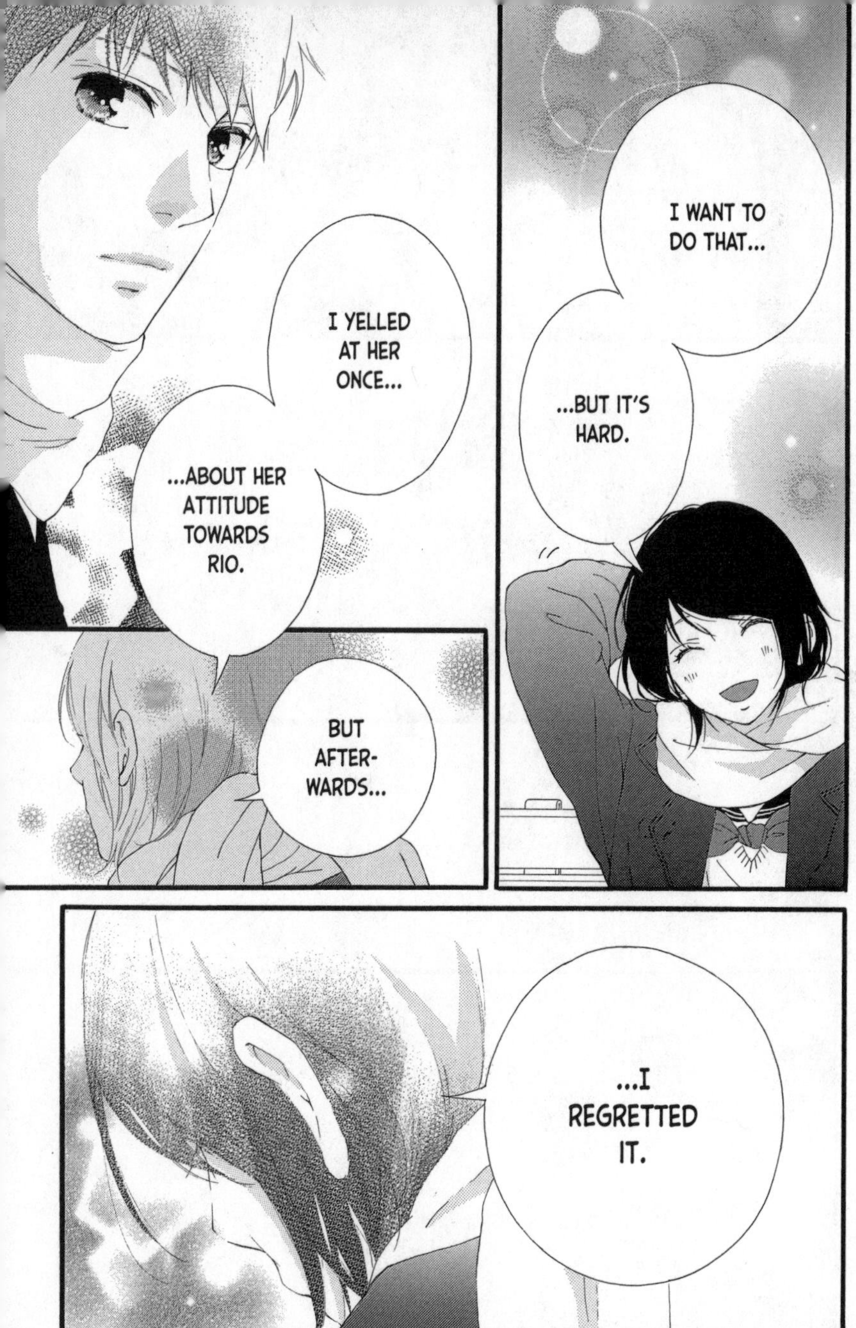
I WANT TO DO THAT...
...BUT IT'S HARD.
I YELLED AT HER ONCE...
...ABOUT HER ATTITUDE TOWARDS RIO.
BUT AFTER-WARDS...
...I REGRETTED IT.

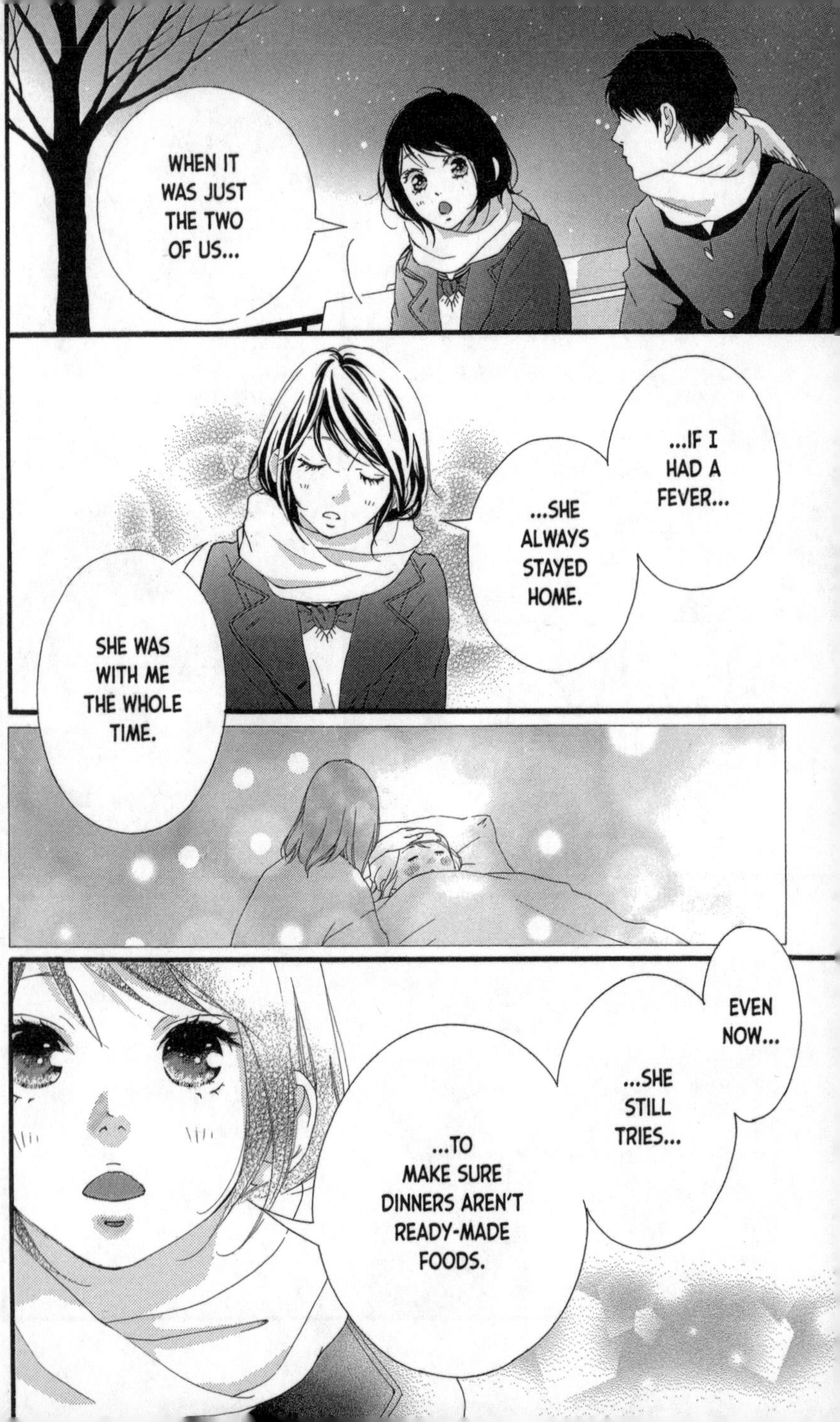
WHEN IT WAS JUST THE TWO OF US...
...IF I HAD A FEVER...
...SHE ALWAYS STAYED HOME.
SHE WAS WITH ME THE WHOLE TIME.
EVEN NOW...
...SHE STILL TRIES...
...TO MAKE SURE DINNERS AREN'T READY-MADE FOODS.

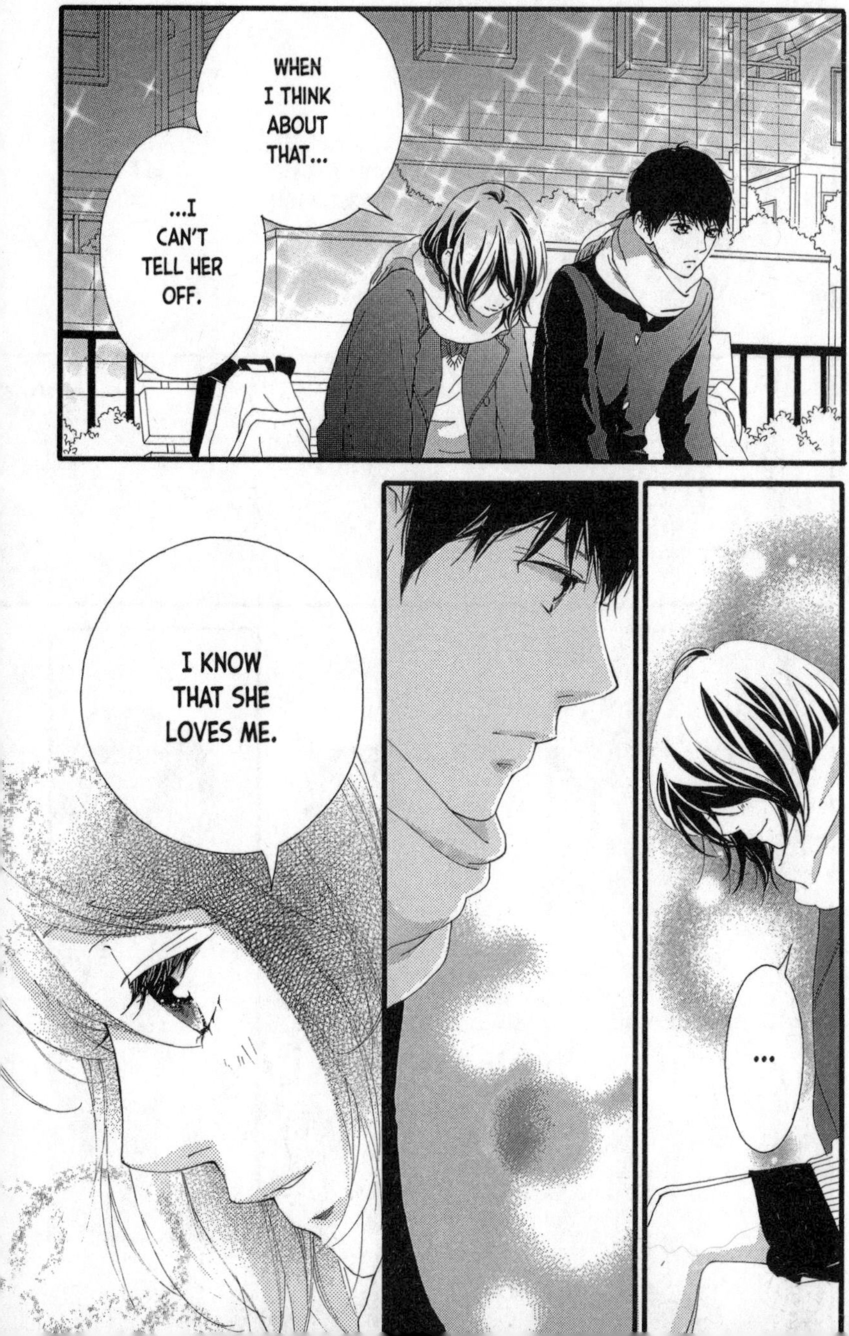
WHEN I THINK ABOUT THAT...
...I CAN'T TELL HER OFF.
...
I KNOW THAT SHE LOVES ME.

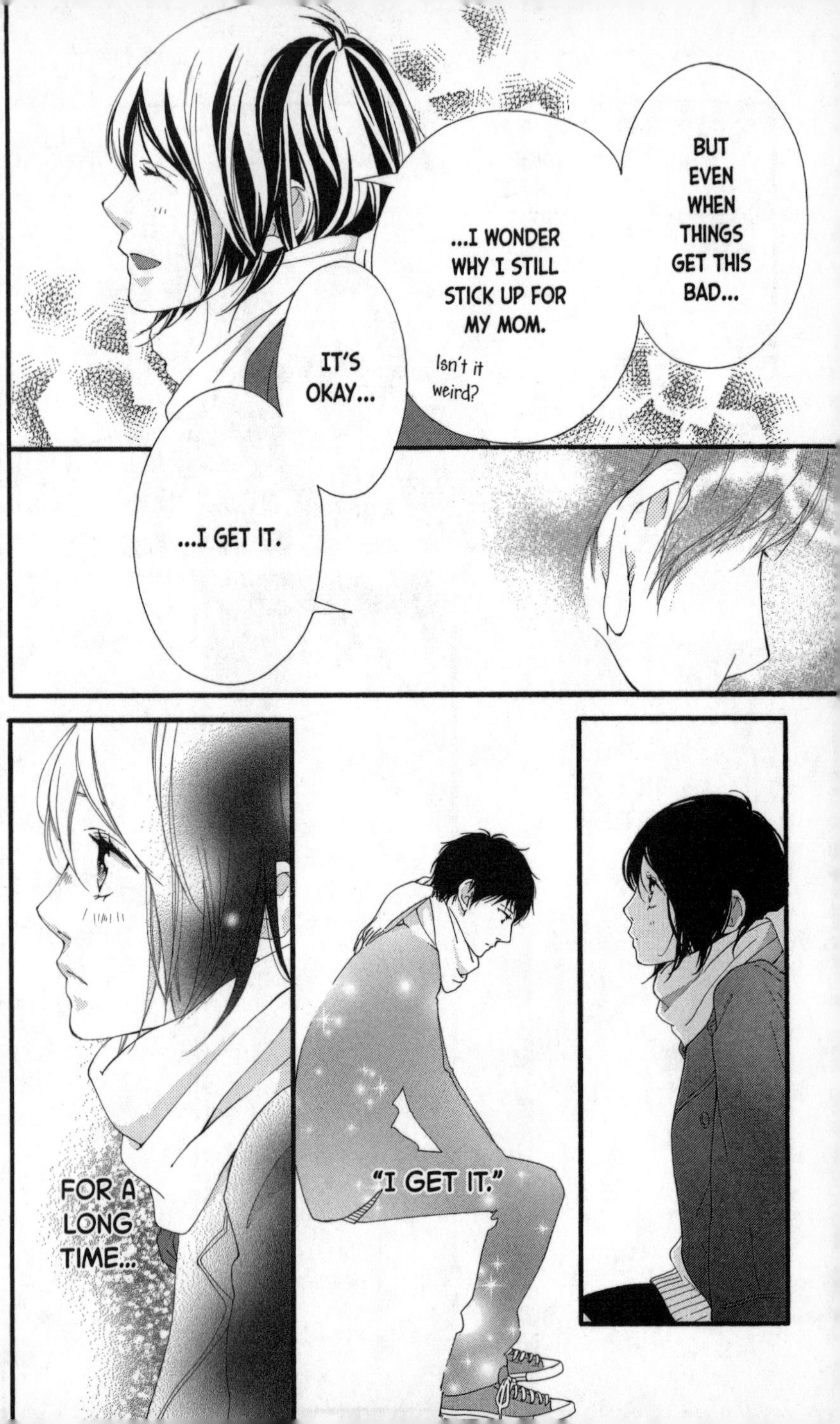
BUT EVEN WHEN THINGS GET THIS BAD...
...I WONDER WHY I STILL STICK UP FOR MY MOM.
Isn't it weird?
IT'S OKAY...
...I GET IT.
"I GET IT."
FOR A LONG TIME...

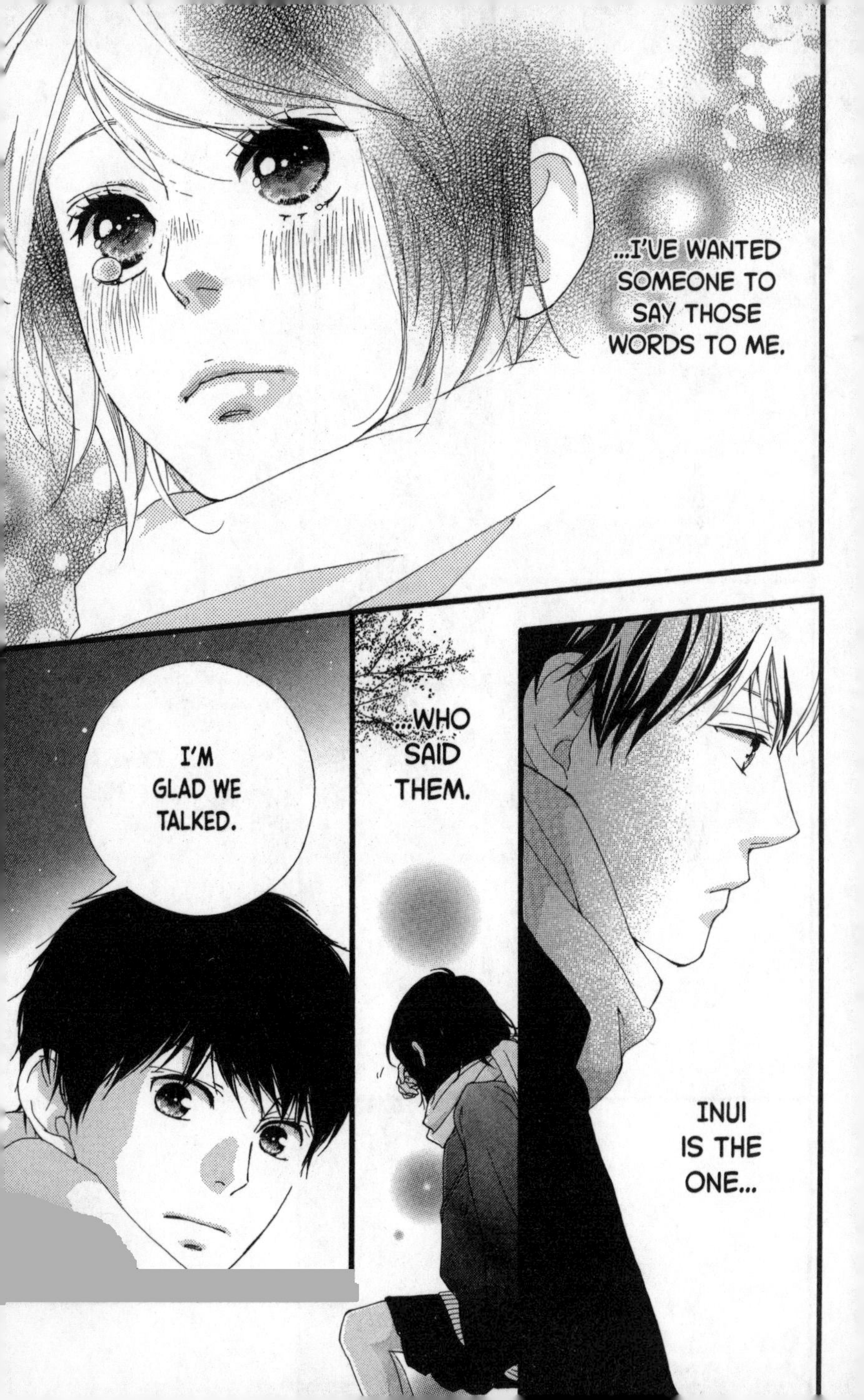
...I'VE WANTED SOMEONE TO SAY THOSE WORDS TO ME.
INUI IS THE ONE...
...WHO SAID THEM.
I'M GLAD WE TALKED.

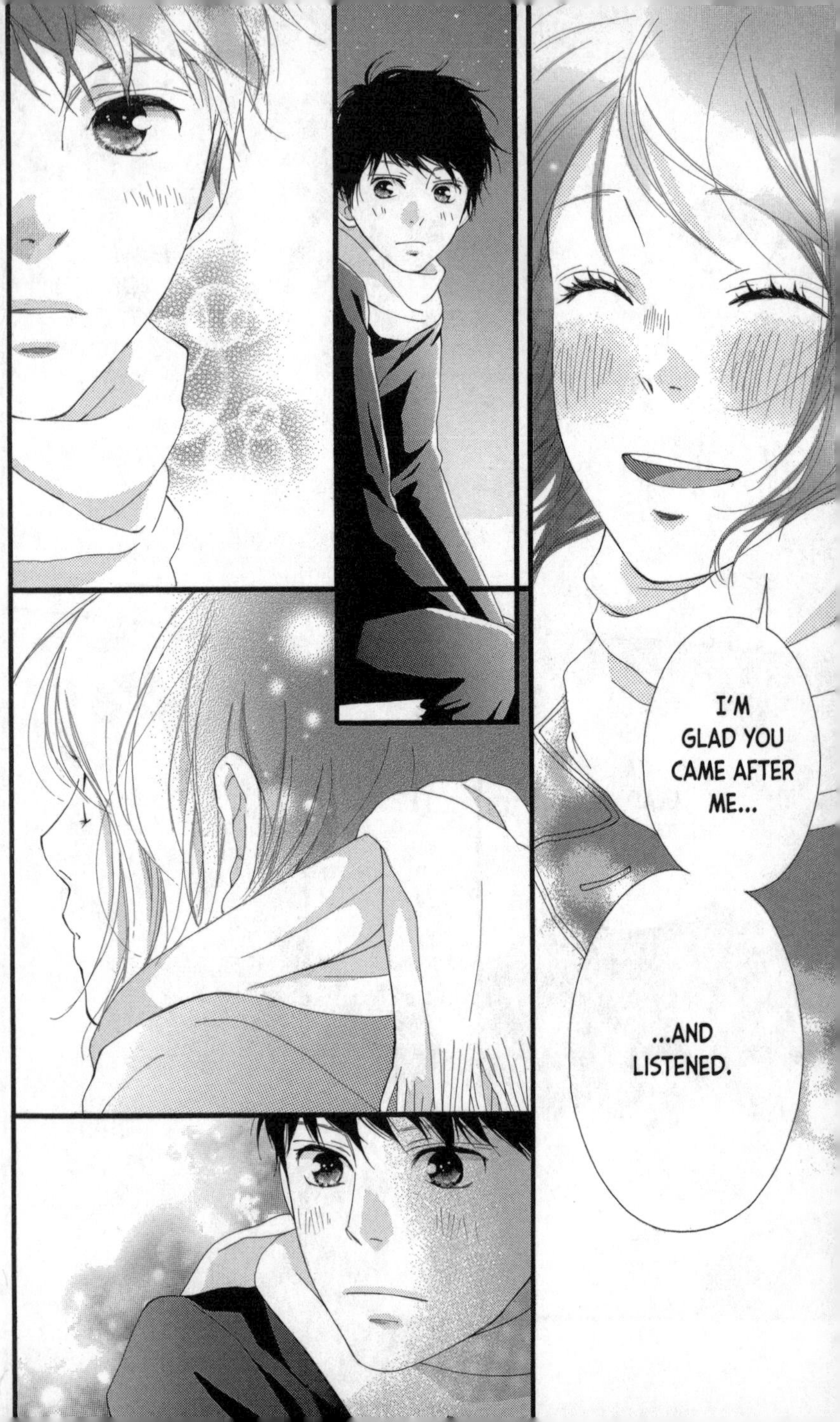
I'M GLAD YOU CAME AFTER ME...
...AND LISTENED.

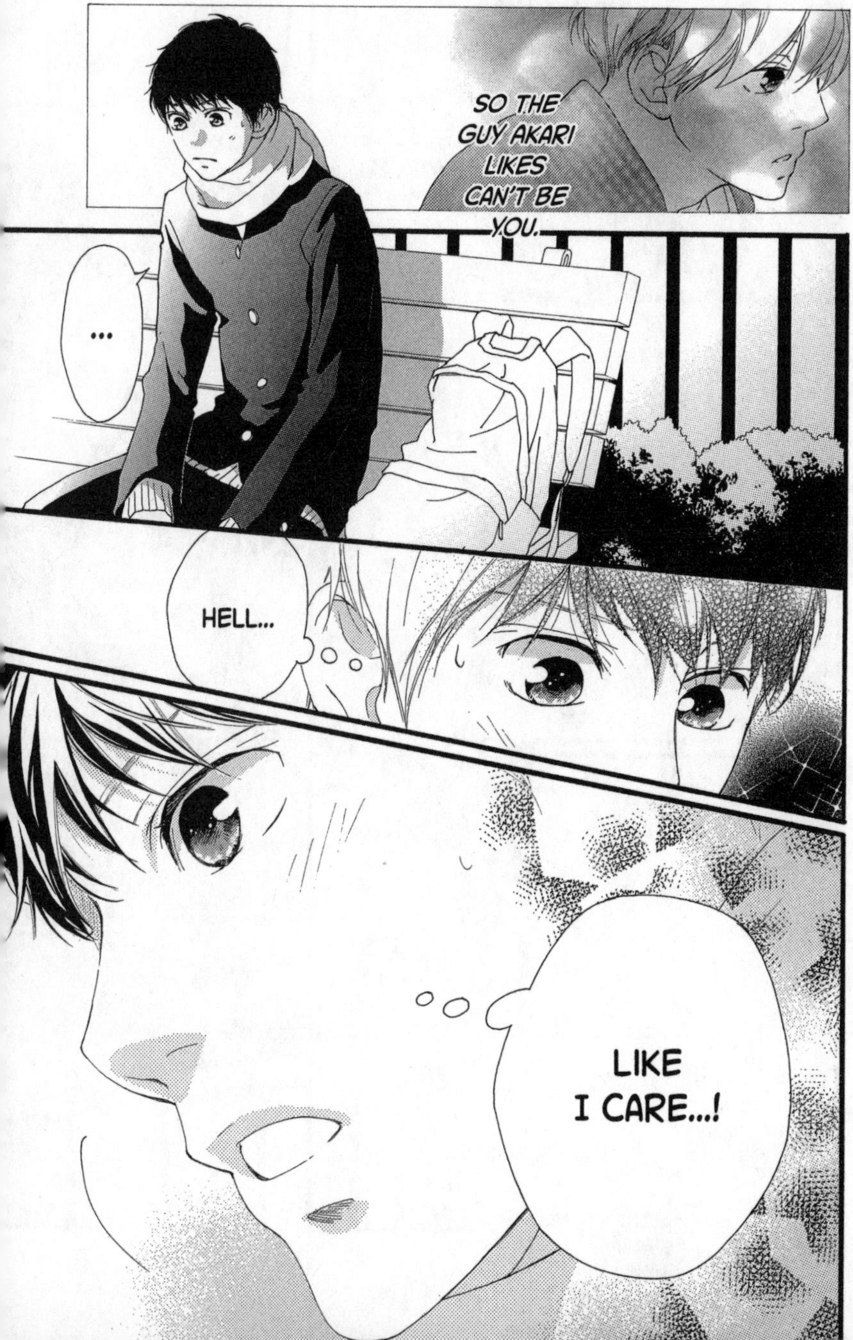
SO THE GUY AKARI LIKES CAN'T BE YOU.
...
HELL...
LIKE I CARE...!

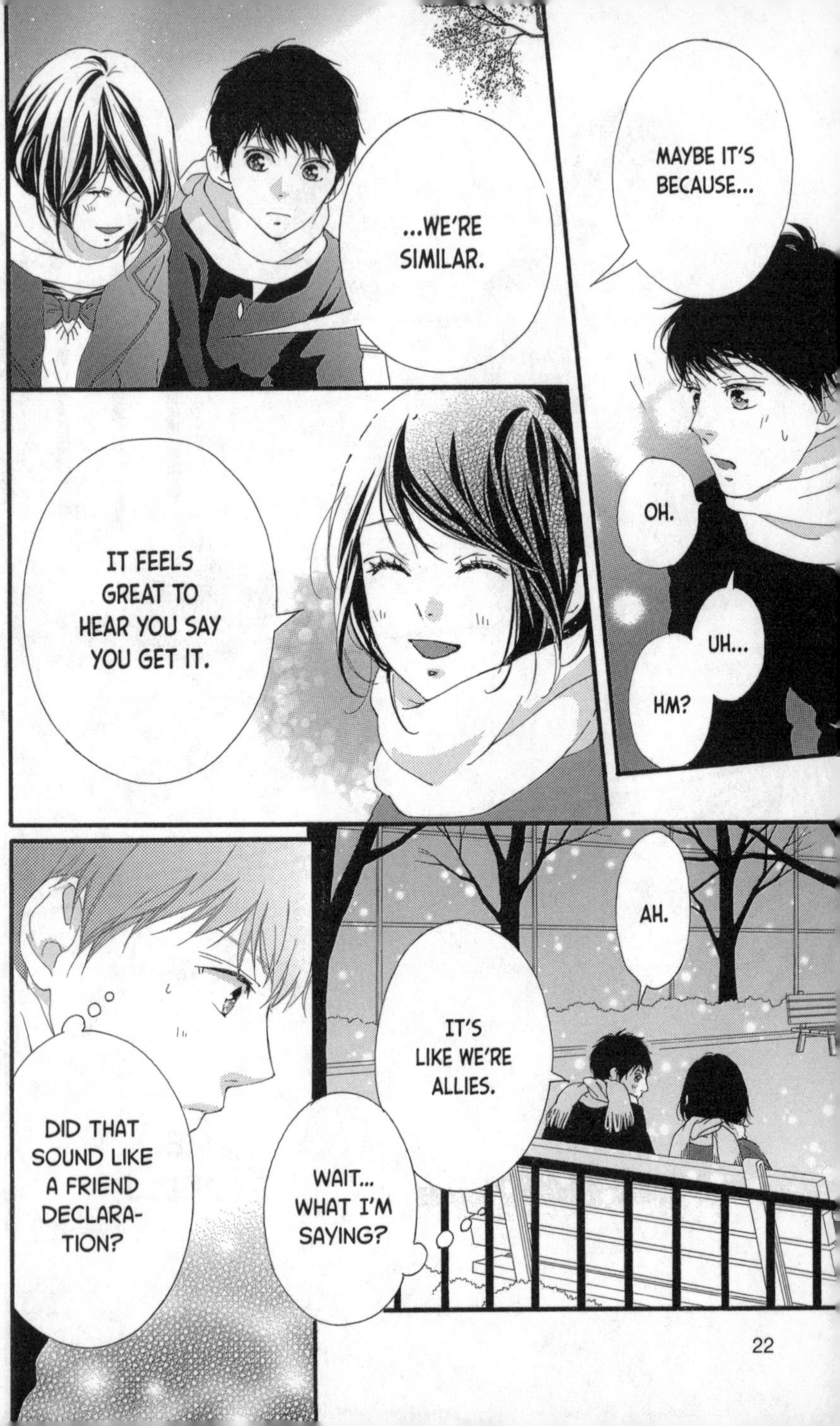
MAYBE IT'S BECAUSE...
OH.
UH...
HM?
...WE'RE SIMILAR.
IT FEELS GREAT TO HEAR YOU SAY YOU GET IT.
AH.
IT'S LIKE WE'RE ALLIES.
WAIT... WHAT I'M SAYING?
DID THAT SOUND LIKE A FRIEND DECLARA-TION?

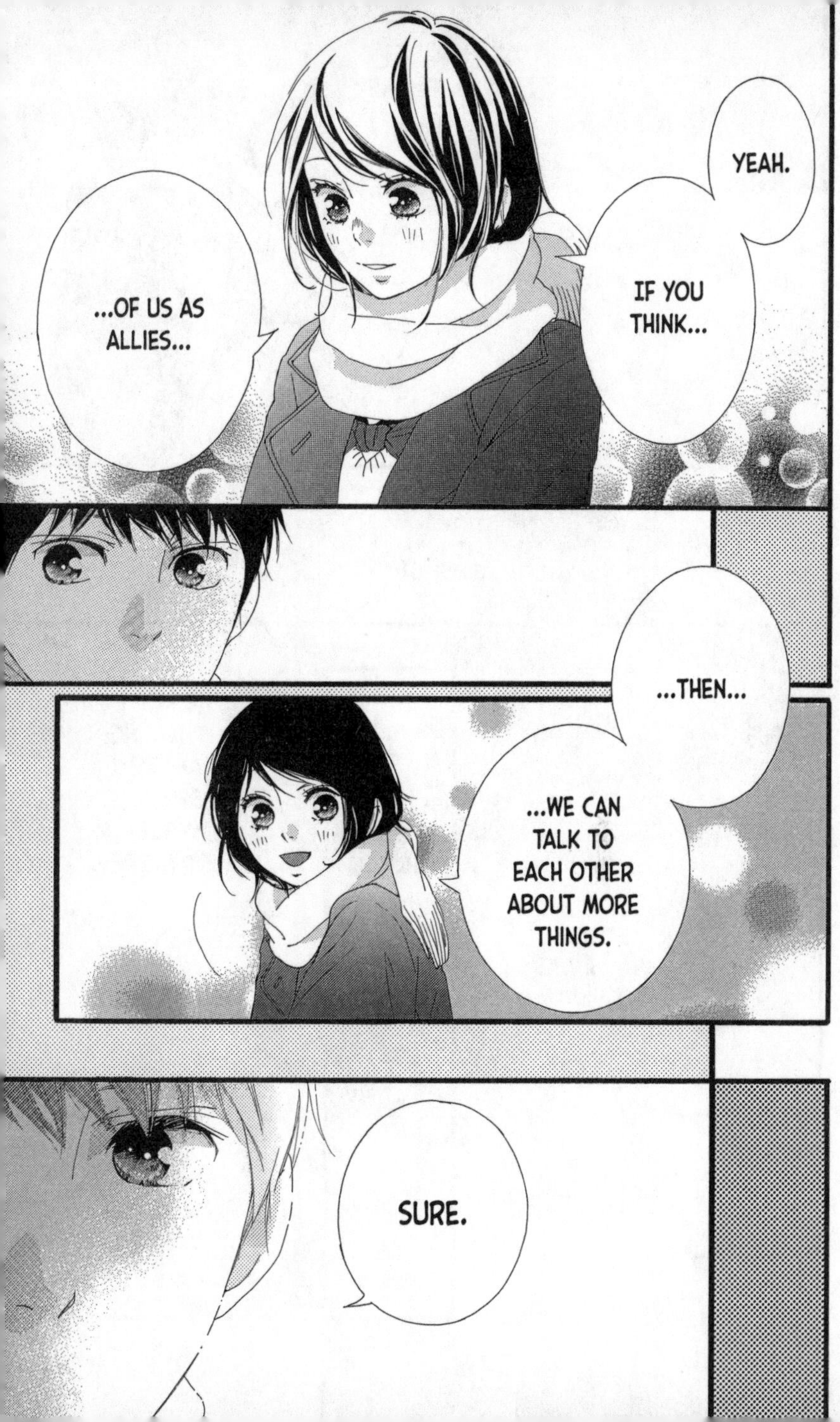
YEAH.
IF YOU THINK...
...OF US AS ALLIES...
...THEN...
...WE CAN TALK TO EACH OTHER ABOUT MORE THINGS.
SURE.

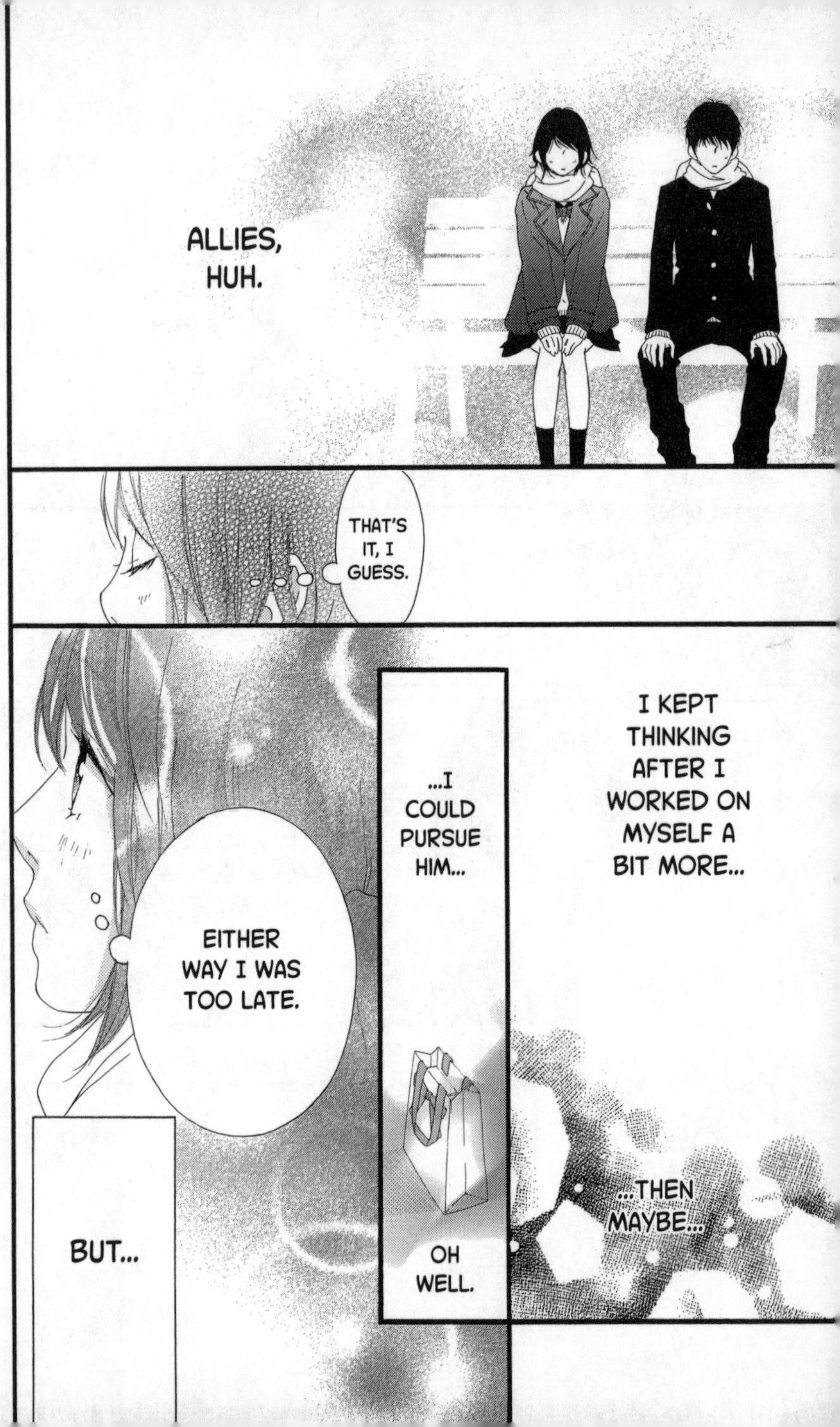
ALLIES, HUH.
THAT'S IT, I GUESS.
I KEPT THINKING AFTER I WORKED ON MYSELF A BIT MORE...
...THEN MAYBE...
...I COULD PURSUE HIM...
OH WELL.
EITHER WAY I WAS TOO LATE.
BUT...

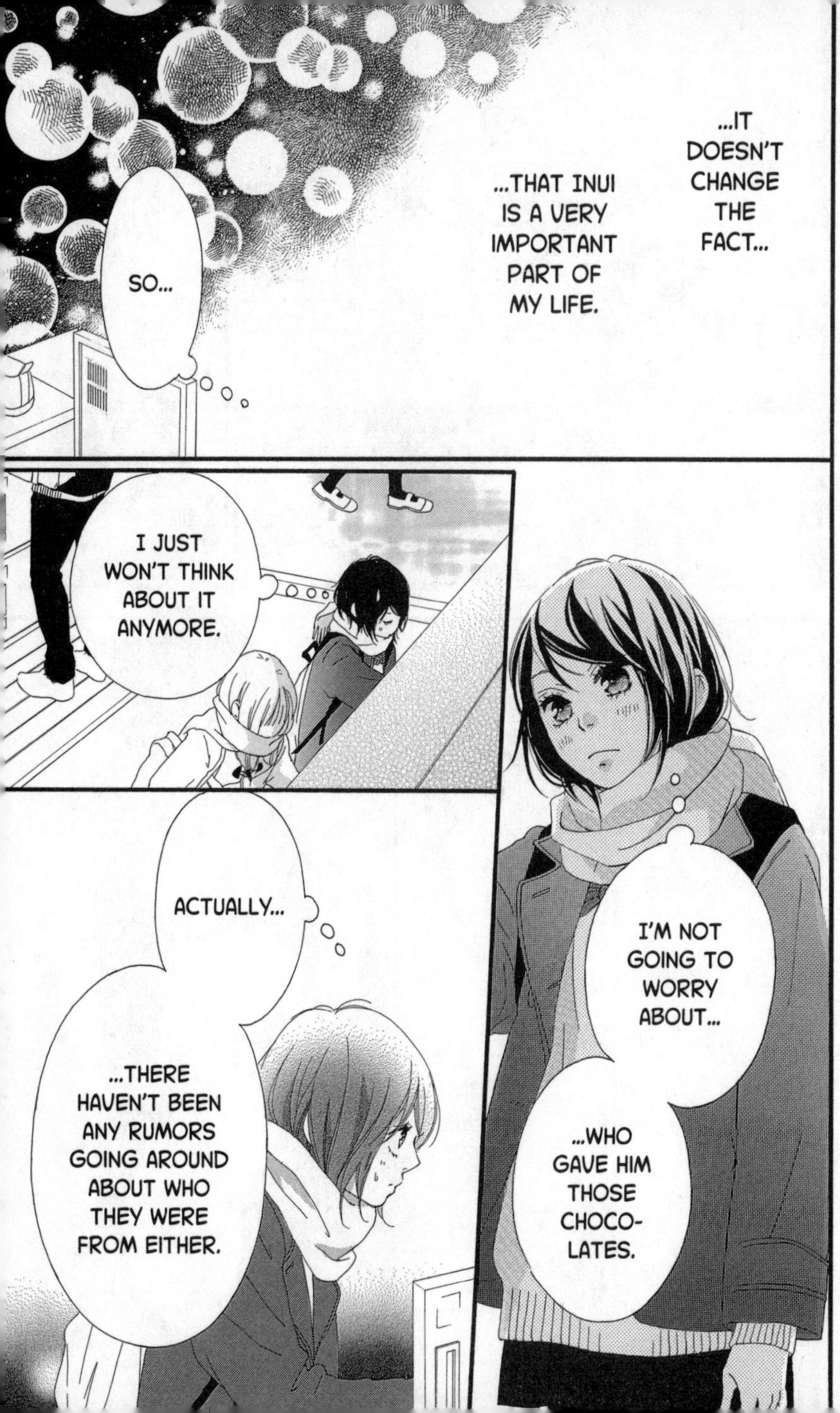
...IT DOESN'T CHANGE THE FACT...
...THAT INUI IS A VERY IMPORTANT PART OF MY LIFE.
SO...
I'M NOT GOING TO WORRY ABOUT...
...WHO GAVE HIM THOSE CHOCO-LATES.
I JUST WON'T THINK ABOUT IT ANYMORE.
ACTUALLY...
...THERE HAVEN'T BEEN ANY RUMORS GOING AROUND ABOUT WHO THEY WERE FROM EITHER.

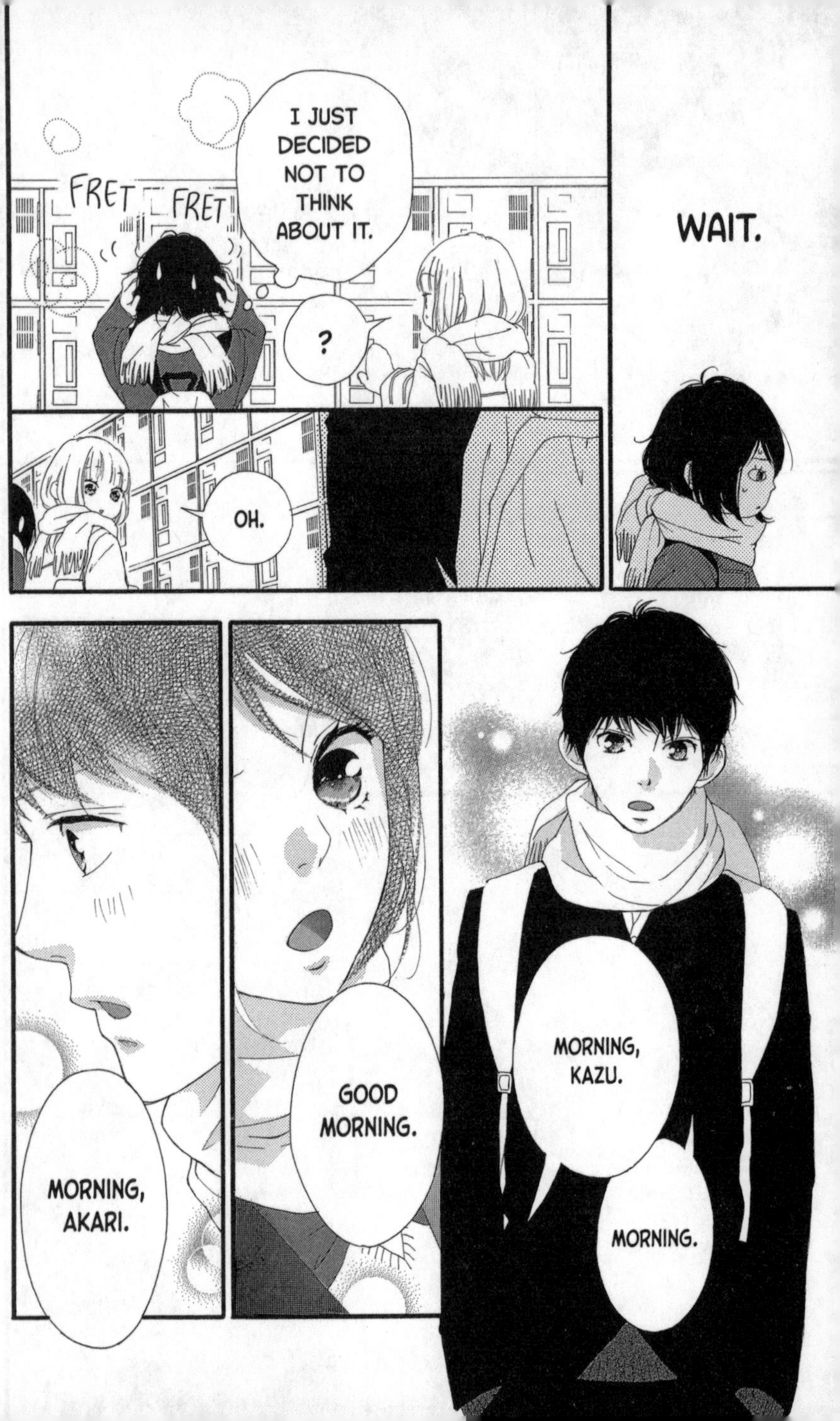
WAIT.
I JUST DECIDED NOT TO THINK ABOUT IT.
FRET FRET
?
OH.
MORNING, KAZU.
MORNING.
GOOD MORNING.
MORNING, AKARI.

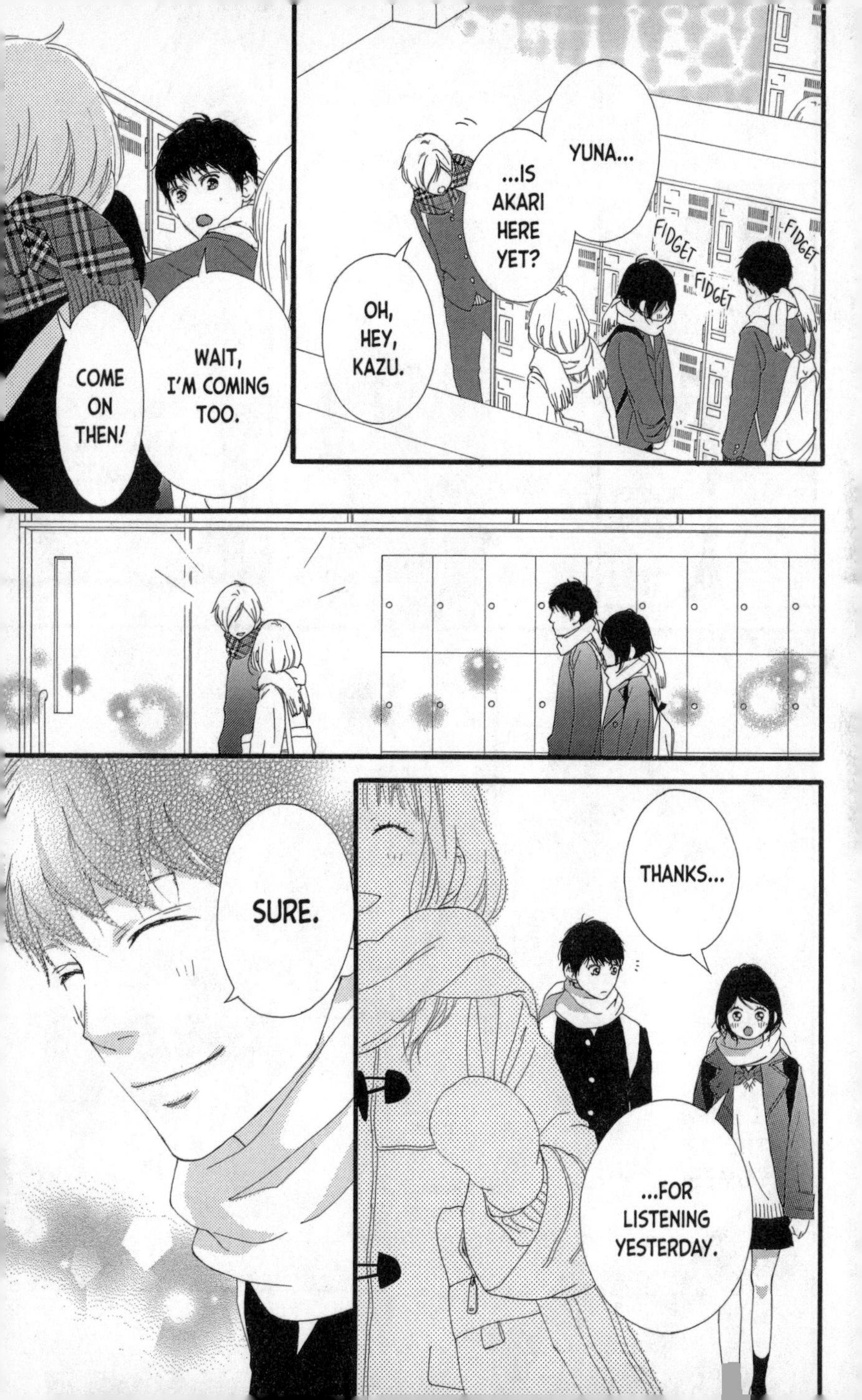
YUNA...
...IS AKARI HERE YET?
FIDGET
FIDGET
FIDGET
OH, HEY, KAZU.
WAIT, I'M COMING TOO.
COME ON THEN!
THANKS...
...FOR LISTENING YESTERDAY.
SURE.

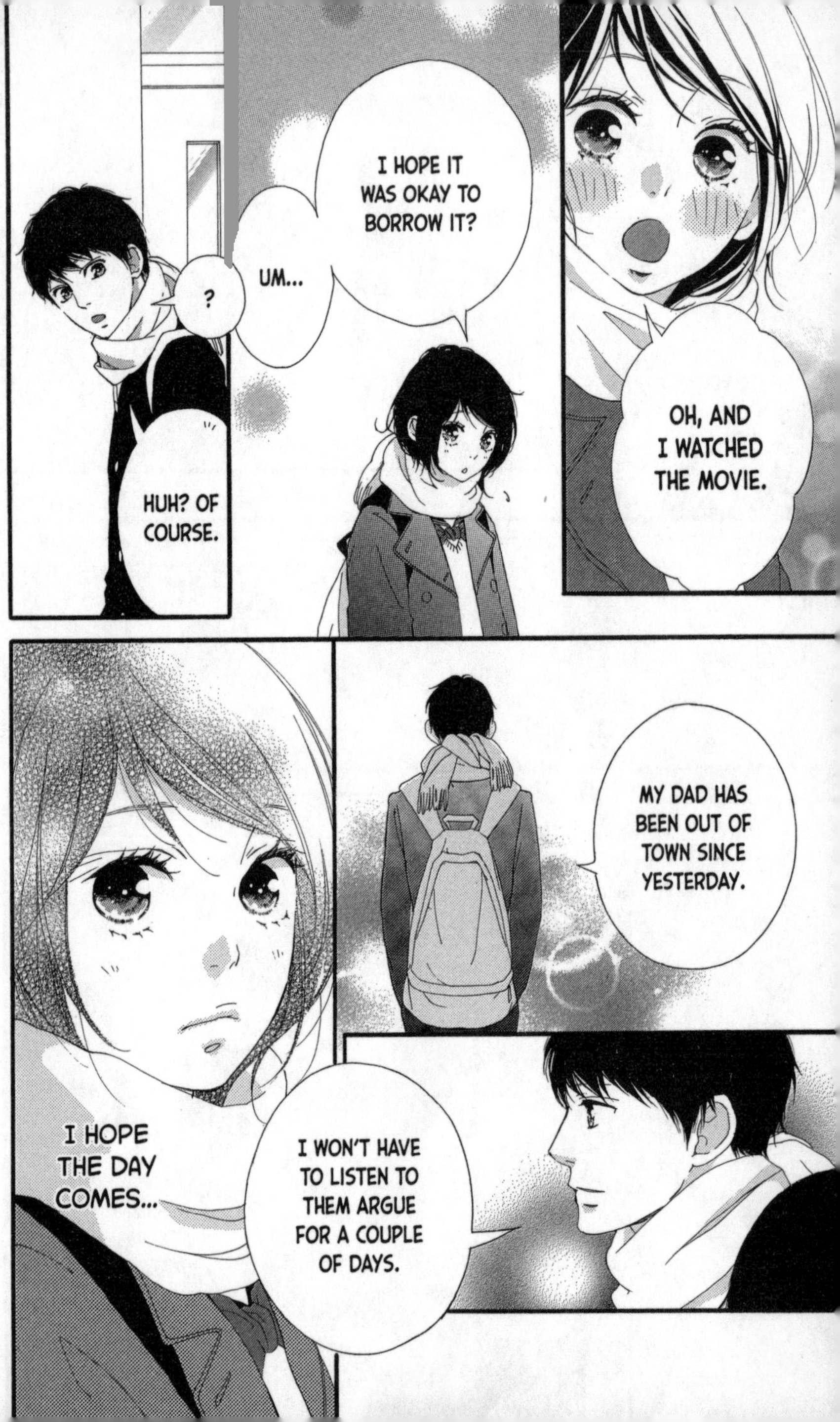
OH, AND I WATCHED THE MOVIE.
I HOPE IT WAS OKAY TO BORROW IT?
UM...
?
HUH? OF COURSE.
MY DAD HAS BEEN OUT OF TOWN SINCE YESTERDAY.
I WON'T HAVE TO LISTEN TO THEM ARGUE FOR A COUPLE OF DAYS.
I HOPE THE DAY COMES...

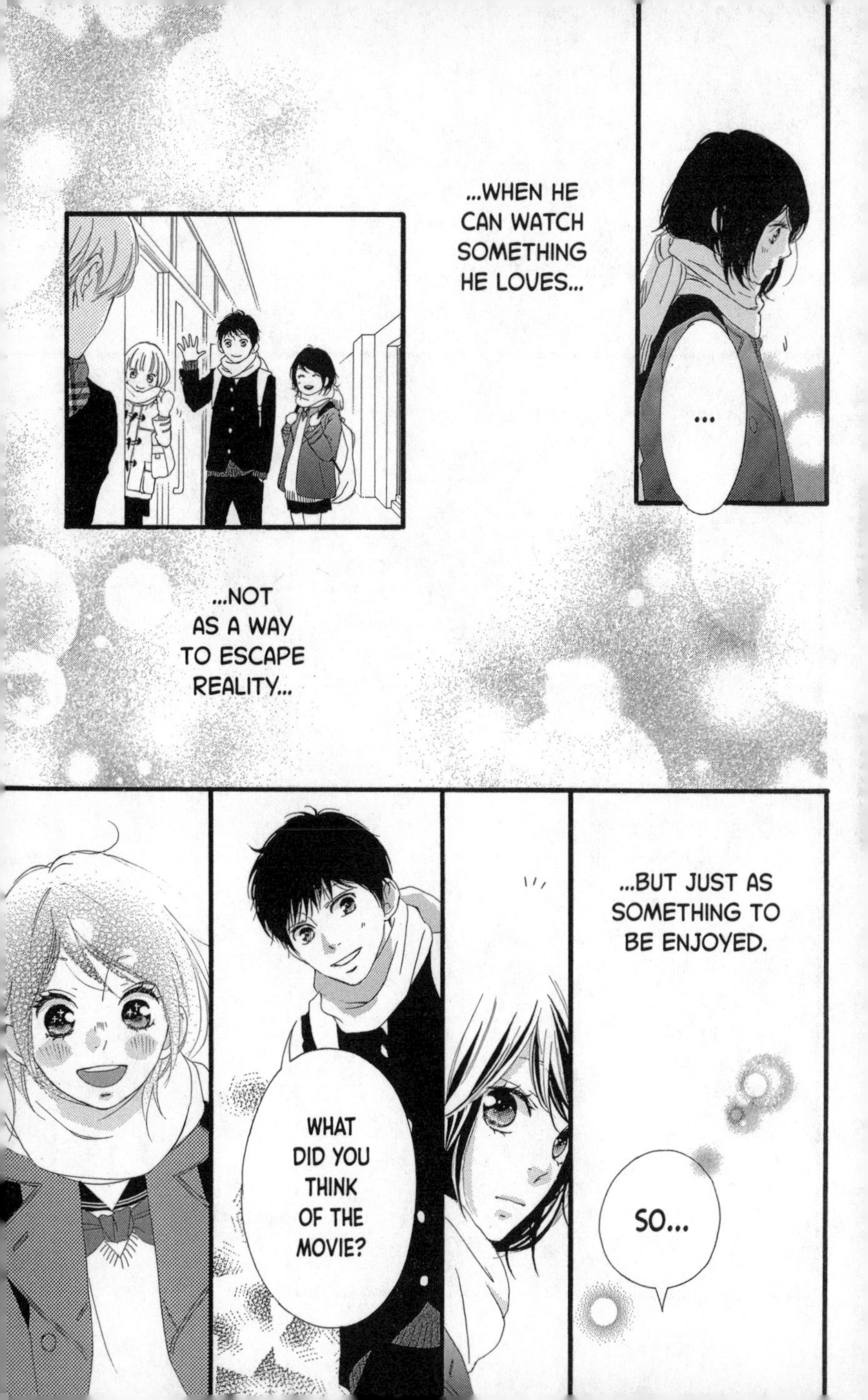
...
...WHEN HE CAN WATCH SOMETHING HE LOVES...
...NOT AS A WAY TO ESCAPE REALITY...
...BUT JUST AS SOMETHING TO BE ENJOYED.
SO...
WHAT DID YOU THINK OF THE MOVIE?

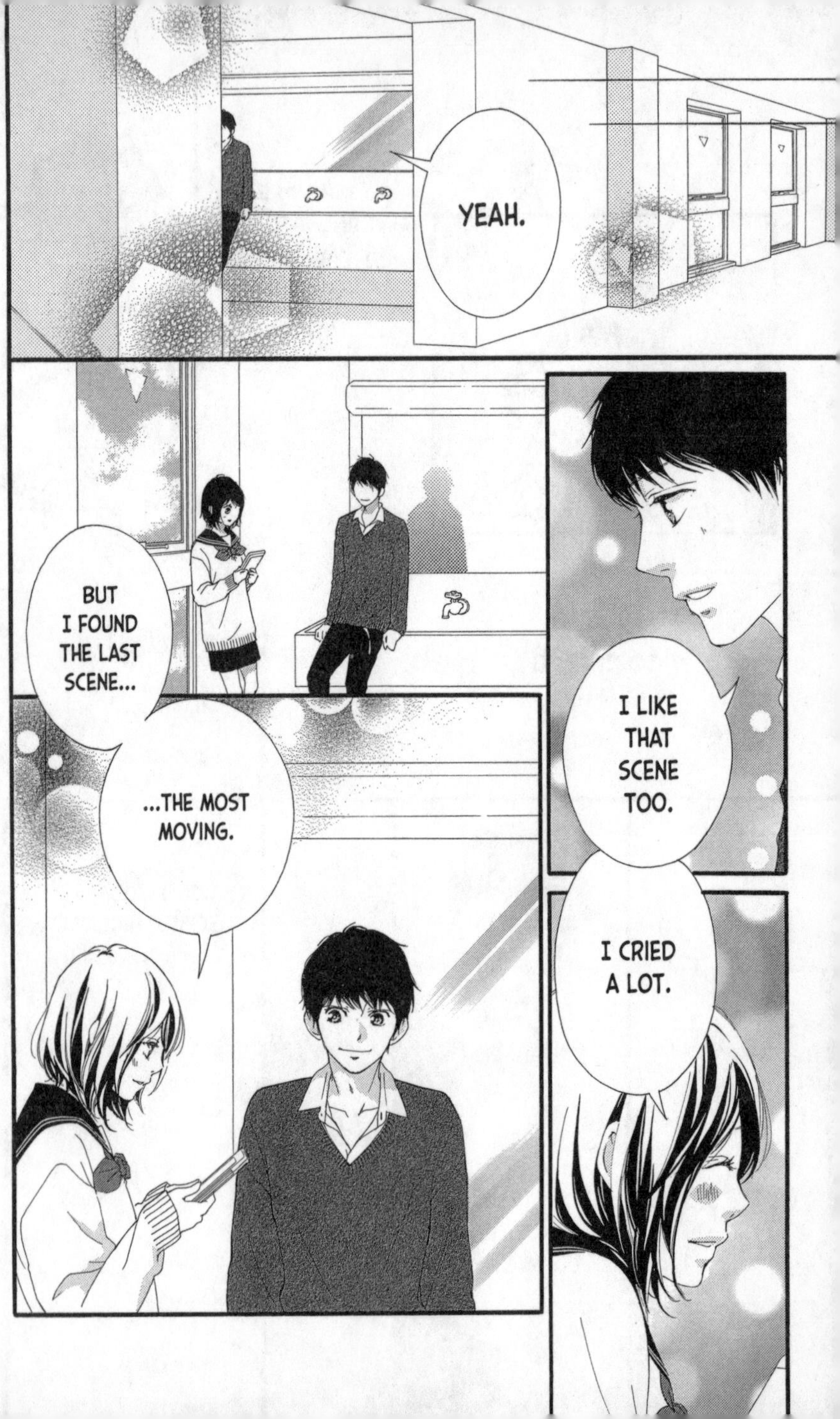
YEAH.
BUT I FOUND THE LAST SCENE...
...THE MOST MOVING.
I LIKE THAT SCENE TOO.
I CRIED A LOT.

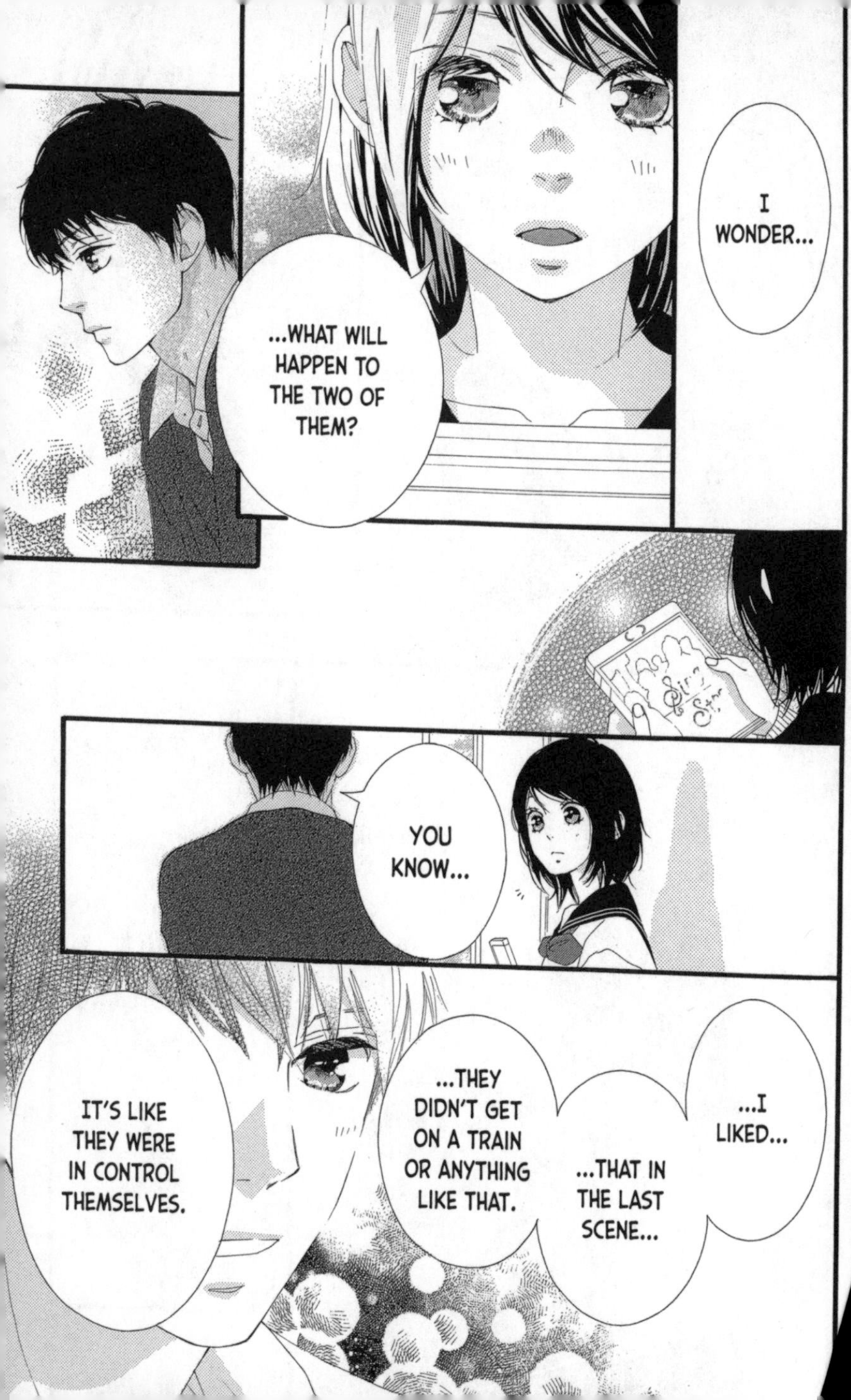
I WONDER...
...WHAT WILL HAPPEN TO THE TWO OF THEM?
YOU KNOW...
...I LIKED...
...THAT IN THE LAST SCENE...
...THEY DIDN'T GET ON A TRAIN OR ANYTHING LIKE THAT.
IT'S LIKE THEY WERE IN CONTROL THEMSELVES.

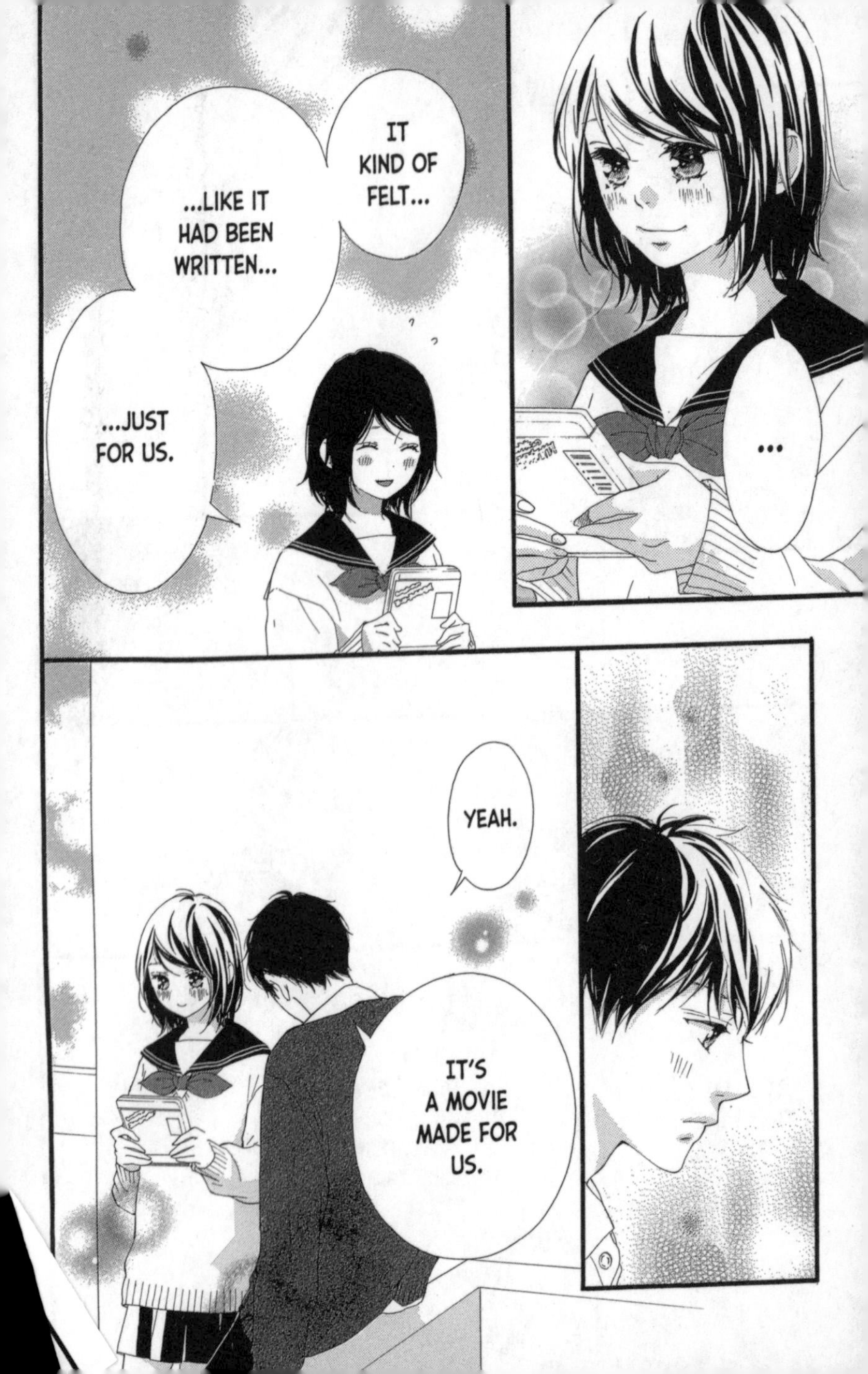
...
IT KIND OF FELT...
...LIKE IT HAD BEEN WRITTEN...
...JUST FOR US.
YEAH.
IT'S A MOVIE MADE FOR US.

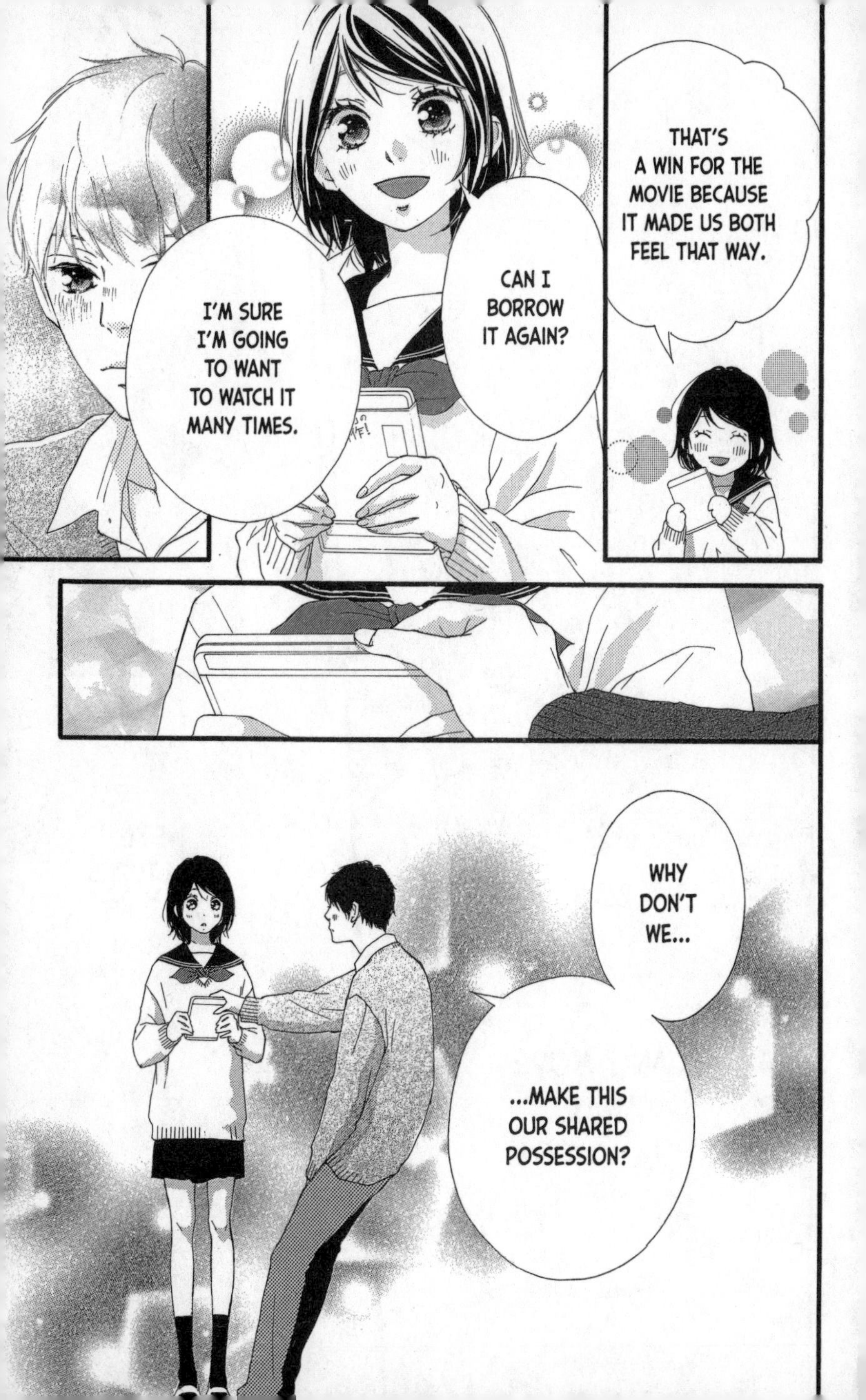
THAT'S A WIN FOR THE MOVIE BECAUSE IT MADE US BOTH FEEL THAT WAY.
CAN I BORROW IT AGAIN?
I'M SURE I'M GOING TO WANT TO WATCH IT MANY TIMES.
WHY DON'T WE...
...MAKE THIS OUR SHARED POSSESSION?

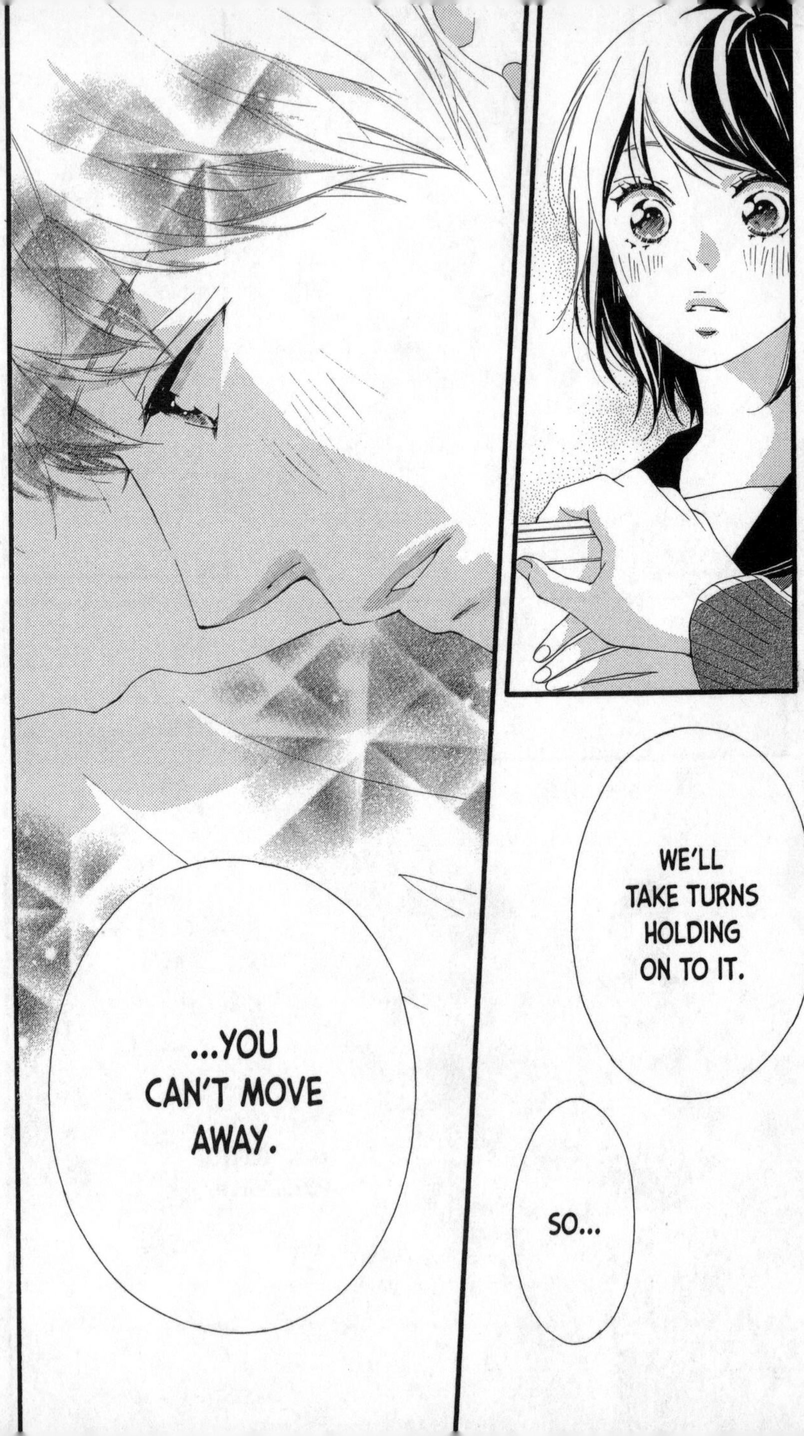
WE'LL TAKE TURNS HOLDING ON TO IT.
SO...
...YOU CAN'T MOVE AWAY.

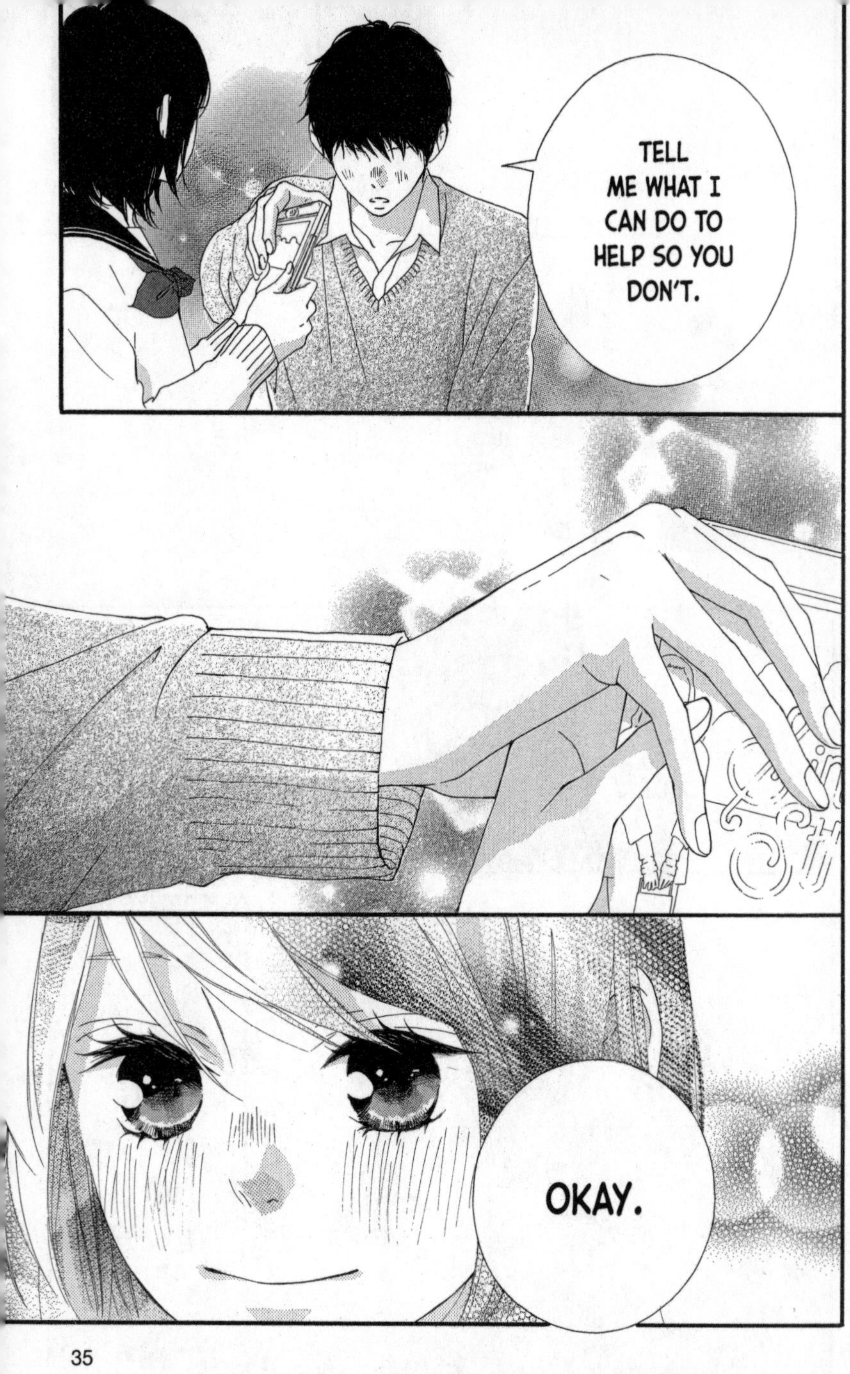
TELL ME WHAT I CAN DO TO HELP SO YOU DON'T.
OKAY.

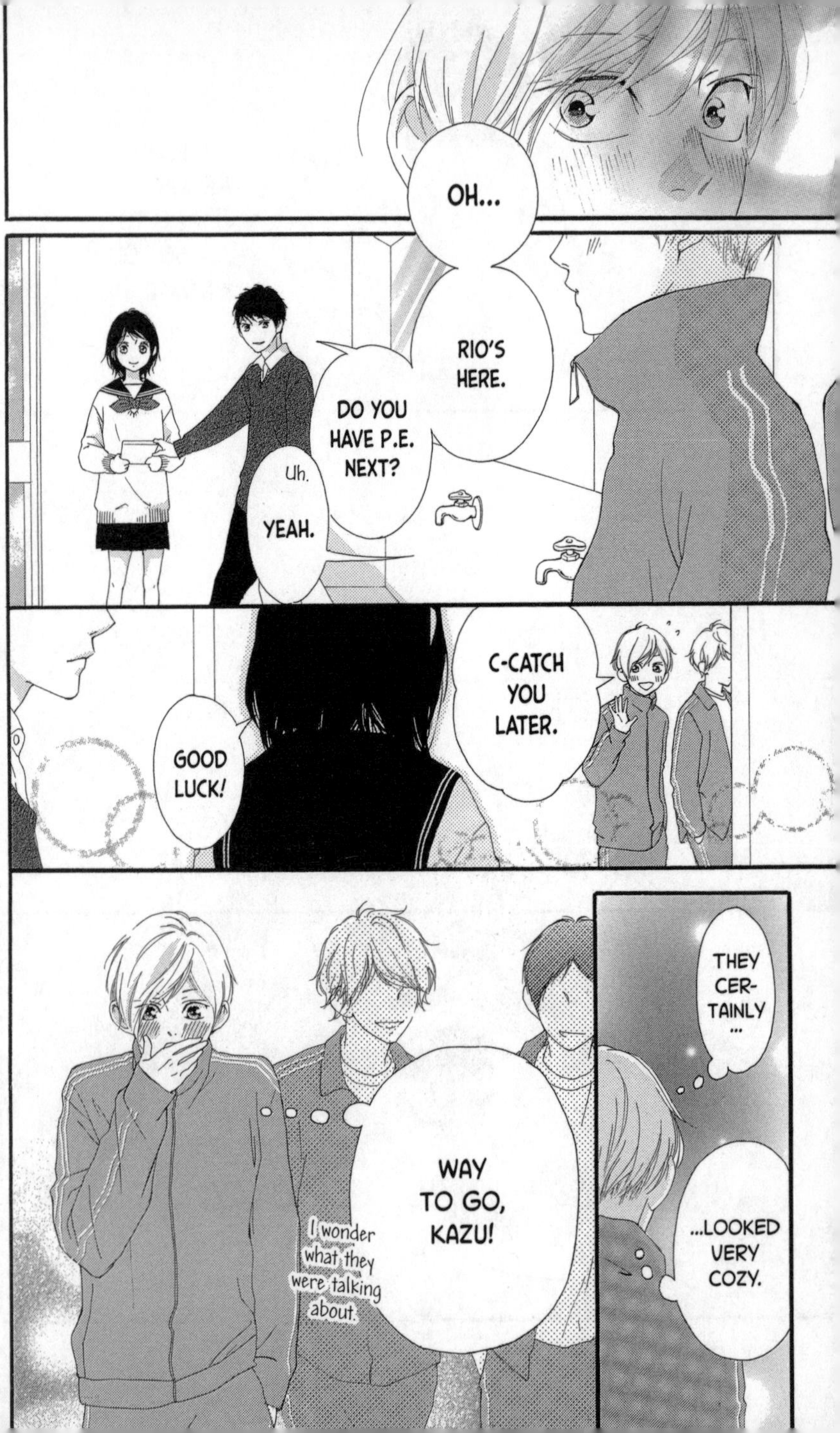
OH...
RIO'S HERE.
DO YOU HAVE P.E. NEXT?
Uh.
YEAH.
C-CATCH YOU LATER.
GOOD LUCK!
THEY CERTAINLY...
...LOOKED VERY COZY.
WAY TO GO, KAZU!
I wonder what they were talking about.

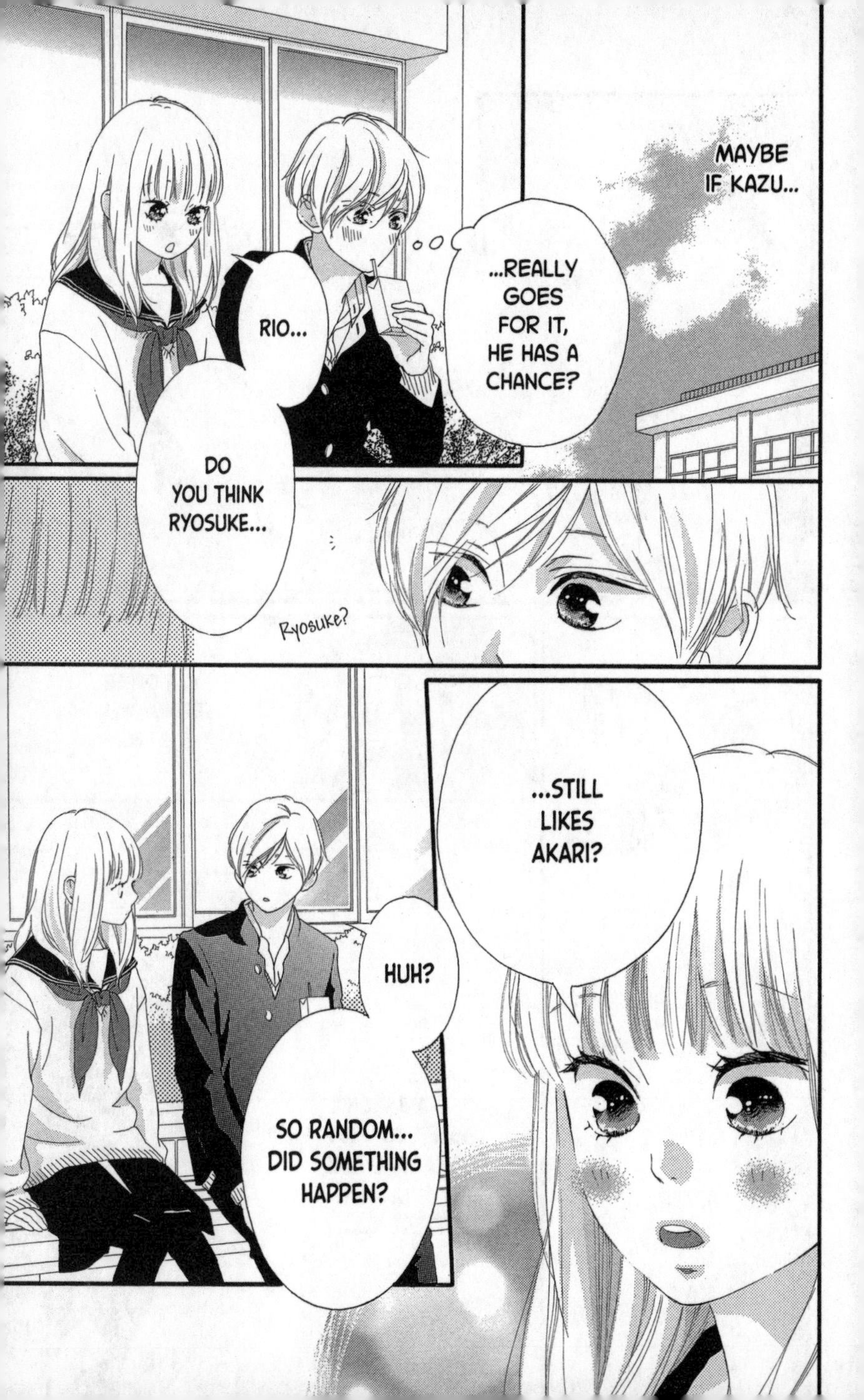
MAYBE IF KAZU...
...REALLY GOES FOR IT, HE HAS A CHANCE?
RIO...
DO YOU THINK RYOSUKE...
Ryosuke?
...STILL LIKES AKARI?
HUH?
SO RANDOM... DID SOMETHING HAPPEN?

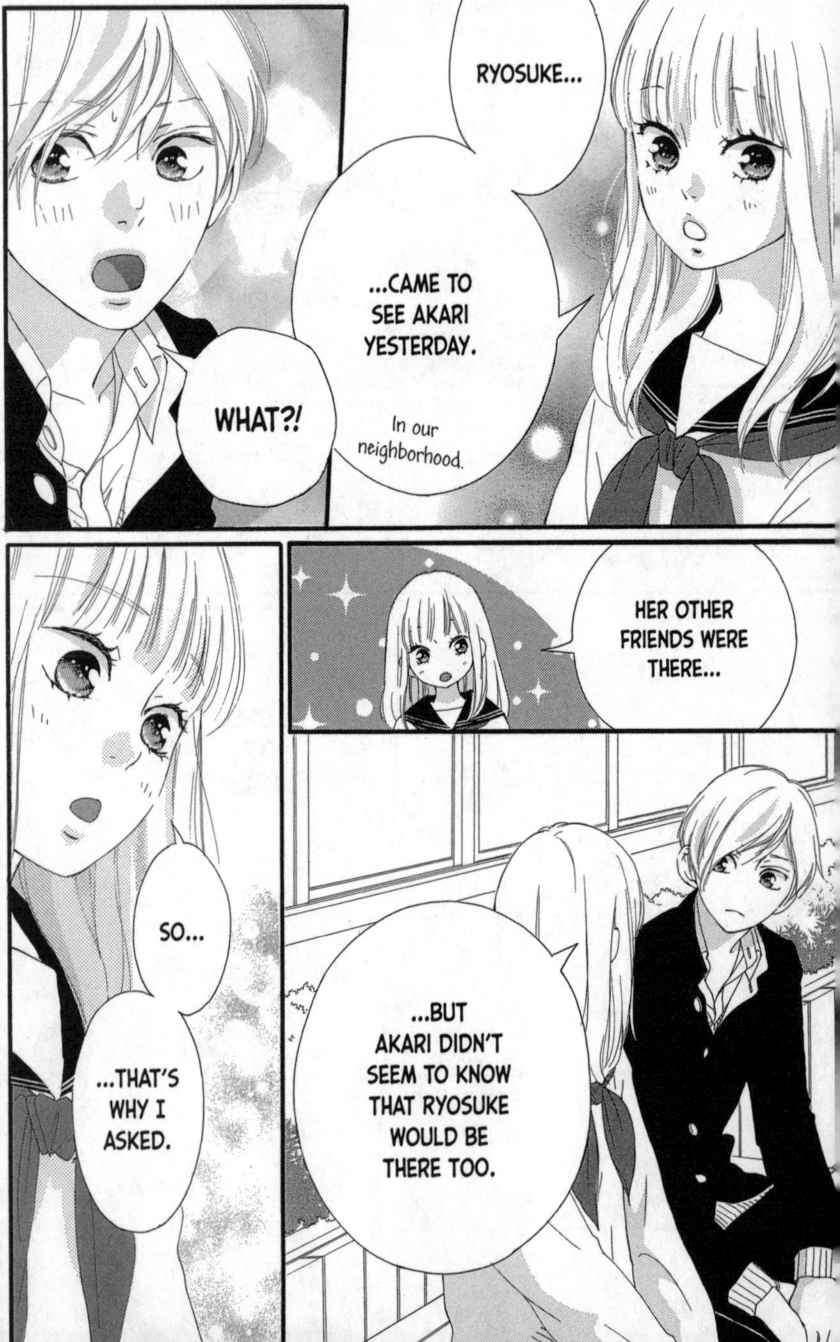
RYOSUKE...
...CAME TO SEE AKARI YESTERDAY.
In our neighborhood.
WHAT?!
HER OTHER FRIENDS WERE THERE...
...BUT AKARI DIDN'T SEEM TO KNOW THAT RYOSUKE WOULD BE THERE TOO.
SO...
...THAT'S WHY I ASKED.

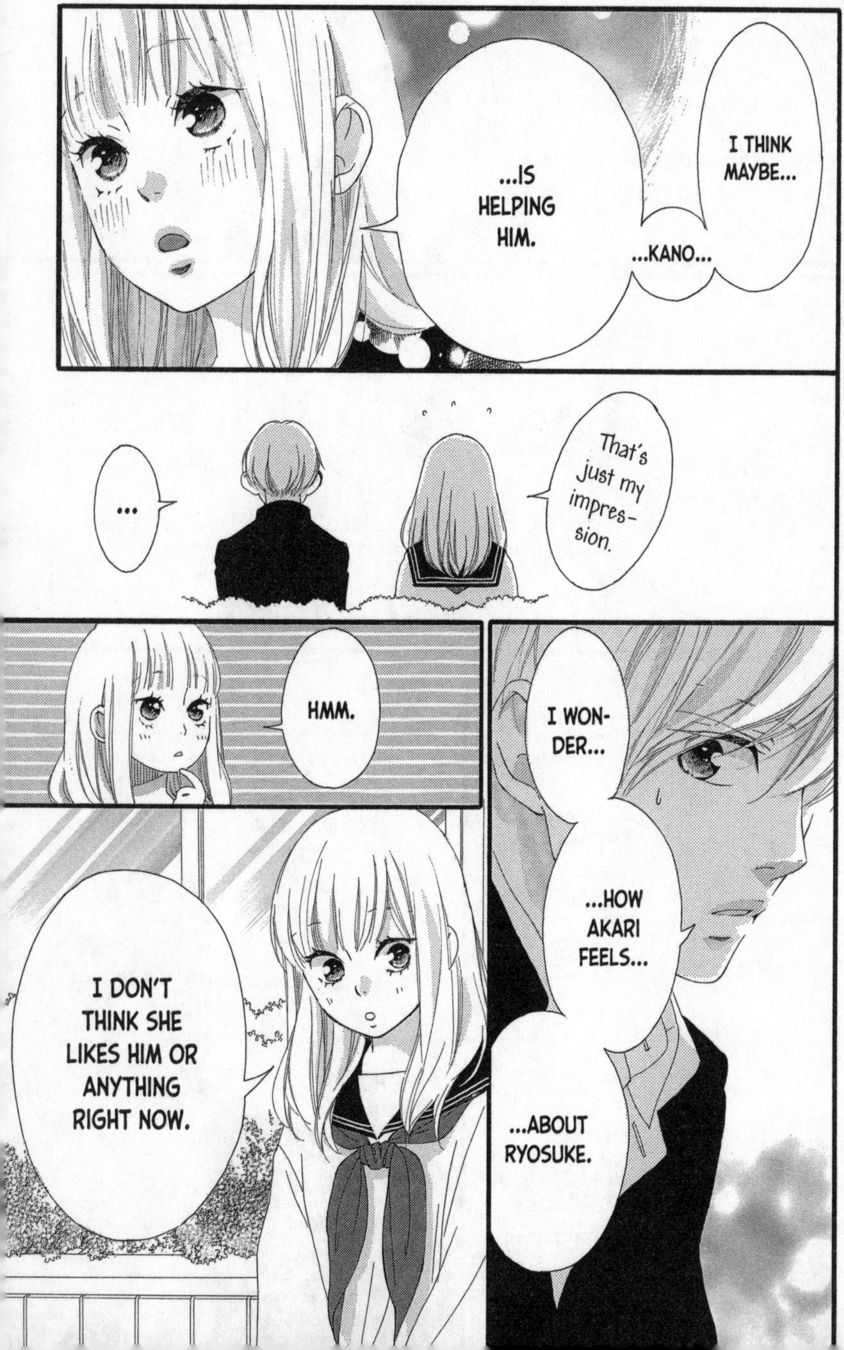
I THINK MAYBE...
...KANO...
...IS HELPING HIM.
That's just my impres-sion.
...
I WON-DER...
...HOW AKARI FEELS...
...ABOUT RYOSUKE.
HMM.
I DON'T THINK SHE LIKES HIM OR ANYTHING RIGHT NOW.

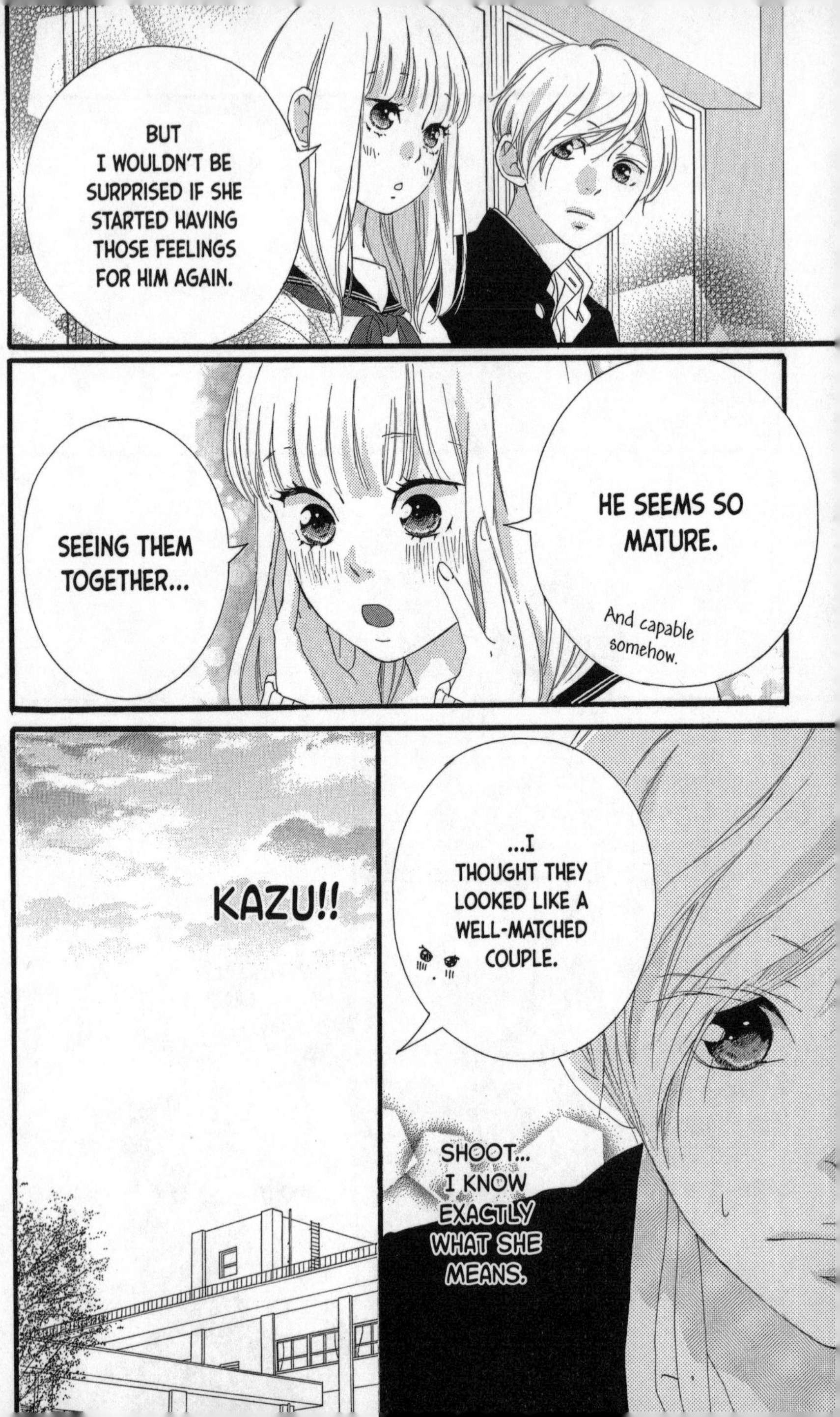
BUT I WOULDN'T BE SURPRISED IF SHE STARTED HAVING THOSE FEELINGS FOR HIM AGAIN.
HE SEEMS SO MATURE.
And capable somehow.
SEEING THEM TOGETHER...
...I THOUGHT THEY LOOKED LIKE A WELL-MATCHED COUPLE.
SHOOT... I KNOW EXACTLY WHAT SHE MEANS.
KAZU!!

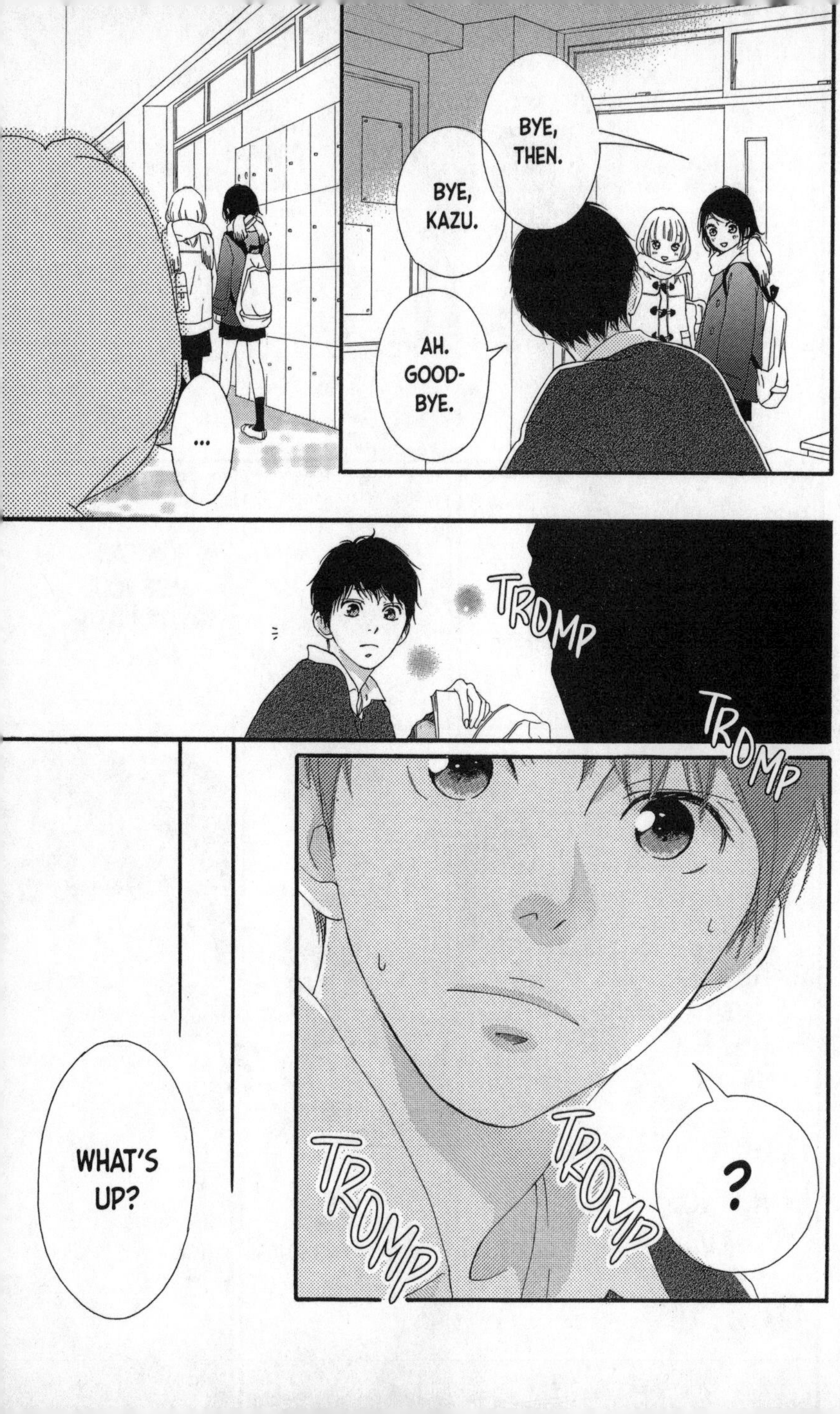
BYE, THEN.
BYE, KAZU.
AH. GOOD-BYE.
...
TROMP
TROMP
?
TROMP
TROMP
WHAT'S UP?

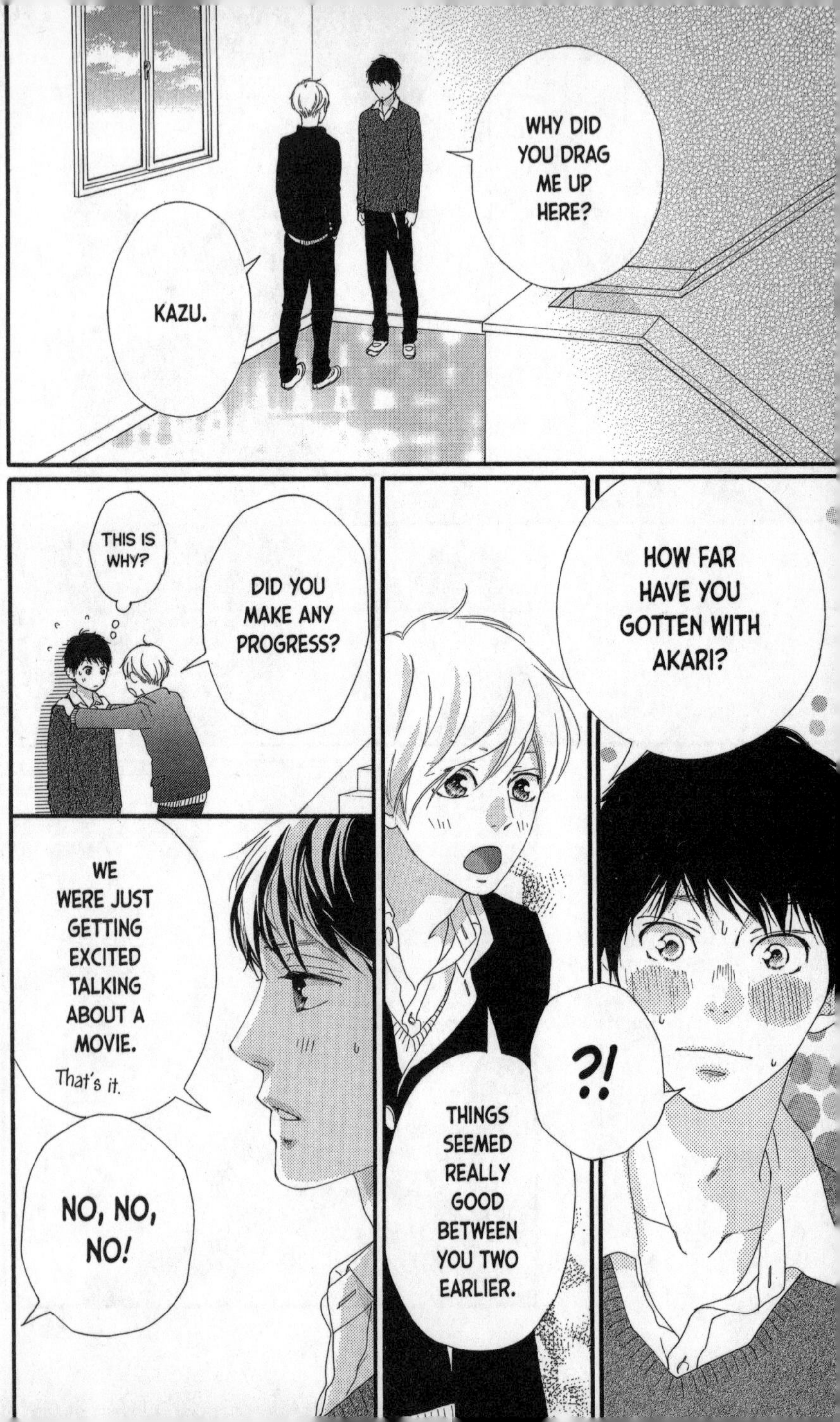
WHY DID YOU DRAG ME UP HERE?
KAZU.
HOW FAR HAVE YOU GOTTEN WITH AKARI?
?!
THINGS SEEMED REALLY GOOD BETWEEN YOU TWO EARLIER.
THIS IS WHY?
DID YOU MAKE ANY PROGRESS?
WE WERE JUST GETTING EXCITED TALKING ABOUT A MOVIE.
That's it.
NO, NO, NO!

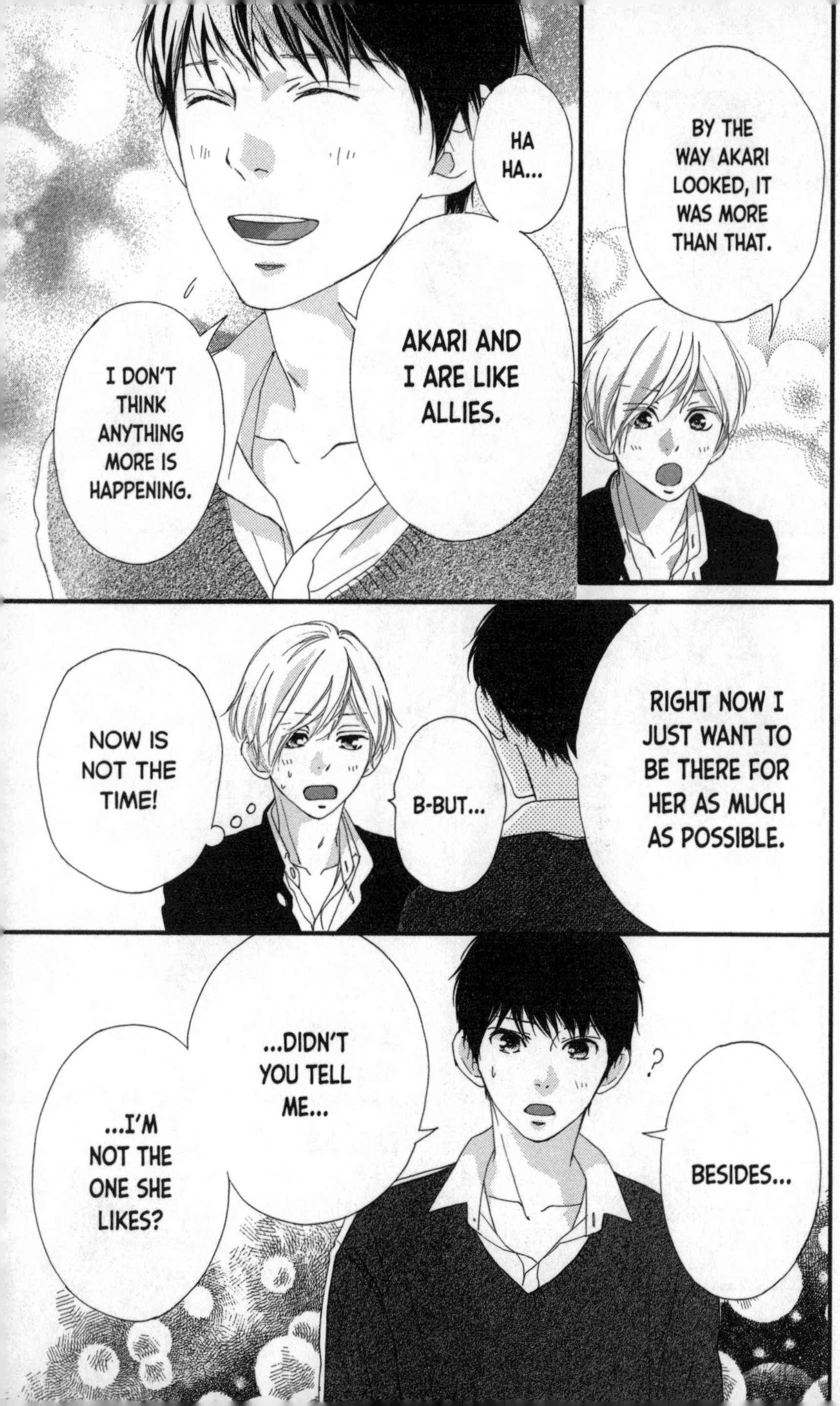
BY THE WAY AKARI LOOKED, IT WAS MORE THAN THAT.
HA HA...
AKARI AND I ARE LIKE ALLIES.
I DON'T THINK ANYTHING MORE IS HAPPENING.
RIGHT NOW I JUST WANT TO BE THERE FOR HER AS MUCH AS POSSIBLE.
B-BUT...
NOW IS NOT THE TIME!
BESIDES...
...DIDN'T YOU TELL ME...
...I'M NOT THE ONE SHE LIKES?

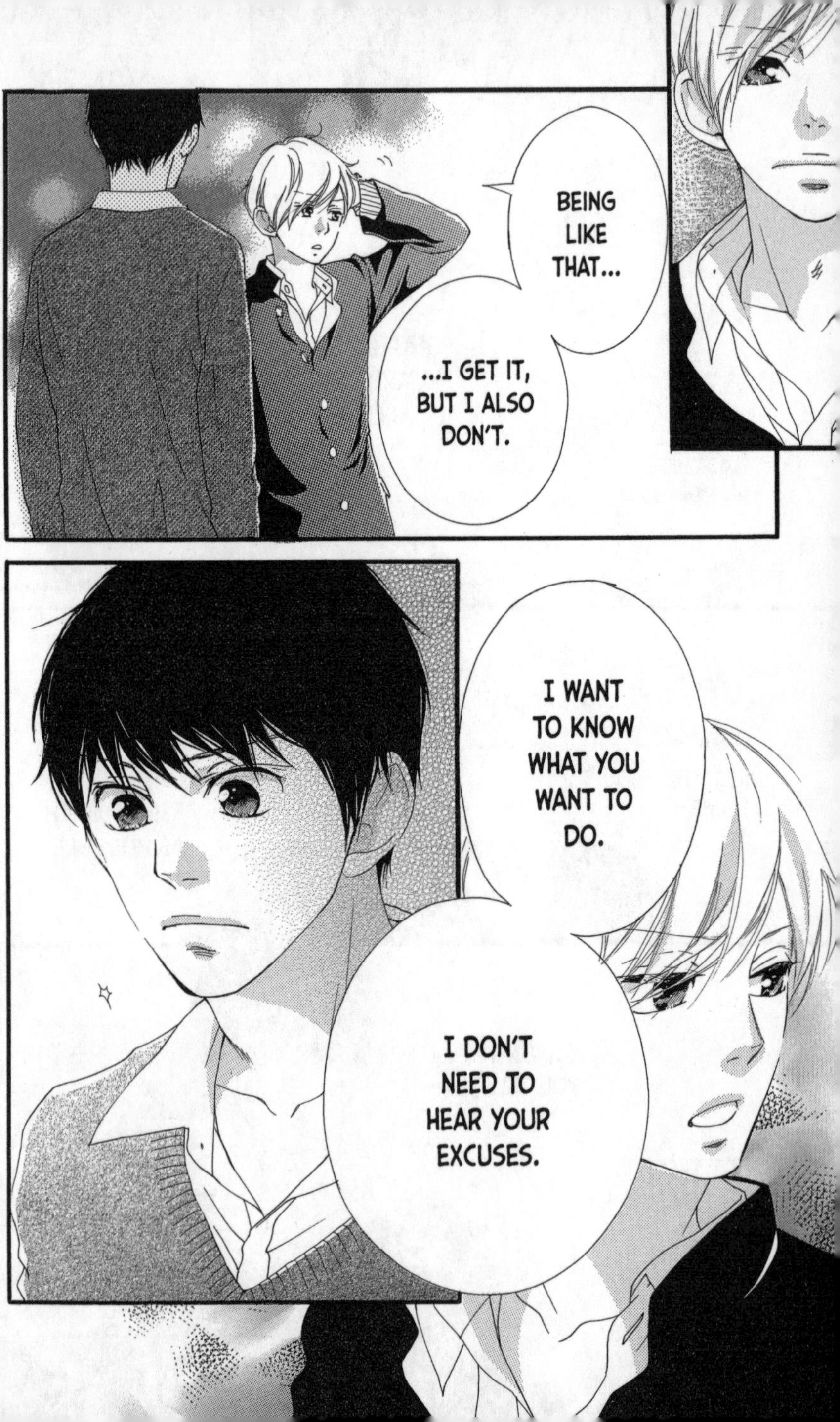
BEING LIKE THAT...
...I GET IT, BUT I ALSO DON'T.
I WANT TO KNOW WHAT YOU WANT TO DO.
I DON'T NEED TO HEAR YOUR EXCUSES.

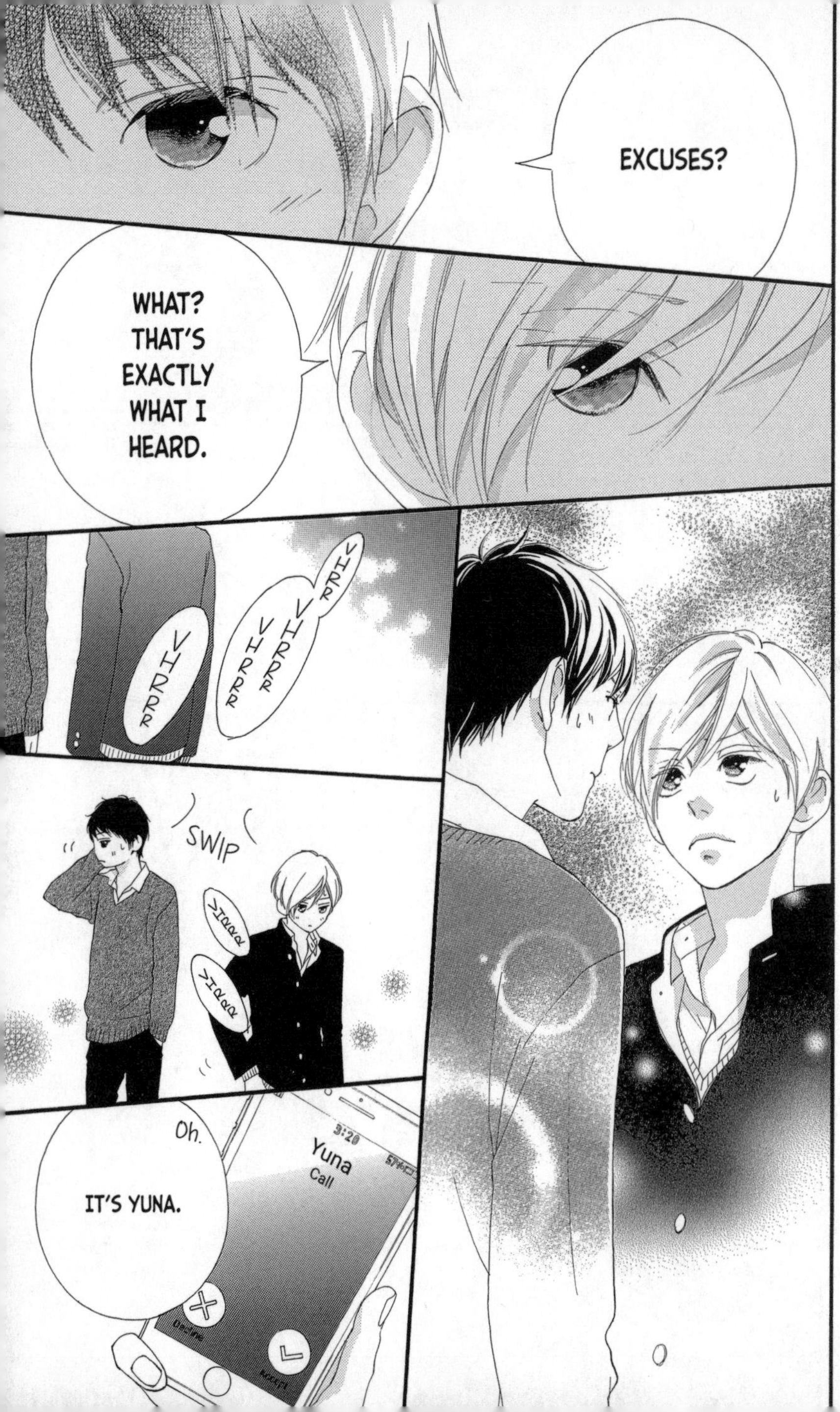
EXCUSES?
WHAT? THAT'S EXACTLY WHAT I HEARD.
VHRR
VHRRR
VHRRR
VHRRR
SWIP
VIRRR
VIRRR
3:20
Yuna
Call
Oh.
IT'S YUNA.

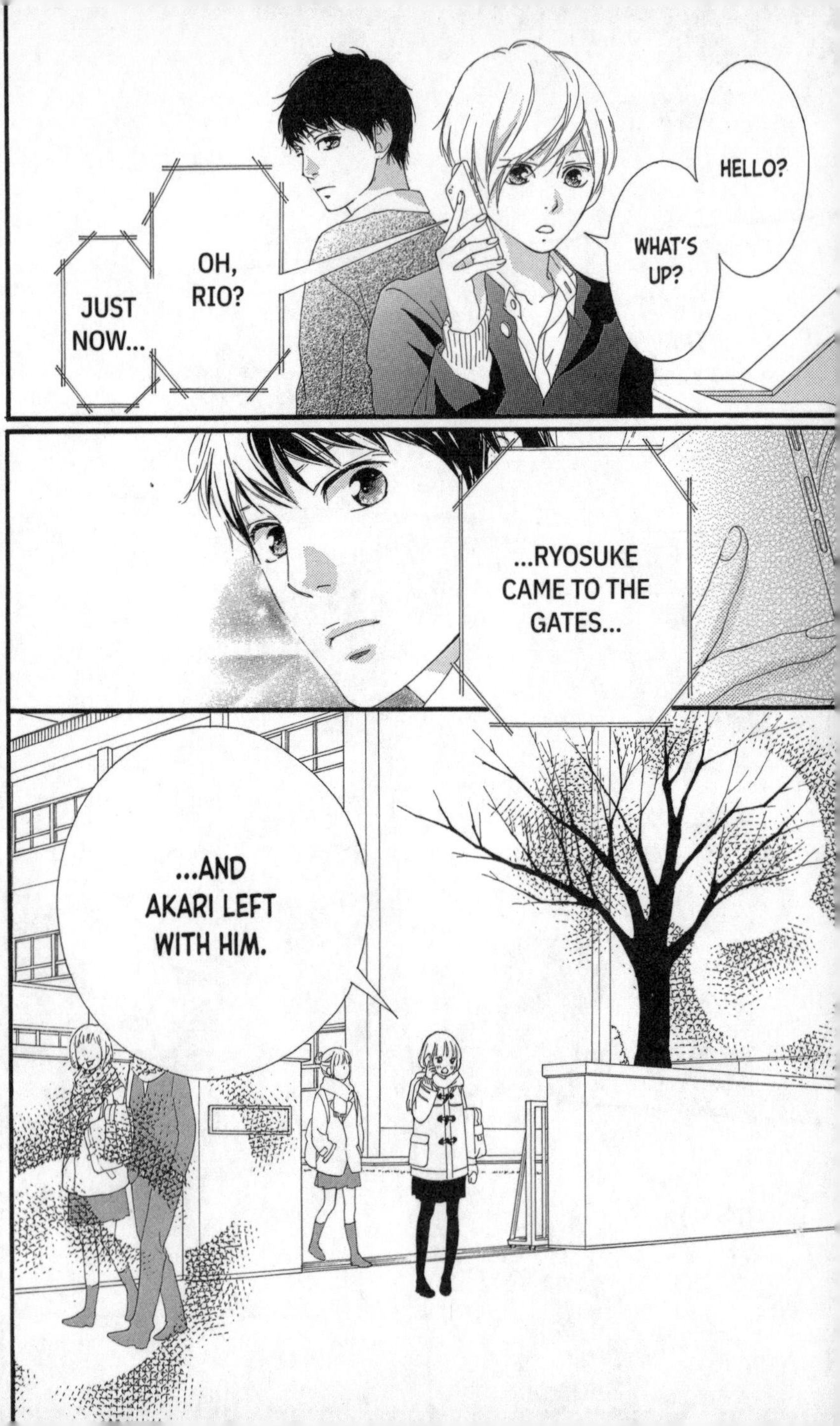
HELLO?
WHAT'S UP?
OH, RIO?
JUST NOW...
...RYOSUKE CAME TO THE GATES...
...AND AKARI LEFT WITH HIM.

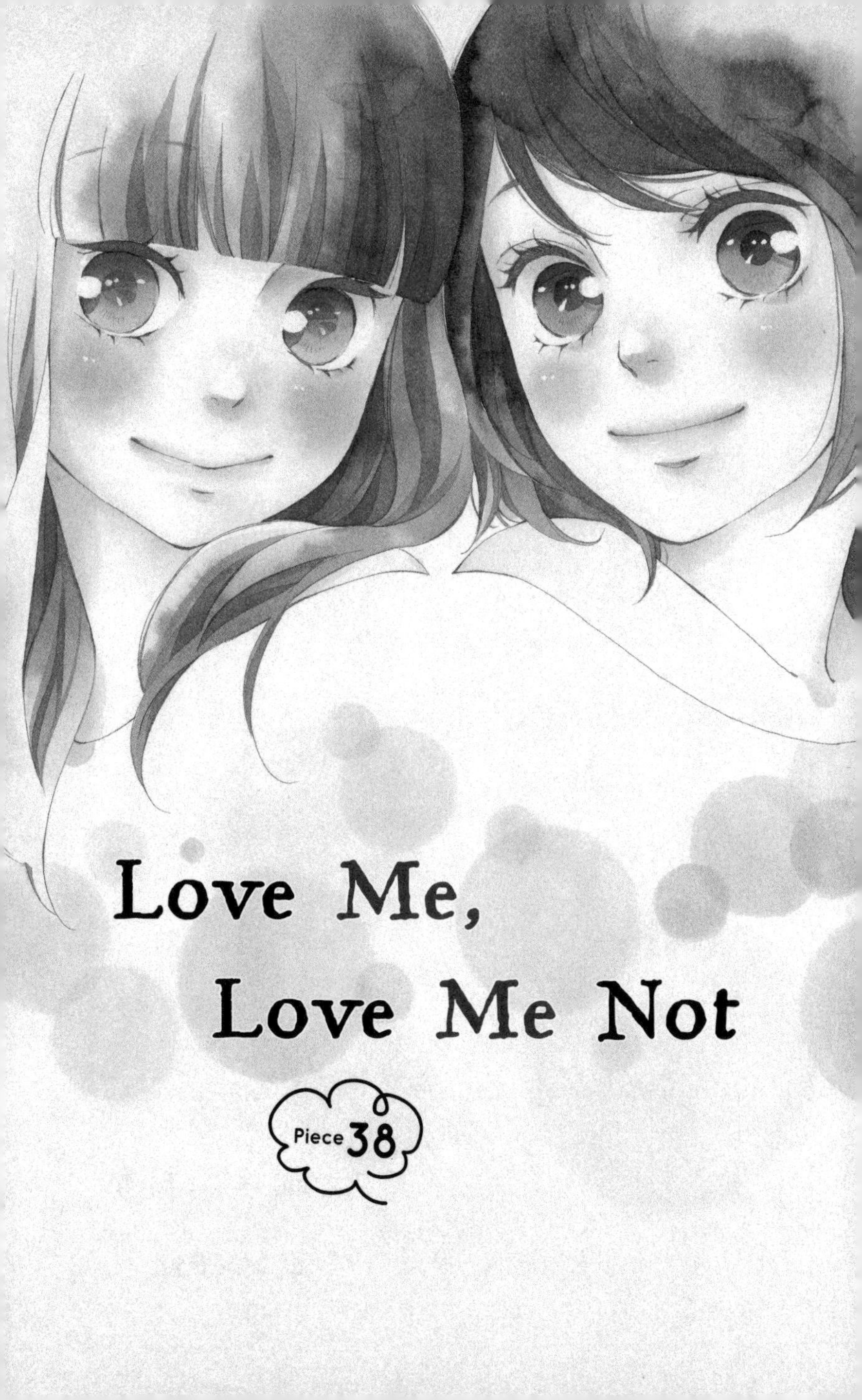
Love Me,
Love Me Not
Piece 38

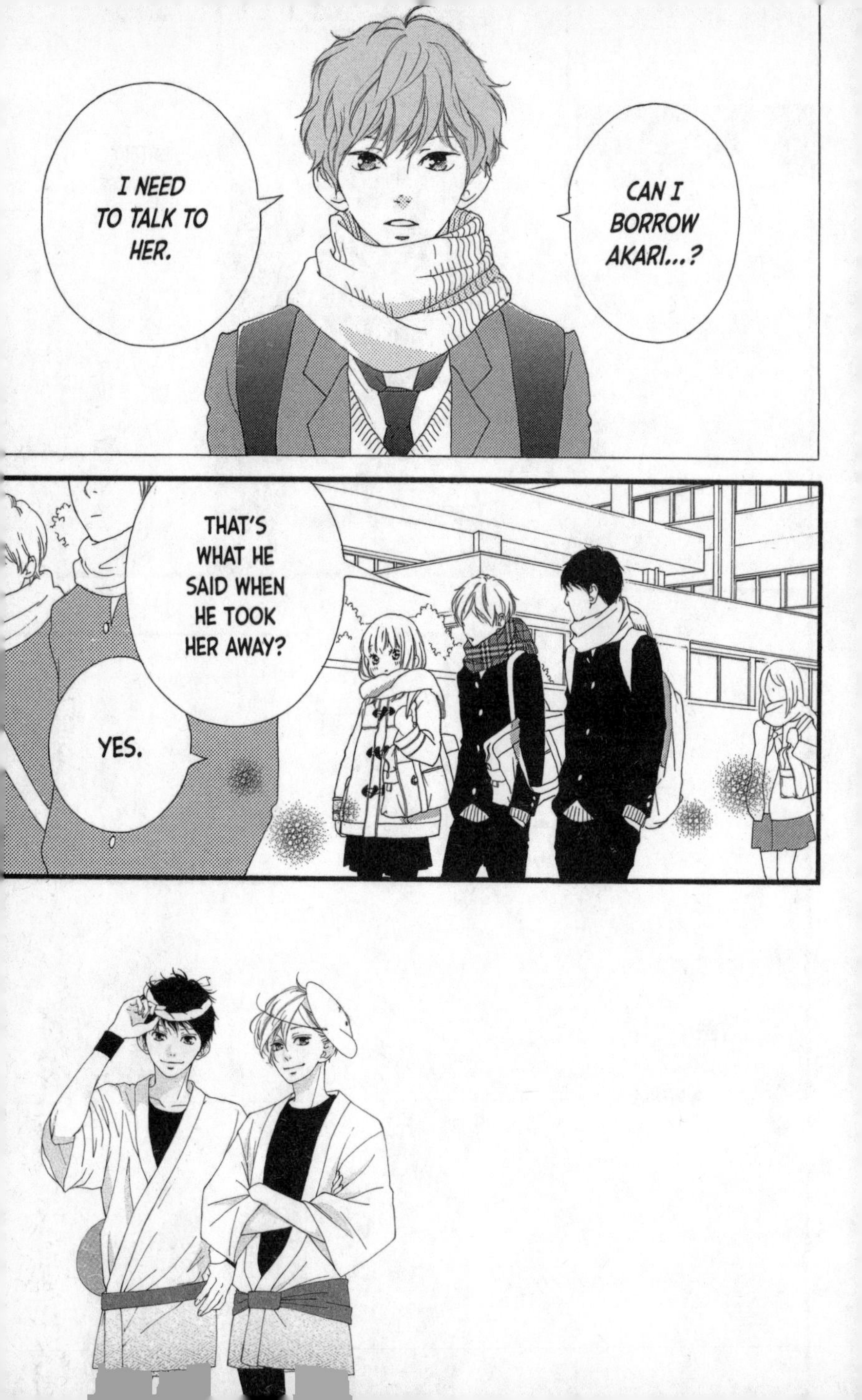
CAN I BORROW AKARI...?
I NEED TO TALK TO HER.
THAT'S WHAT HE SAID WHEN HE TOOK HER AWAY?
YES.

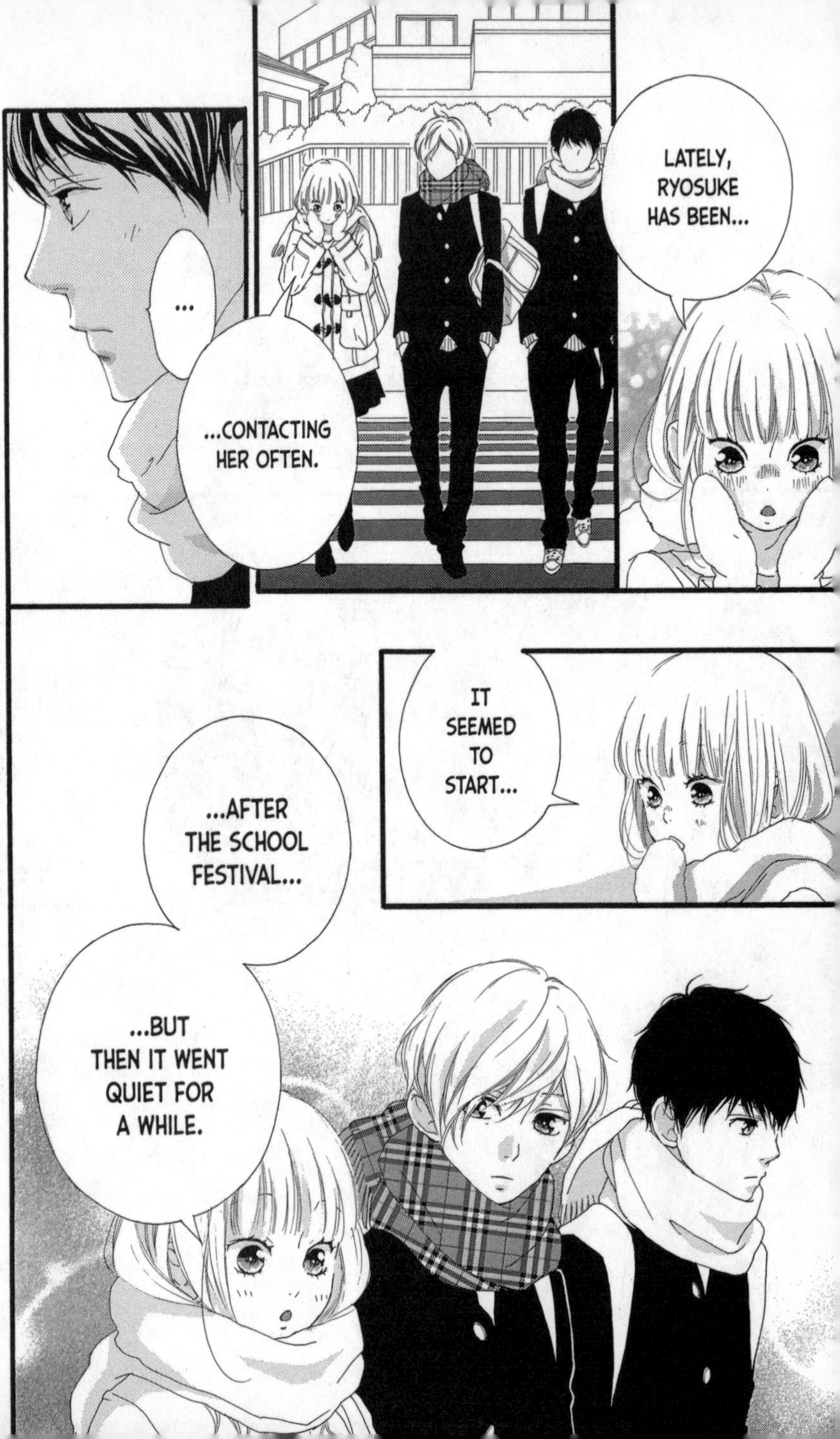
LATELY, RYOSUKE HAS BEEN...
...CONTACTING HER OFTEN.
...
IT SEEMED TO START...
...AFTER THE SCHOOL FESTIVAL...
...BUT THEN IT WENT QUIET FOR A WHILE.

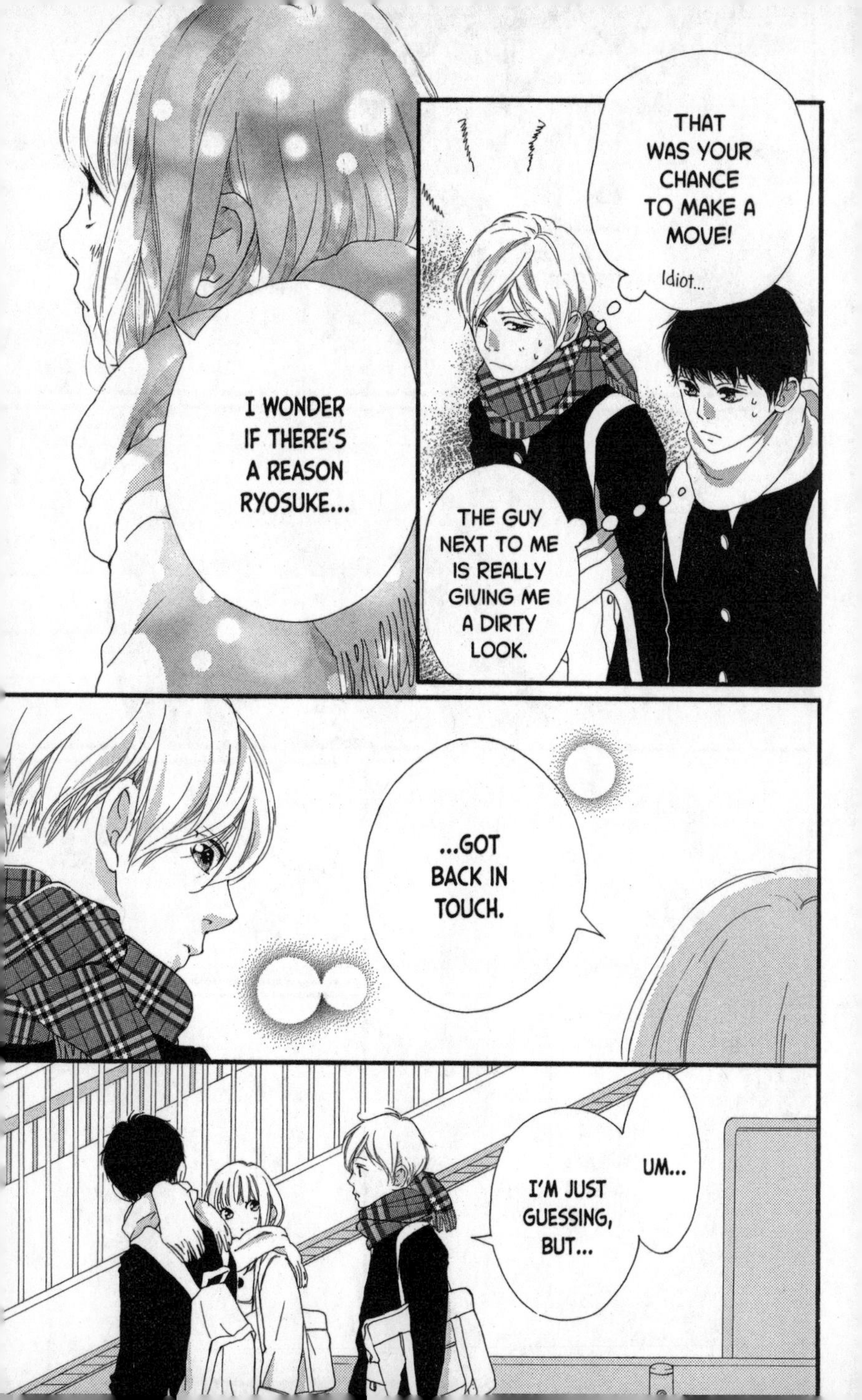
THAT WAS YOUR CHANCE TO MAKE A MOVE!
Idiot...
THE GUY NEXT TO ME IS REALLY GIVING ME A DIRTY LOOK.
I WONDER IF THERE'S A REASON RYOSUKE...
...GOT BACK IN TOUCH.
UM...
I'M JUST GUESSING, BUT...

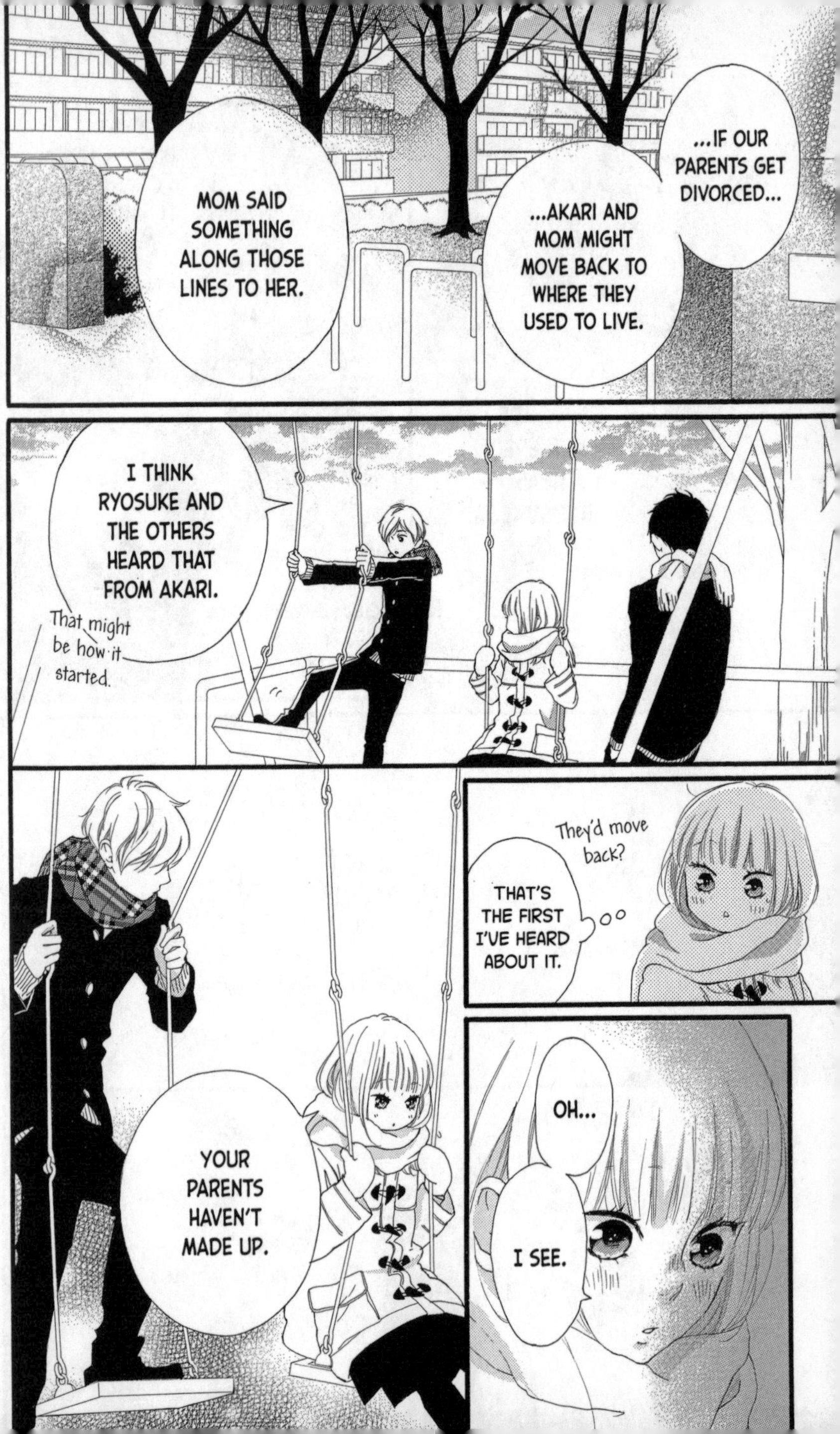
...IF OUR PARENTS GET DIVORCED...
...AKARI AND MOM MIGHT MOVE BACK TO WHERE THEY USED TO LIVE.
MOM SAID SOMETHING ALONG THOSE LINES TO HER.
I THINK RYOSUKE AND THE OTHERS HEARD THAT FROM AKARI.
That might be how it started.
They'd move back?
THAT'S THE FIRST I'VE HEARD ABOUT IT.
OH...
I SEE.
YOUR PARENTS HAVEN'T MADE UP.

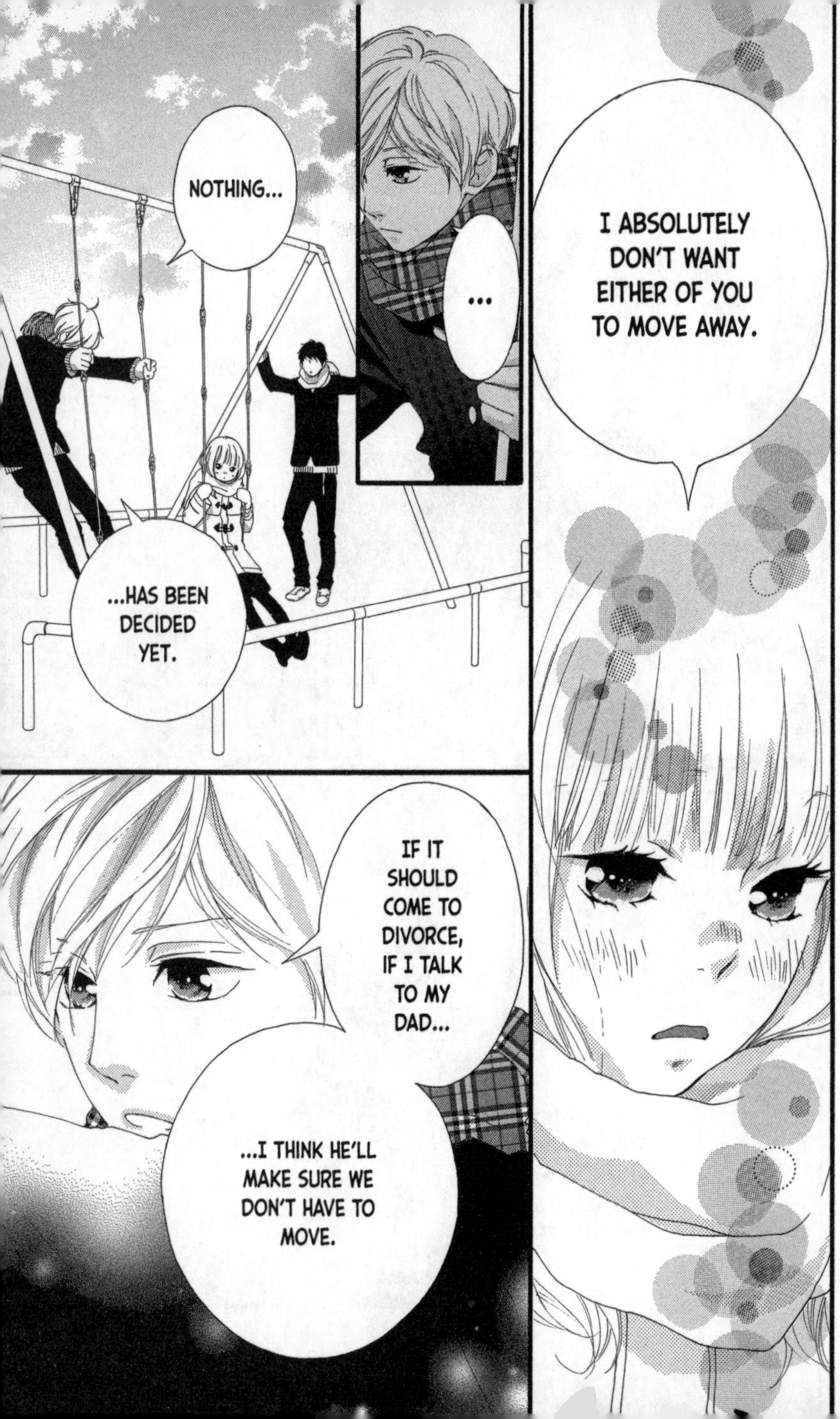
I ABSOLUTELY DON'T WANT EITHER OF YOU TO MOVE AWAY.
...
NOTHING...
...HAS BEEN DECIDED YET.
IF IT SHOULD COME TO DIVORCE, IF I TALK TO MY DAD...
...I THINK HE'LL MAKE SURE WE DON'T HAVE TO MOVE.

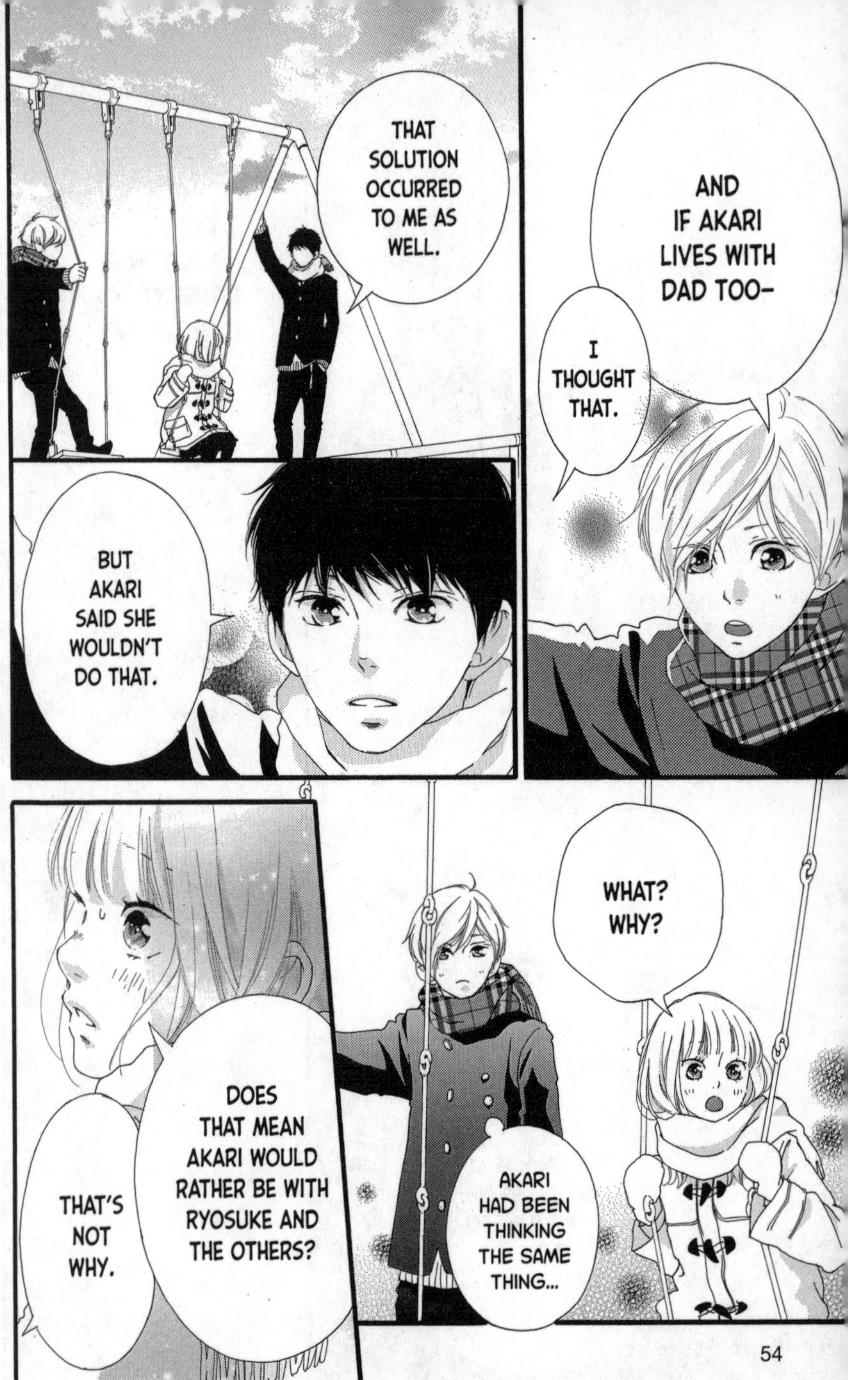
AND IF AKARI LIVES WITH DAD TOO—
I THOUGHT THAT.
THAT SOLUTION OCCURRED TO ME AS WELL.
BUT AKARI SAID SHE WOULDN'T DO THAT.
WHAT? WHY?
AKARI HAD BEEN THINKING THE SAME THING...
DOES THAT MEAN AKARI WOULD RATHER BE WITH RYOSUKE AND THE OTHERS?
THAT'S NOT WHY.

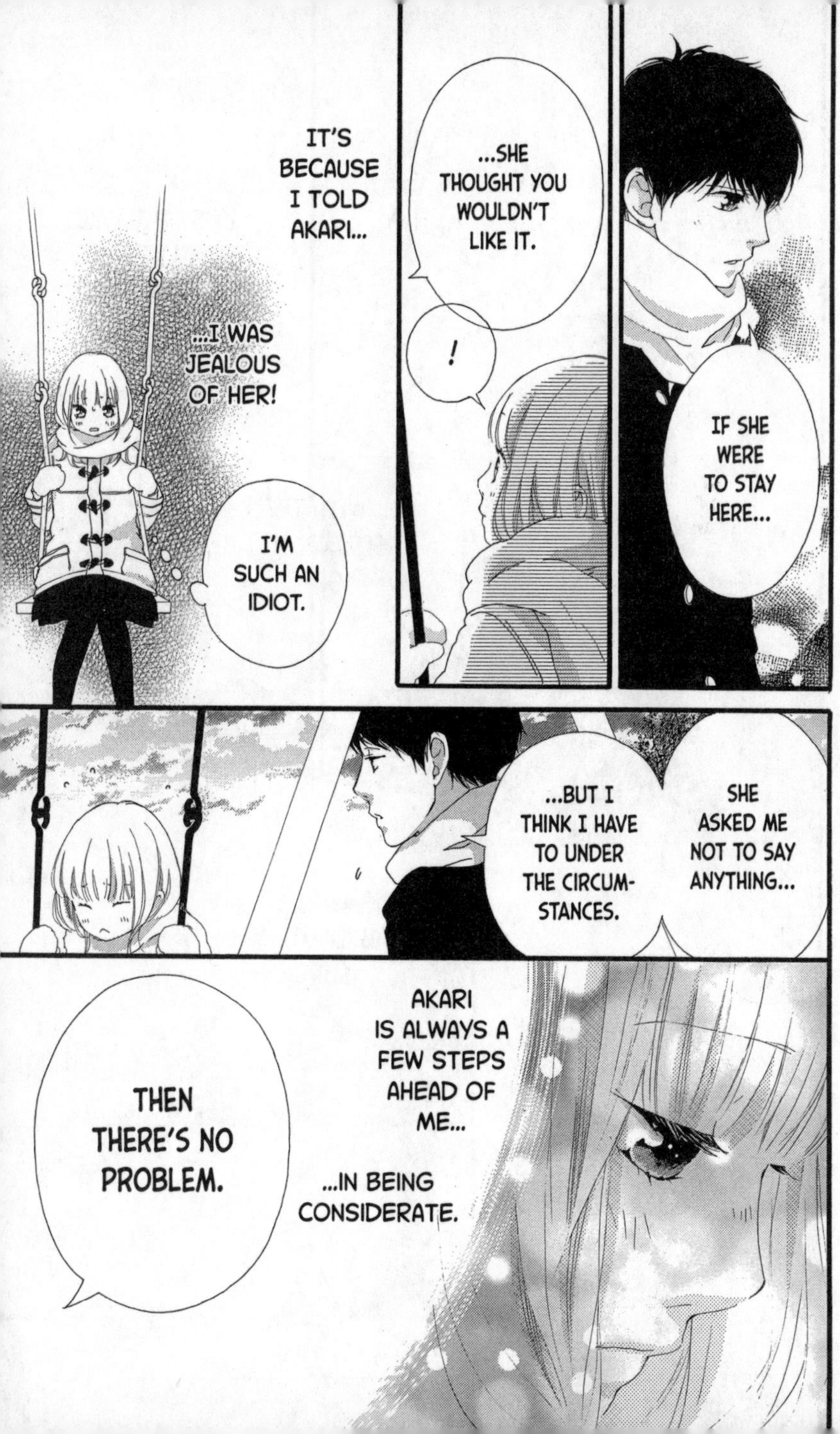
IF SHE WERE TO STAY HERE...
...SHE THOUGHT YOU WOULDN'T LIKE IT.
!
IT'S BECAUSE I TOLD AKARI...
...I WAS JEALOUS OF HER!
I'M SUCH AN IDIOT.
SHE ASKED ME NOT TO SAY ANYTHING...
...BUT I THINK I HAVE TO UNDER THE CIRCUM-STANCES.
AKARI IS ALWAYS A FEW STEPS AHEAD OF ME...
...IN BEING CONSIDERATE.
THEN THERE'S NO PROBLEM.

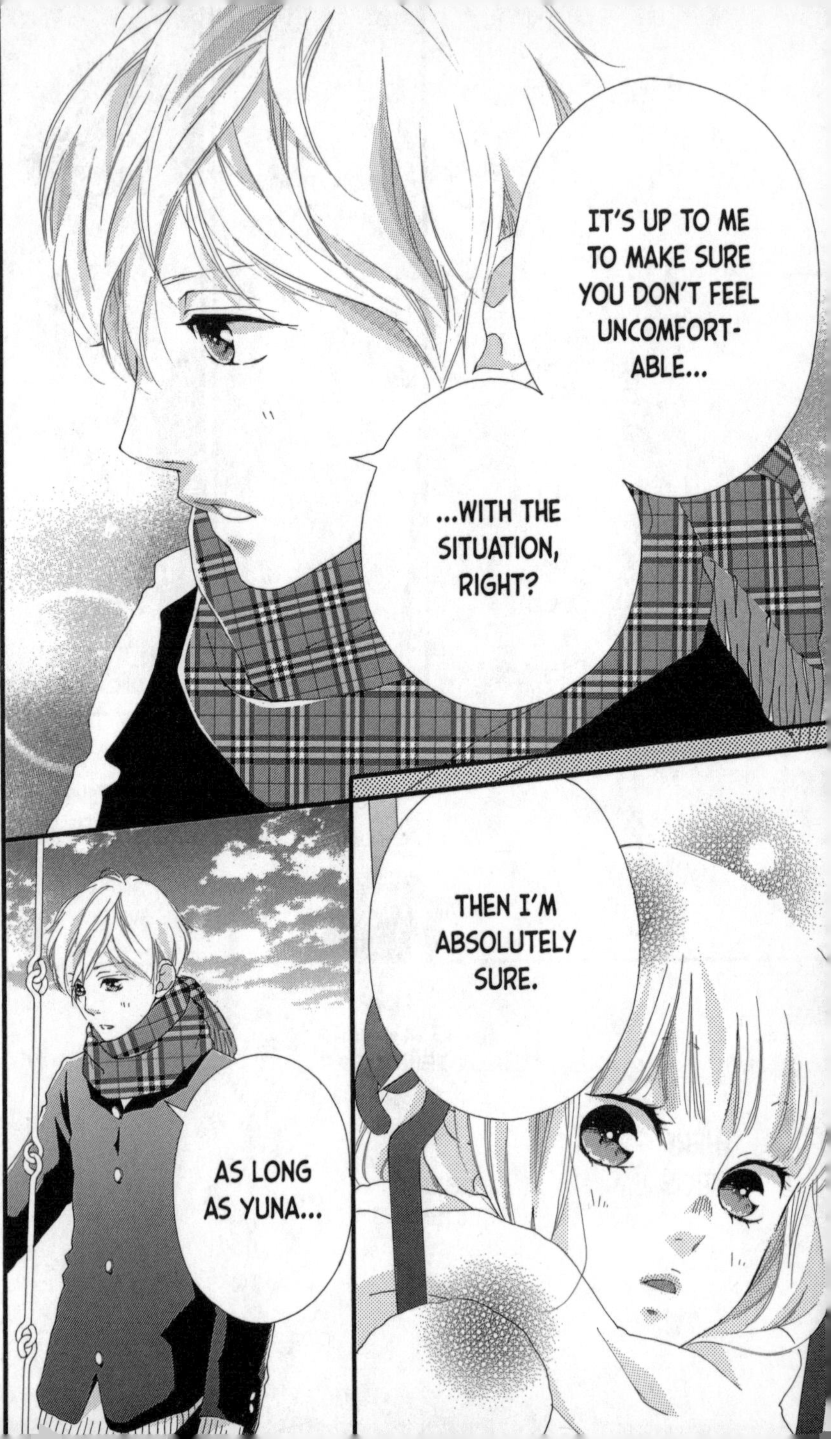
IT'S UP TO ME TO MAKE SURE YOU DON'T FEEL UNCOMFORT-ABLE...
...WITH THE SITUATION, RIGHT?
THEN I'M ABSOLUTELY SURE.
AS LONG AS YUNA...

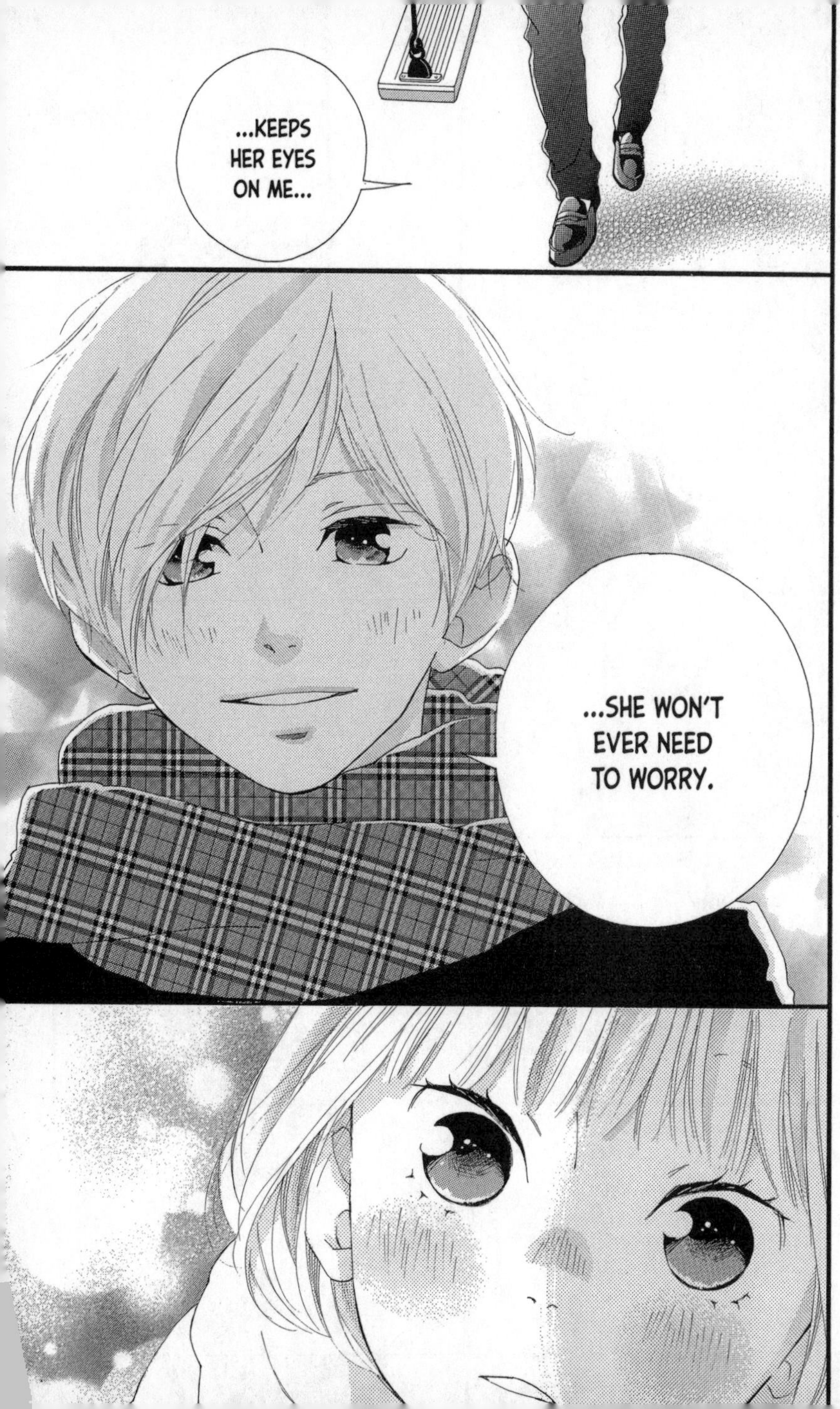
...KEEPS HER EYES ON ME...
...SHE WON'T EVER NEED TO WORRY.

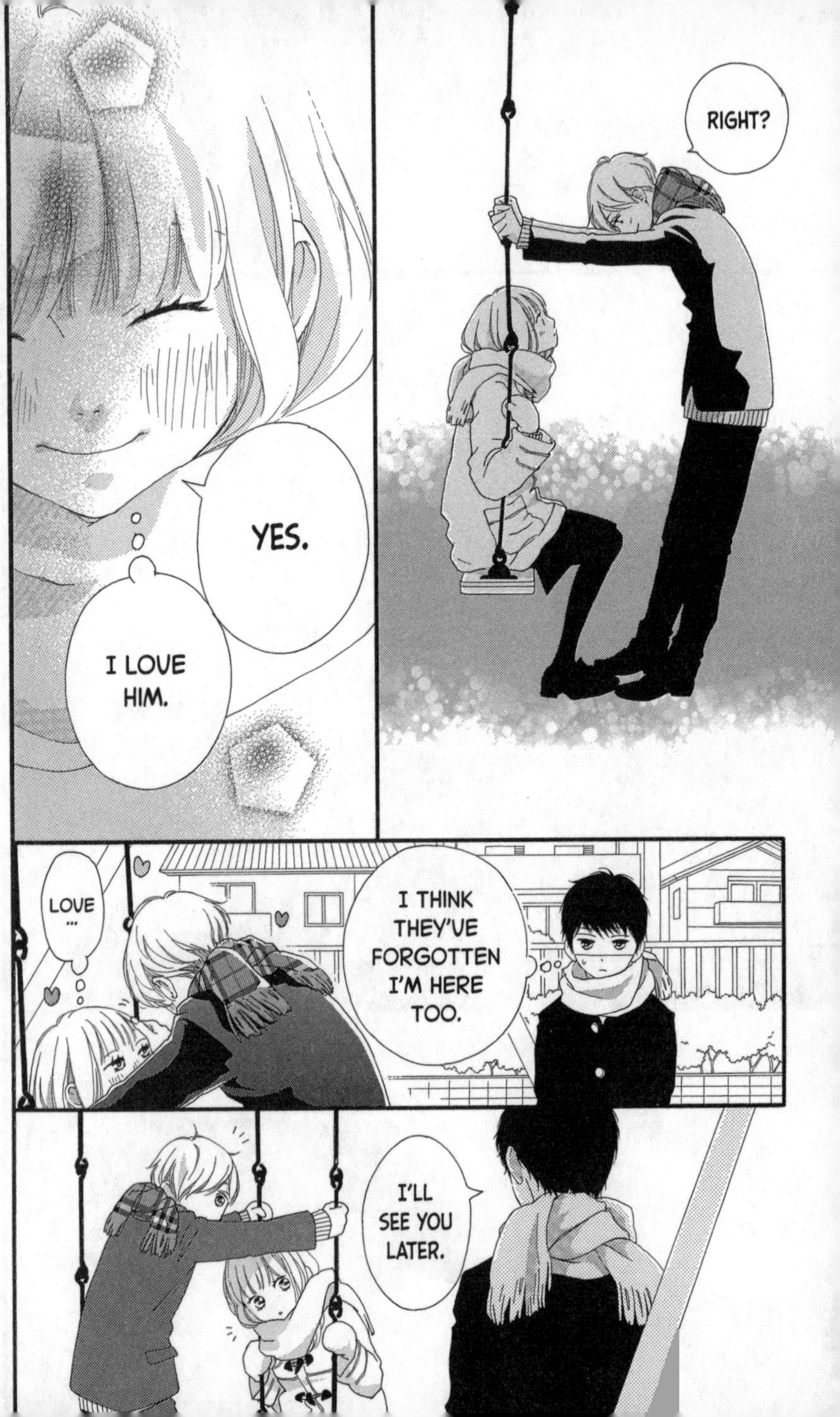
RIGHT?
YES.
I LOVE HIM.
I THINK THEY'VE FORGOTTEN I'M HERE TOO.
LOVE...
I'LL SEE YOU LATER.

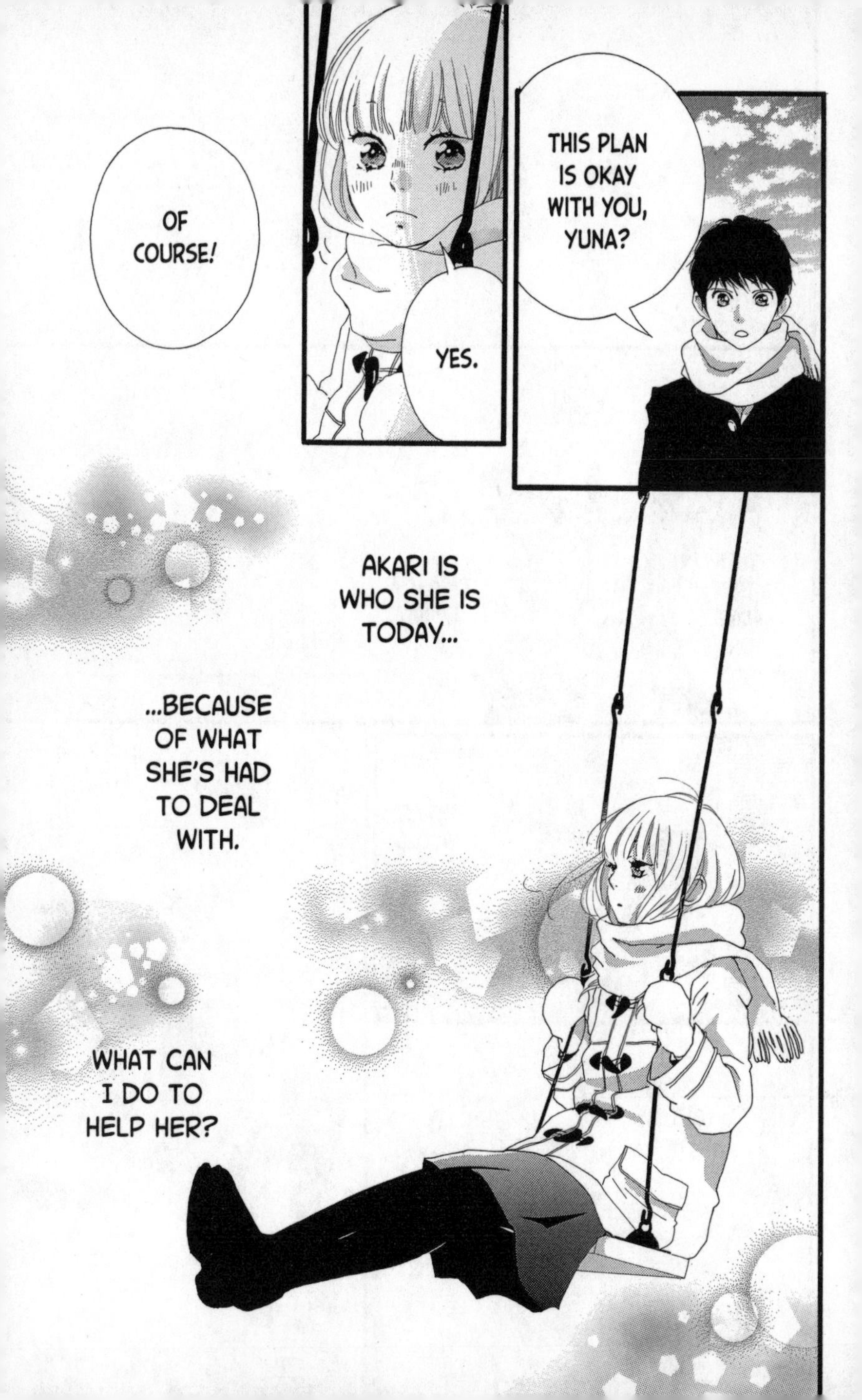
THIS PLAN IS OKAY WITH YOU, YUNA?
YES.
OF COURSE!
AKARI IS WHO SHE IS TODAY...
...BECAUSE OF WHAT SHE'S HAD TO DEAL WITH.
WHAT CAN I DO TO HELP HER?

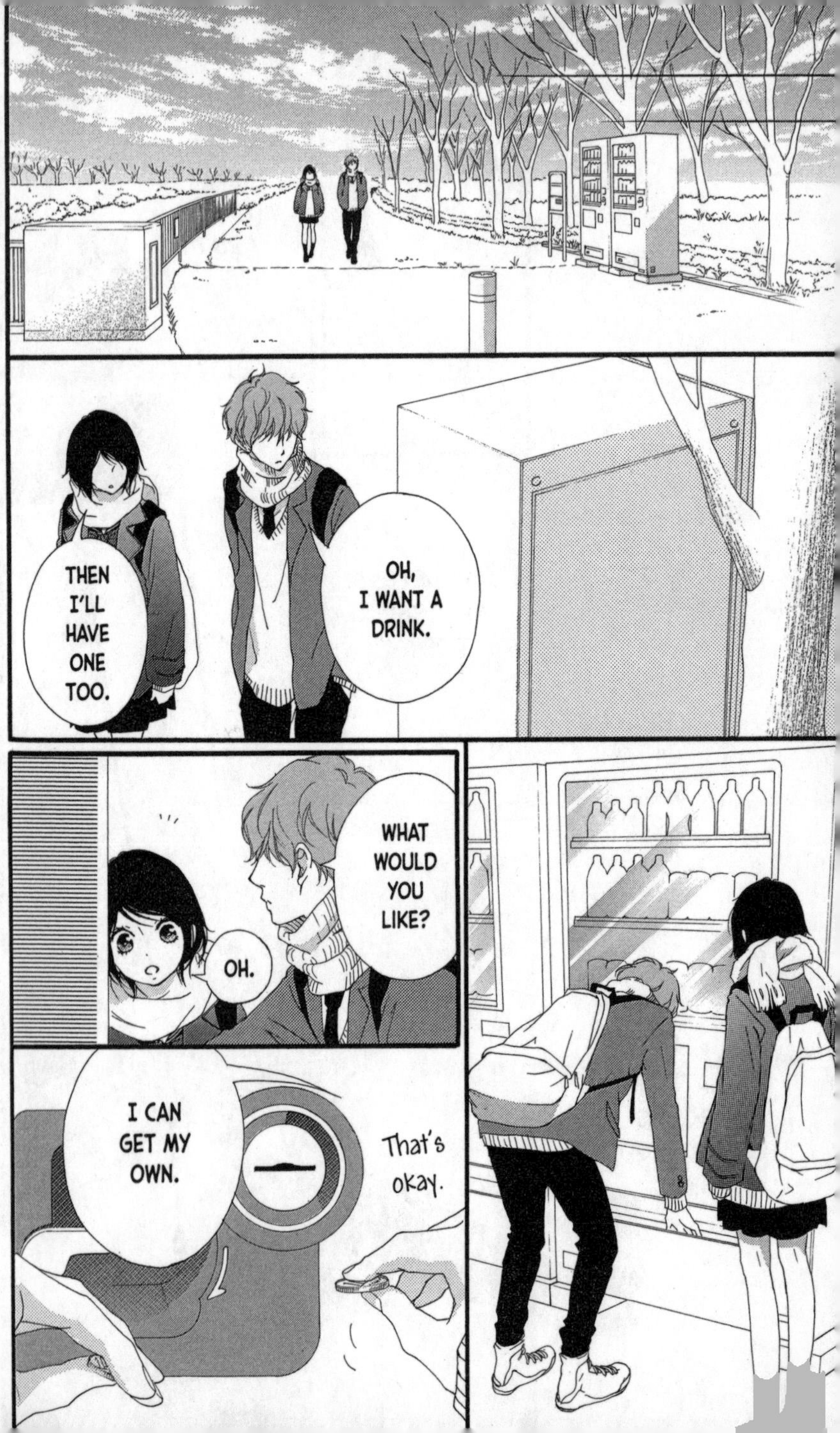
OH, I WANT A DRINK.
THEN I'LL HAVE ONE TOO.
WHAT WOULD YOU LIKE?
OH.
That's okay.
I CAN GET MY OWN.

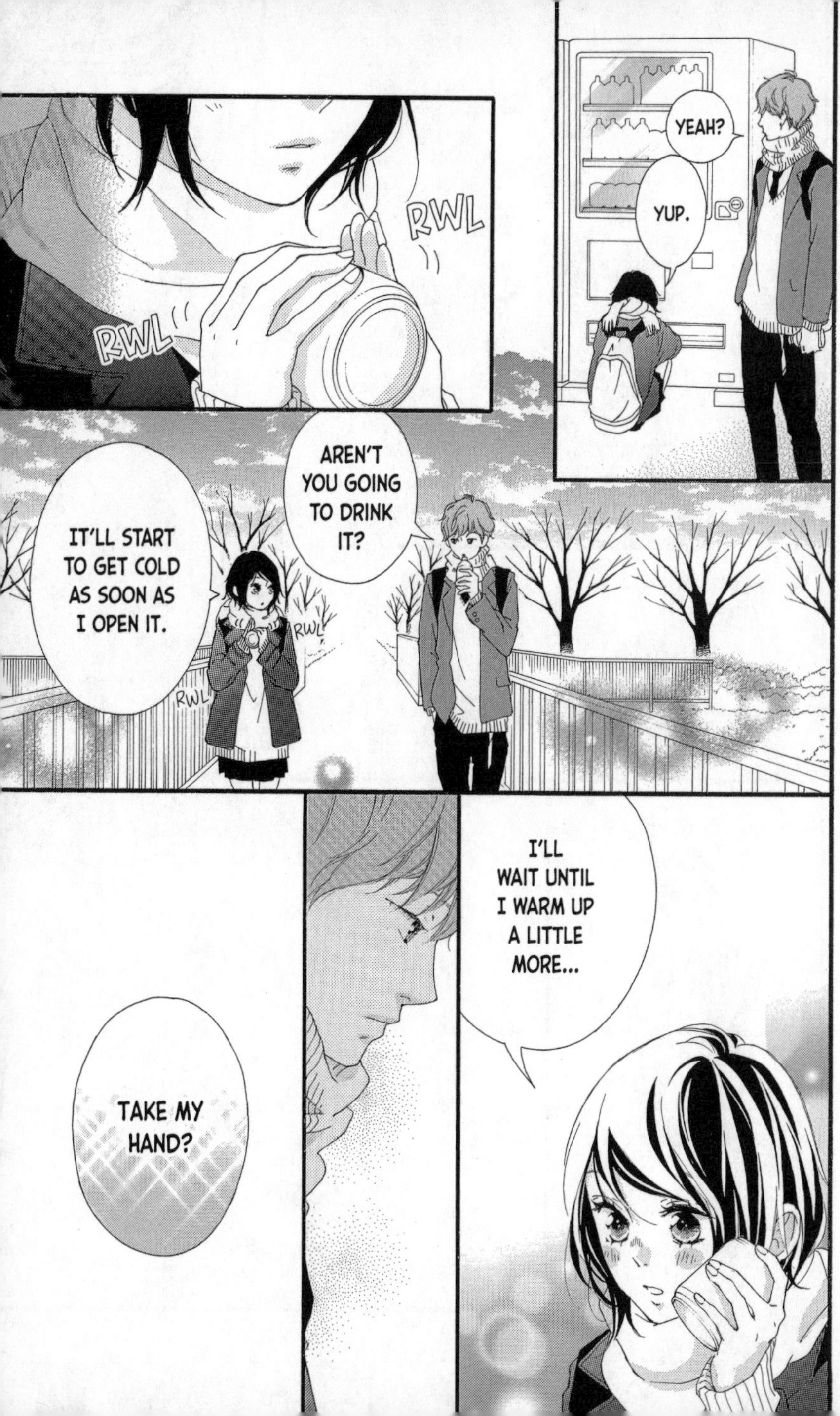
YEAH?
YUP.
RWL
RWL
AREN'T YOU GOING TO DRINK IT?
IT'LL START TO GET COLD AS SOON AS I OPEN IT.
RWL
RWL
I'LL WAIT UNTIL I WARM UP A LITTLE MORE...
TAKE MY HAND?

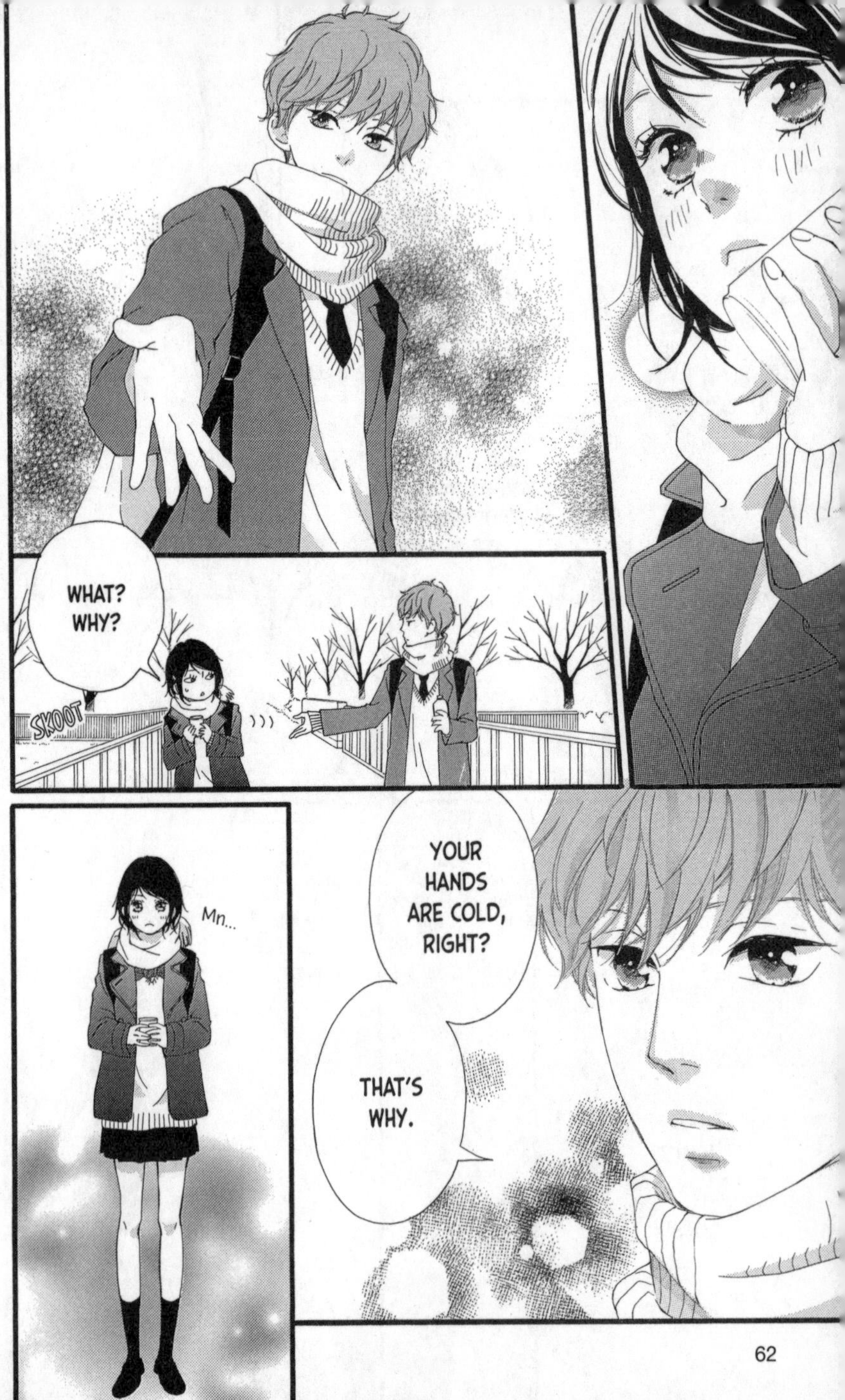
WHAT? WHY?
SKOOT
YOUR HANDS ARE COLD, RIGHT?
THAT'S WHY.
Mn...

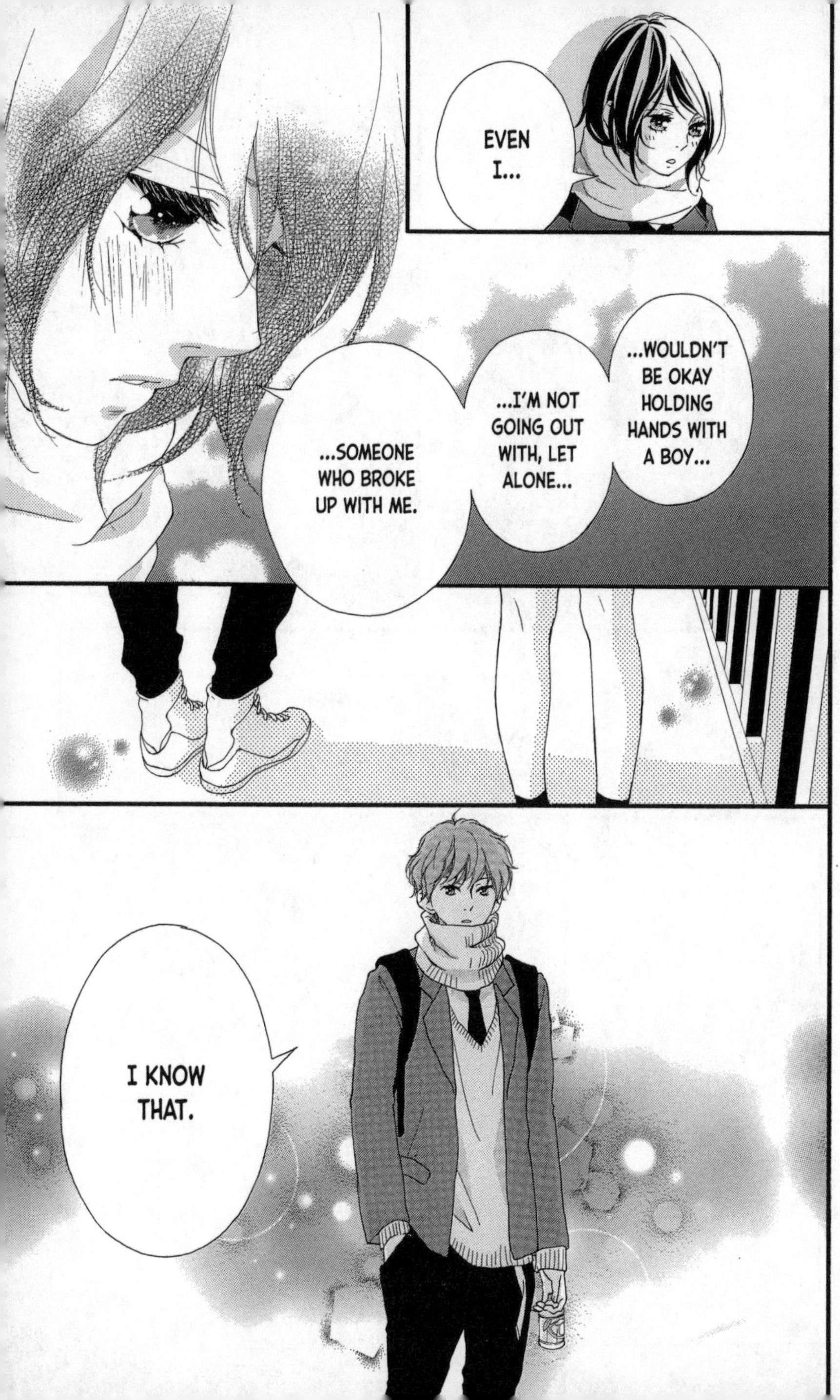
EVEN I...
...WOULDN'T BE OKAY HOLDING HANDS WITH A BOY...
...I'M NOT GOING OUT WITH, LET ALONE...
...SOMEONE WHO BROKE UP WITH ME.
I KNOW THAT.

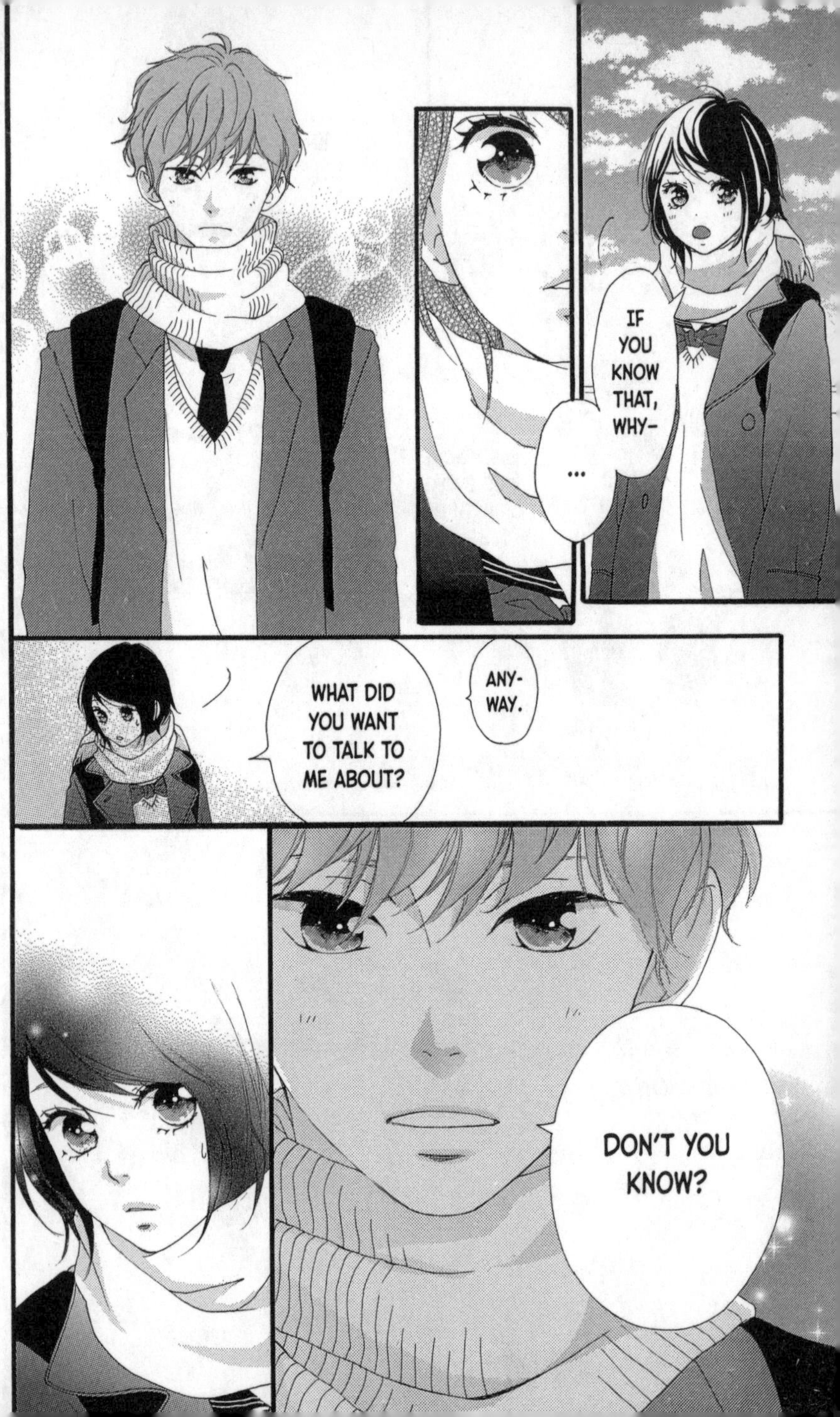
IF YOU KNOW THAT, WHY-
...
ANY-WAY.
WHAT DID YOU WANT TO TALK TO ME ABOUT?
DON'T YOU KNOW?

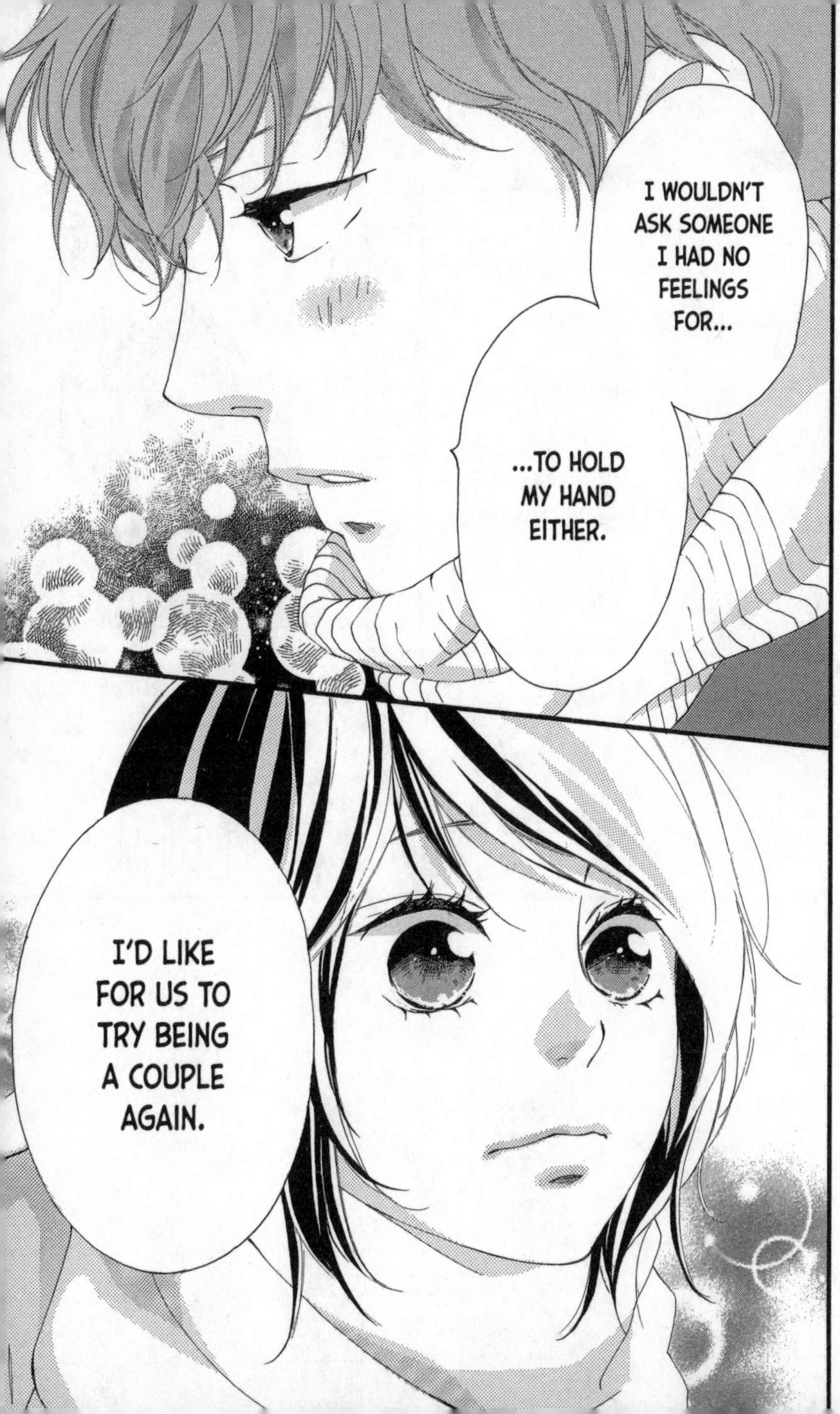
I WOULDN'T ASK SOMEONE I HAD NO FEELINGS FOR...
...TO HOLD MY HAND EITHER.
I'D LIKE FOR US TO TRY BEING A COUPLE AGAIN.

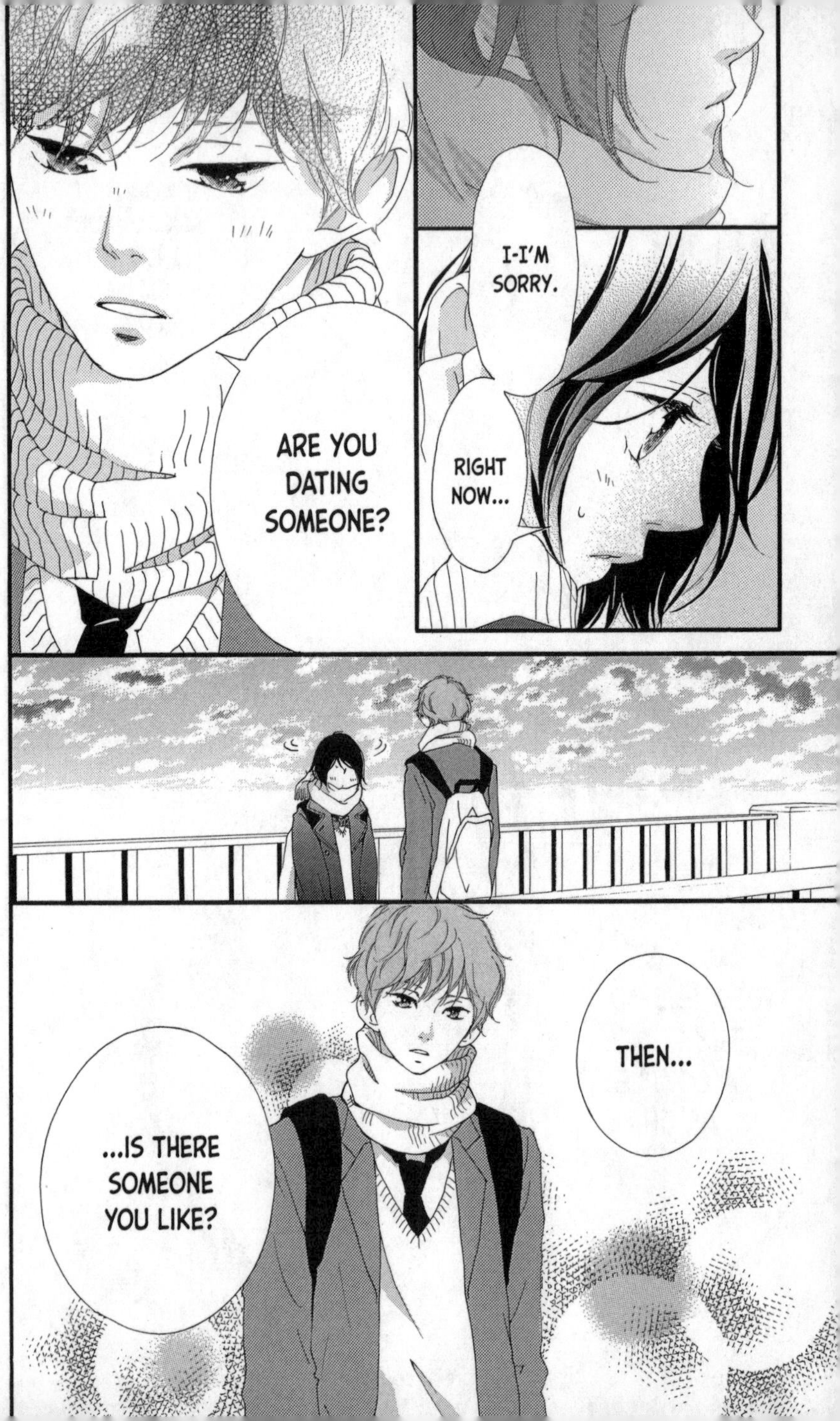
I-I'M SORRY.
RIGHT NOW...
ARE YOU DATING SOMEONE?
THEN...
...IS THERE SOMEONE YOU LIKE?

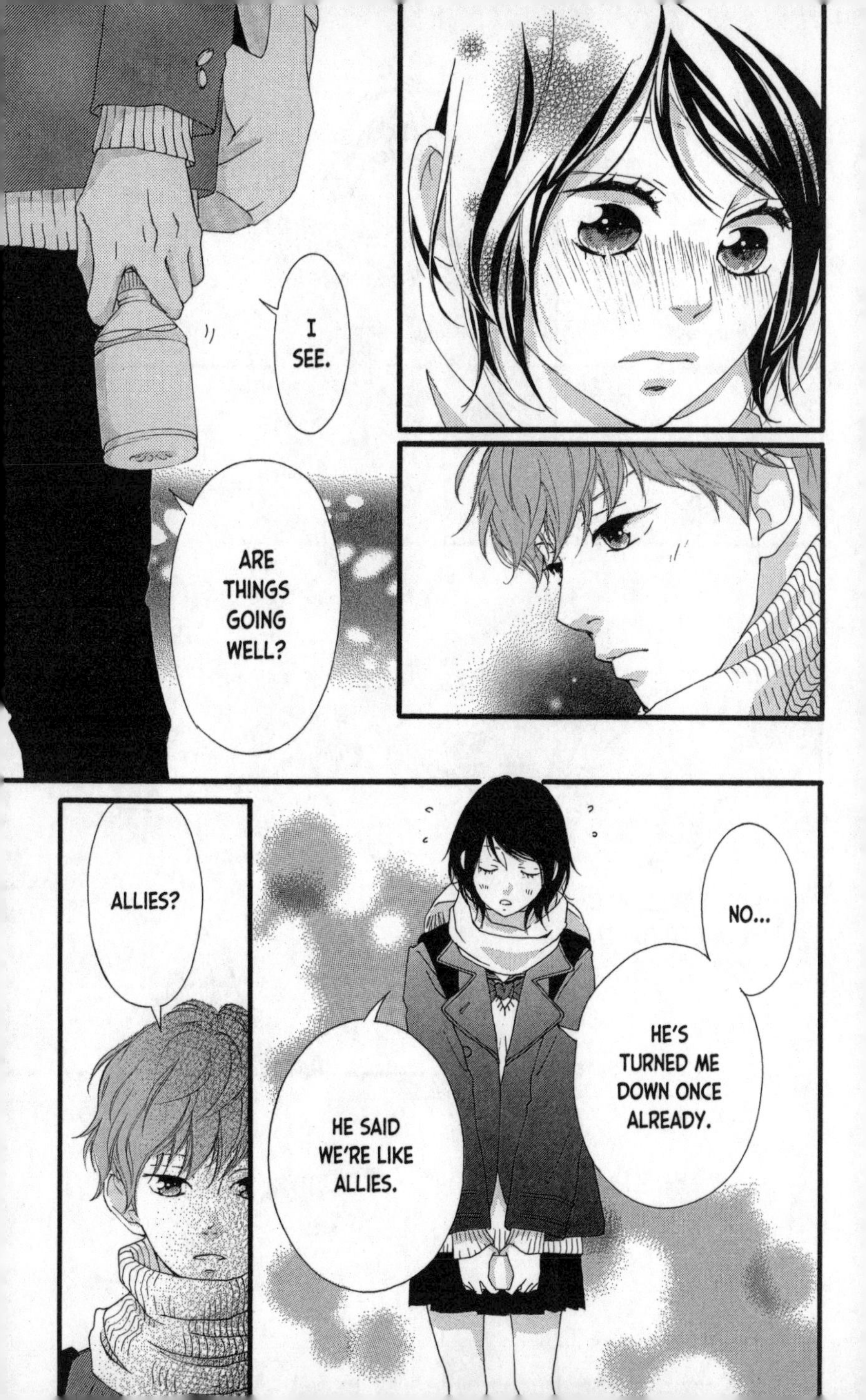
I SEE.
ARE THINGS GOING WELL?
NO...
HE'S TURNED ME DOWN ONCE ALREADY.
HE SAID WE'RE LIKE ALLIES.
ALLIES?

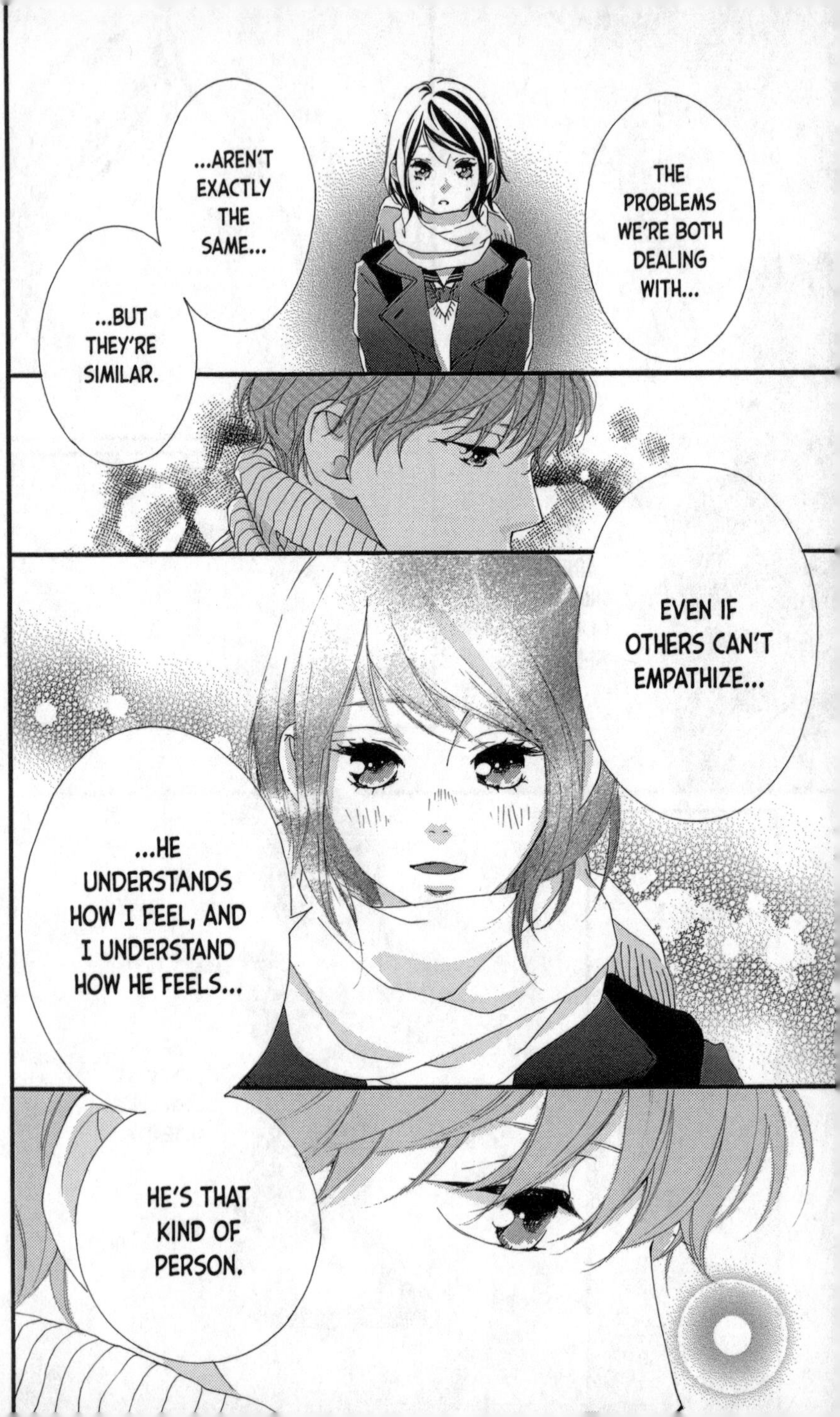
THE PROBLEMS WE'RE BOTH DEALING WITH...
...AREN'T EXACTLY THE SAME...
...BUT THEY'RE SIMILAR.
EVEN IF OTHERS CAN'T EMPATHIZE...
...HE UNDERSTANDS HOW I FEEL, AND I UNDERSTAND HOW HE FEELS...
HE'S THAT KIND OF PERSON.

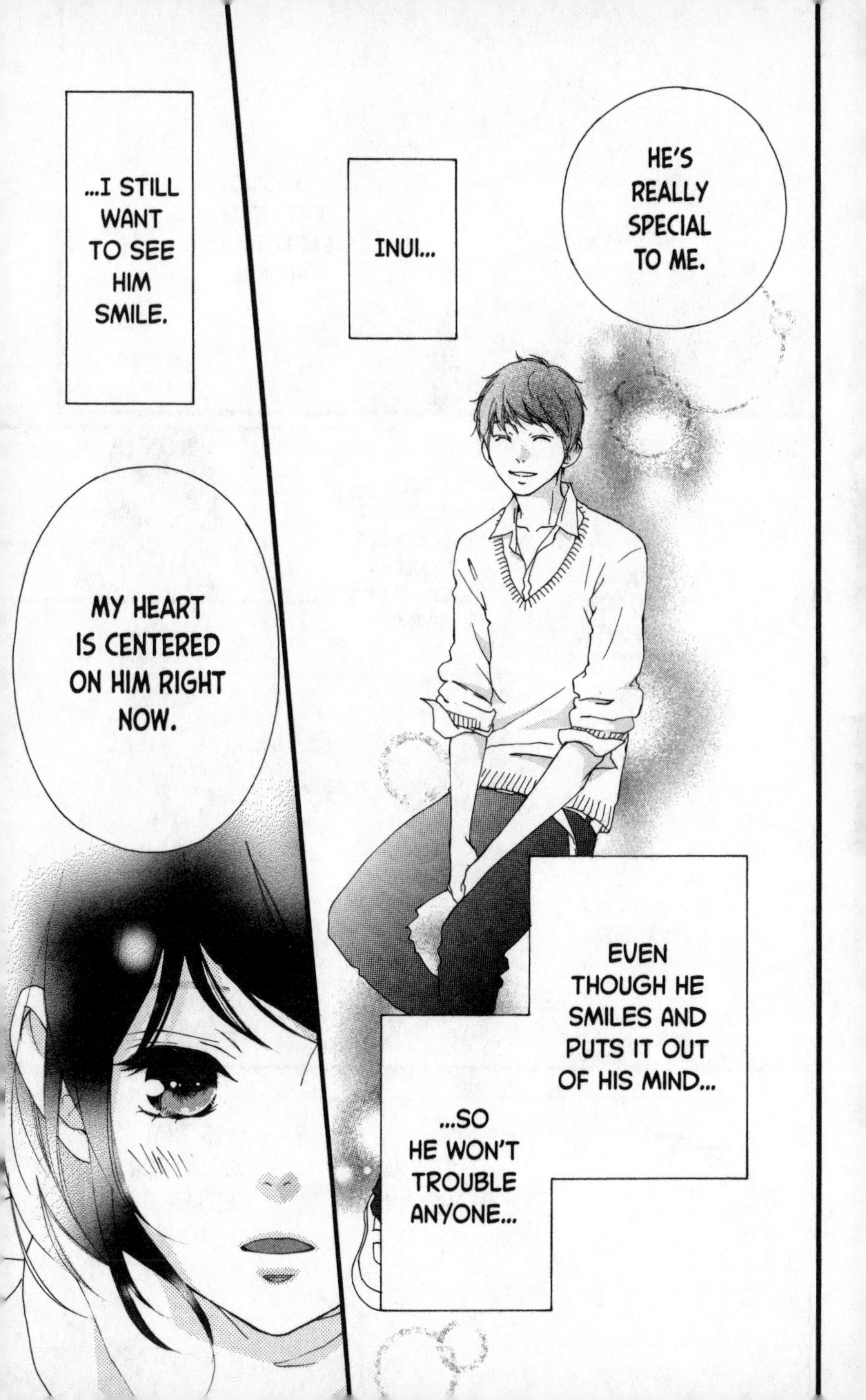
HE'S REALLY SPECIAL TO ME.
INUI...
EVEN THOUGH HE SMILES AND PUTS IT OUT OF HIS MIND...
...SO HE WON'T TROUBLE ANYONE...
...I STILL WANT TO SEE HIM SMILE.
MY HEART IS CENTERED ON HIM RIGHT NOW.

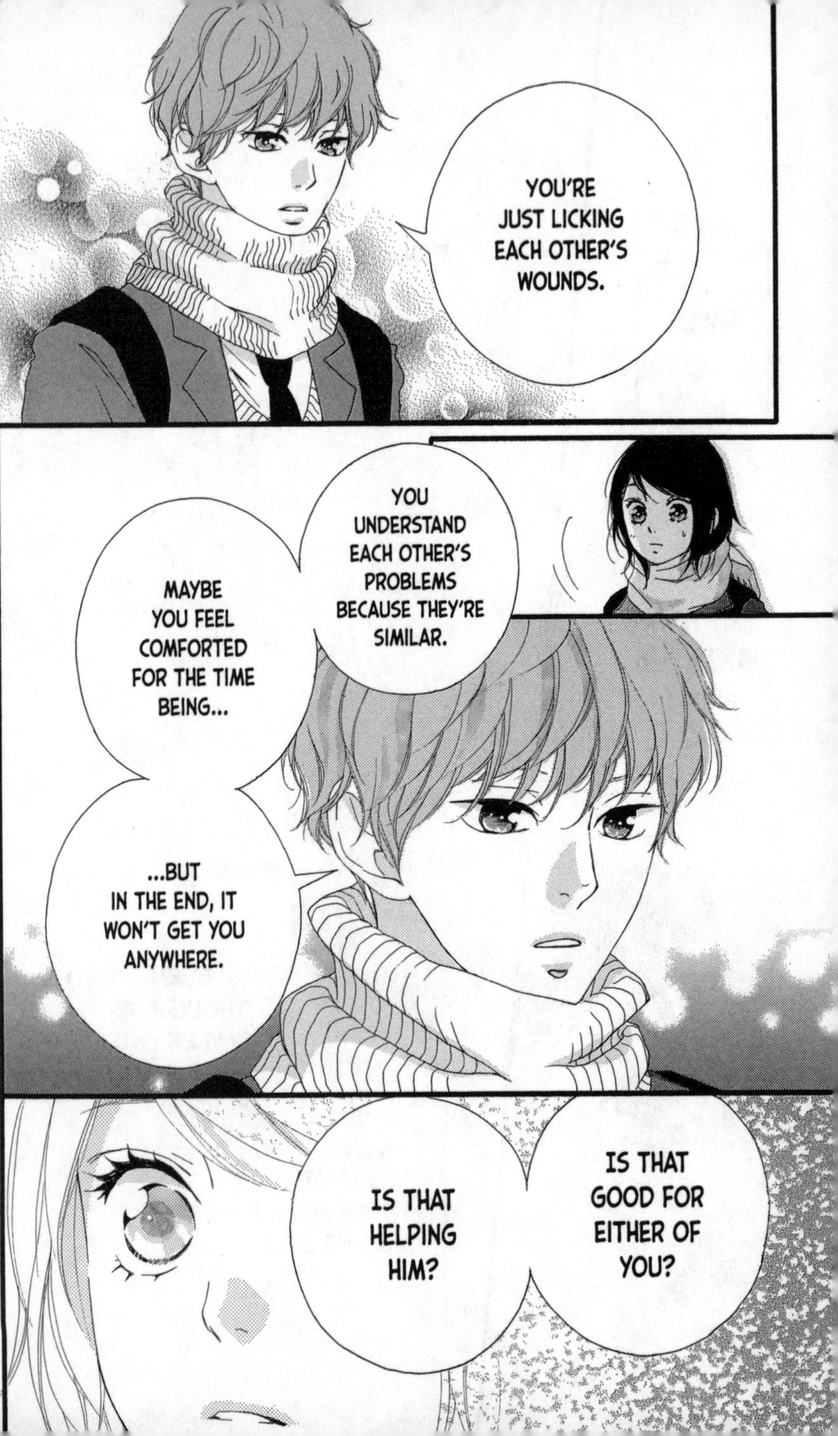
YOU'RE JUST LICKING EACH OTHER'S WOUNDS.
YOU UNDERSTAND EACH OTHER'S PROBLEMS BECAUSE THEY'RE SIMILAR.
MAYBE YOU FEEL COMFORTED FOR THE TIME BEING...
...BUT IN THE END, IT WON'T GET YOU ANYWHERE.
IS THAT GOOD FOR EITHER OF YOU?
IS THAT HELPING HIM?

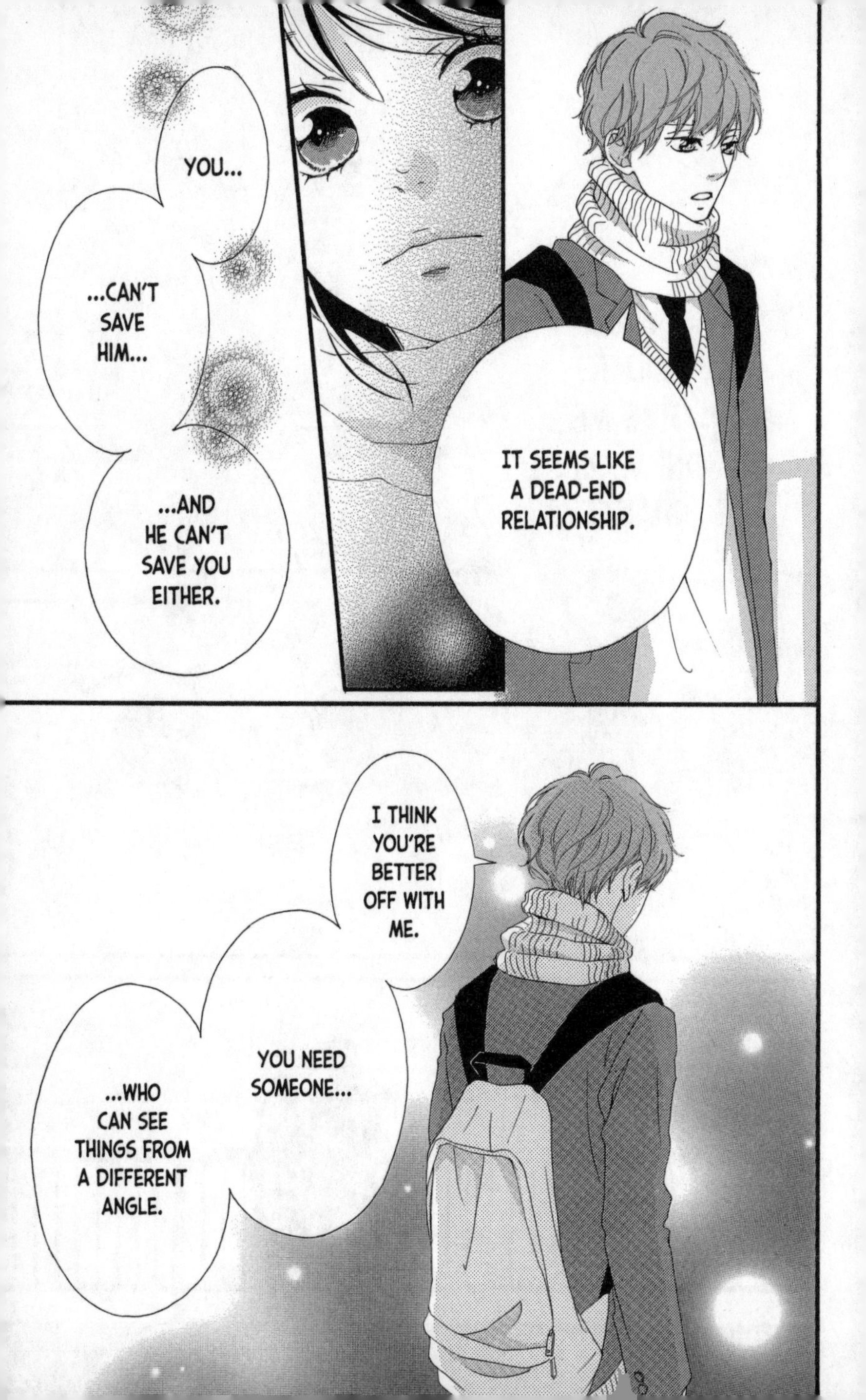
IT SEEMS LIKE A DEAD-END RELATIONSHIP.
YOU...
...CAN'T SAVE HIM...
...AND HE CAN'T SAVE YOU EITHER.
I THINK YOU'RE BETTER OFF WITH ME.
YOU NEED SOMEONE...
...WHO CAN SEE THINGS FROM A DIFFERENT ANGLE.

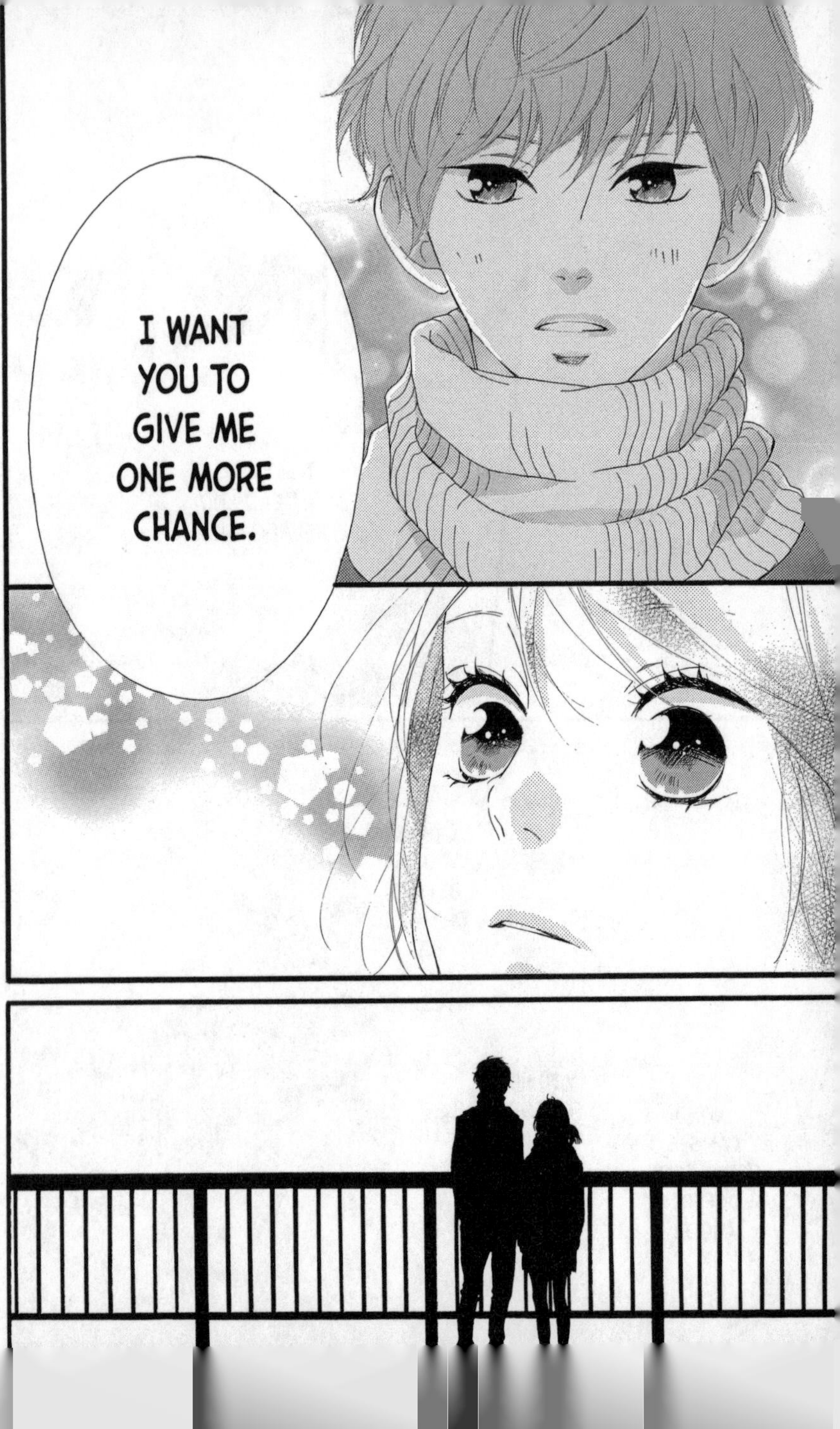
I WANT YOU TO GIVE ME ONE MORE CHANCE.

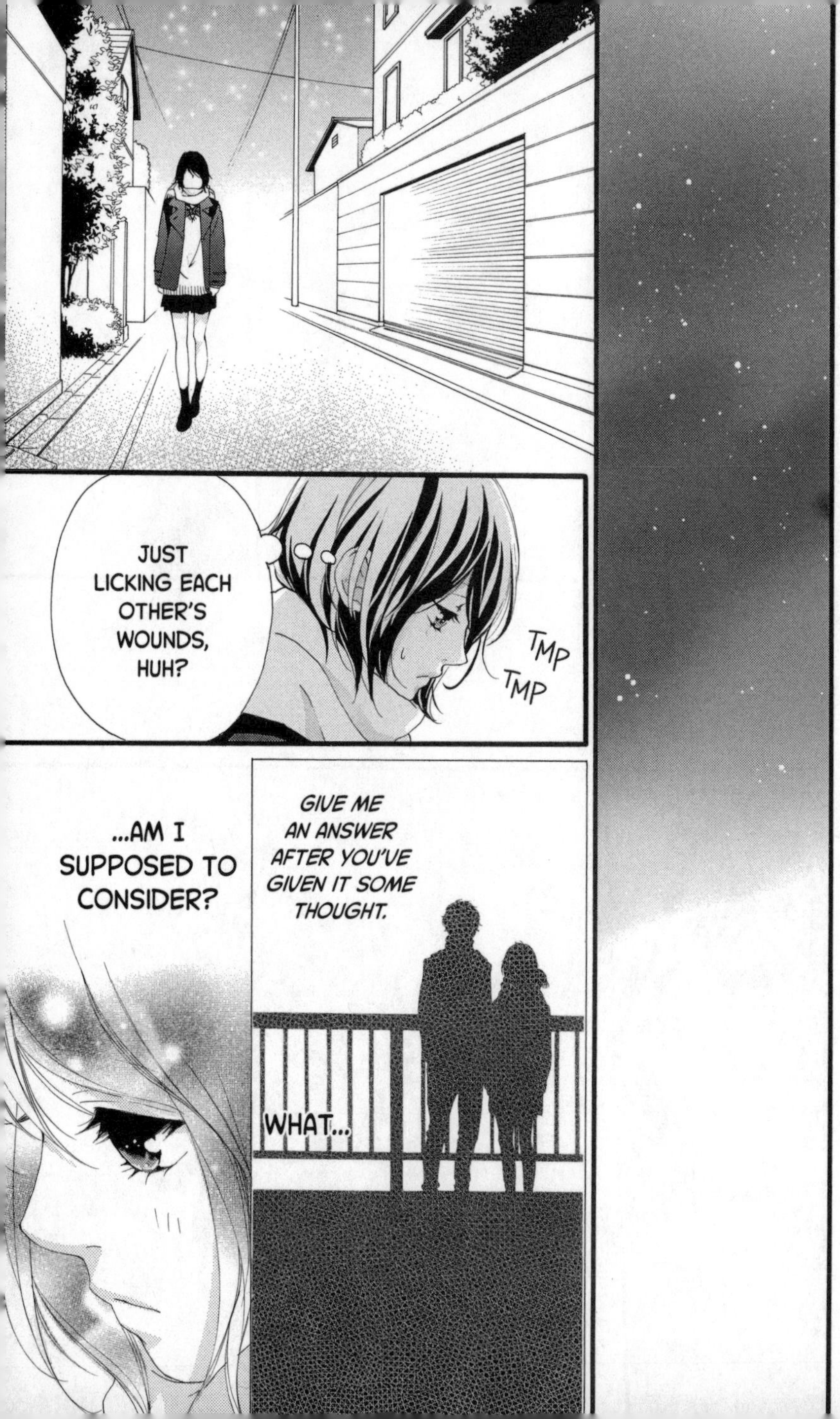
JUST LICKING EACH OTHER'S WOUNDS, HUH?
TMP TMP
GIVE ME AN ANSWER AFTER YOU'VE GIVEN IT SOME THOUGHT.
WHAT...
...AM I SUPPOSED TO CONSIDER?

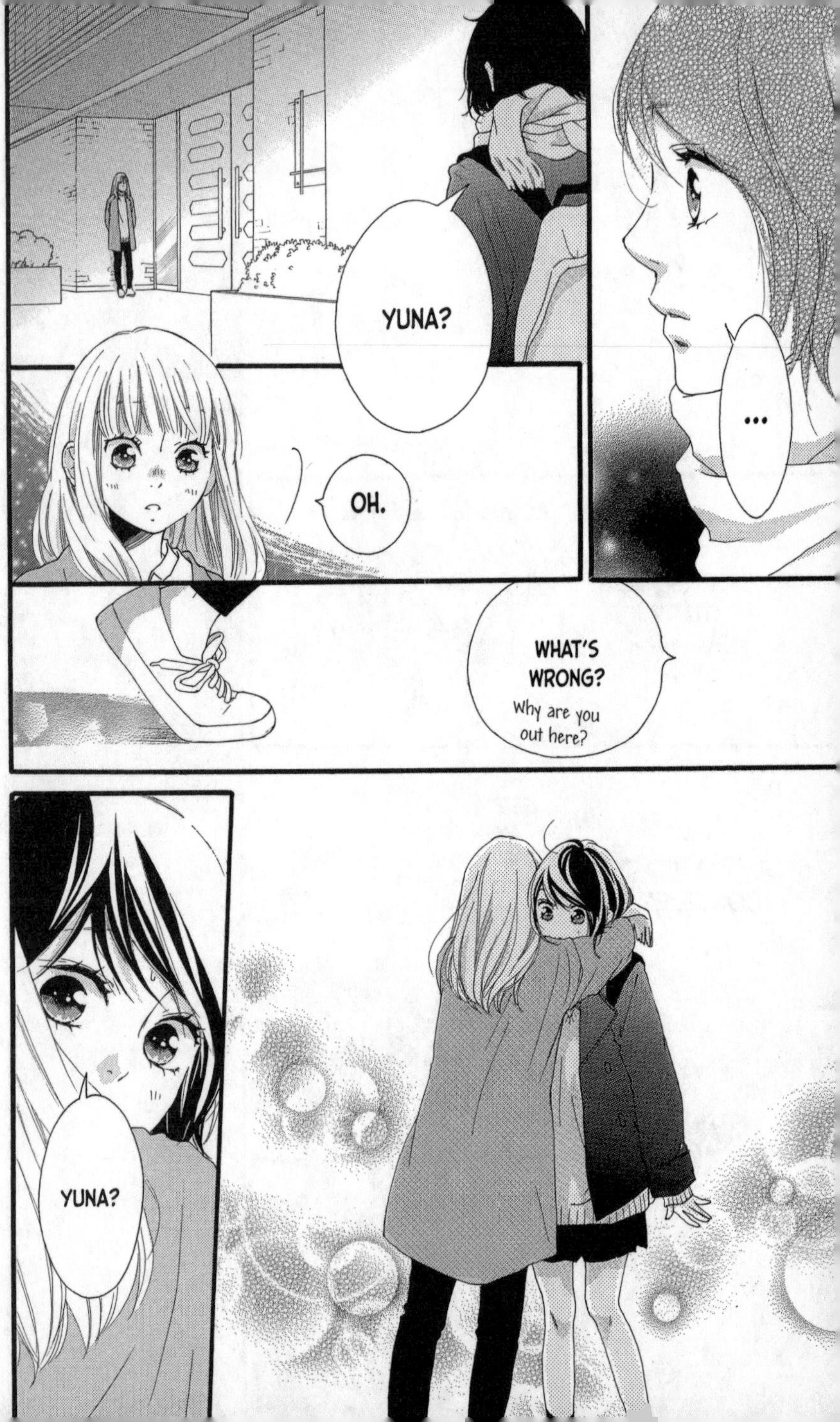
...
YUNA?
OH.
WHAT'S WRONG?
Why are you out here?
YUNA?

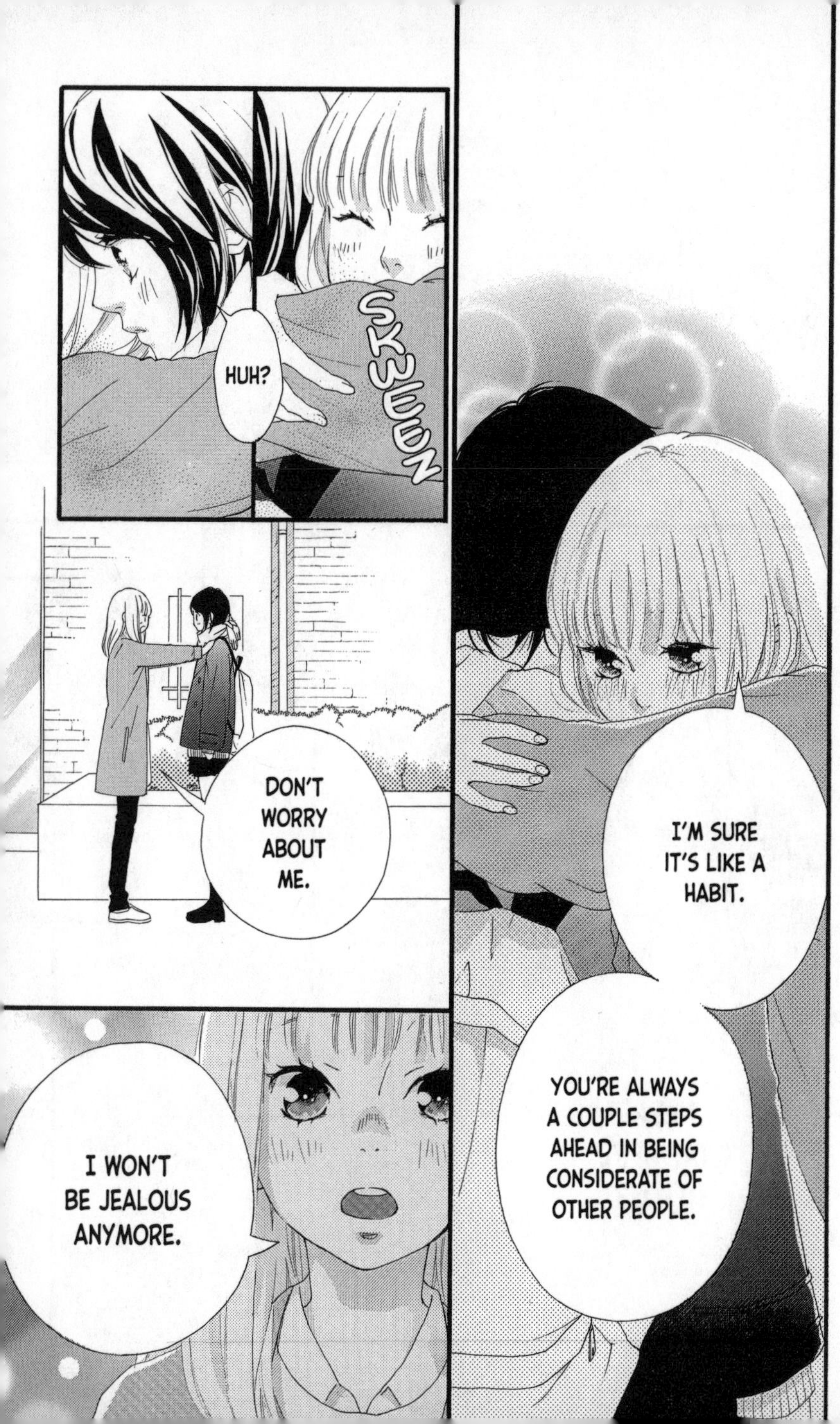
I'M SURE IT'S LIKE A HABIT.
YOU'RE ALWAYS A COUPLE STEPS AHEAD IN BEING CONSIDERATE OF OTHER PEOPLE.
SKWEEN
HUH?
DON'T WORRY ABOUT ME.
I WON'T BE JEALOUS ANYMORE.

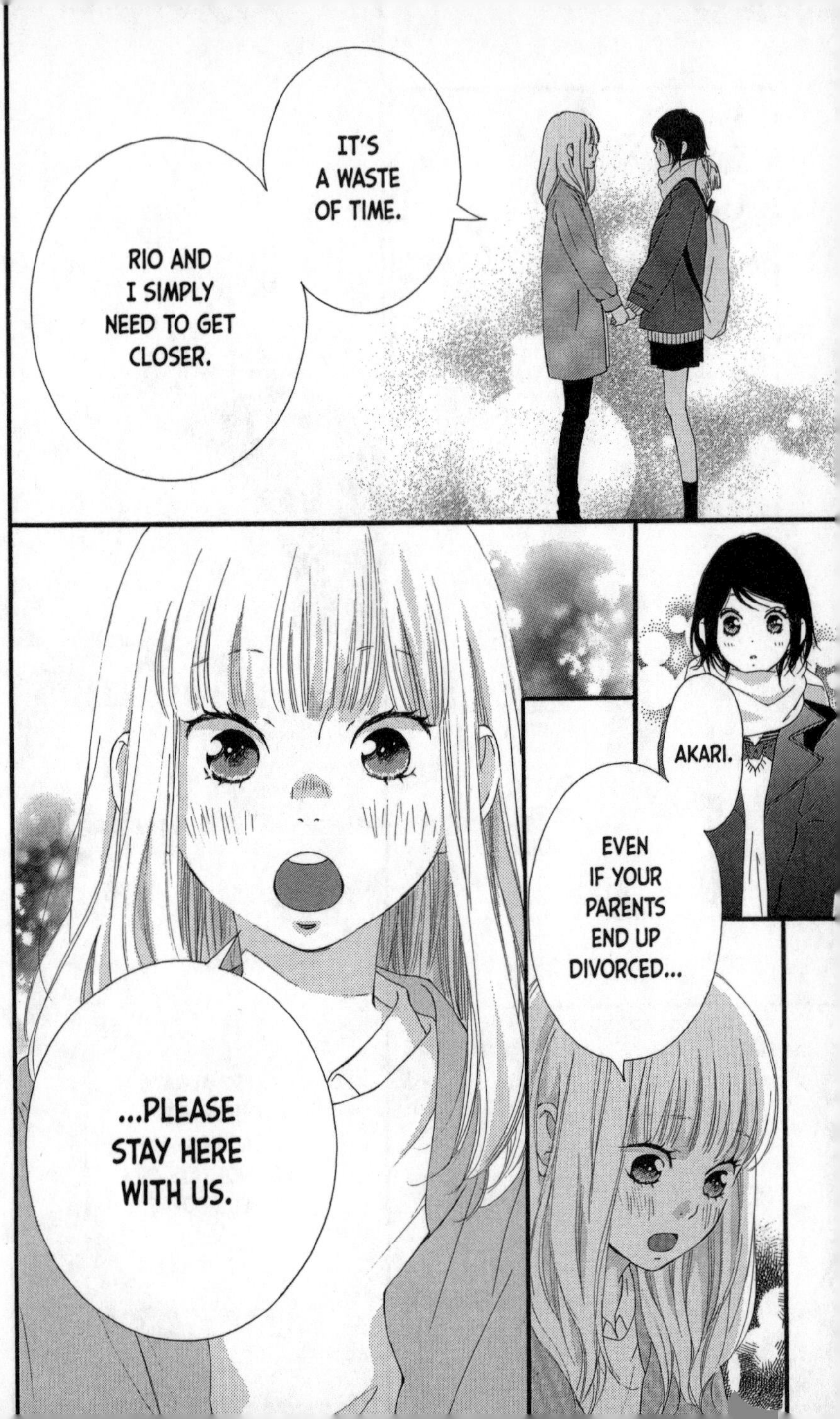
IT'S A WASTE OF TIME.
RIO AND I SIMPLY NEED TO GET CLOSER.
AKARI.
EVEN IF YOUR PARENTS END UP DIVORCED...
...PLEASE STAY HERE WITH US.

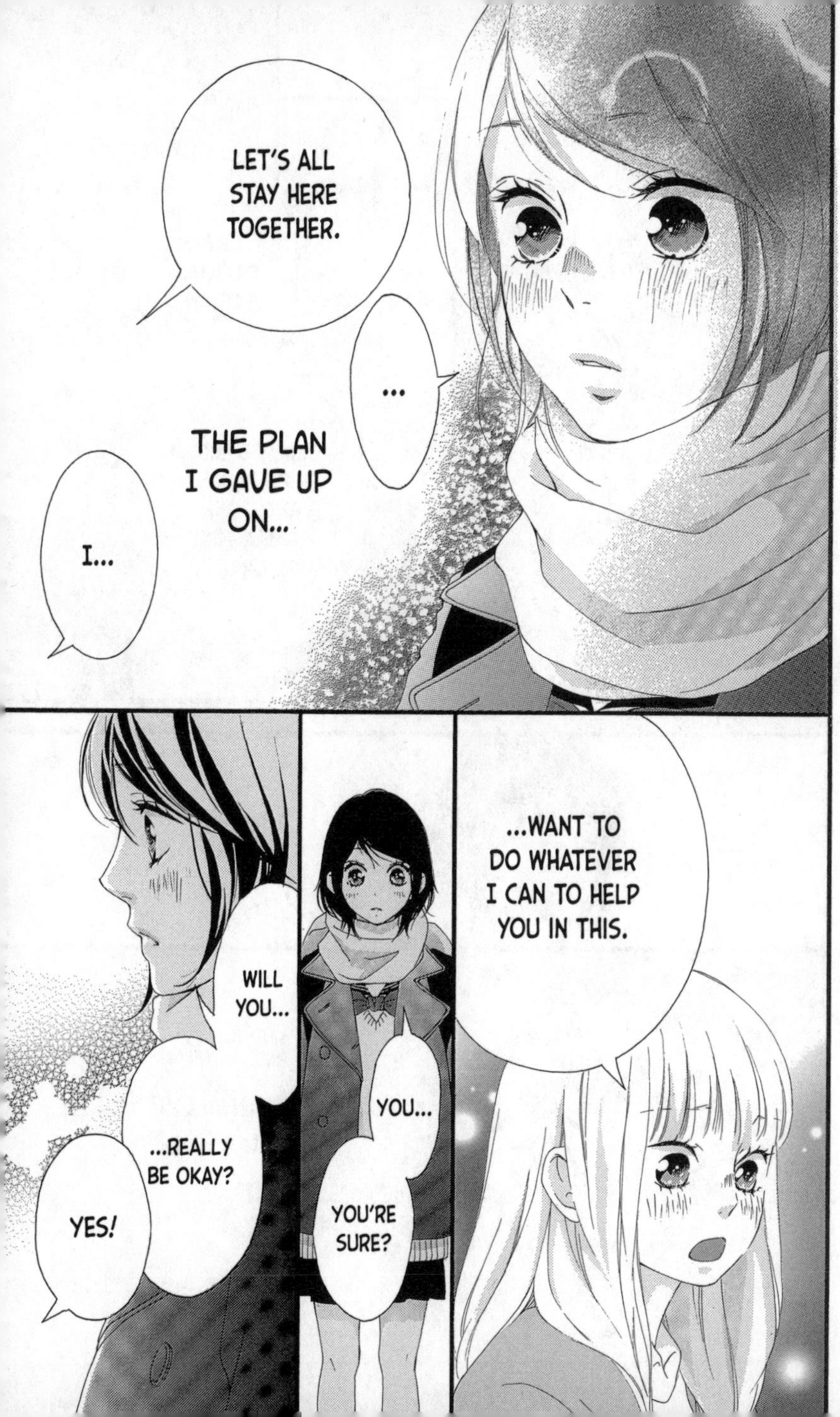
LET'S ALL STAY HERE TOGETHER.
...
THE PLAN I GAVE UP ON...
I...
...WANT TO DO WHATEVER I CAN TO HELP YOU IN THIS.
YOU...
YOU'RE SURE?
WILL YOU...
...REALLY BE OKAY?
YES!

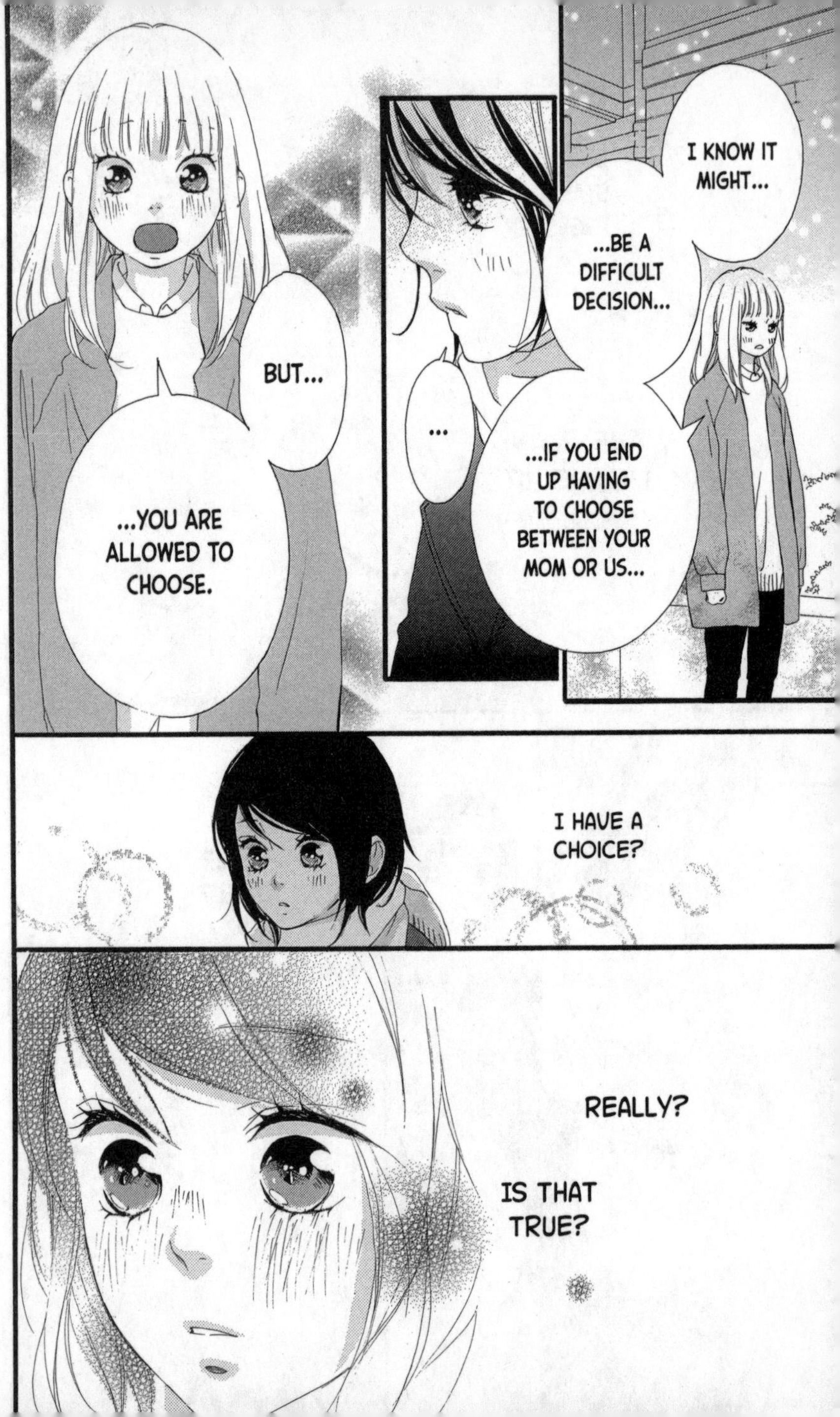
I KNOW IT MIGHT...
...BE A DIFFICULT DECISION...
...IF YOU END UP HAVING TO CHOOSE BETWEEN YOUR MOM OR US...
...
BUT...
...YOU ARE ALLOWED TO CHOOSE.
I HAVE A CHOICE?
REALLY?
IS THAT TRUE?

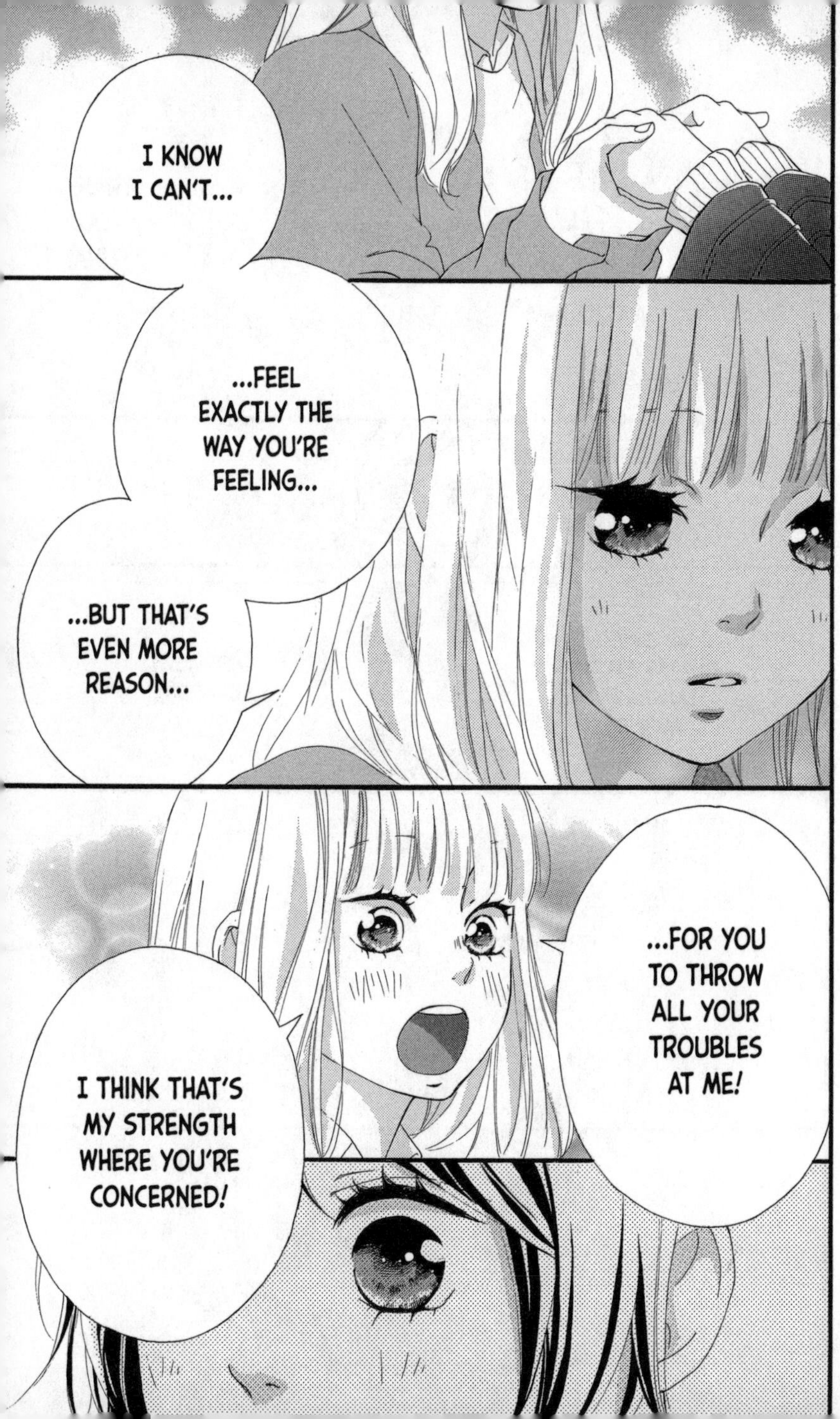
I KNOW I CAN'T...
...FEEL EXACTLY THE WAY YOU'RE FEELING...
...BUT THAT'S EVEN MORE REASON...
...FOR YOU TO THROW ALL YOUR TROUBLES AT ME!
I THINK THAT'S MY STRENGTH WHERE YOU'RE CONCERNED!

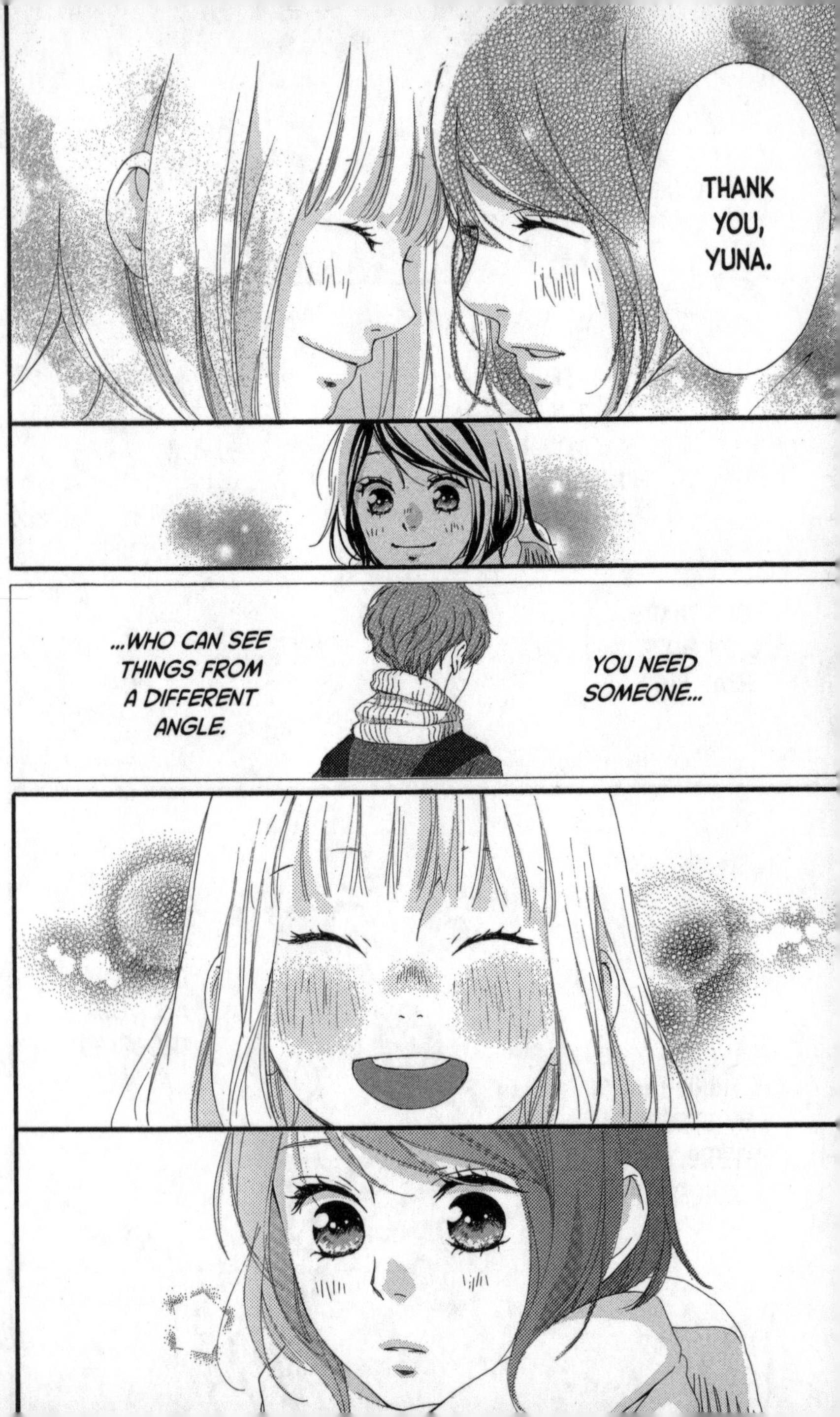
THANK YOU, YUNA.
YOU NEED SOMEONE...
...WHO CAN SEE THINGS FROM A DIFFERENT ANGLE.

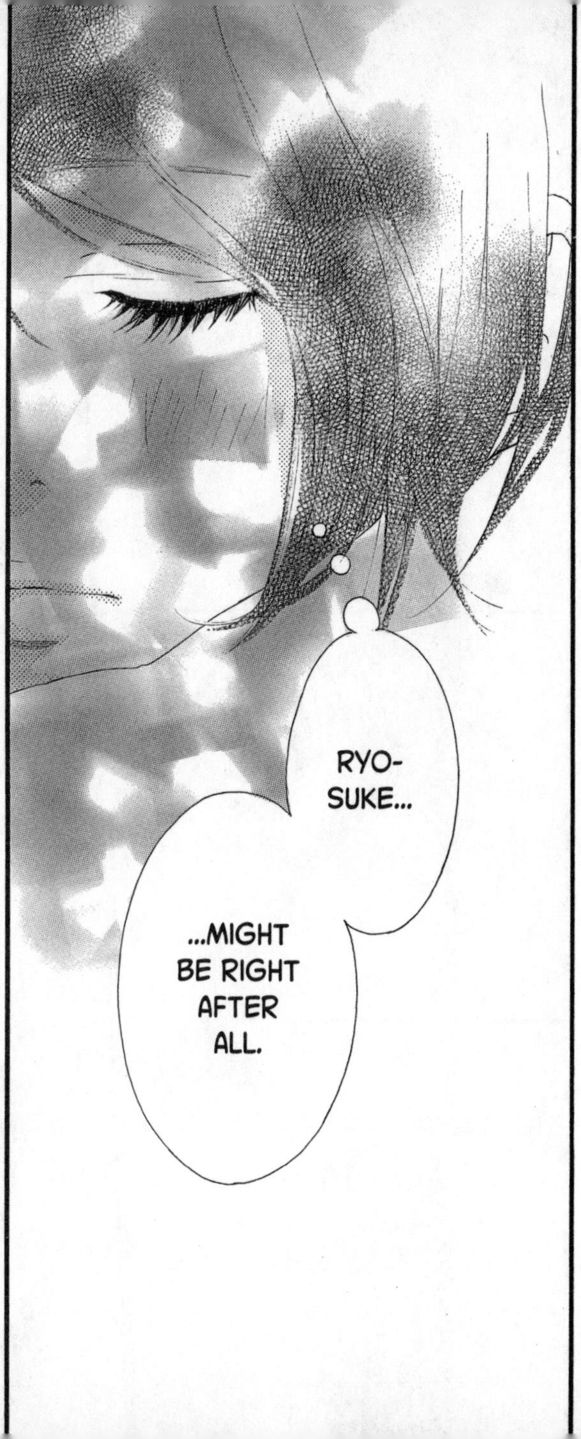
RYO-SUKE...
...MIGHT BE RIGHT AFTER ALL.

The condo I live in now has workmen who periodically come to wash the outside of the windows. I'll get a notice saying, "Please protect your privacy by drawing your curtains on this day." But I'm very lazy about going to check my mailbox, so the window-cleaning days often arrive without me noticing. The other day I didn't realize it was cleaning day, and I was working with the curtains open. Out of nowhere, a workman appeared on my balcony and scared me to death. I thought, "Isn't it rude to close the curtains now?" So I pretended not to notice that he was there (very difficult) and sat at my desk. When I thought about it afterwards, I realized it would've made it easier for him to do his job if I had closed the curtain. We both felt awkward and neither of us benefited.

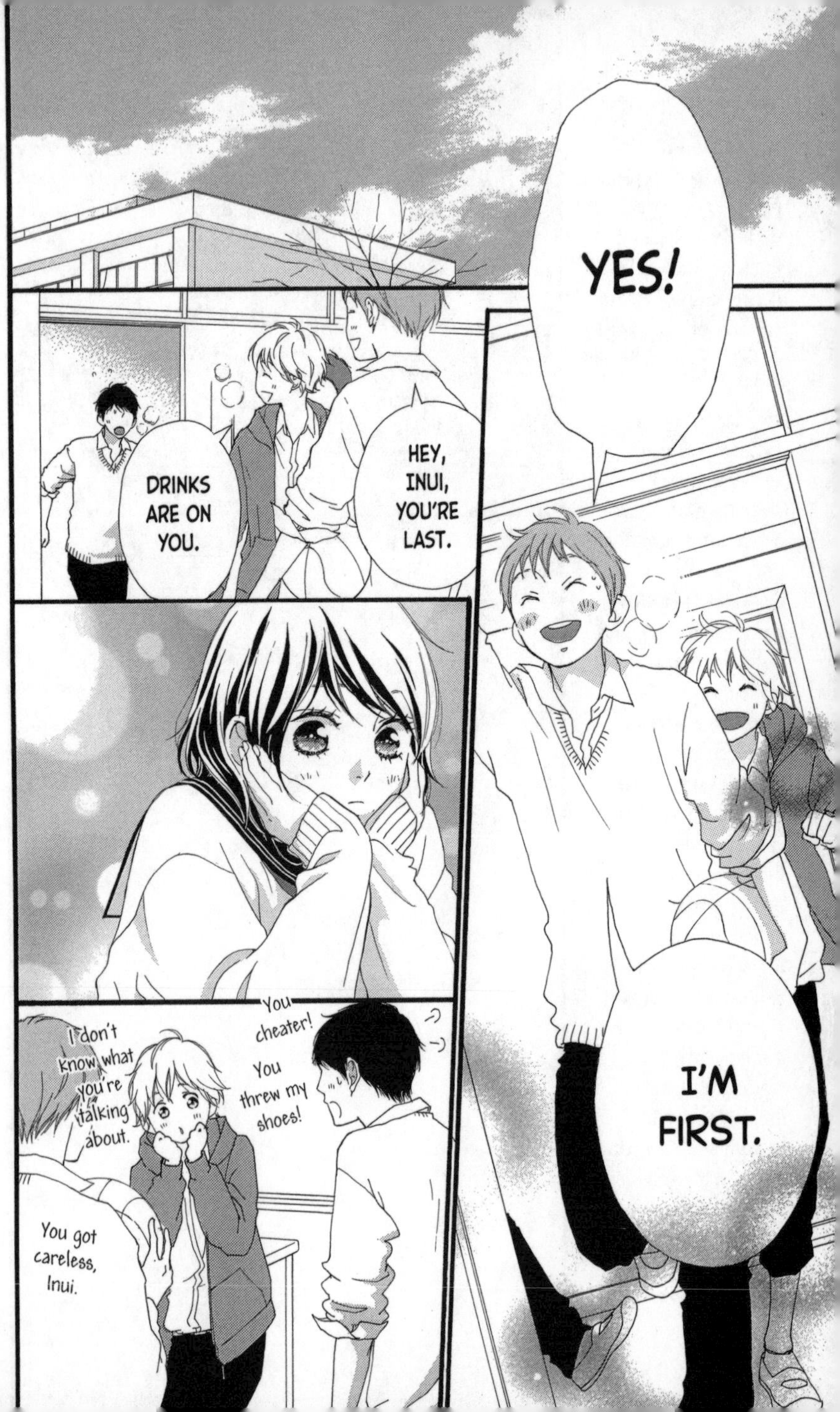
YES!
I'M FIRST.
HEY, INUI, YOU'RE LAST.
DRINKS ARE ON YOU.
You cheater!
You threw my shoes!
I don't know what you're talking about.
You got careless, Inui.

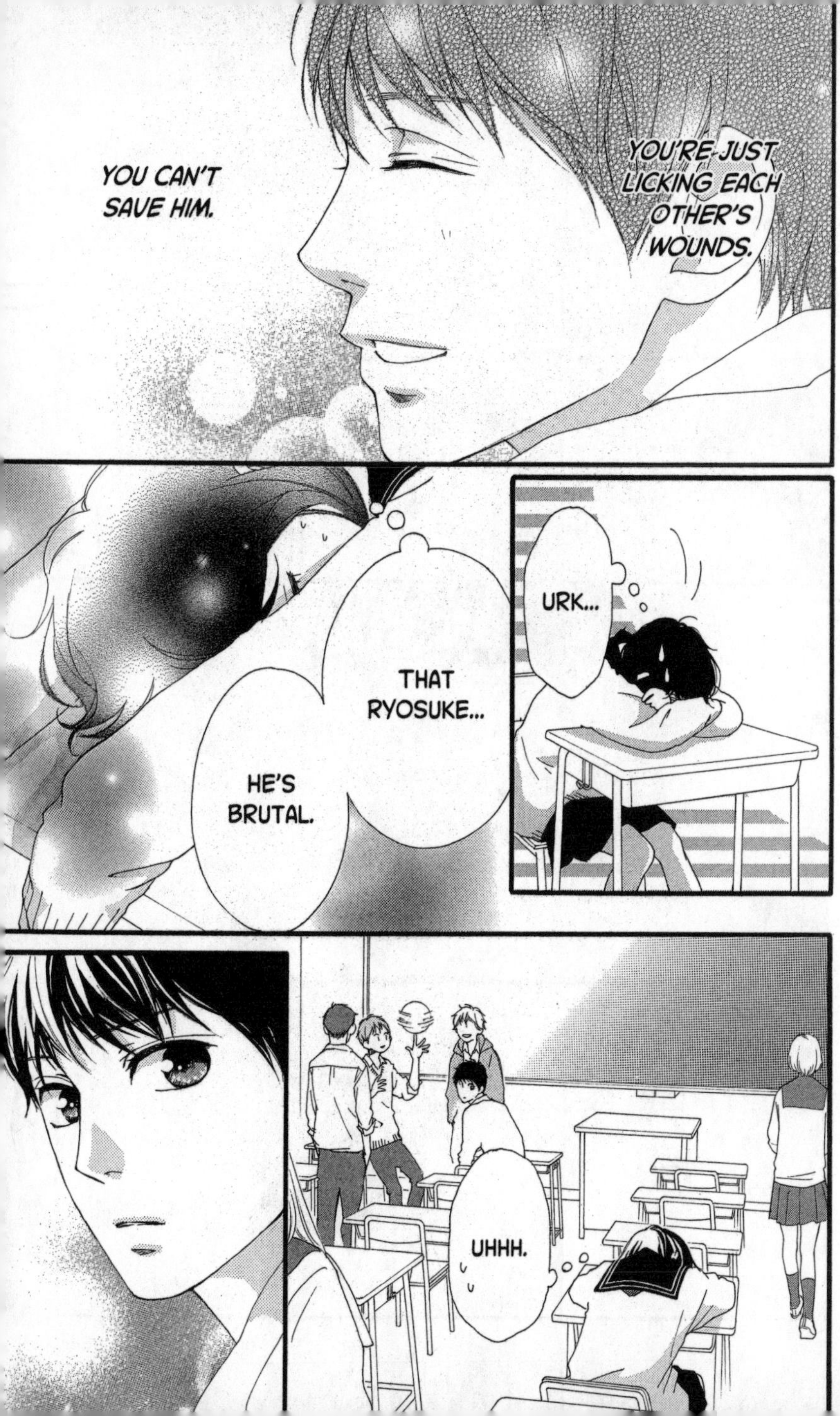
YOU'RE JUST LICKING EACH OTHER'S WOUNDS.
YOU CAN'T SAVE HIM.
URK...
THAT RYOSUKE...
HE'S BRUTAL.
UHHH.

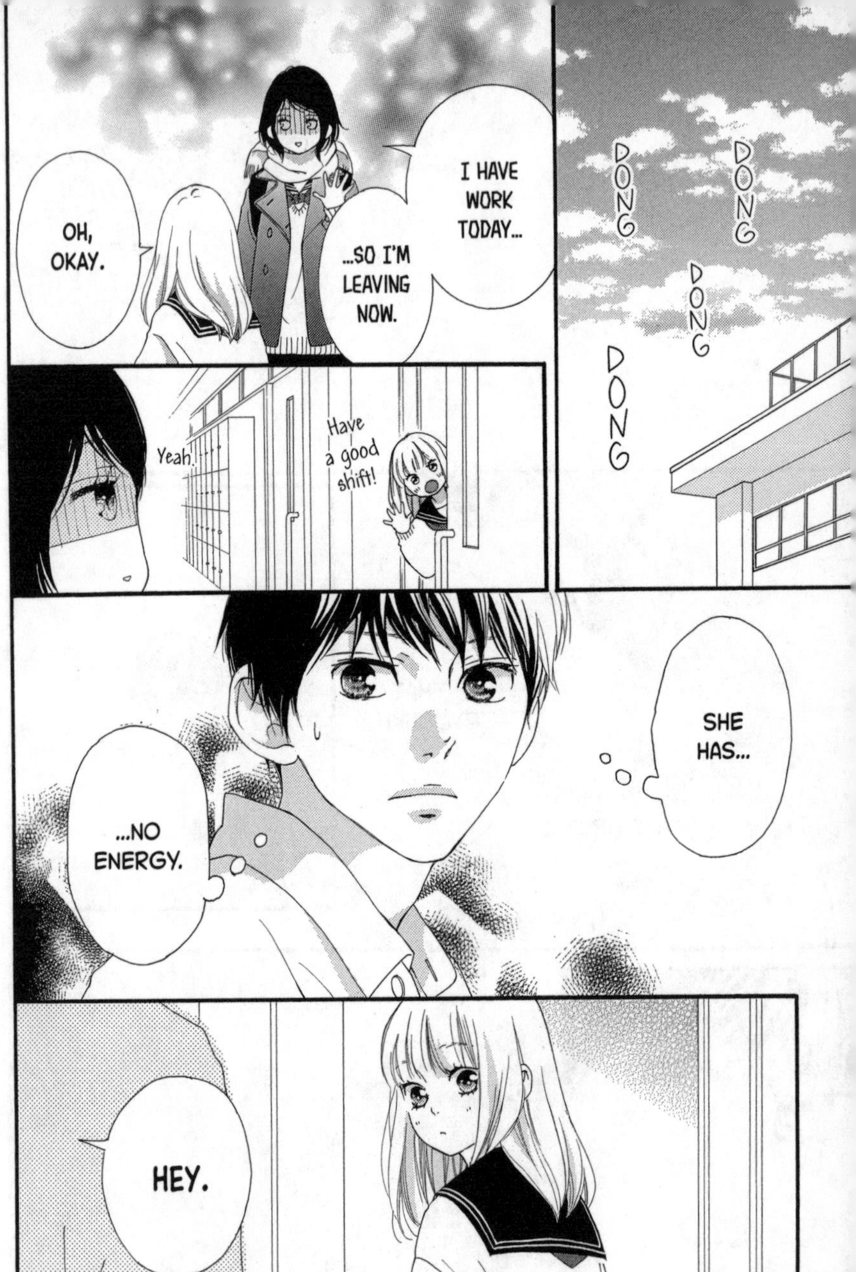
DONG
DONG
DONG
DONG
I HAVE WORK TODAY...
...SO I'M LEAVING NOW.
OH, OKAY.
Have a good shift!
Yeah.
SHE HAS...
...NO ENERGY.
HEY.

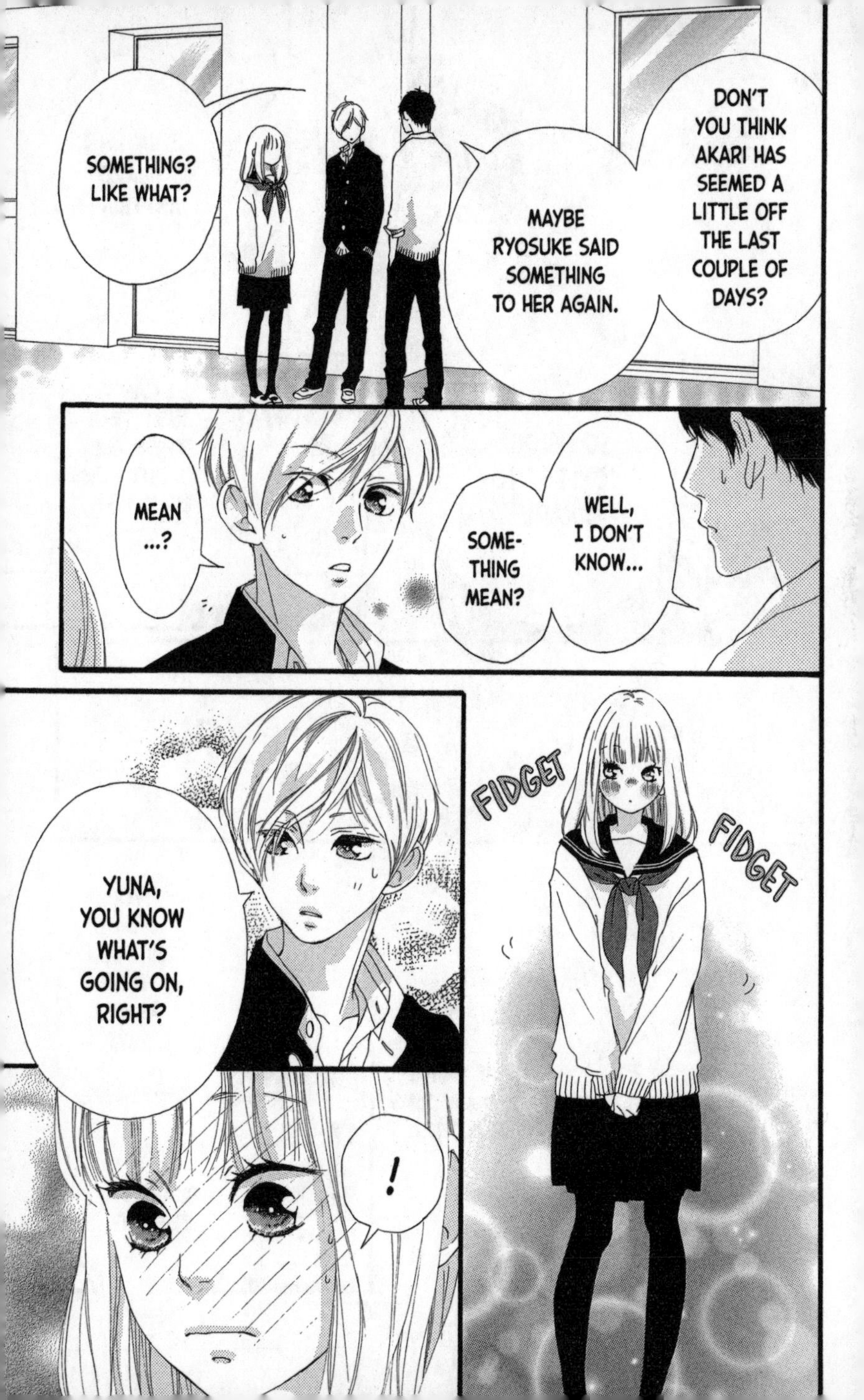
DON'T YOU THINK AKARI HAS SEEMED A LITTLE OFF THE LAST COUPLE OF DAYS?
MAYBE RYOSUKE SAID SOMETHING TO HER AGAIN.
SOMETHING? LIKE WHAT?
WELL, I DON'T KNOW...
SOME-THING MEAN?
MEAN ...?
FIDGET
FIDGET
YUNA, YOU KNOW WHAT'S GOING ON, RIGHT?
!

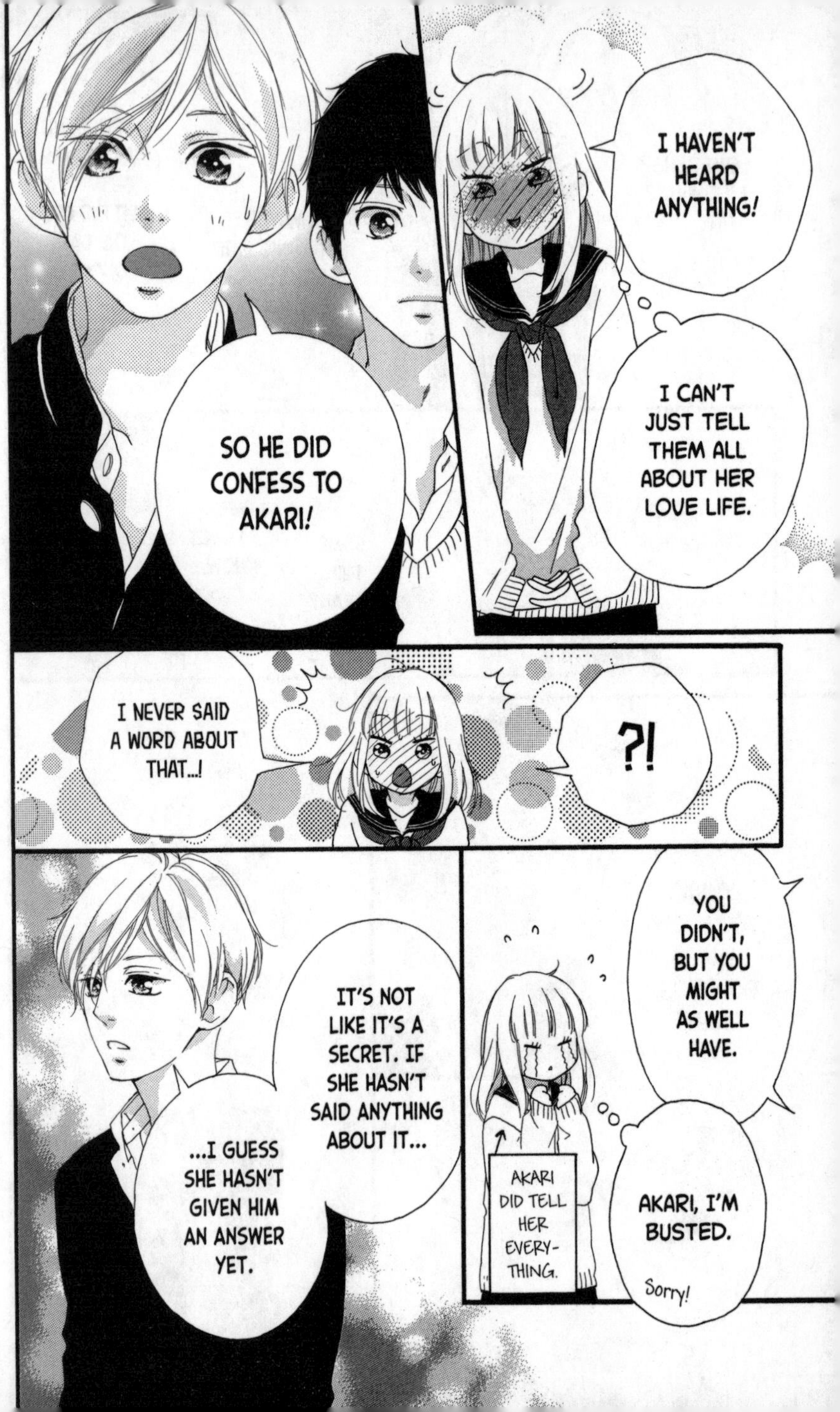

I HAVEN'T HEARD ANYTHING!
I CAN'T JUST TELL THEM ALL ABOUT HER LOVE LIFE.
SO HE DID CONFESS TO AKARI!
?!
I NEVER SAID A WORD ABOUT THAT...!
YOU DIDN'T, BUT YOU MIGHT AS WELL HAVE.
IT'S NOT LIKE IT'S A SECRET. IF SHE HASN'T SAID ANYTHING ABOUT IT...
...I GUESS SHE HASN'T GIVEN HIM AN ANSWER YET.
AKARI DID TELL HER EVERY-THING.
AKARI, I'M BUSTED.
Sorry!

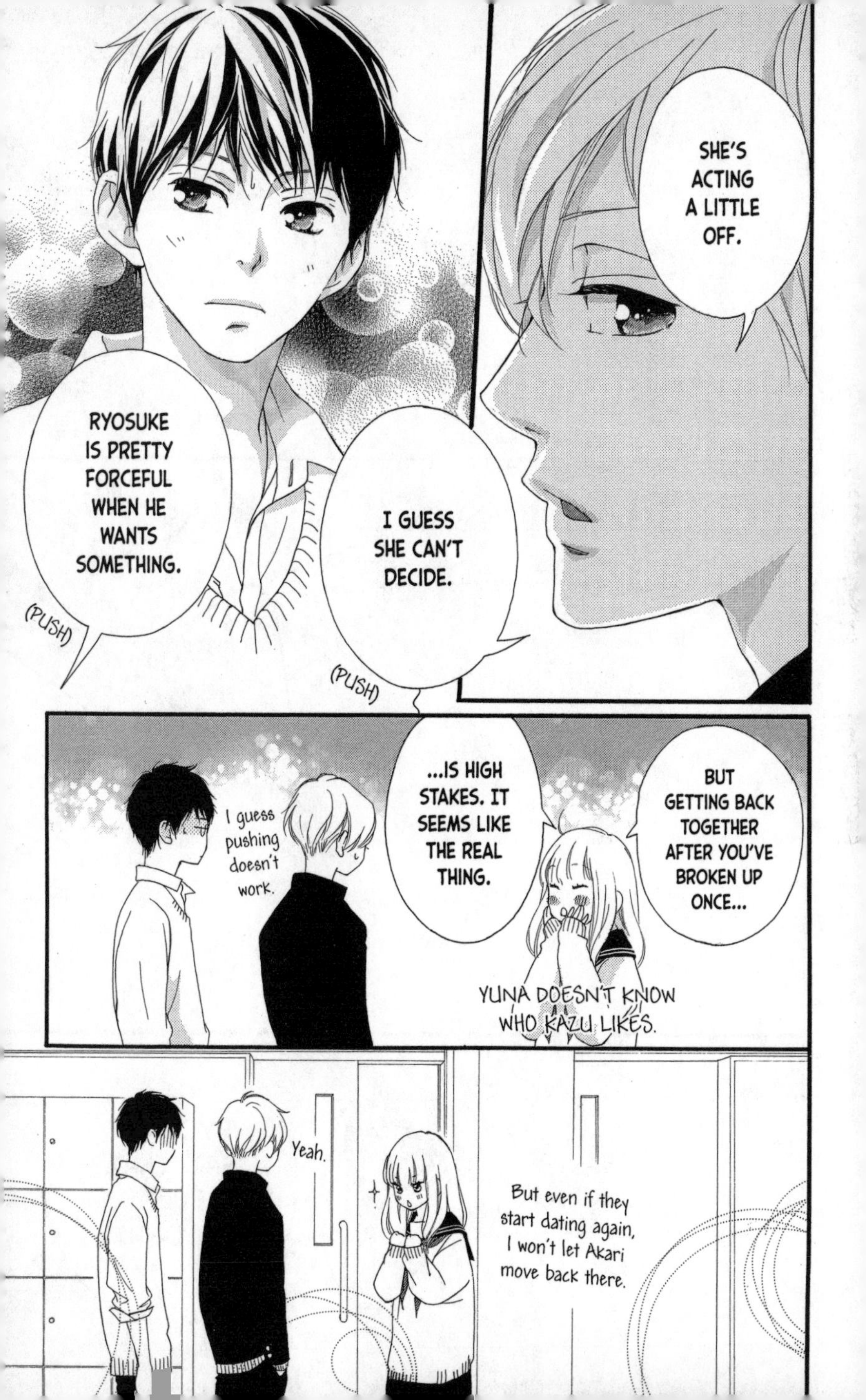
SHE'S ACTING A LITTLE OFF.
RYOSUKE IS PRETTY FORCEFUL WHEN HE WANTS SOMETHING.
(PUSH)
I GUESS SHE CAN'T DECIDE.
(PUSH)
BUT GETTING BACK TOGETHER AFTER YOU'VE BROKEN UP ONCE...
...IS HIGH STAKES. IT SEEMS LIKE THE REAL THING.
YUNA DOESN'T KNOW WHO KAZU LIKES.
I guess pushing doesn't work.
But even if they start dating again, I won't let Akari move back there.
Yeah.

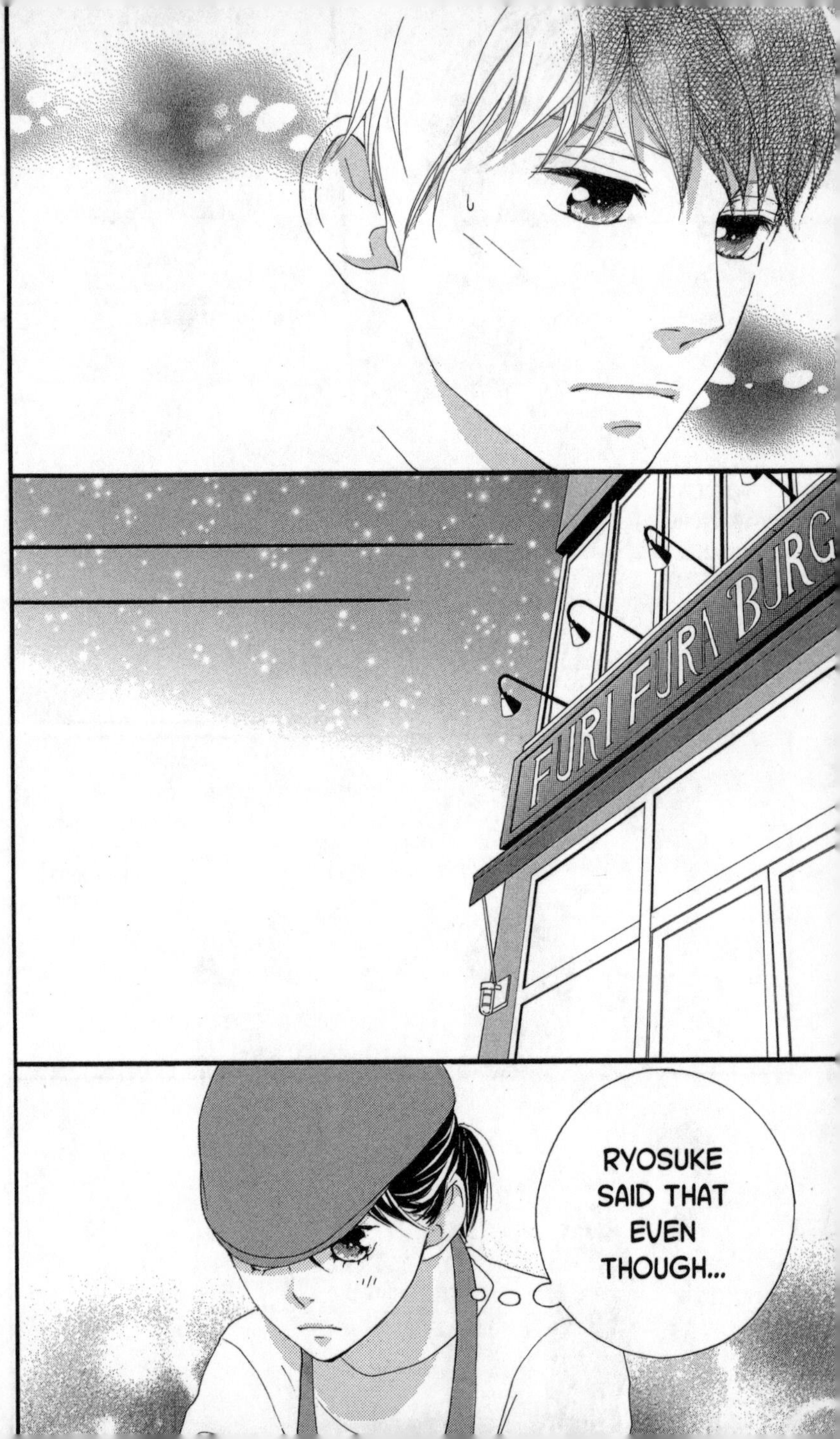
FURI FURA BURG
RYOSUKE SAID THAT EVEN THOUGH...

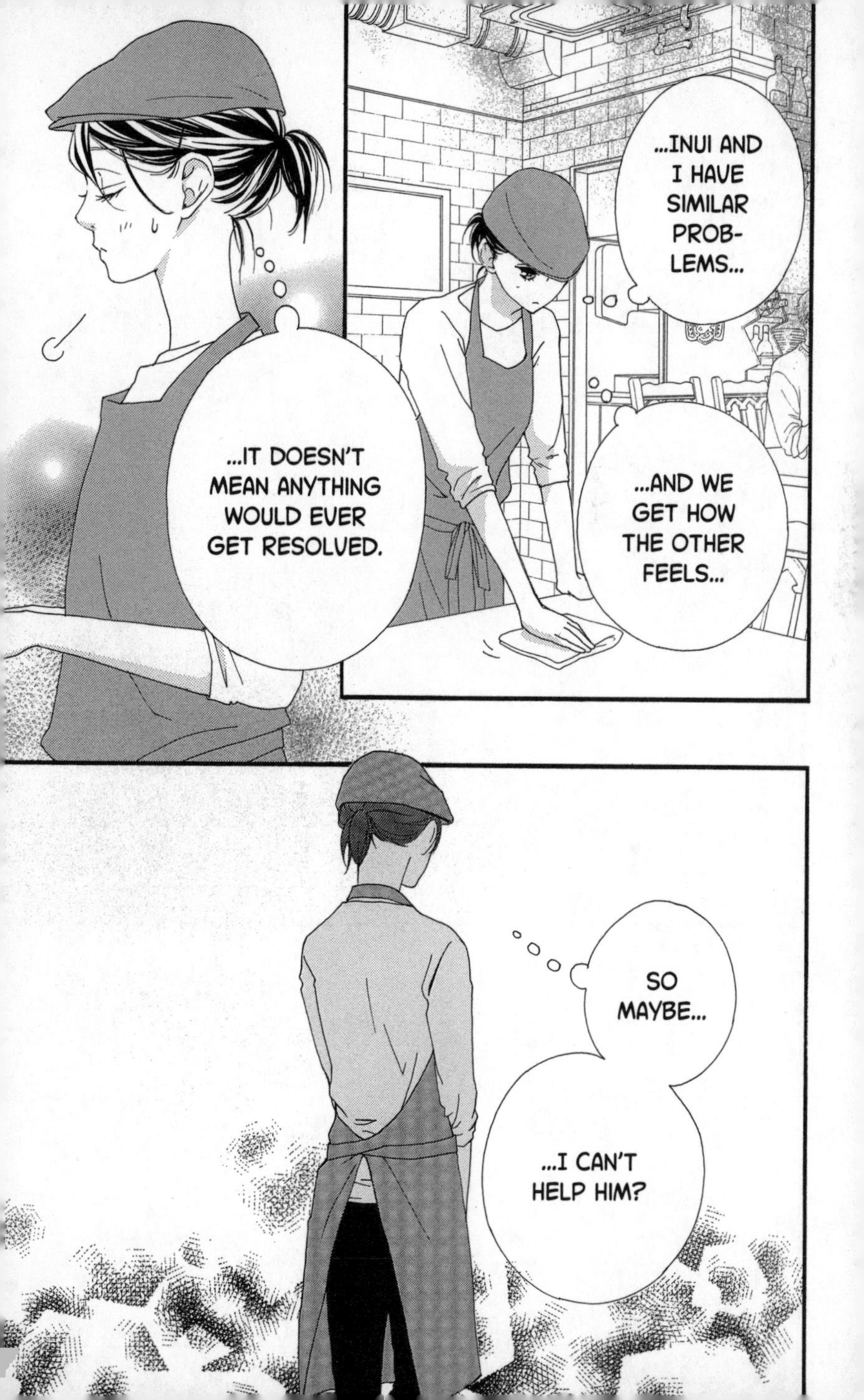
...INUI AND I HAVE SIMILAR PROB-LEMS...
...AND WE GET HOW THE OTHER FEELS...
...IT DOESN'T MEAN ANYTHING WOULD EVER GET RESOLVED.
SO MAYBE...
...I CAN'T HELP HIM?

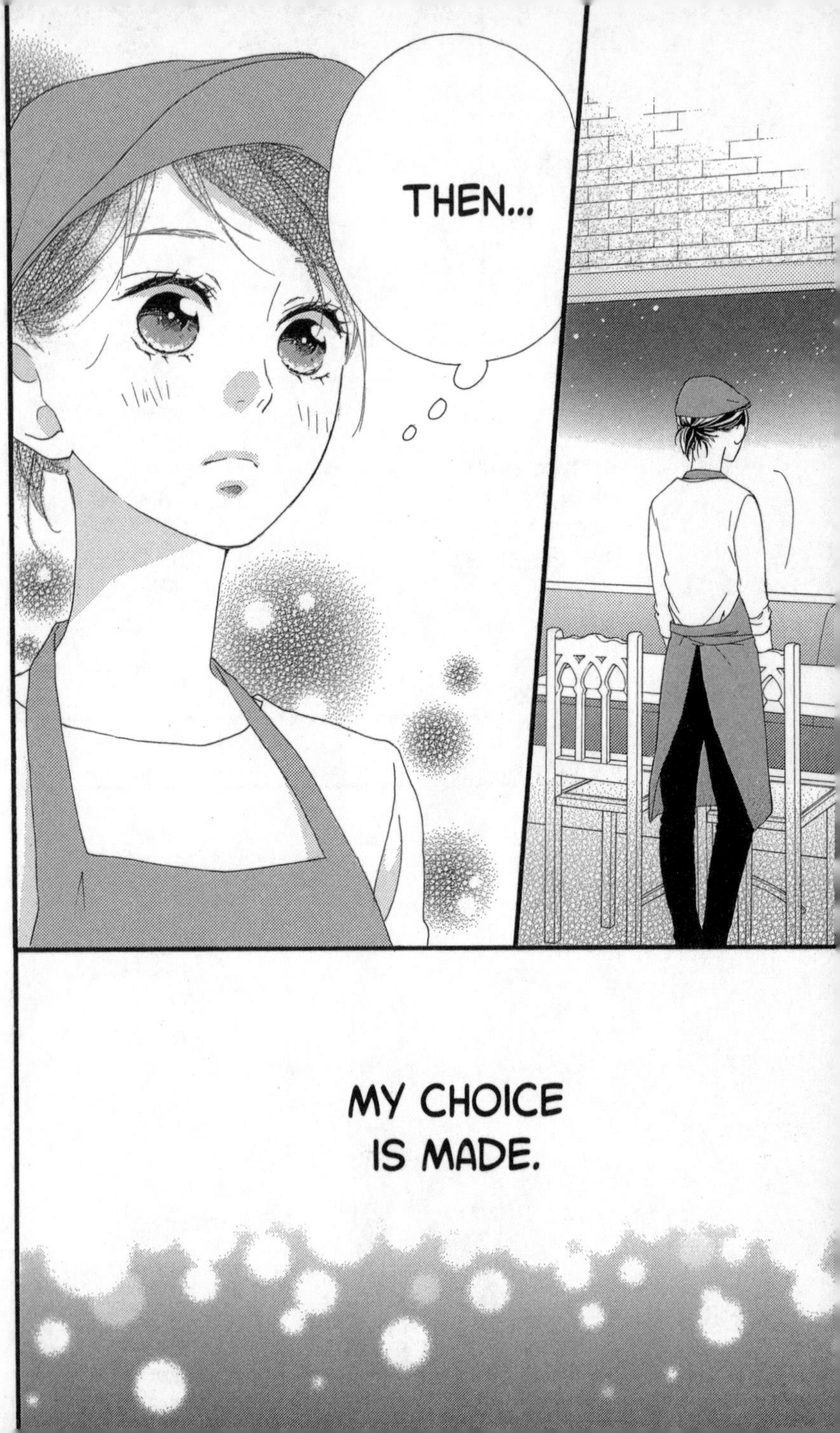
THEN...
MY CHOICE IS MADE.

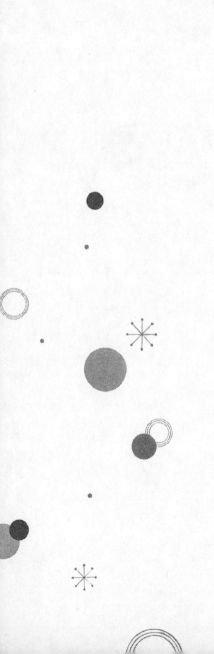

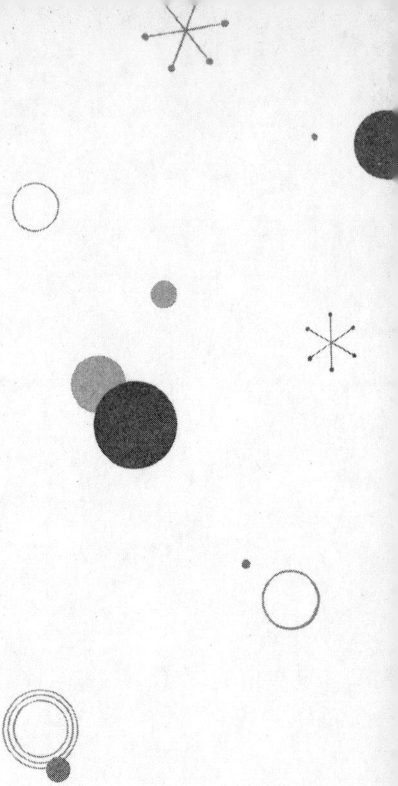

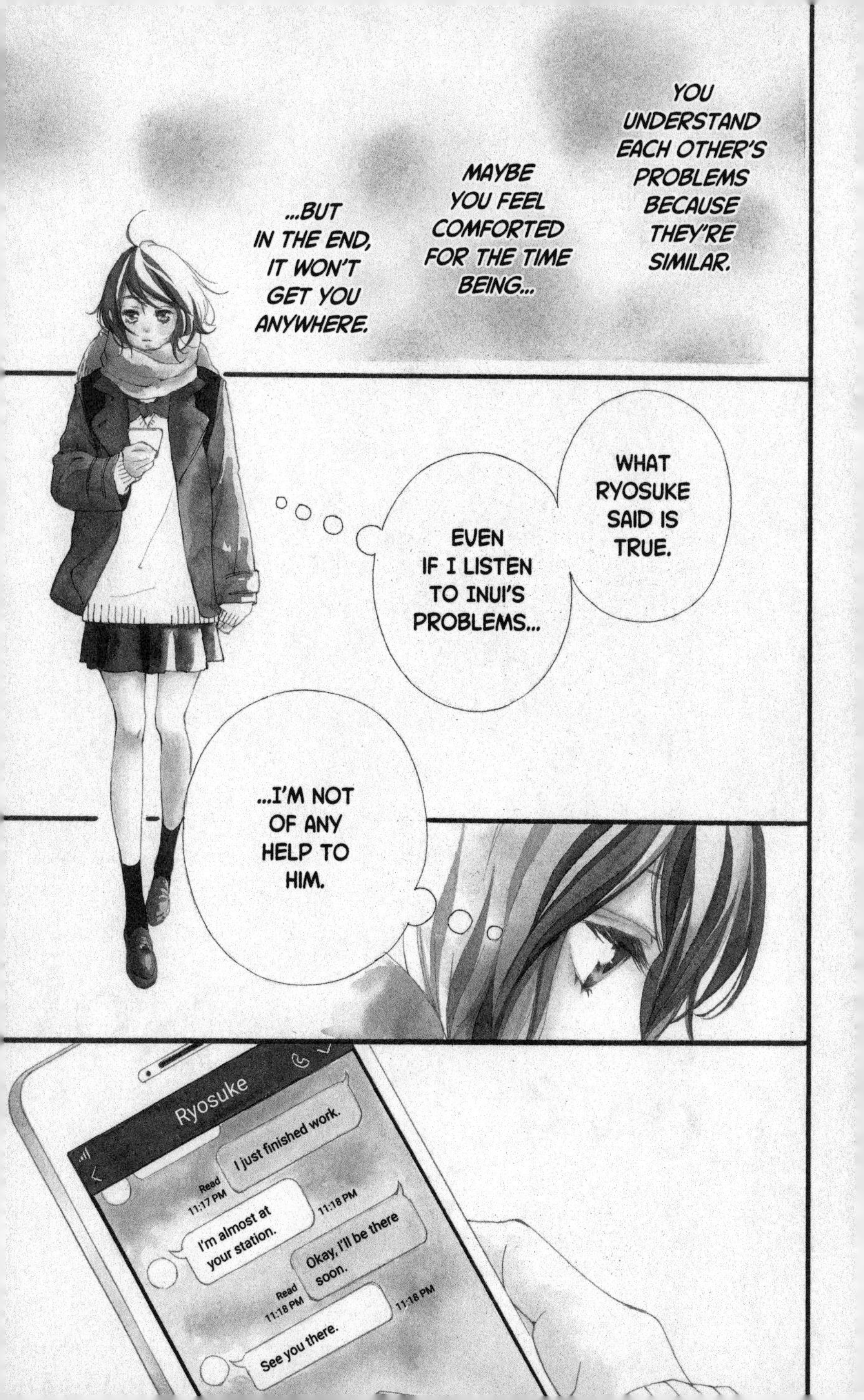
YOU UNDERSTAND EACH OTHER'S PROBLEMS BECAUSE THEY'RE SIMILAR.
MAYBE YOU FEEL COMFORTED FOR THE TIME BEING...
...BUT IN THE END, IT WON'T GET YOU ANYWHERE.
WHAT RYOSUKE SAID IS TRUE.
EVEN IF I LISTEN TO INUI'S PROBLEMS...
...I'M NOT OF ANY HELP TO HIM.
Ryosuke
I just finished work.
Read 11:17 PM
I'm almost at your station.
11:18 PM
Okay, I'll be there soon.
Read 11:18 PM
See you there.
11:18 PM

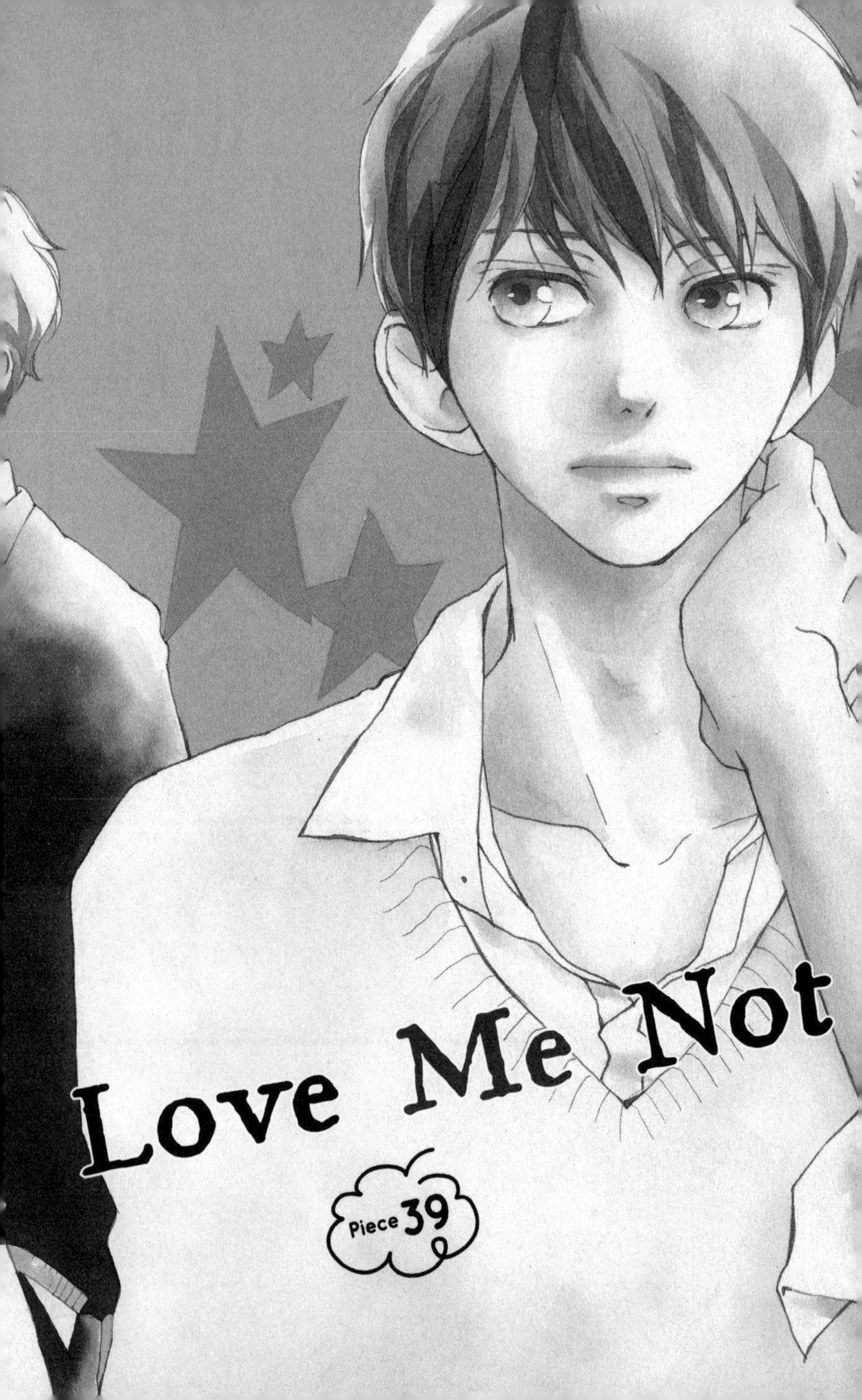
Love Me Not
Piece 39

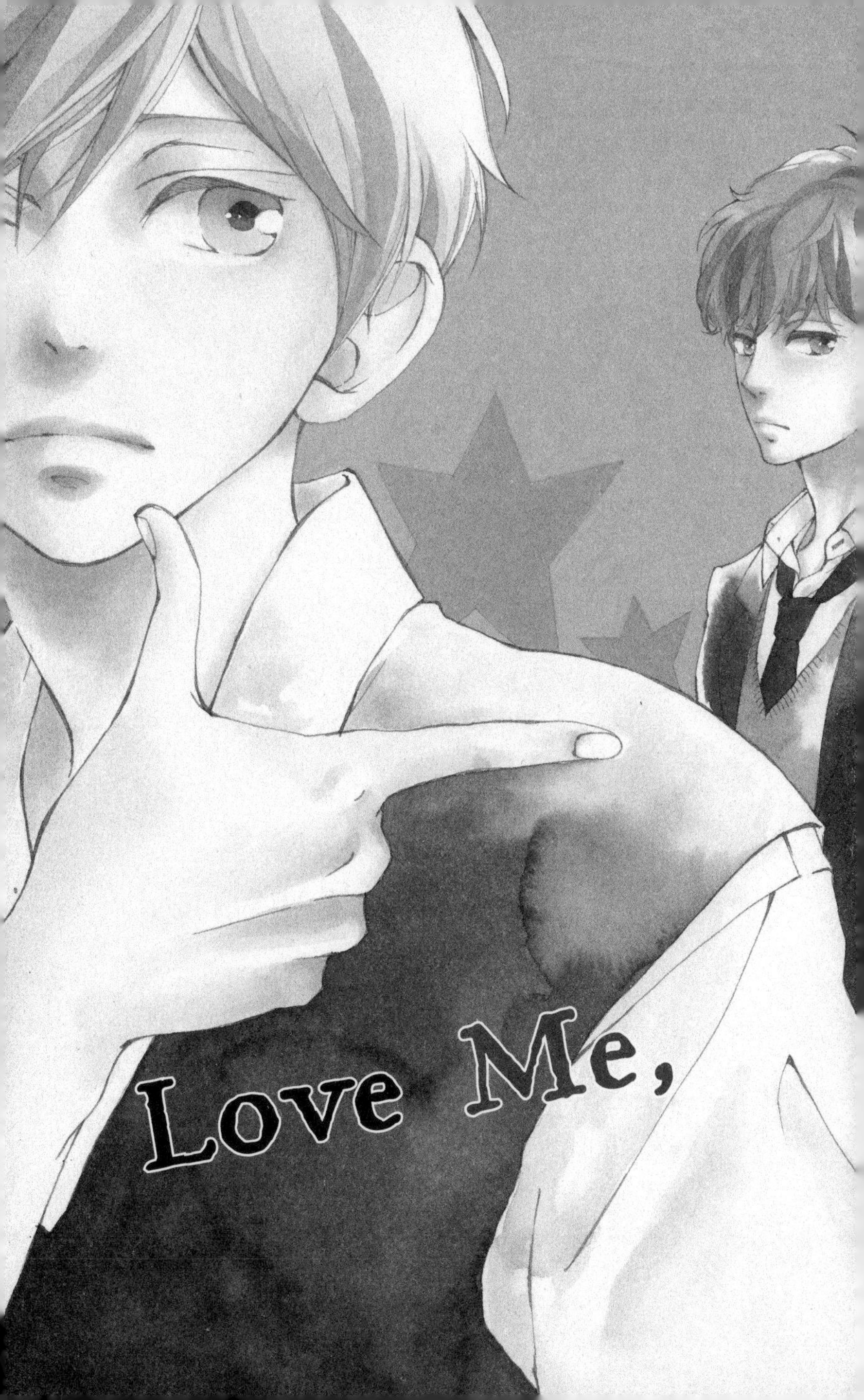
Love Me,

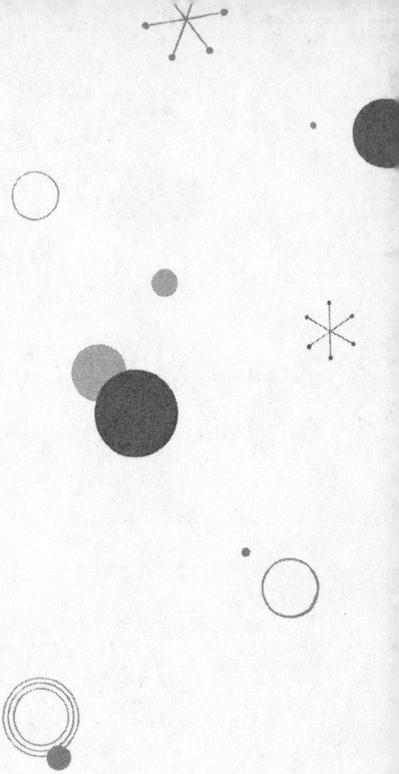

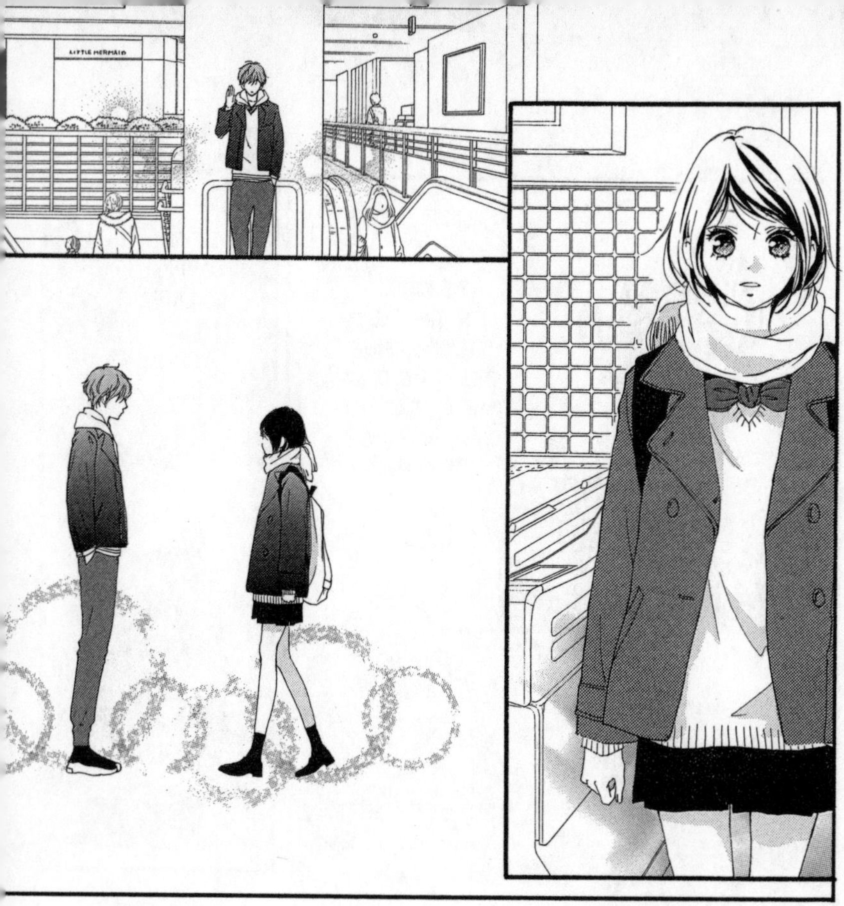
LITTLE MERMAID

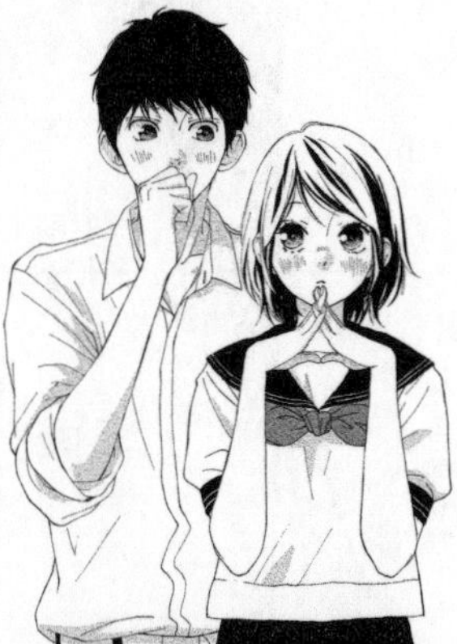

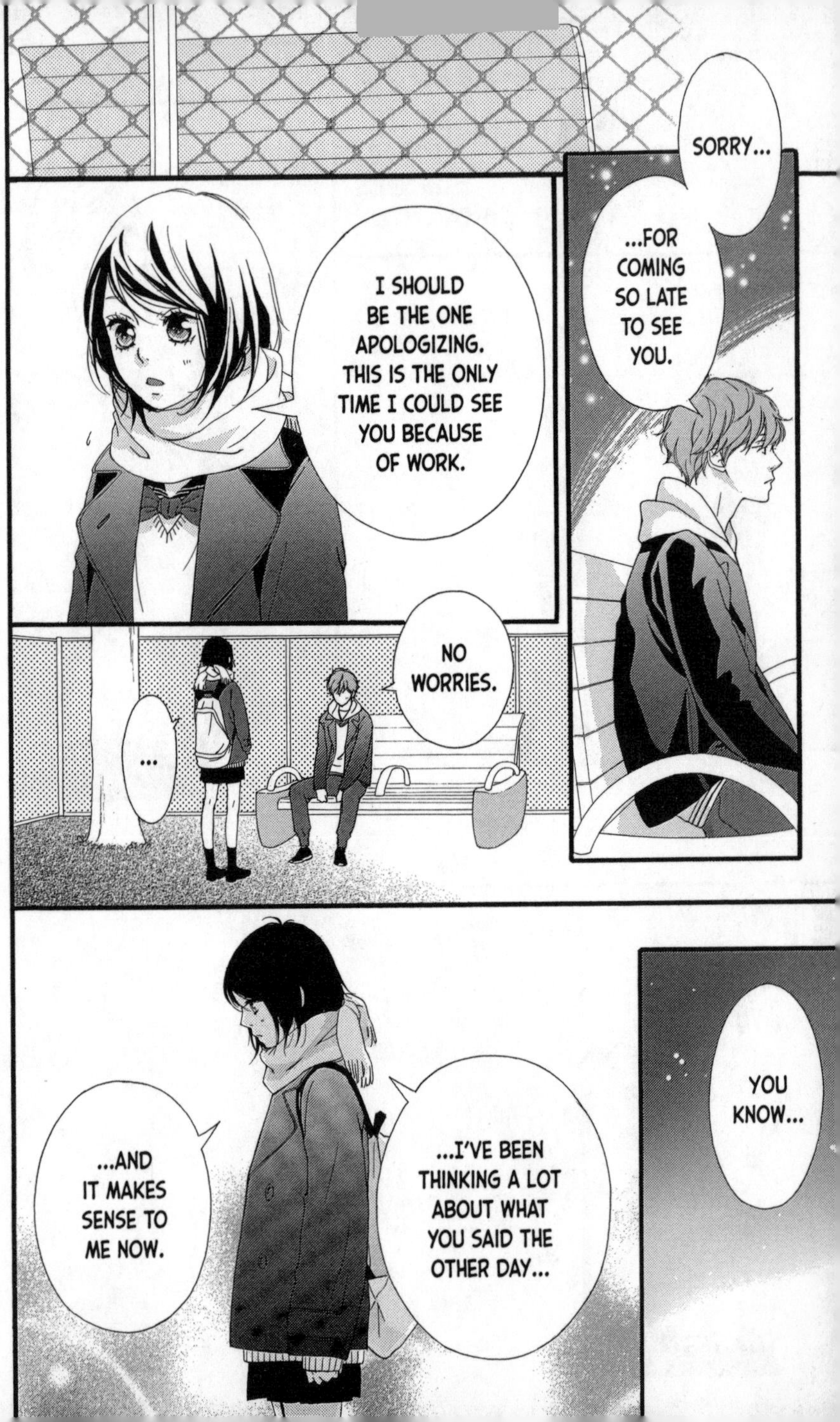
SORRY...
...FOR COMING SO LATE TO SEE YOU.
I SHOULD BE THE ONE APOLOGIZING. THIS IS THE ONLY TIME I COULD SEE YOU BECAUSE OF WORK.
NO WORRIES.
...
YOU KNOW...
...I'VE BEEN THINKING A LOT ABOUT WHAT YOU SAID THE OTHER DAY...
...AND IT MAKES SENSE TO ME NOW.

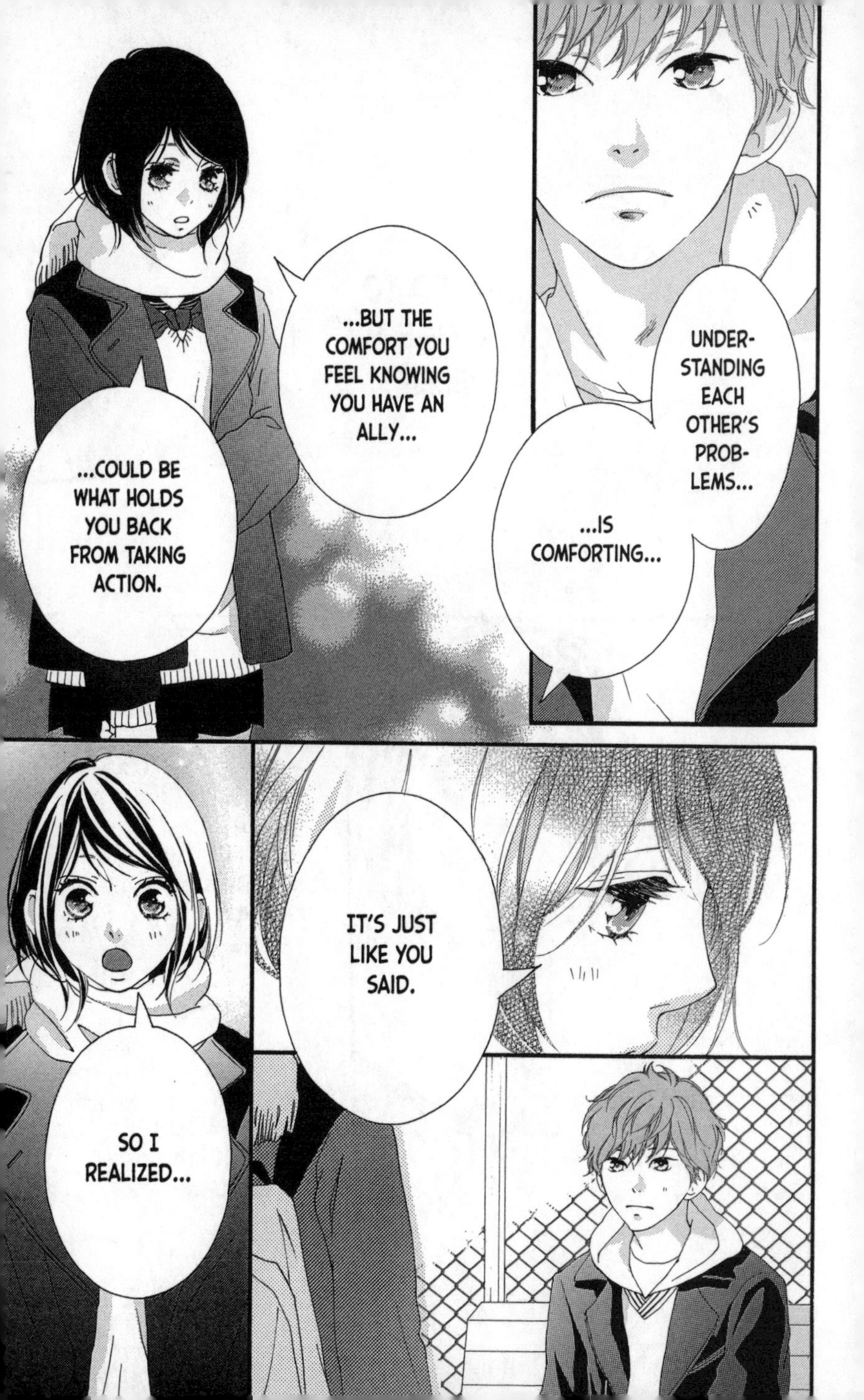
UNDER-STANDING EACH OTHER'S PROB-LEMS...
...IS COMFORTING...
...BUT THE COMFORT YOU FEEL KNOWING YOU HAVE AN ALLY...
...COULD BE WHAT HOLDS YOU BACK FROM TAKING ACTION.
IT'S JUST LIKE YOU SAID.
SO I REALIZED...

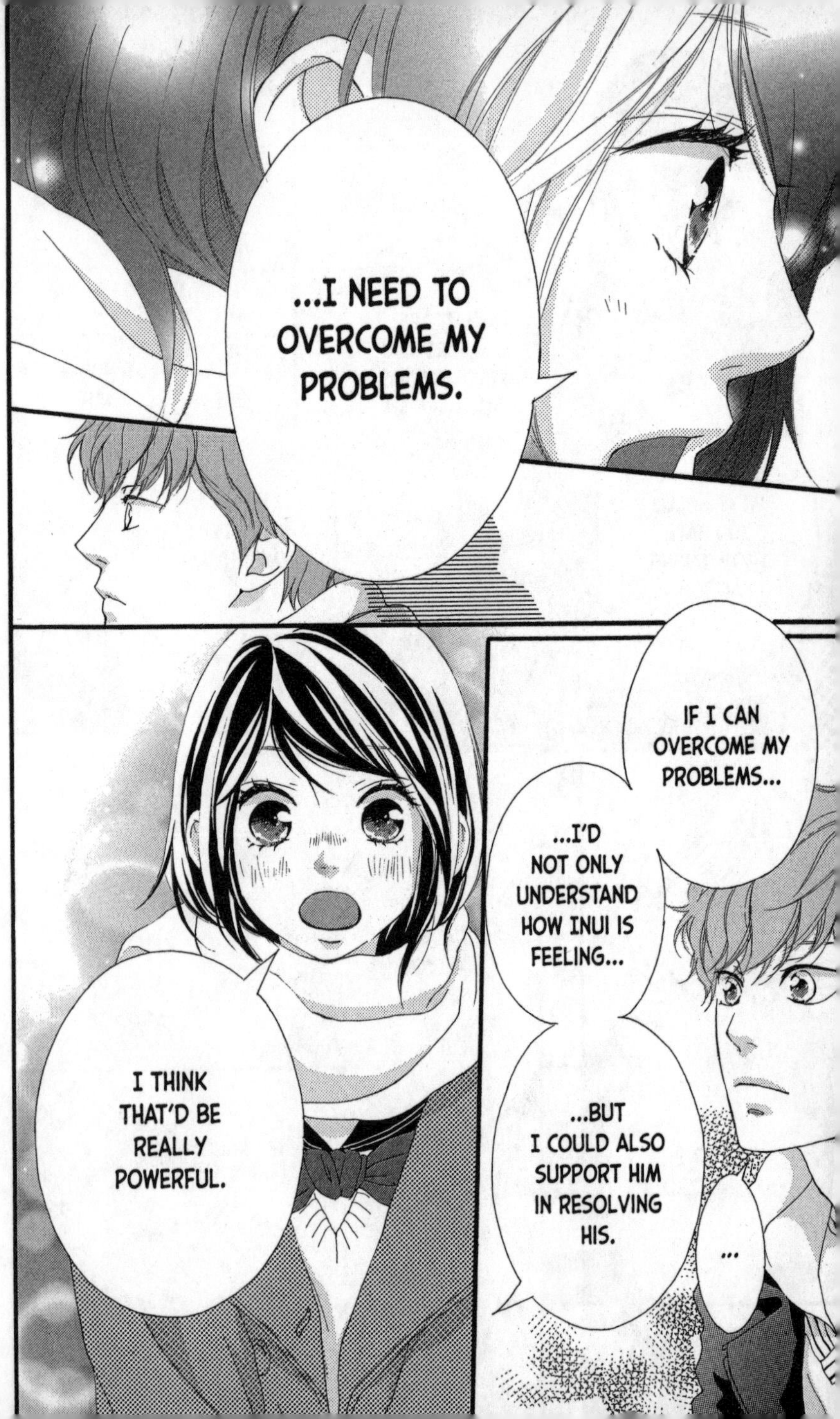
...I NEED TO OVERCOME MY PROBLEMS.
IF I CAN OVERCOME MY PROBLEMS...
...I'D NOT ONLY UNDERSTAND HOW INUI IS FEELING...
...BUT I COULD ALSO SUPPORT HIM IN RESOLVING HIS.
...
I THINK THAT'D BE REALLY POWERFUL.

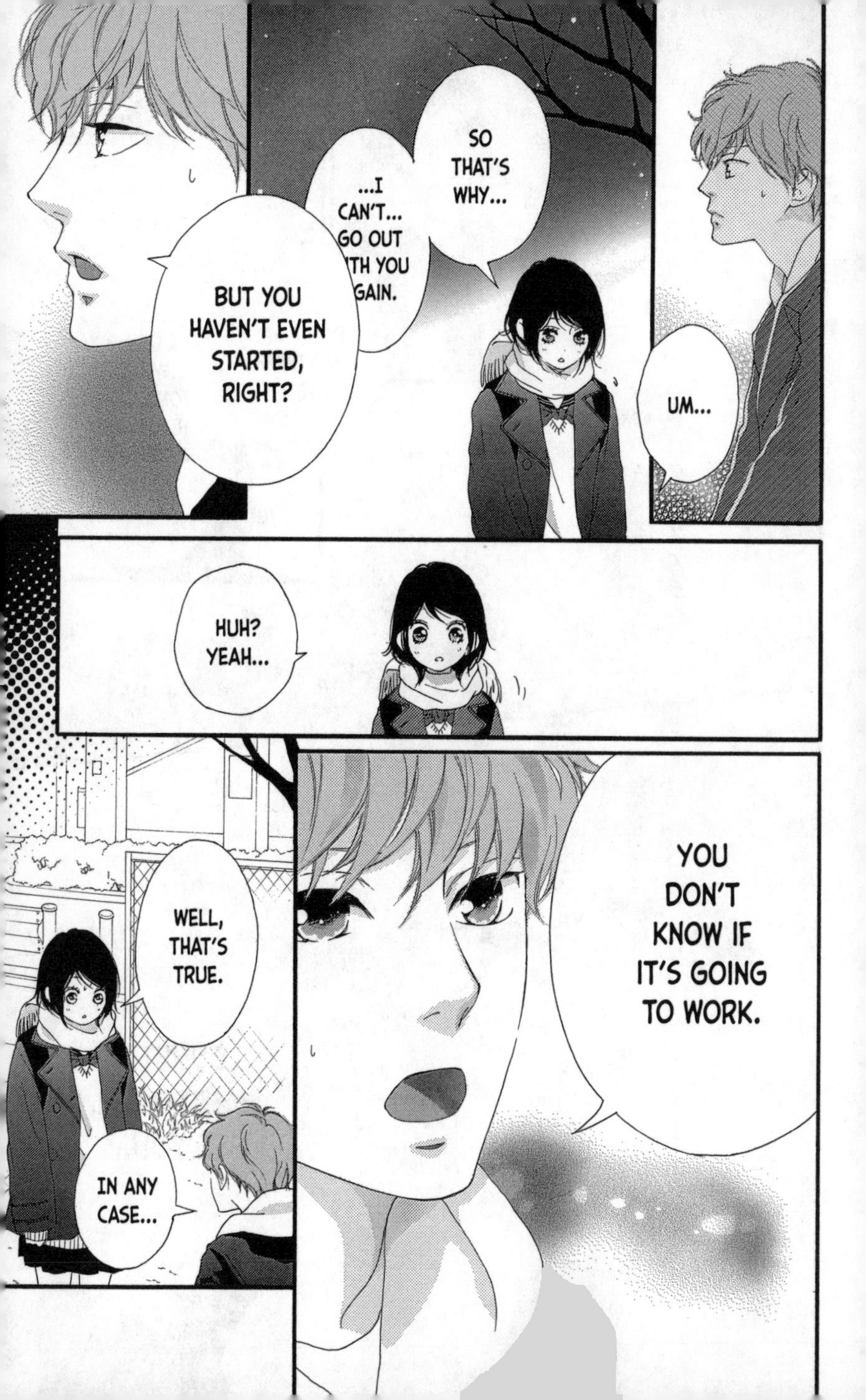
UM...
SO THAT'S WHY...
...I CAN'T... GO OUT ITH YOU GAIN.
BUT YOU HAVEN'T EVEN STARTED, RIGHT?
HUH? YEAH...
YOU DON'T KNOW IF IT'S GOING TO WORK.
WELL, THAT'S TRUE.
IN ANY CASE...

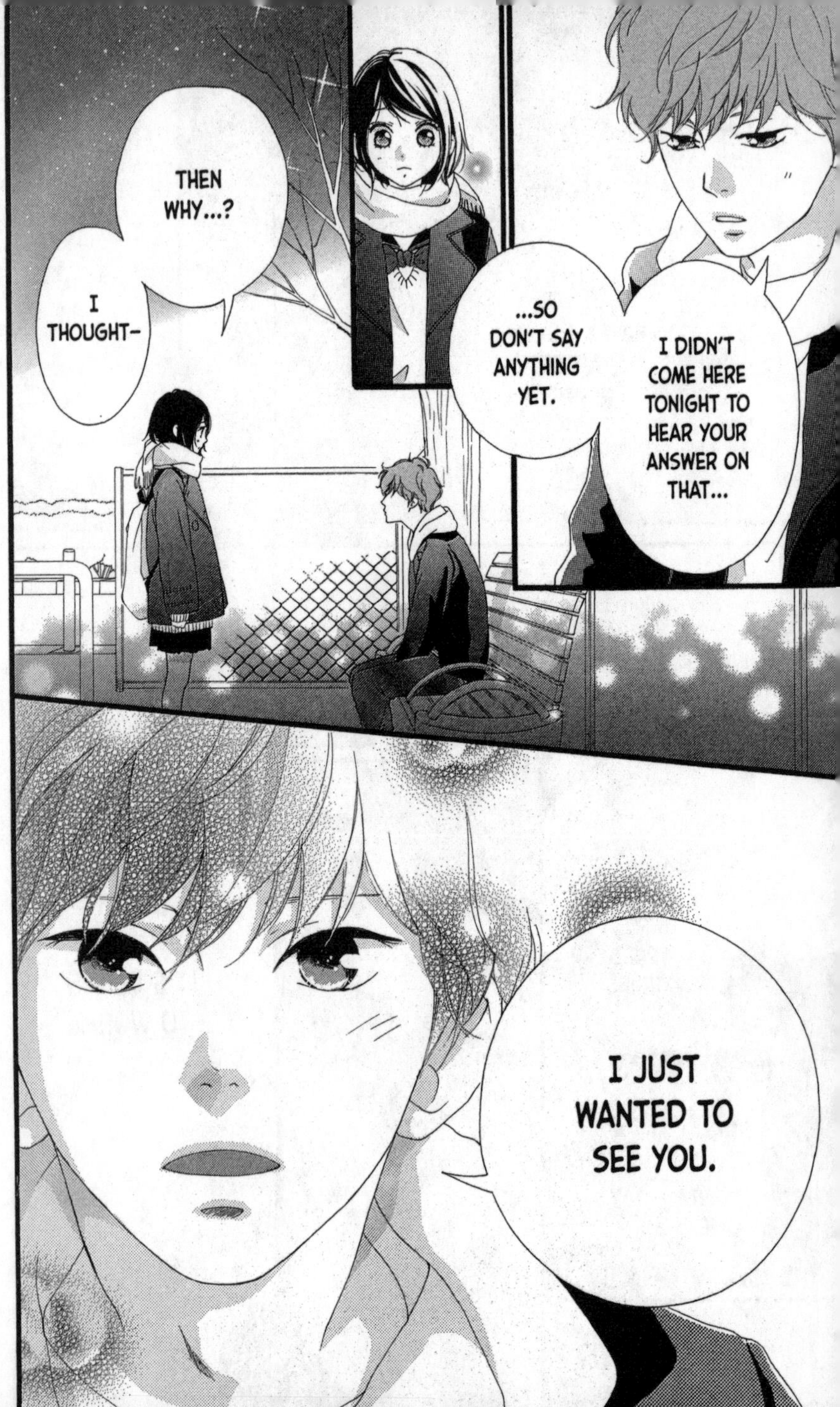
I DIDN'T COME HERE TONIGHT TO HEAR YOUR ANSWER ON THAT...
...SO DON'T SAY ANYTHING YET.
THEN WHY...?
I THOUGHT-
I JUST WANTED TO SEE YOU.

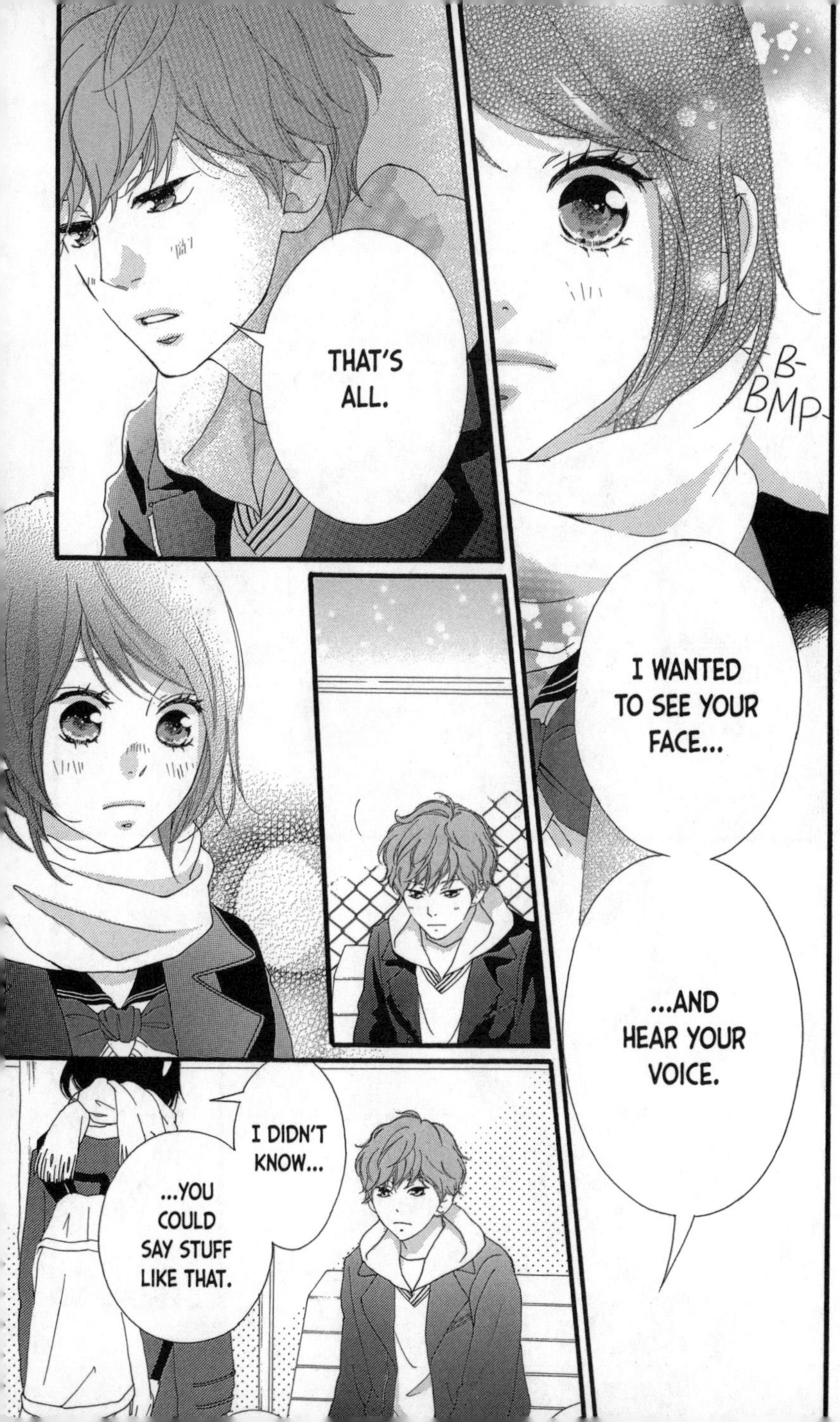
B-BMP
I WANTED TO SEE YOUR FACE...
...AND HEAR YOUR VOICE.
THAT'S ALL.
I DIDN'T KNOW...
...YOU COULD SAY STUFF LIKE THAT.

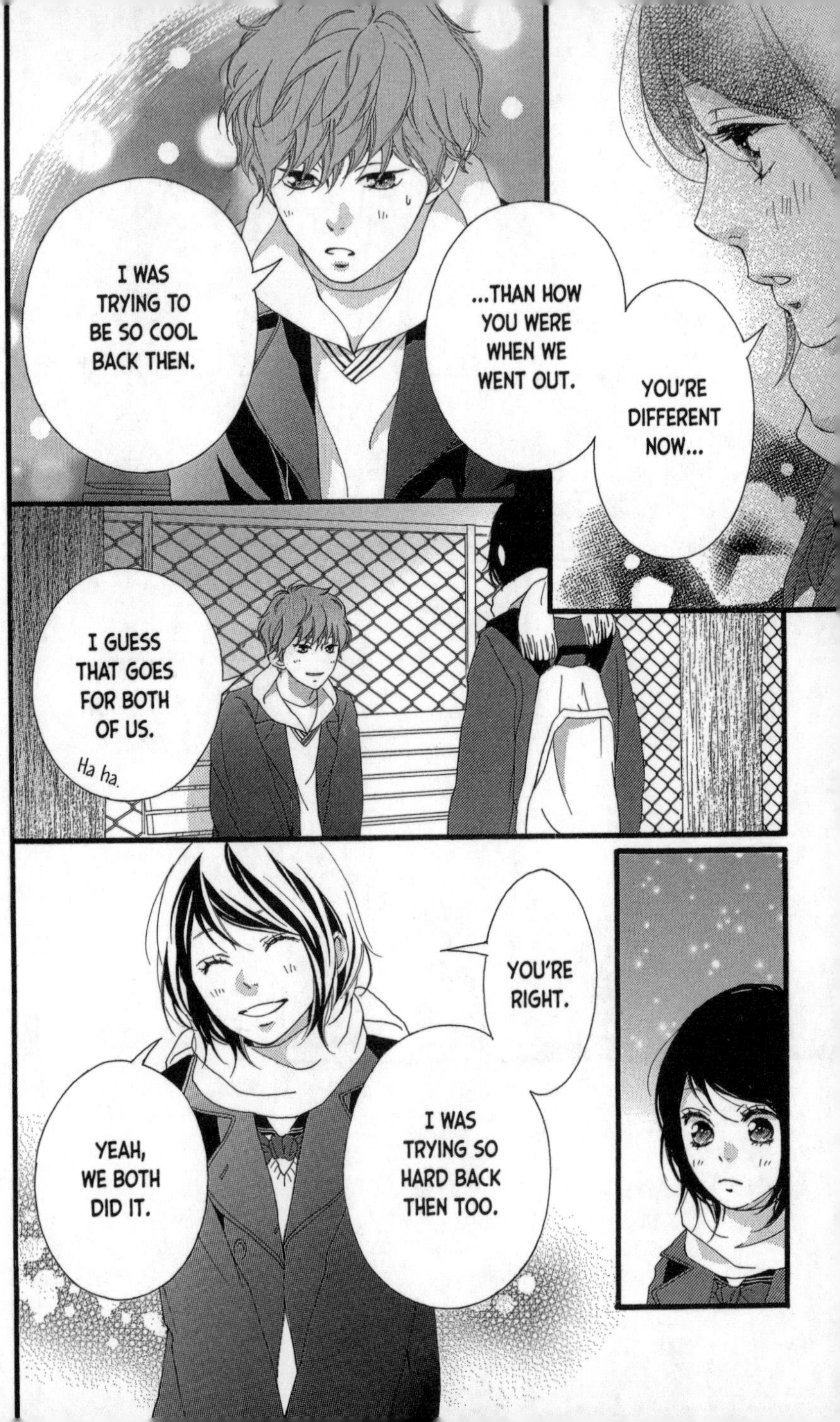
YOU'RE DIFFERENT NOW...
...THAN HOW YOU WERE WHEN WE WENT OUT.
I WAS TRYING TO BE SO COOL BACK THEN.
I GUESS THAT GOES FOR BOTH OF US.
Ha ha.
YOU'RE RIGHT.
I WAS TRYING SO HARD BACK THEN TOO.
YEAH, WE BOTH DID IT.

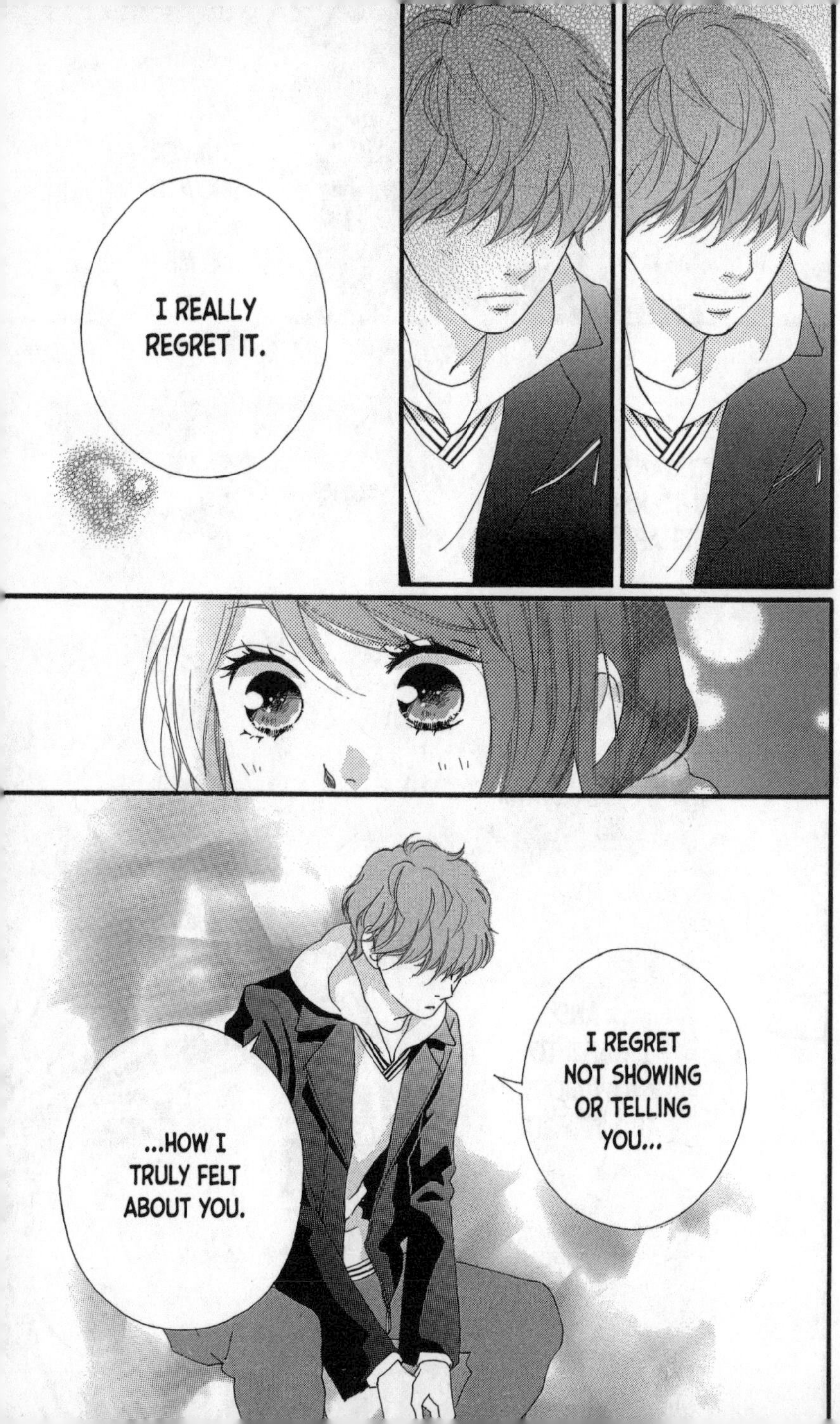
I REALLY REGRET IT.
I REGRET NOT SHOWING OR TELLING YOU...
...HOW I TRULY FELT ABOUT YOU.

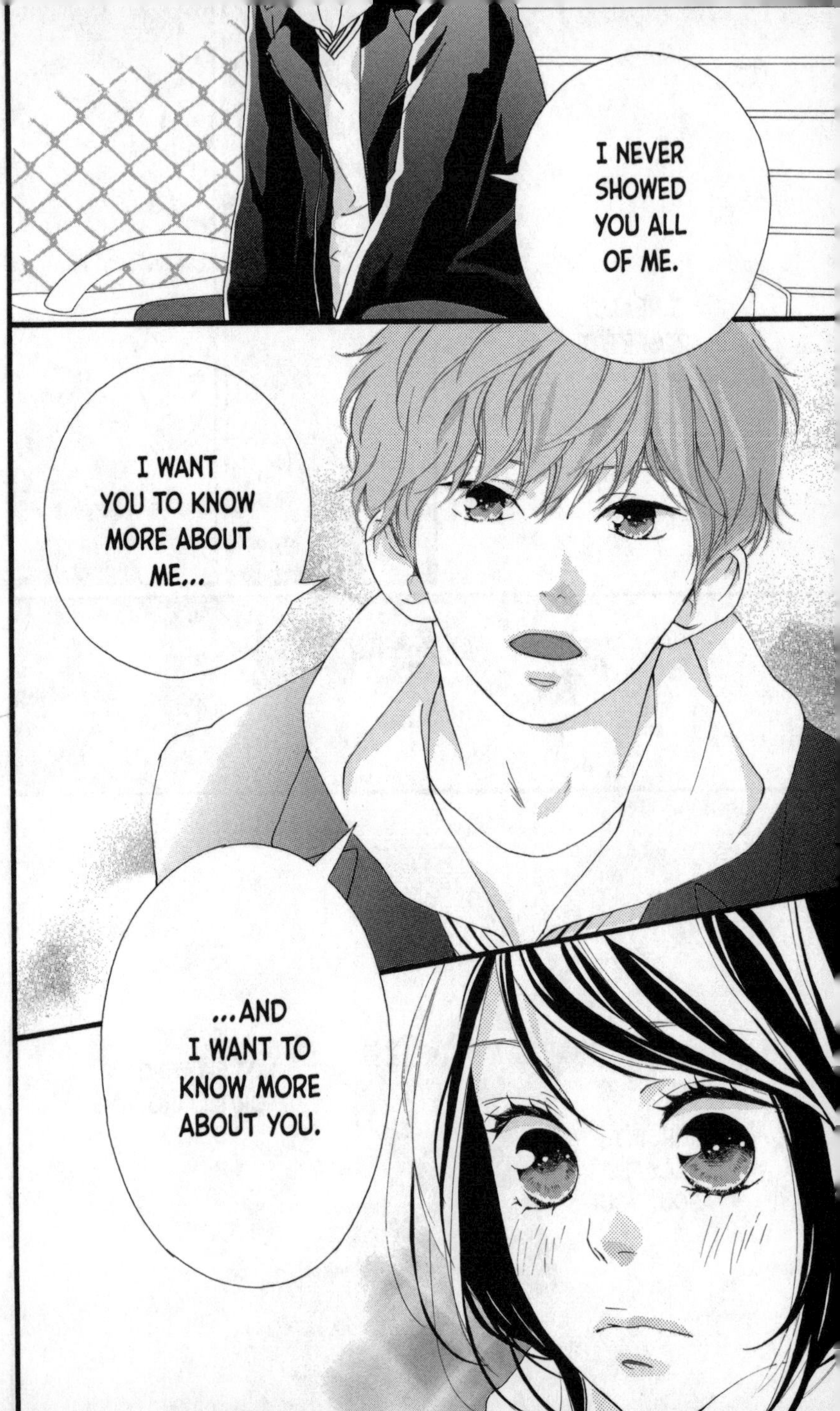
I NEVER SHOWED YOU ALL OF ME.
I WANT YOU TO KNOW MORE ABOUT ME...
...AND I WANT TO KNOW MORE ABOUT YOU.

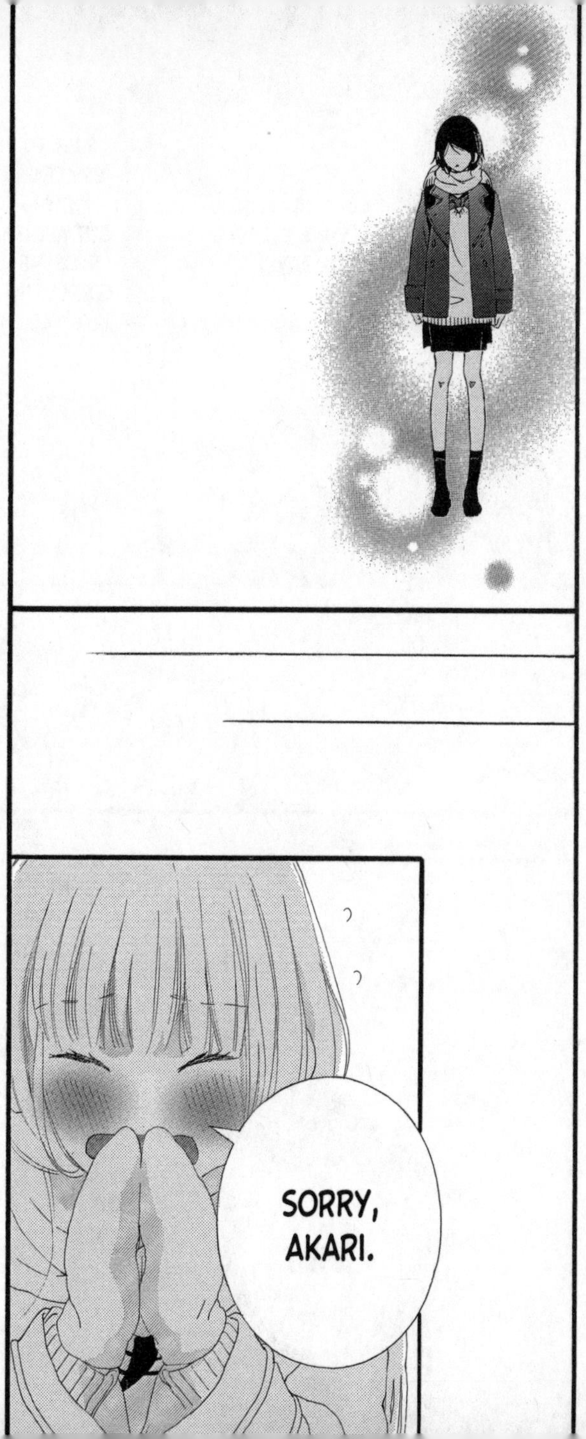
SORRY, AKARI.

Recently during breaks from work, I've started playing games on my phone with my assistants. I rarely play games, but for the first time in about a dozen years, I'm completely hooked. It's fun for us all to play together, and it's just as much fun to play on my own. I find myself playing in the little pockets of time I have. I play more than anyone else at work. The other day, by the time I'd noticed, I had been playing for an entire day. Even I was taken aback. I wonder why I'm still not very good considering all the time I put in. But I realize that it's cutting into my reading time, so I need some self-restraint. I know that, but... I'm impressed by all the people of the world out there who can control themselves. It's very admirable.

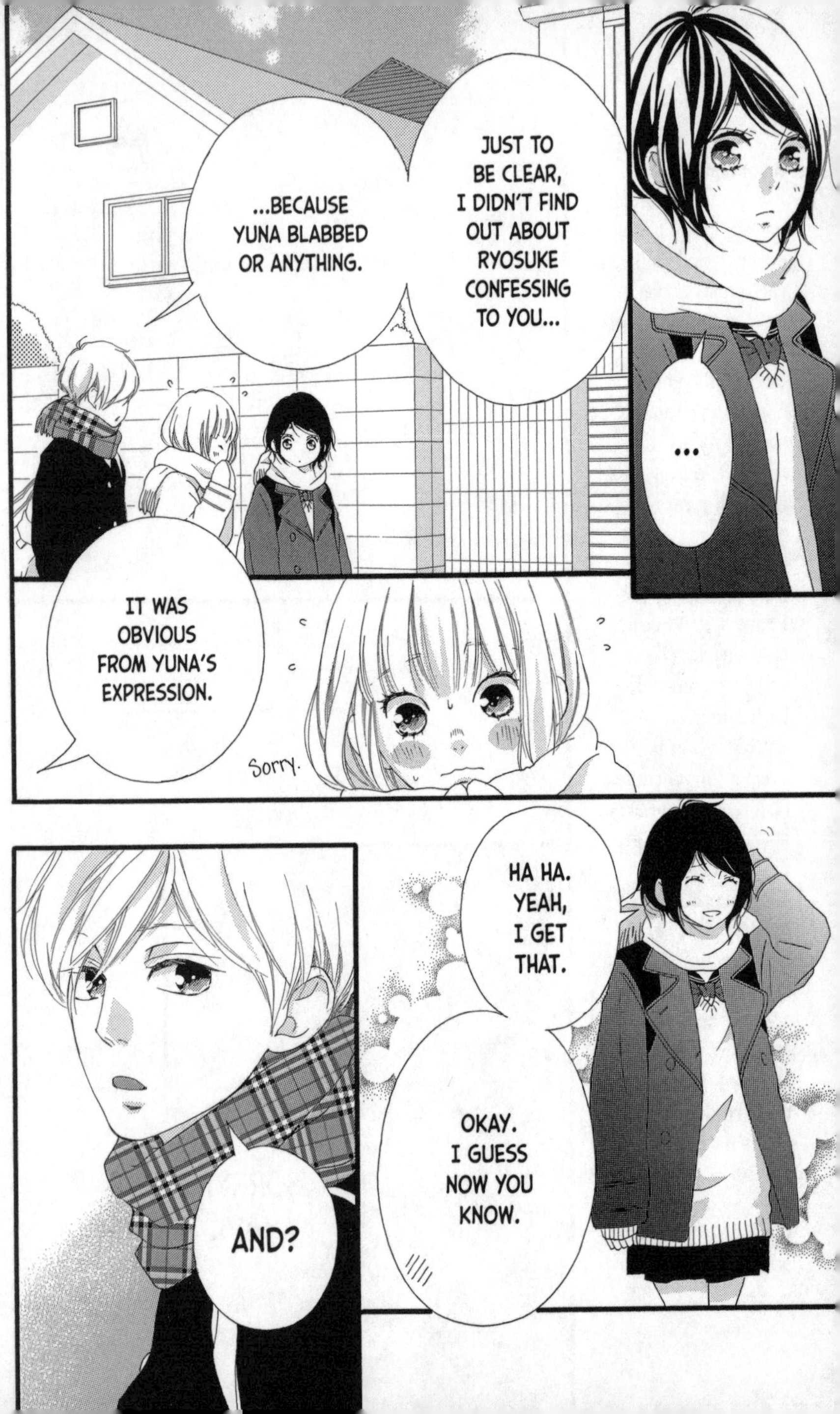
...
JUST TO BE CLEAR, I DIDN'T FIND OUT ABOUT RYOSUKE CONFESSING TO YOU...
...BECAUSE YUNA BLABBED OR ANYTHING.
IT WAS OBVIOUS FROM YUNA'S EXPRESSION.
Sorry.
HA HA. YEAH, I GET THAT.
OKAY. I GUESS NOW YOU KNOW.
AND?

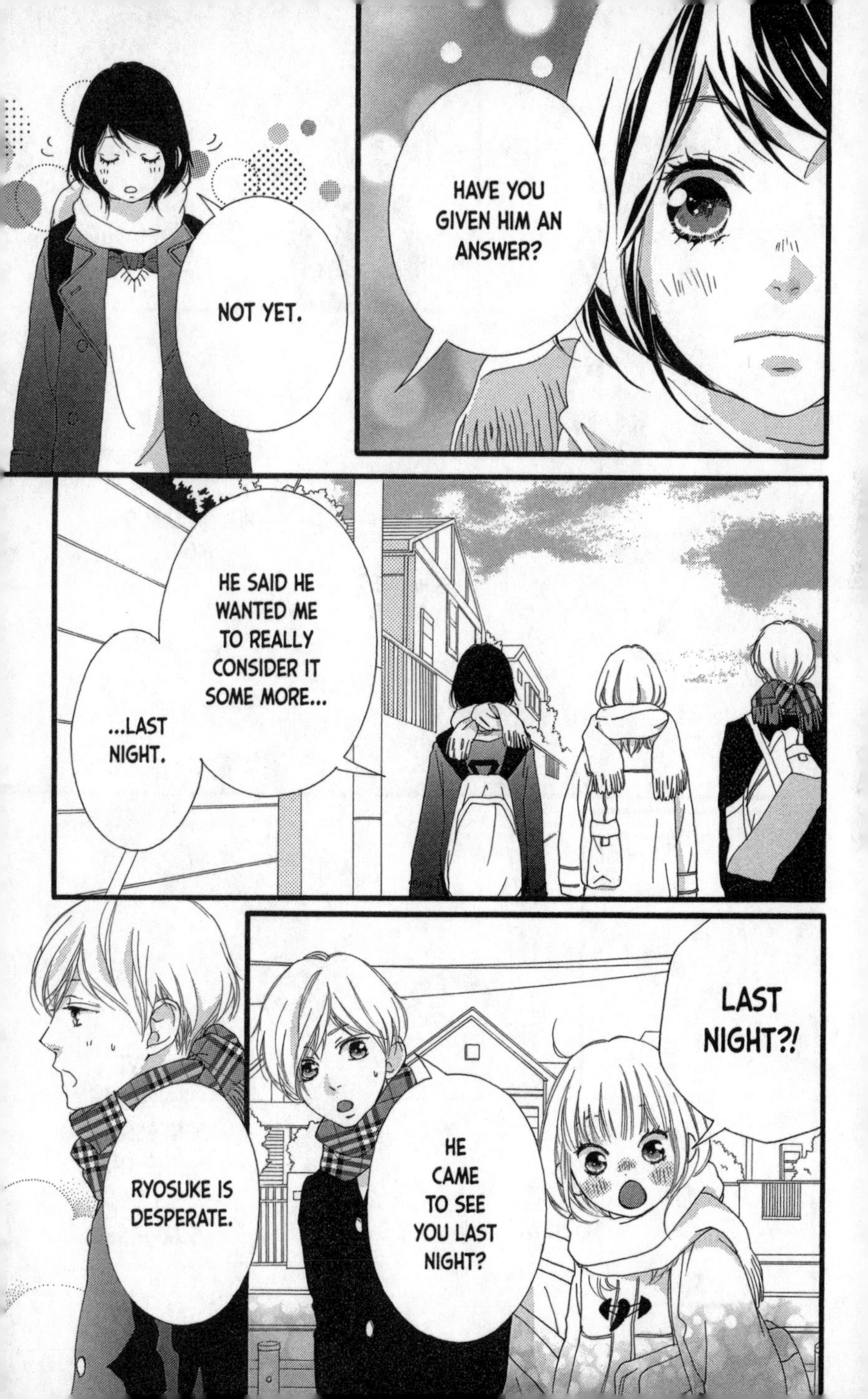
HAVE YOU GIVEN HIM AN ANSWER?
NOT YET.
HE SAID HE WANTED ME TO REALLY CONSIDER IT SOME MORE...
...LAST NIGHT.
LAST NIGHT?!
HE CAME TO SEE YOU LAST NIGHT?
RYOSUKE IS DESPERATE.

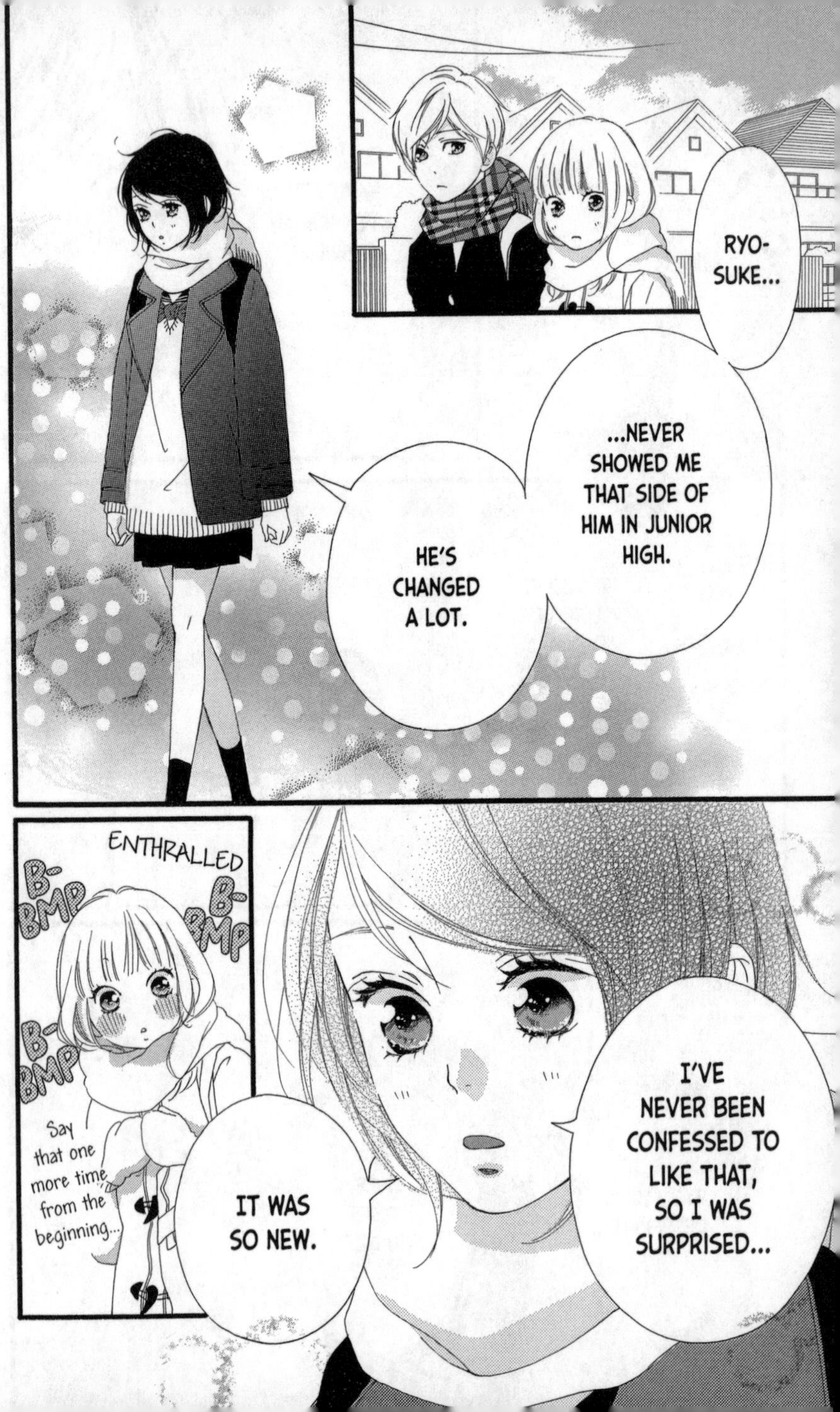
RYO-SUKE...
...NEVER SHOWED ME THAT SIDE OF HIM IN JUNIOR HIGH.
HE'S CHANGED A LOT.
I'VE NEVER BEEN CONFESSED TO LIKE THAT, SO I WAS SURPRISED...
IT WAS SO NEW.
ENTHRALLED
B-BMP
B-BMP
B-BMP
Say that one more time from the beginning...

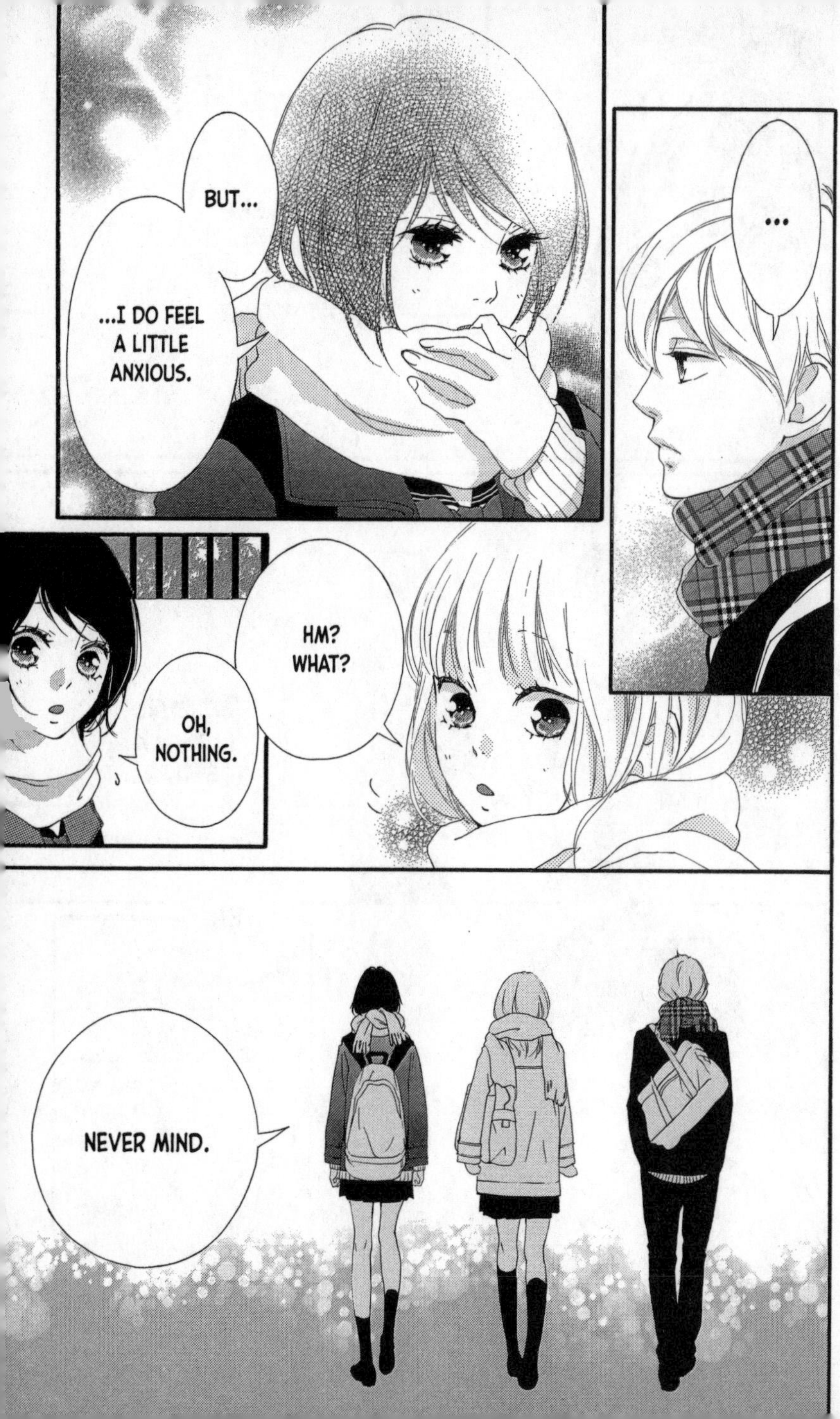
...
BUT...
...I DO FEEL A LITTLE ANXIOUS.
HM? WHAT?
OH, NOTHING.
NEVER MIND.

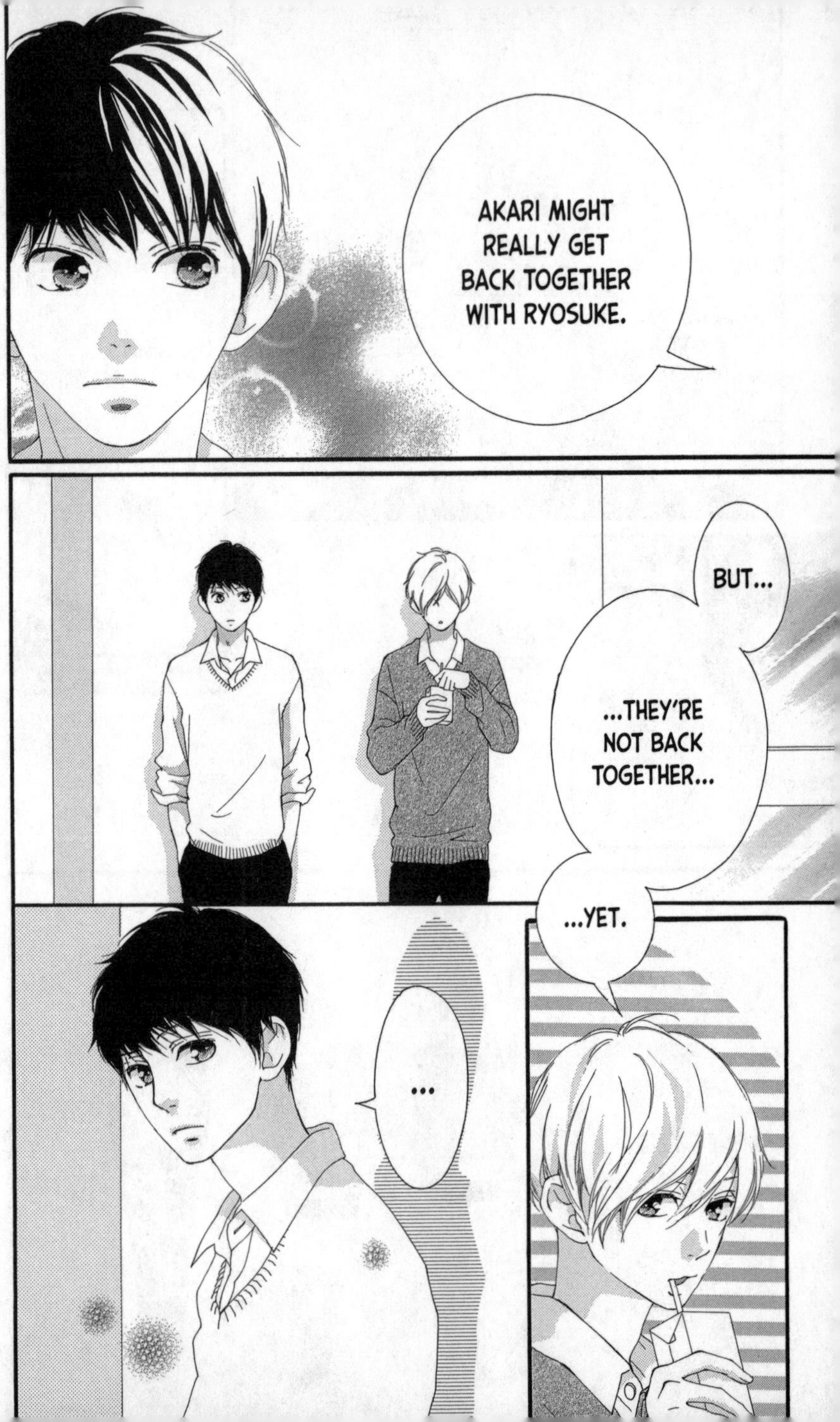
AKARI MIGHT REALLY GET BACK TOGETHER WITH RYOSUKE.
BUT...
...THEY'RE NOT BACK TOGETHER...
...YET.
...

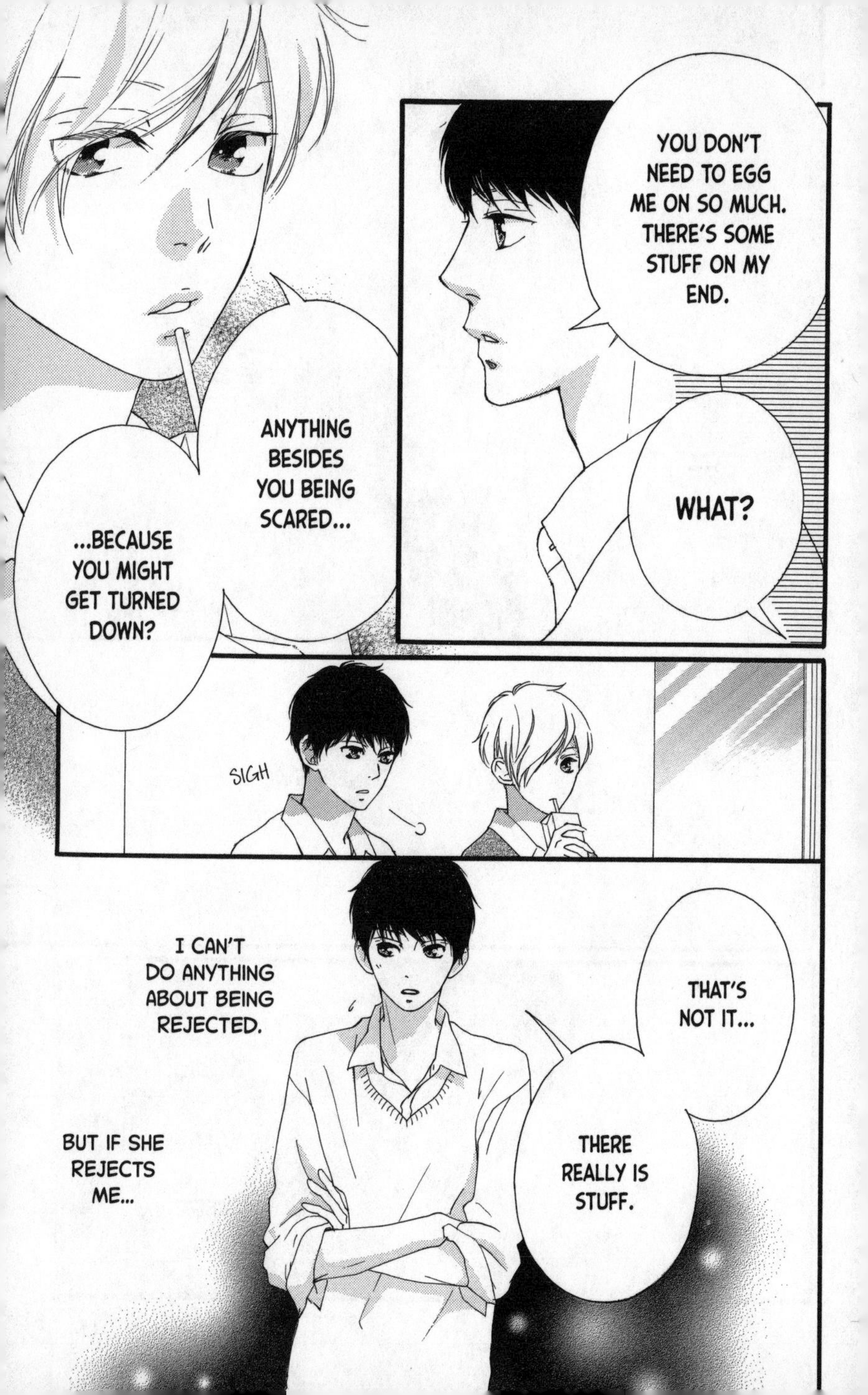
YOU DON'T NEED TO EGG ME ON SO MUCH. THERE'S SOME STUFF ON MY END.
WHAT?
ANYTHING BESIDES YOU BEING SCARED...
...BECAUSE YOU MIGHT GET TURNED DOWN?
SIGH
THAT'S NOT IT...
THERE REALLY IS STUFF.
I CAN'T DO ANYTHING ABOUT BEING REJECTED.
BUT IF SHE REJECTS ME...

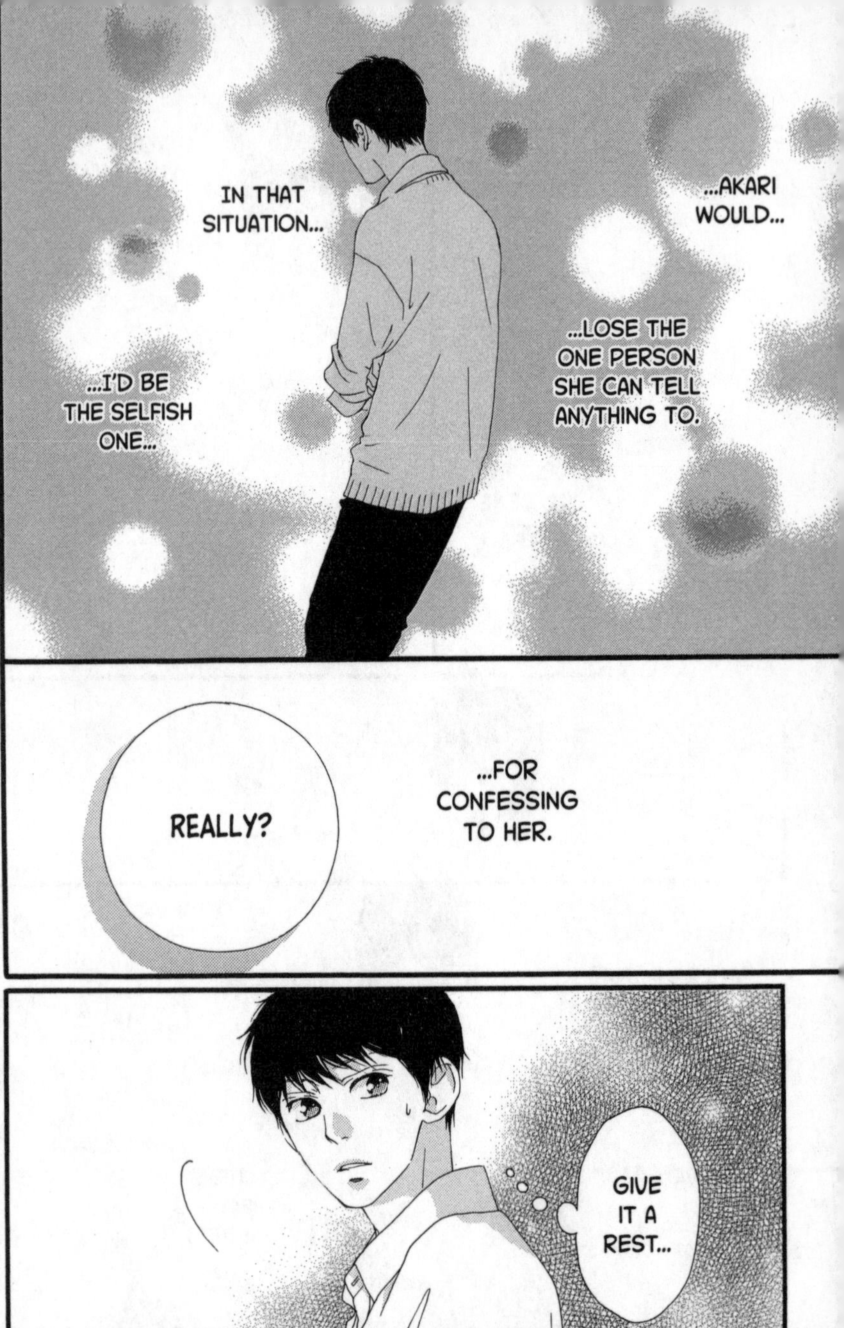
...AKARI WOULD...
...LOSE THE ONE PERSON SHE CAN TELL ANYTHING TO.
IN THAT SITUATION...
...I'D BE THE SELFISH ONE...
...FOR CONFESSING TO HER.
REALLY?
GIVE IT A REST...

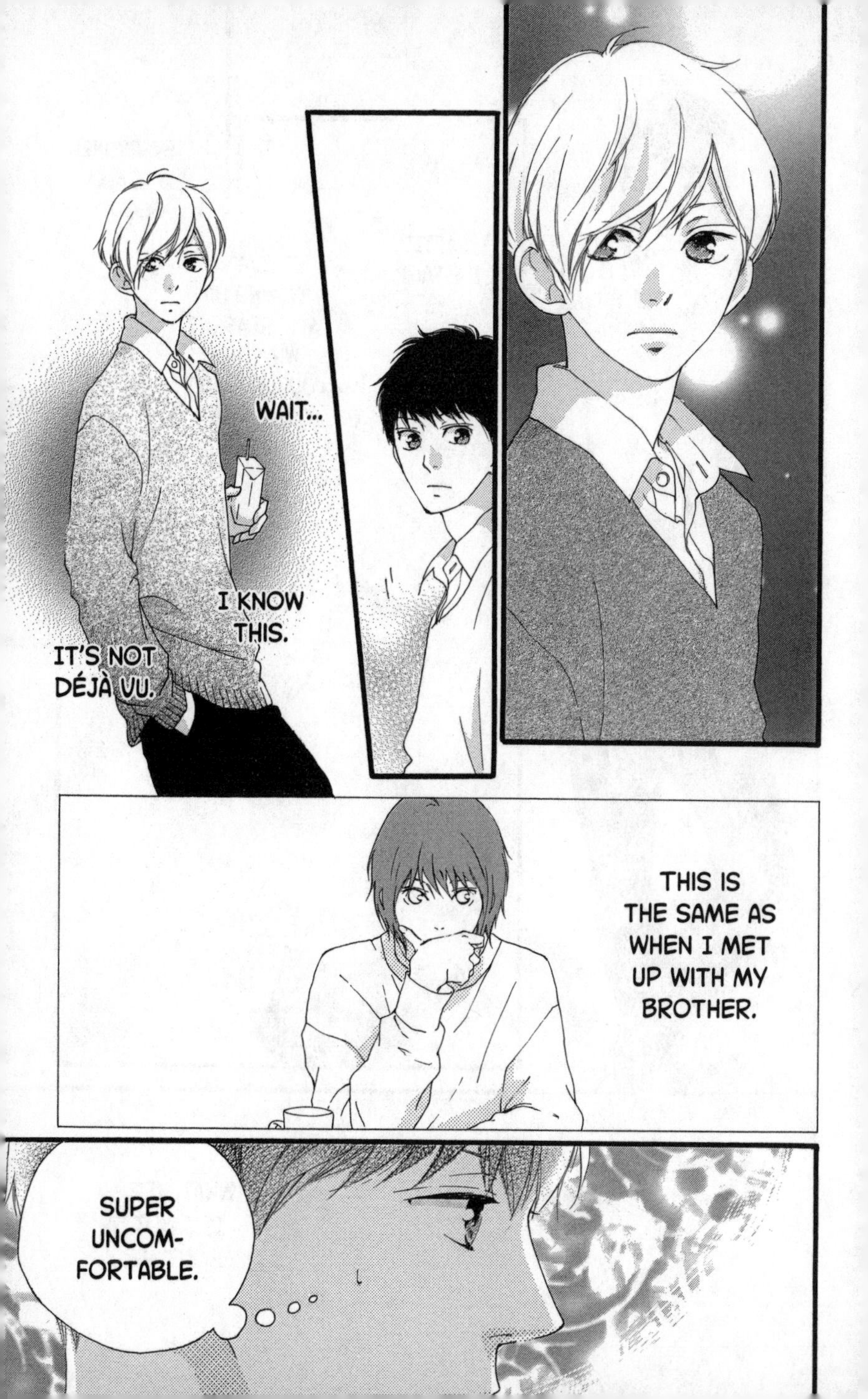
WAIT...
I KNOW THIS.
IT'S NOT DÉJÀ VU.
THIS IS THE SAME AS WHEN I MET UP WITH MY BROTHER.
SUPER UNCOM-FORTABLE.

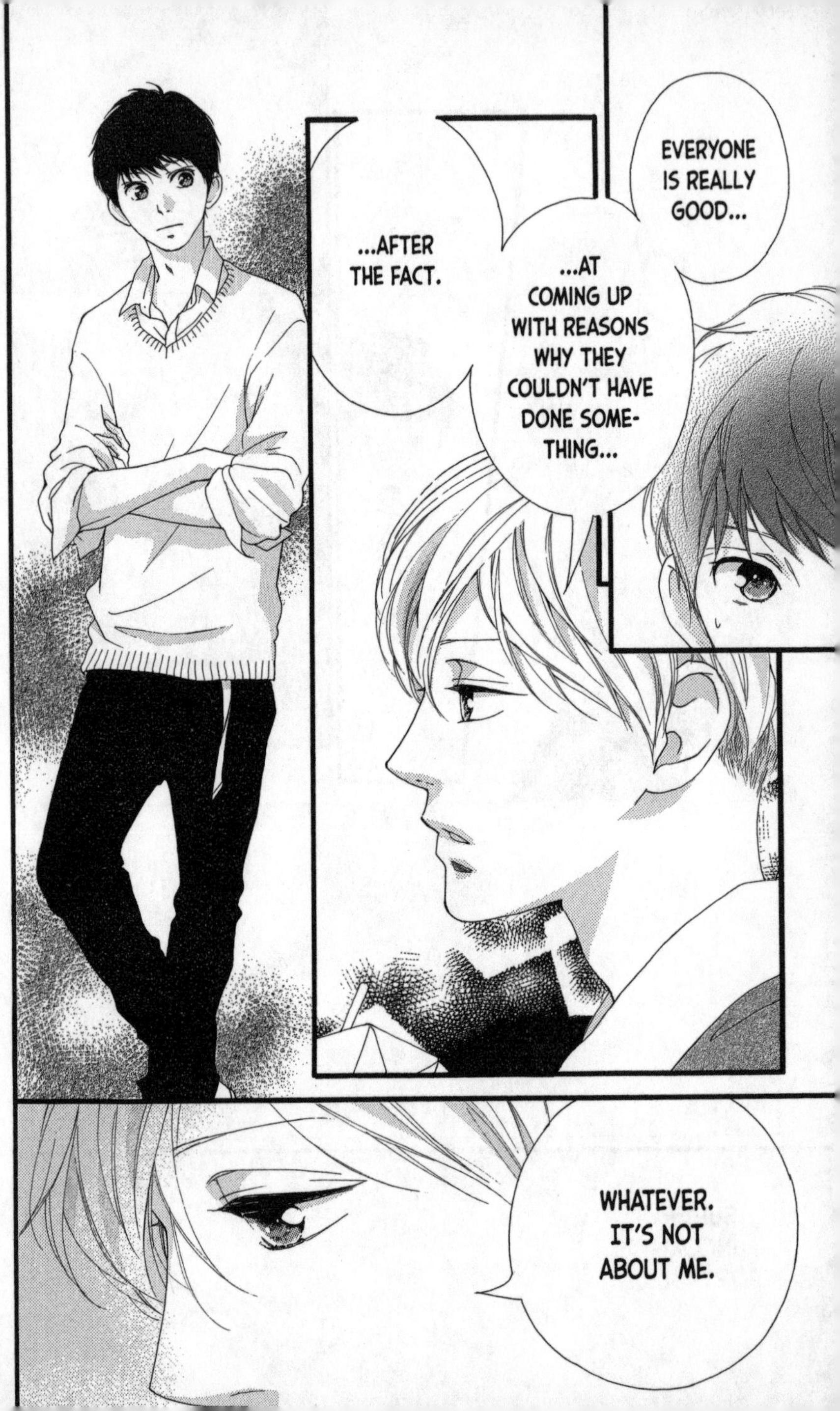
EVERYONE IS REALLY GOOD...
...AT COMING UP WITH REASONS WHY THEY COULDN'T HAVE DONE SOME-THING...
...AFTER THE FACT.
WHATEVER. IT'S NOT ABOUT ME.

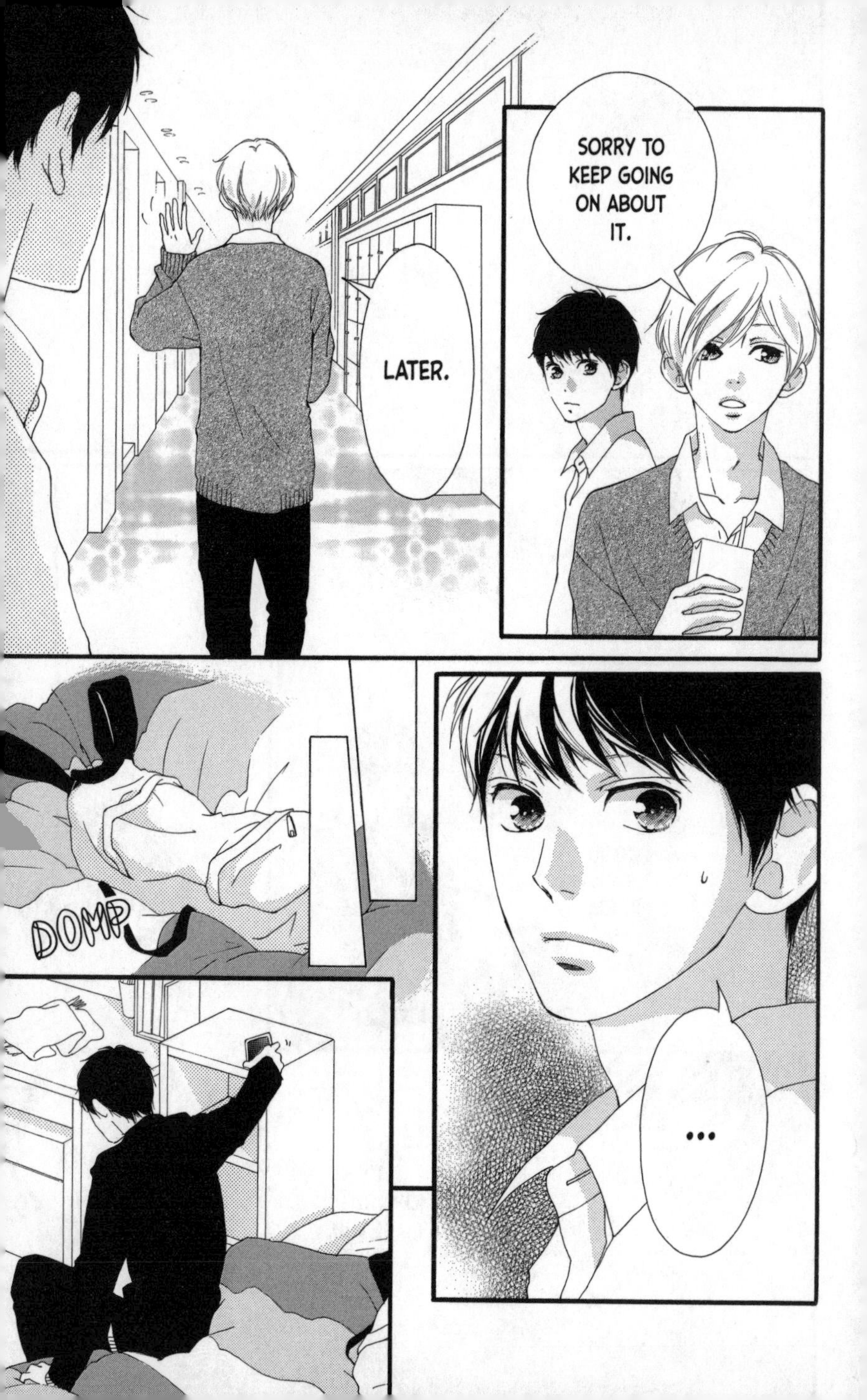
SORRY TO KEEP GOING ON ABOUT IT.
LATER.
...
DOMP

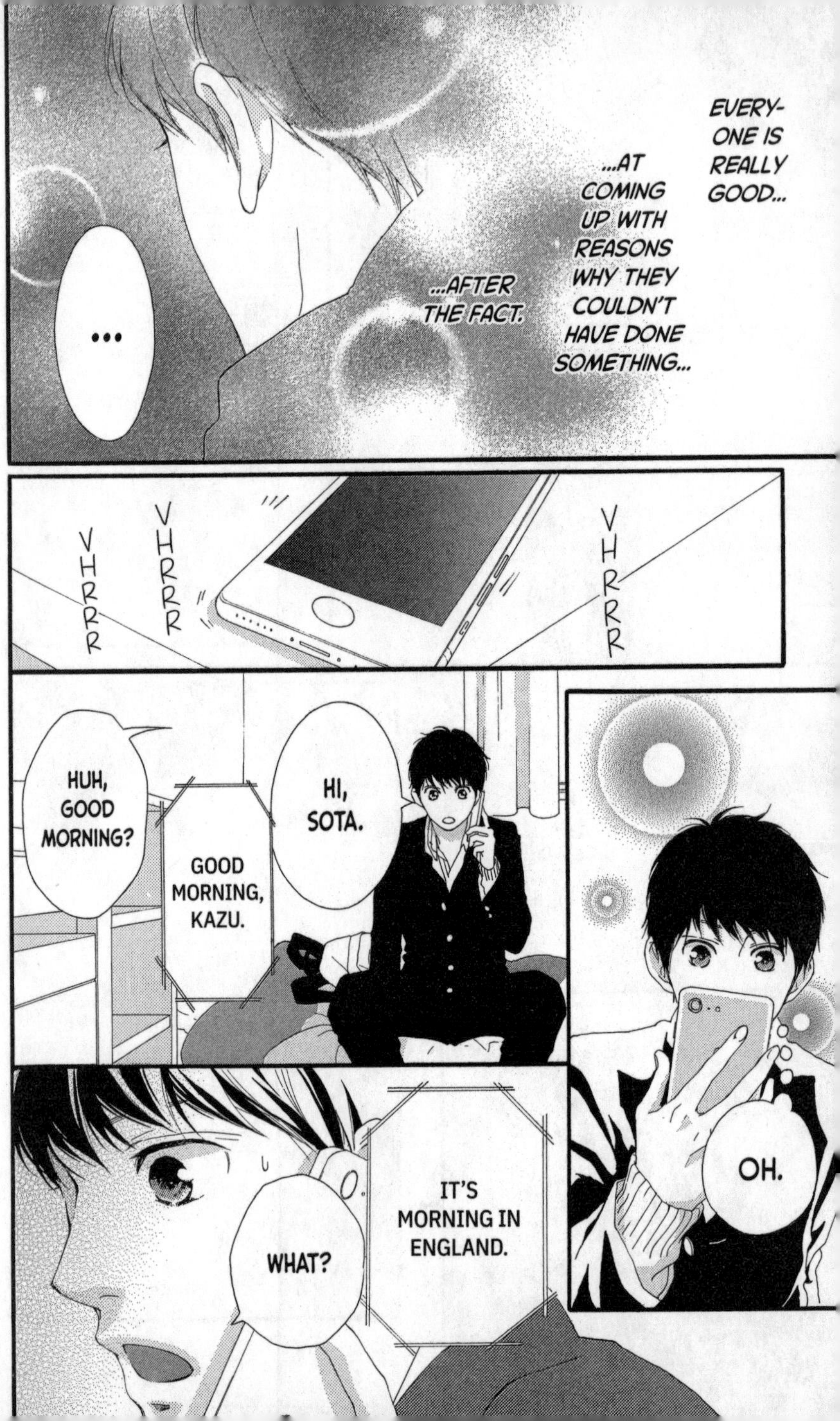
EVERY-ONE IS REALLY GOOD...
...AT COMING UP WITH REASONS WHY THEY COULDN'T HAVE DONE SOMETHING...
...AFTER THE FACT.
...
VHRRR
VHRRR
VHRRR
OH.
HI, SOTA.
GOOD MORNING, KAZU.
HUH, GOOD MORNING?
IT'S MORNING IN ENGLAND.
WHAT?

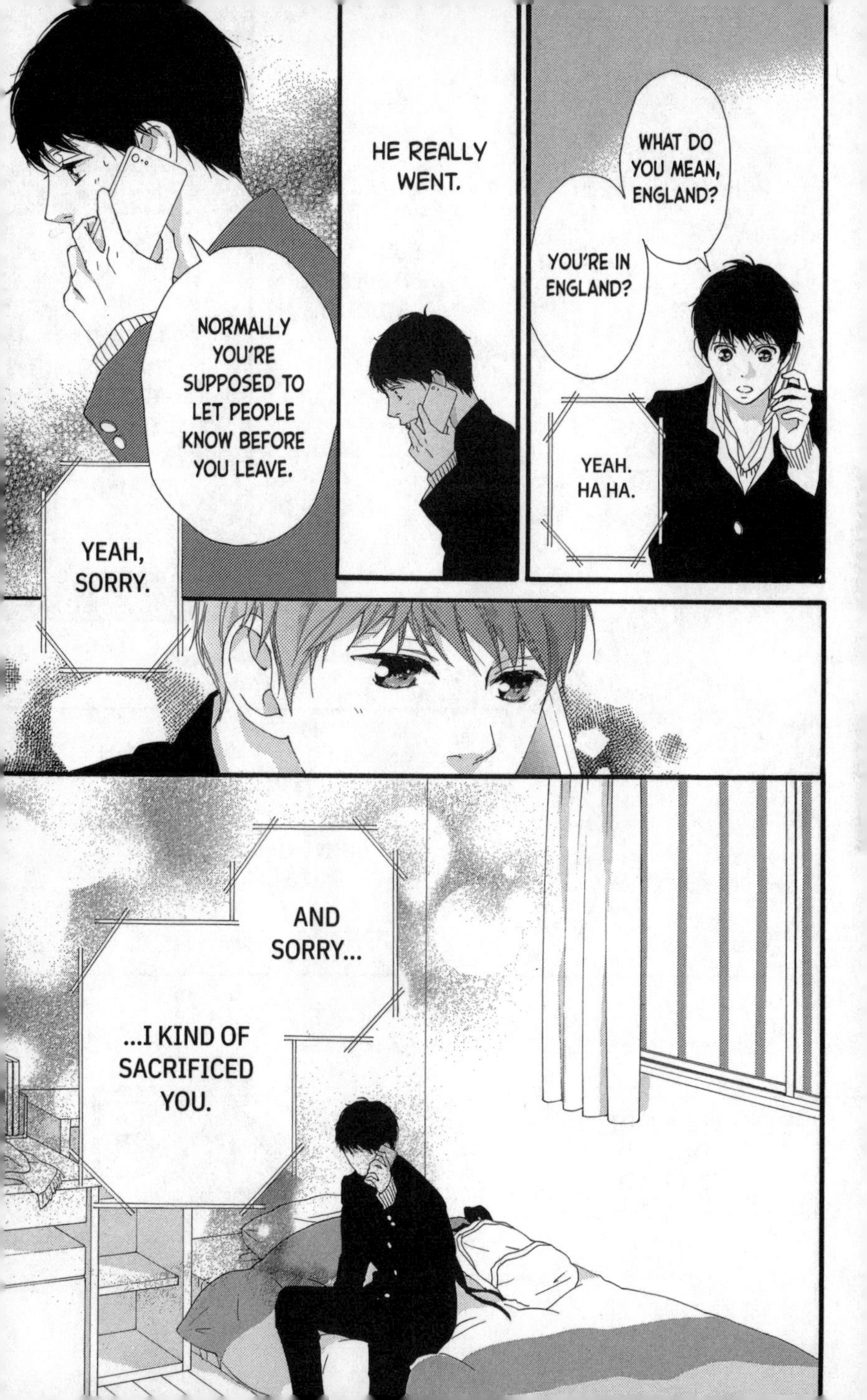
WHAT DO YOU MEAN, ENGLAND?
YOU'RE IN ENGLAND?
YEAH. HA HA.
HE REALLY WENT.
NORMALLY YOU'RE SUPPOSED TO LET PEOPLE KNOW BEFORE YOU LEAVE.
YEAH, SORRY.
AND SORRY...
...I KIND OF SACRIFICED YOU.

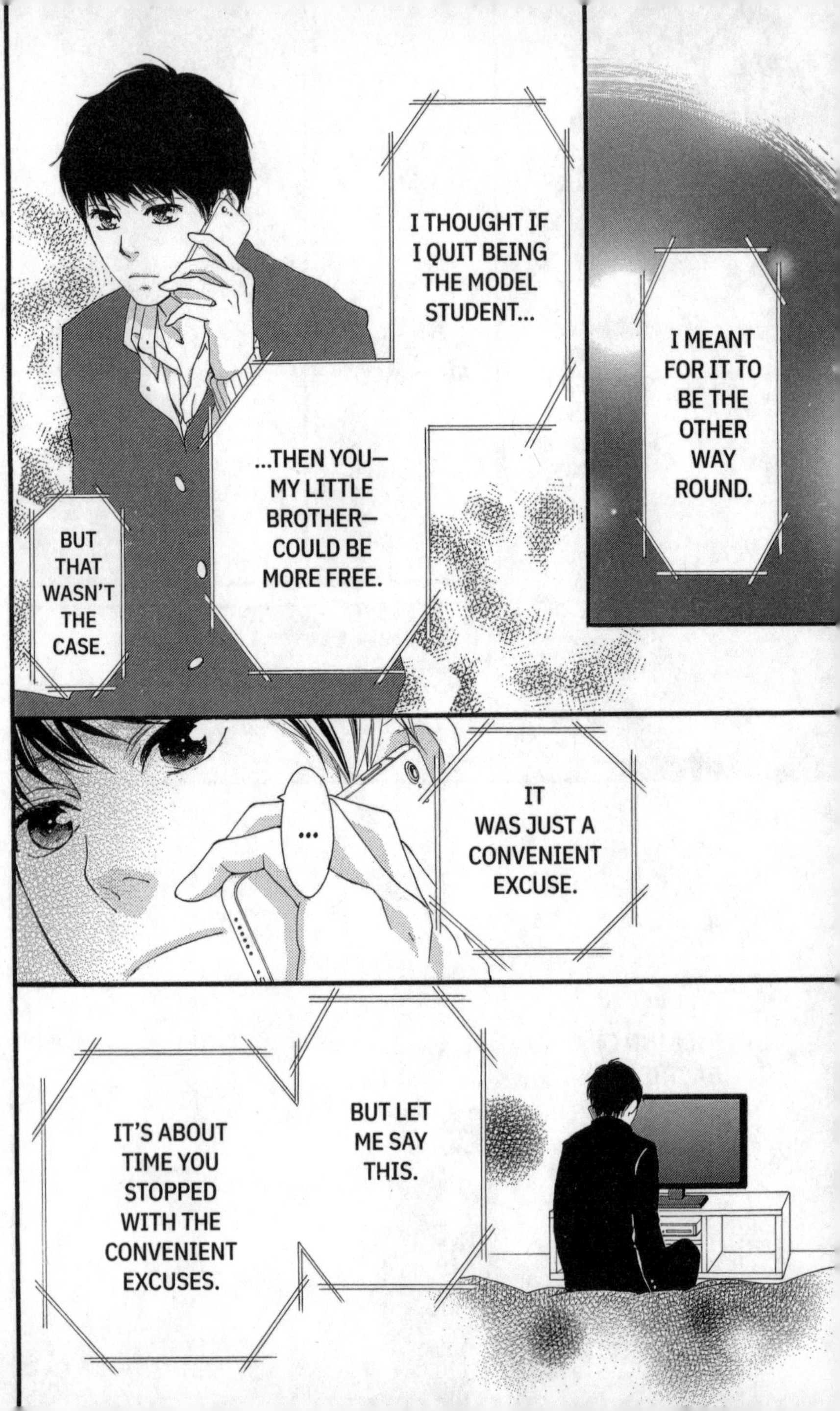
I MEANT FOR IT TO BE THE OTHER WAY ROUND.
I THOUGHT IF I QUIT BEING THE MODEL STUDENT...
...THEN YOU— MY LITTLE BROTHER— COULD BE MORE FREE.
BUT THAT WASN'T THE CASE.
IT WAS JUST A CONVENIENT EXCUSE.
...
BUT LET ME SAY THIS.
IT'S ABOUT TIME YOU STOPPED WITH THE CONVENIENT EXCUSES.

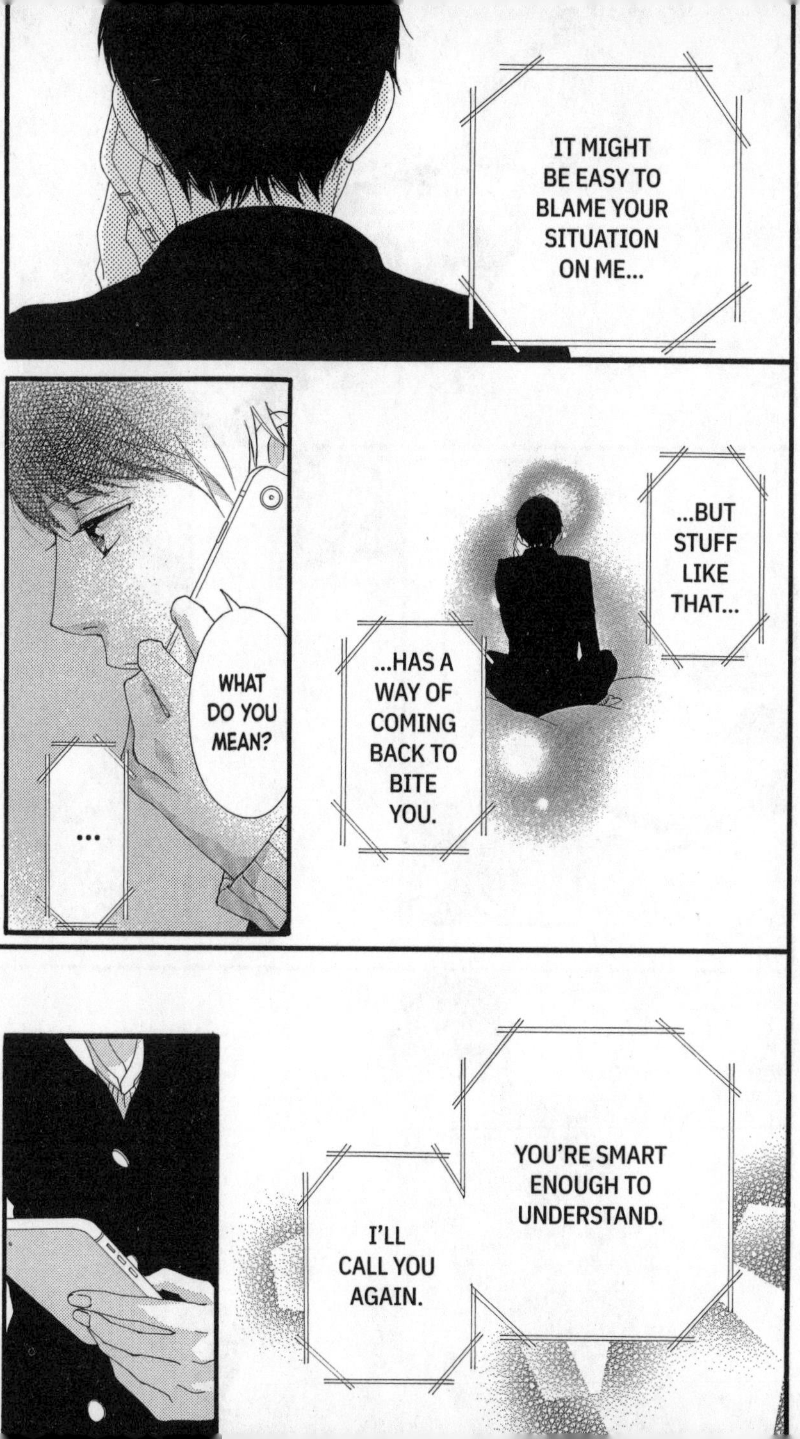
IT MIGHT BE EASY TO BLAME YOUR SITUATION ON ME...
...BUT STUFF LIKE THAT...
...HAS A WAY OF COMING BACK TO BITE YOU.
WHAT DO YOU MEAN?
...
YOU'RE SMART ENOUGH TO UNDERSTAND.
I'LL CALL YOU AGAIN.

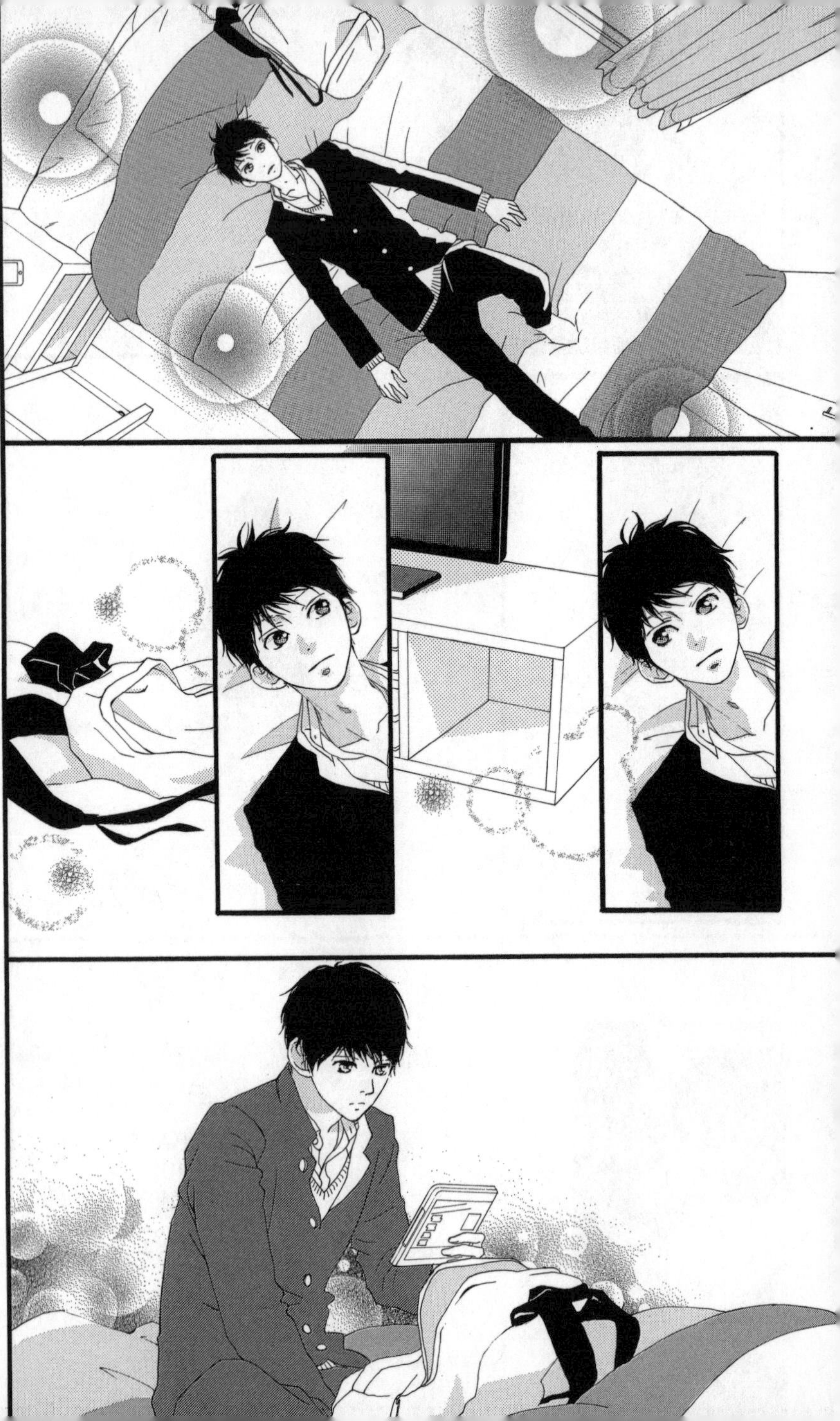

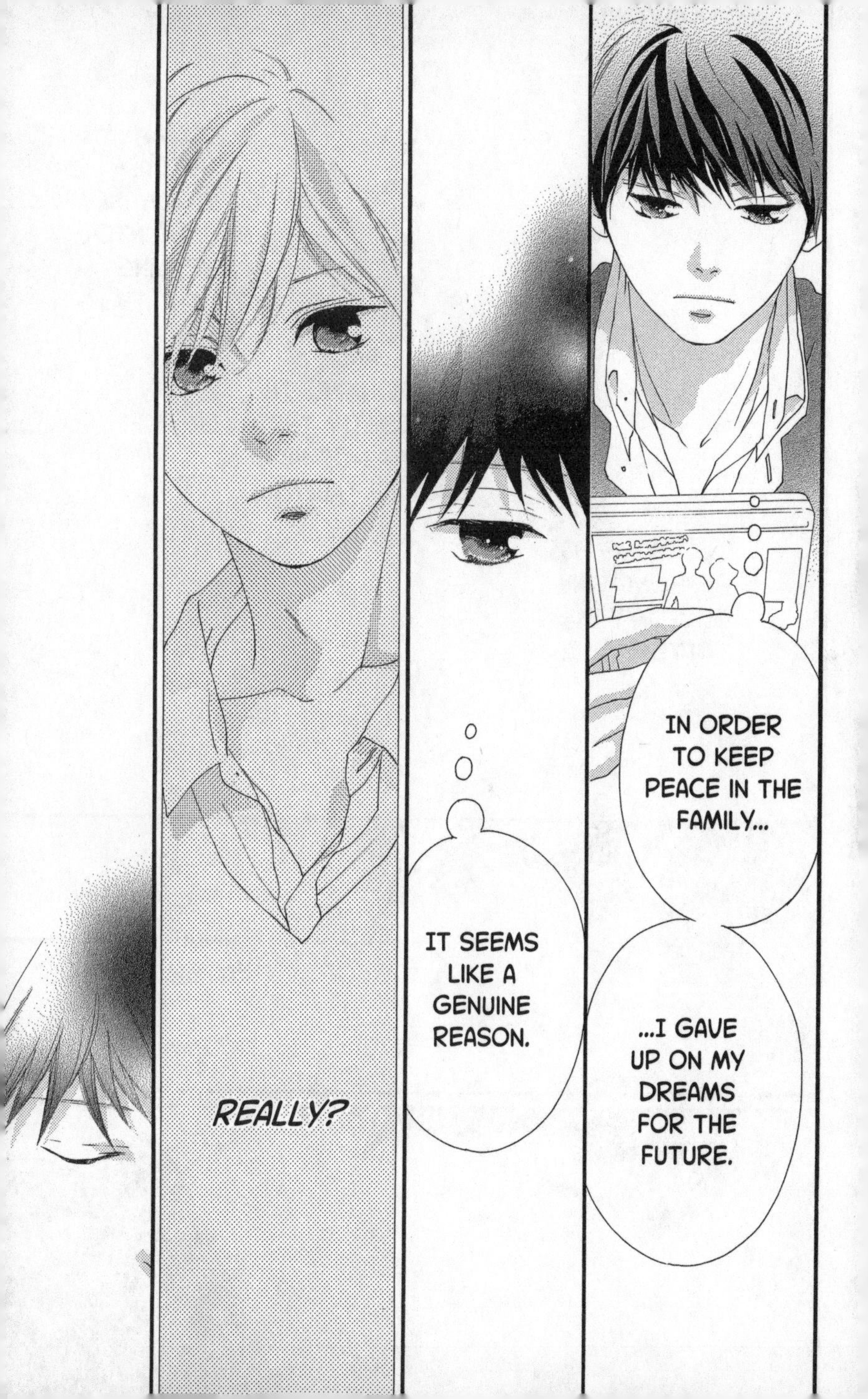
IN ORDER TO KEEP PEACE IN THE FAMILY...
...I GAVE UP ON MY DREAMS FOR THE FUTURE.
IT SEEMS LIKE A GENUINE REASON.
REALLY?

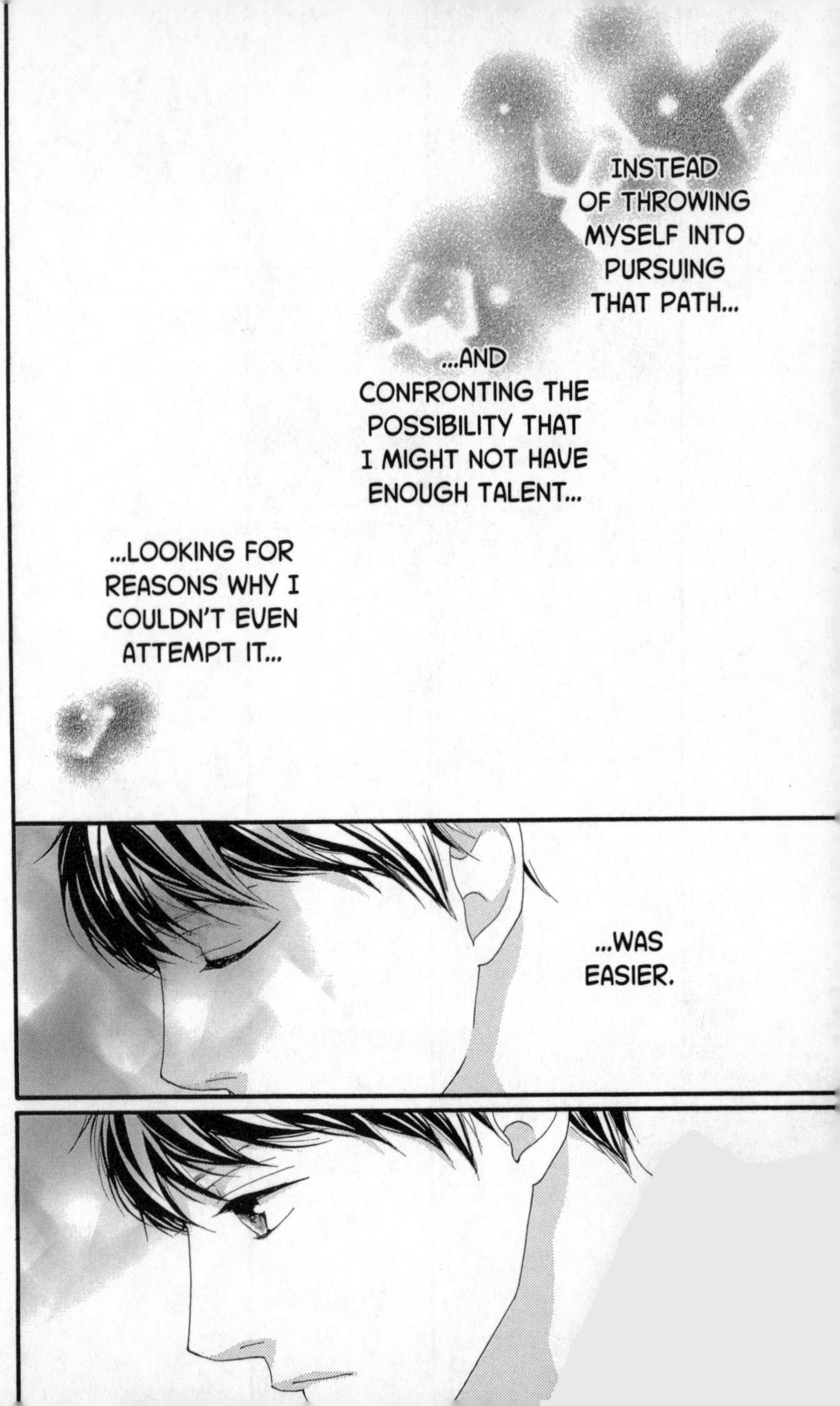
INSTEAD OF THROWING MYSELF INTO PURSUING THAT PATH...
...AND CONFRONTING THE POSSIBILITY THAT I MIGHT NOT HAVE ENOUGH TALENT...
...LOOKING FOR REASONS WHY I COULDN'T EVEN ATTEMPT IT...
...WAS EASIER.

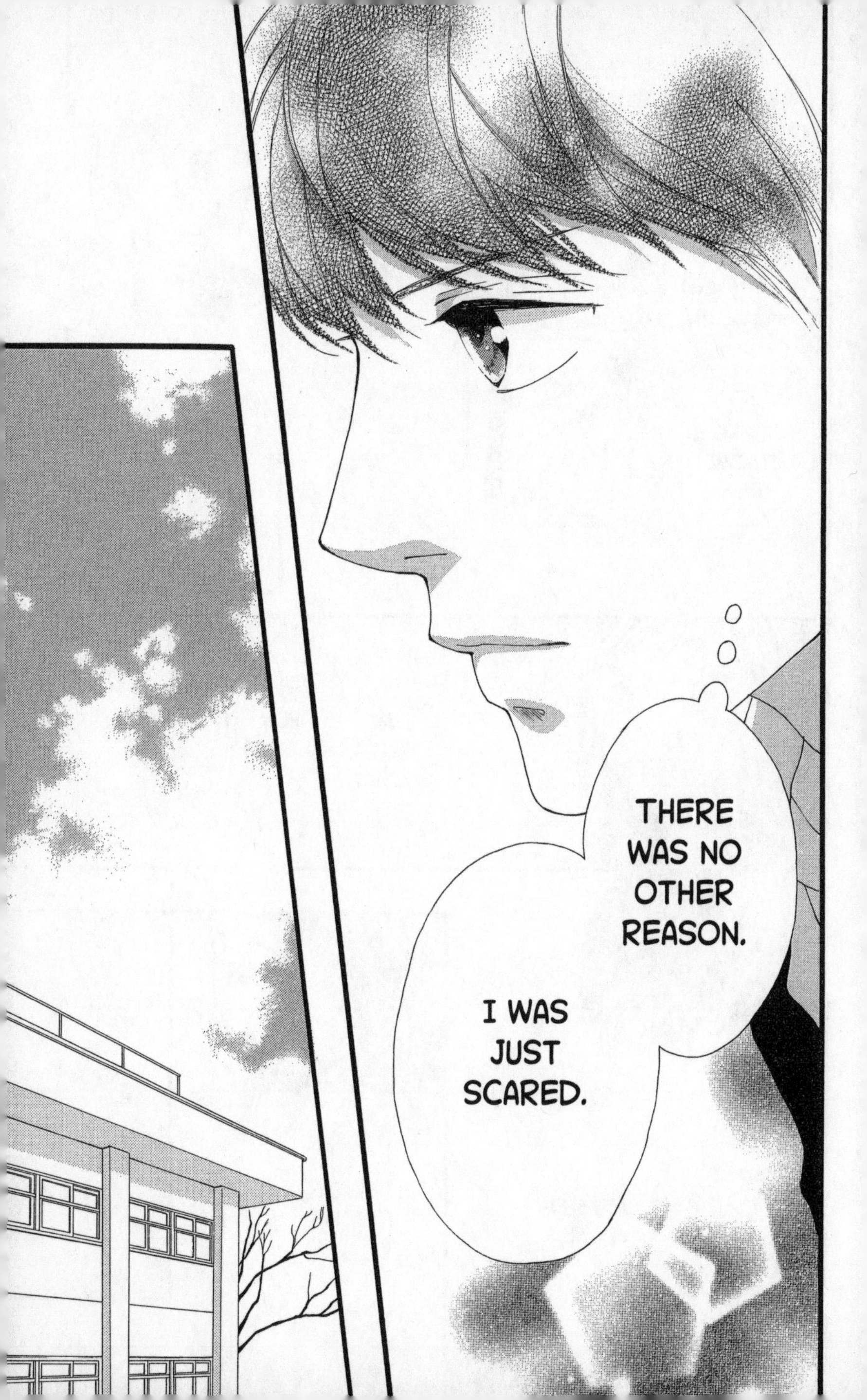
THERE WAS NO OTHER REASON.
I WAS JUST SCARED.

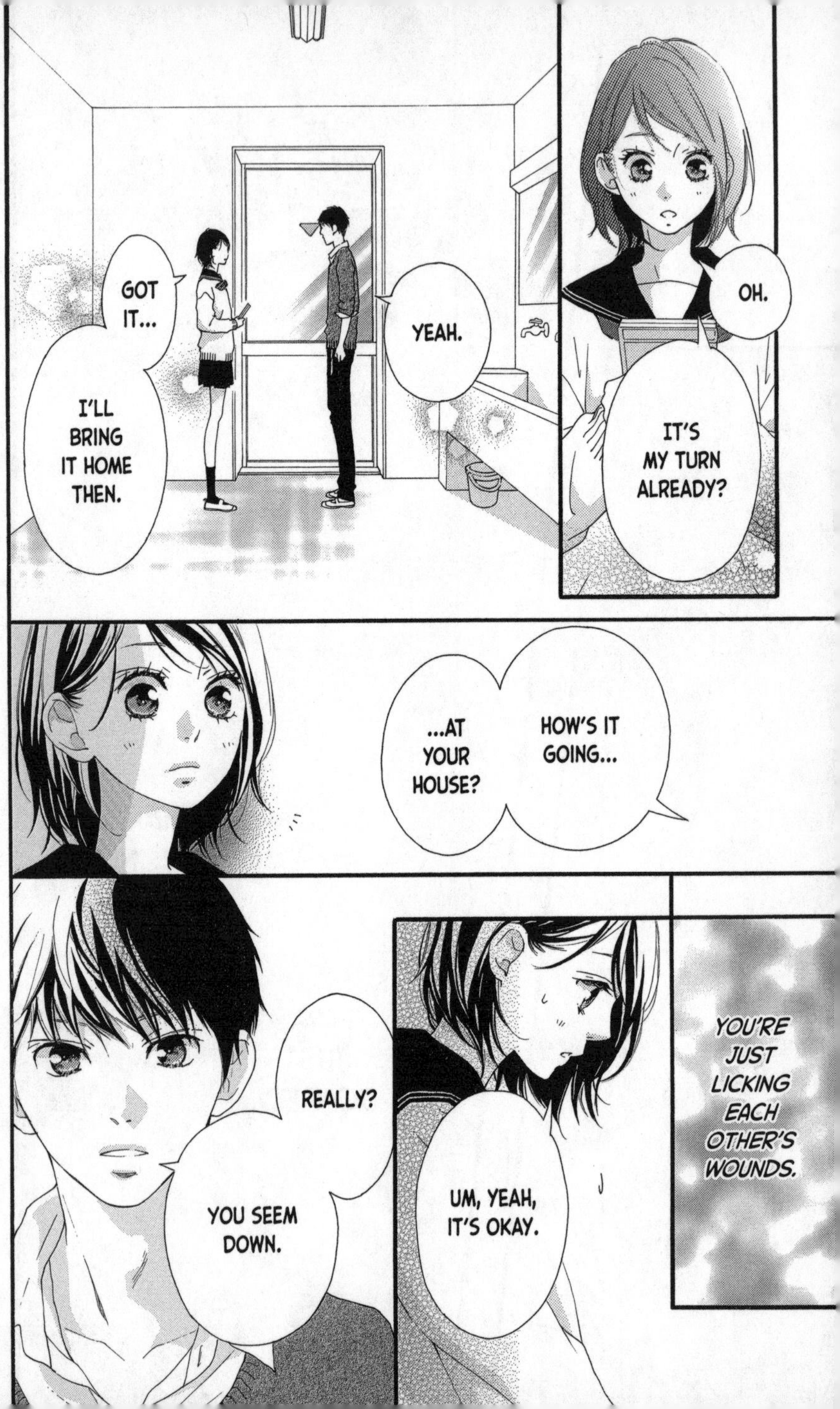
OH.
IT'S MY TURN ALREADY?
YEAH.
GOT IT...
I'LL BRING IT HOME THEN.
HOW'S IT GOING...
...AT YOUR HOUSE?
YOU'RE JUST LICKING EACH OTHER'S WOUNDS.
UM, YEAH, IT'S OKAY.
REALLY?
YOU SEEM DOWN.

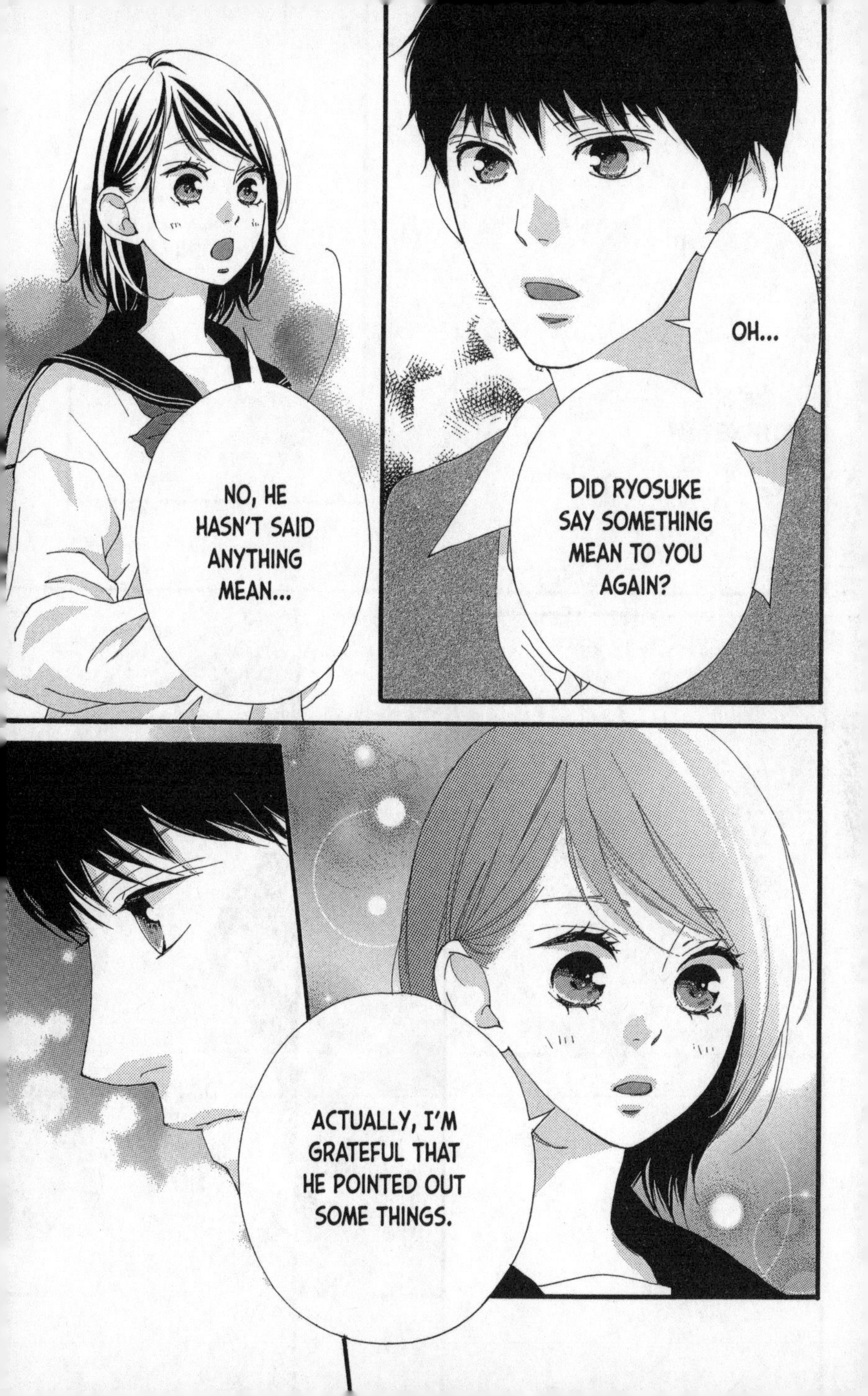
OH...
DID RYOSUKE SAY SOMETHING MEAN TO YOU AGAIN?
NO, HE HASN'T SAID ANYTHING MEAN...
ACTUALLY, I'M GRATEFUL THAT HE POINTED OUT SOME THINGS.

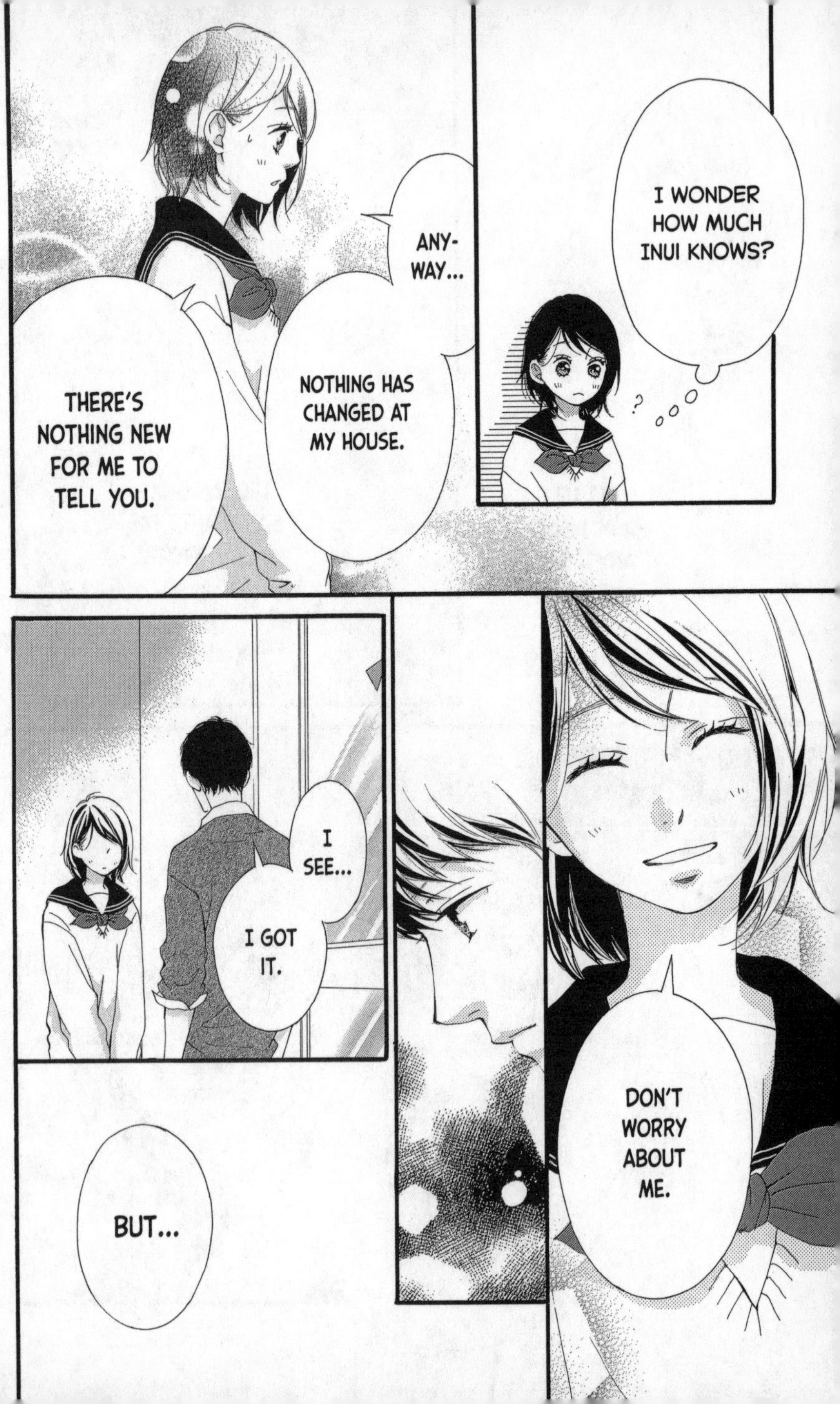
I WONDER HOW MUCH INUI KNOWS?
ANY-WAY...
NOTHING HAS CHANGED AT MY HOUSE.
THERE'S NOTHING NEW FOR ME TO TELL YOU.
DON'T WORRY ABOUT ME.
I SEE...
I GOT IT.
BUT...

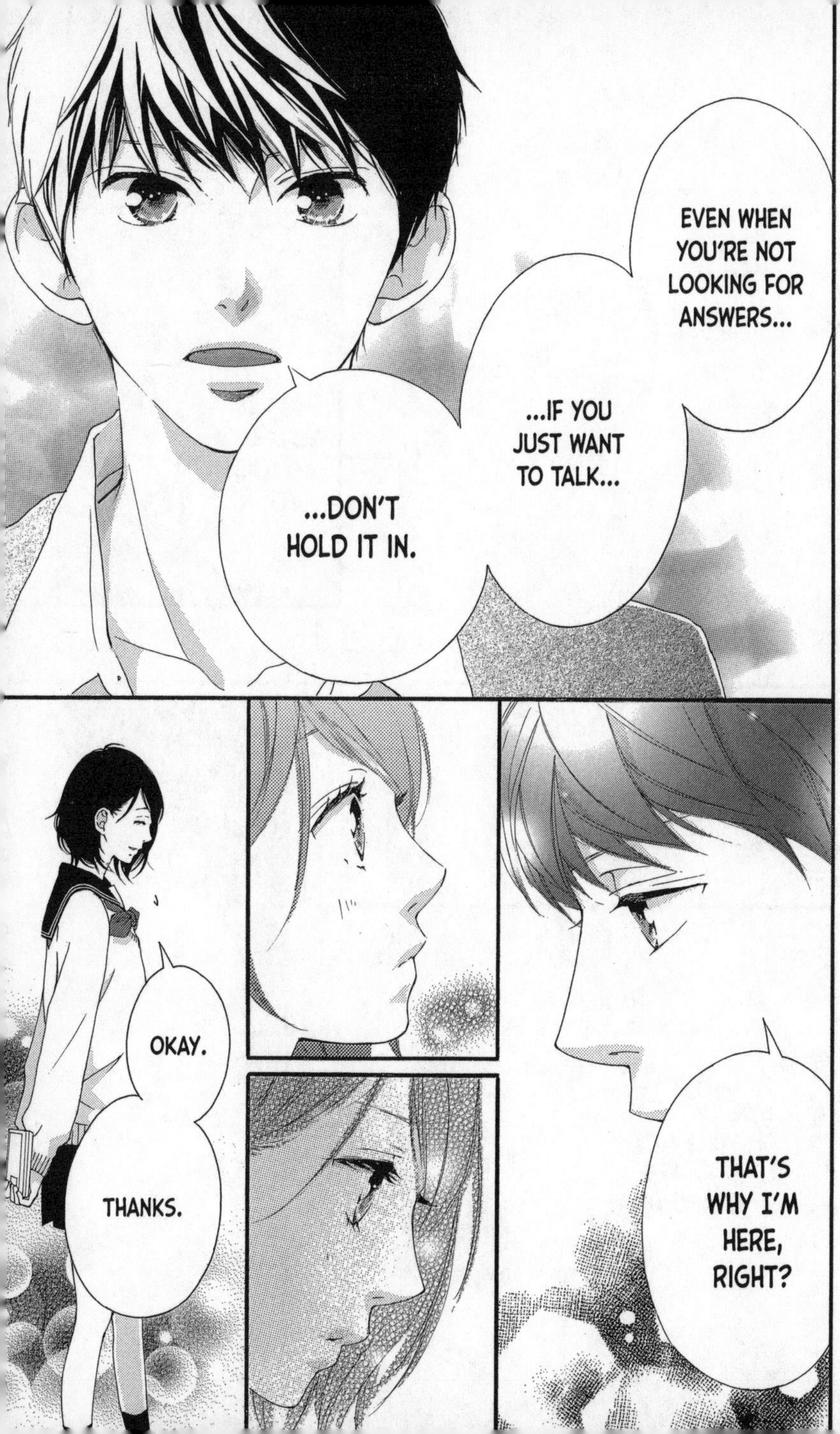
EVEN WHEN YOU'RE NOT LOOKING FOR ANSWERS...
...IF YOU JUST WANT TO TALK...
...DON'T HOLD IT IN.
THAT'S WHY I'M HERE, RIGHT?
OKAY.
THANKS.

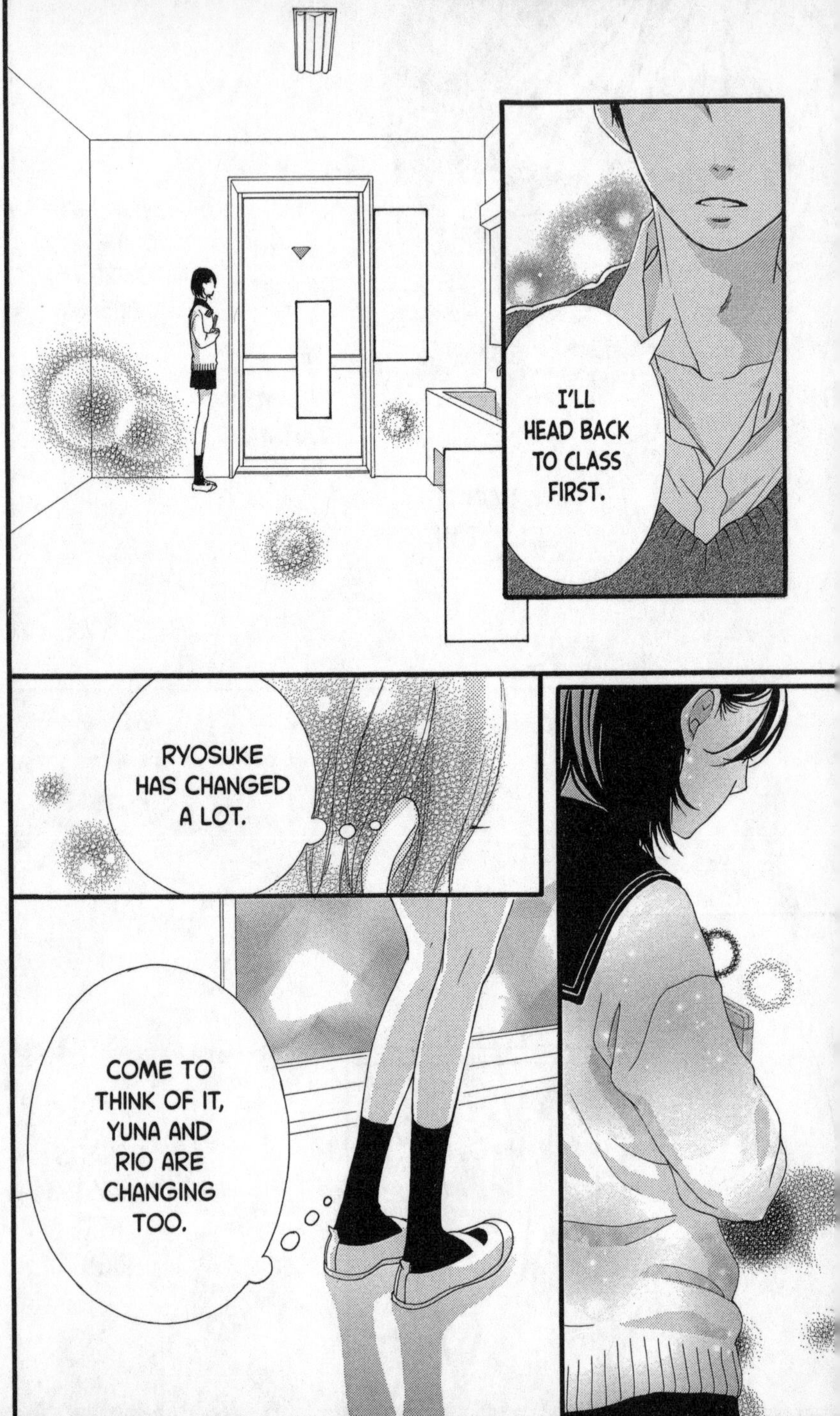
I'LL HEAD BACK TO CLASS FIRST.
RYOSUKE HAS CHANGED A LOT.
COME TO THINK OF IT, YUNA AND RIO ARE CHANGING TOO.

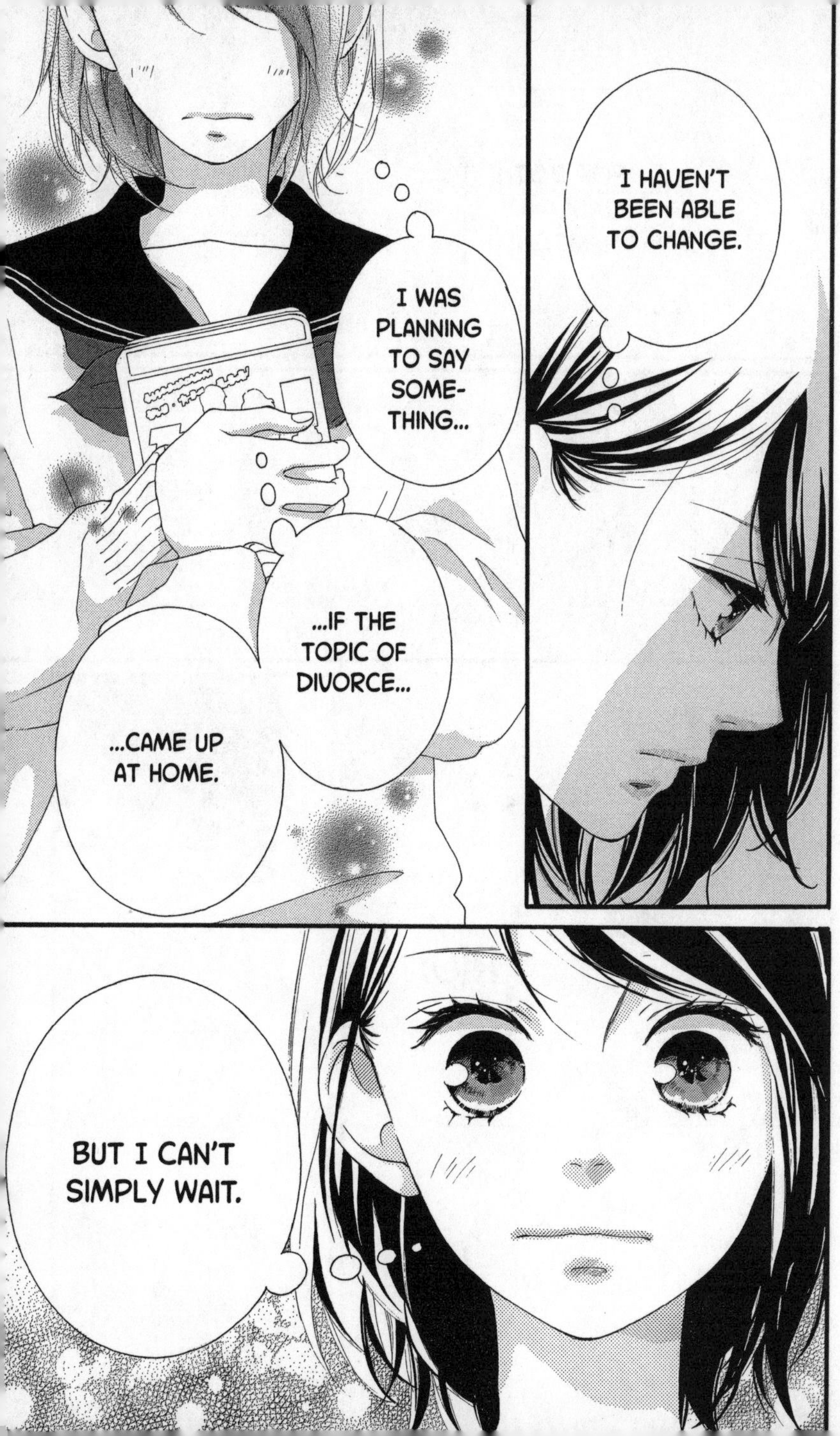
I HAVEN'T BEEN ABLE TO CHANGE.
I WAS PLANNING TO SAY SOME-THING...
...IF THE TOPIC OF DIVORCE...
...CAME UP AT HOME.
BUT I CAN'T SIMPLY WAIT.

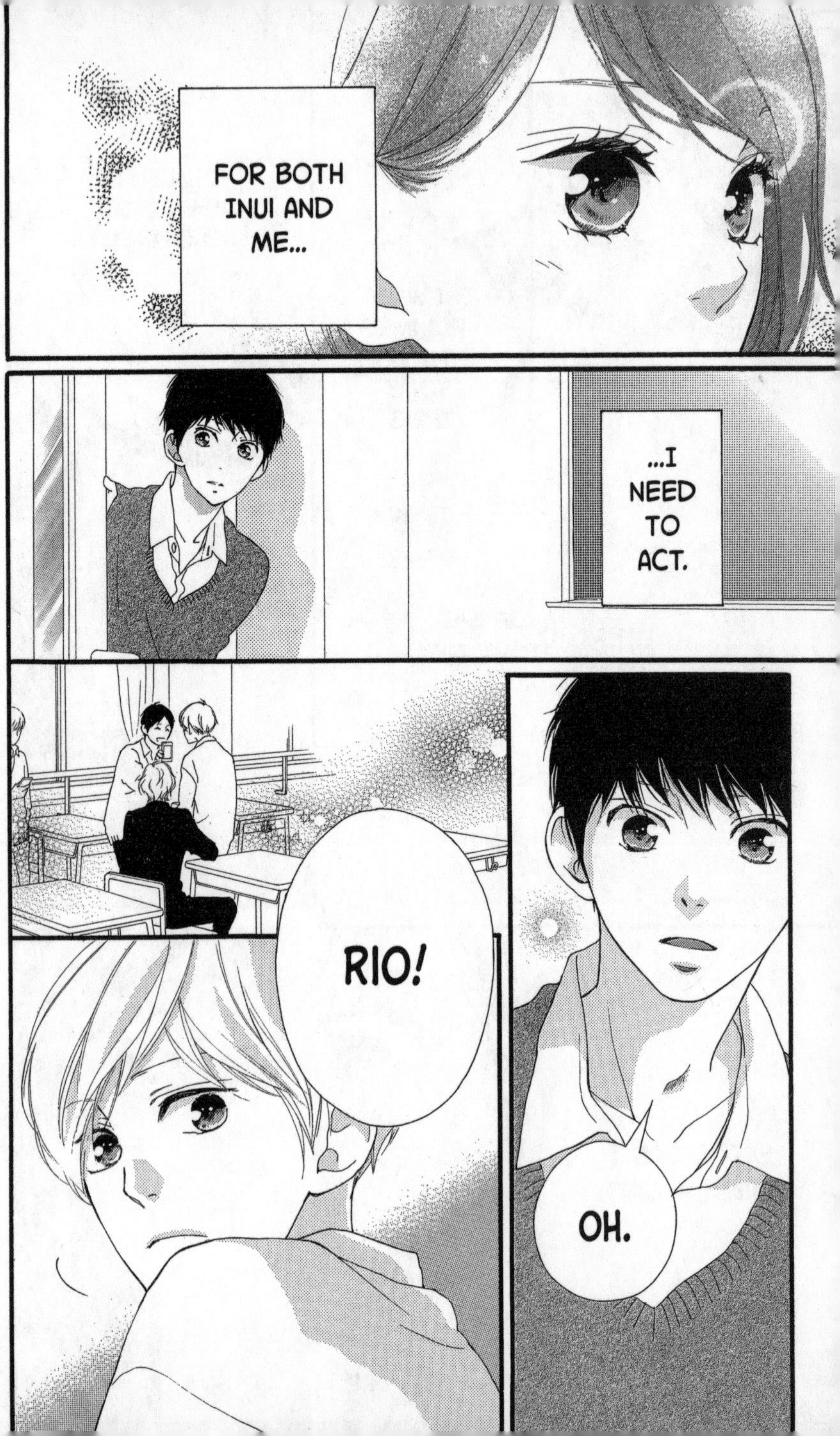
FOR BOTH INUI AND ME...
...I NEED TO ACT.
OH.
RIO!

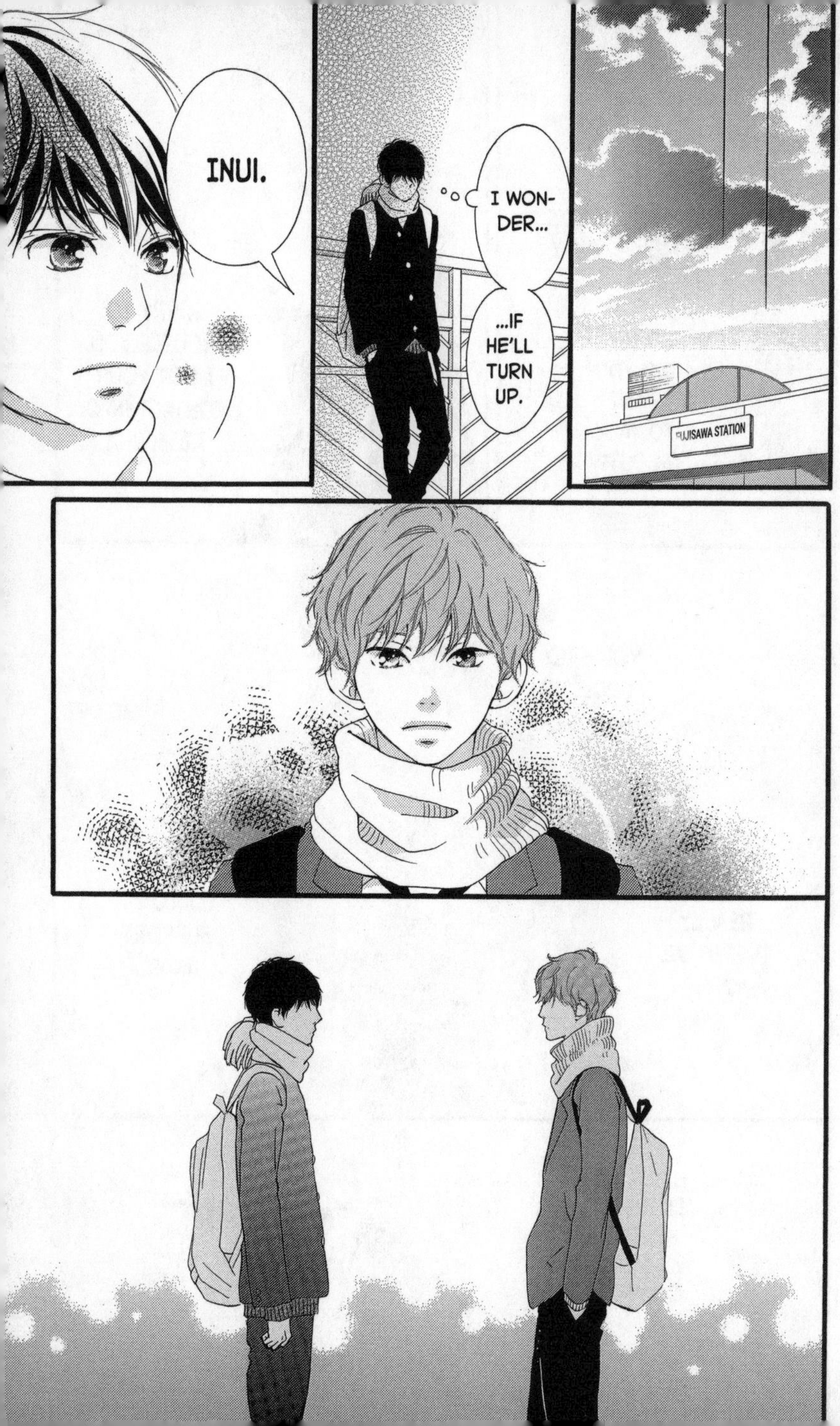
FUJISAWA STATION
I WONDER...
...IF HE'LL TURN UP.
INUI.

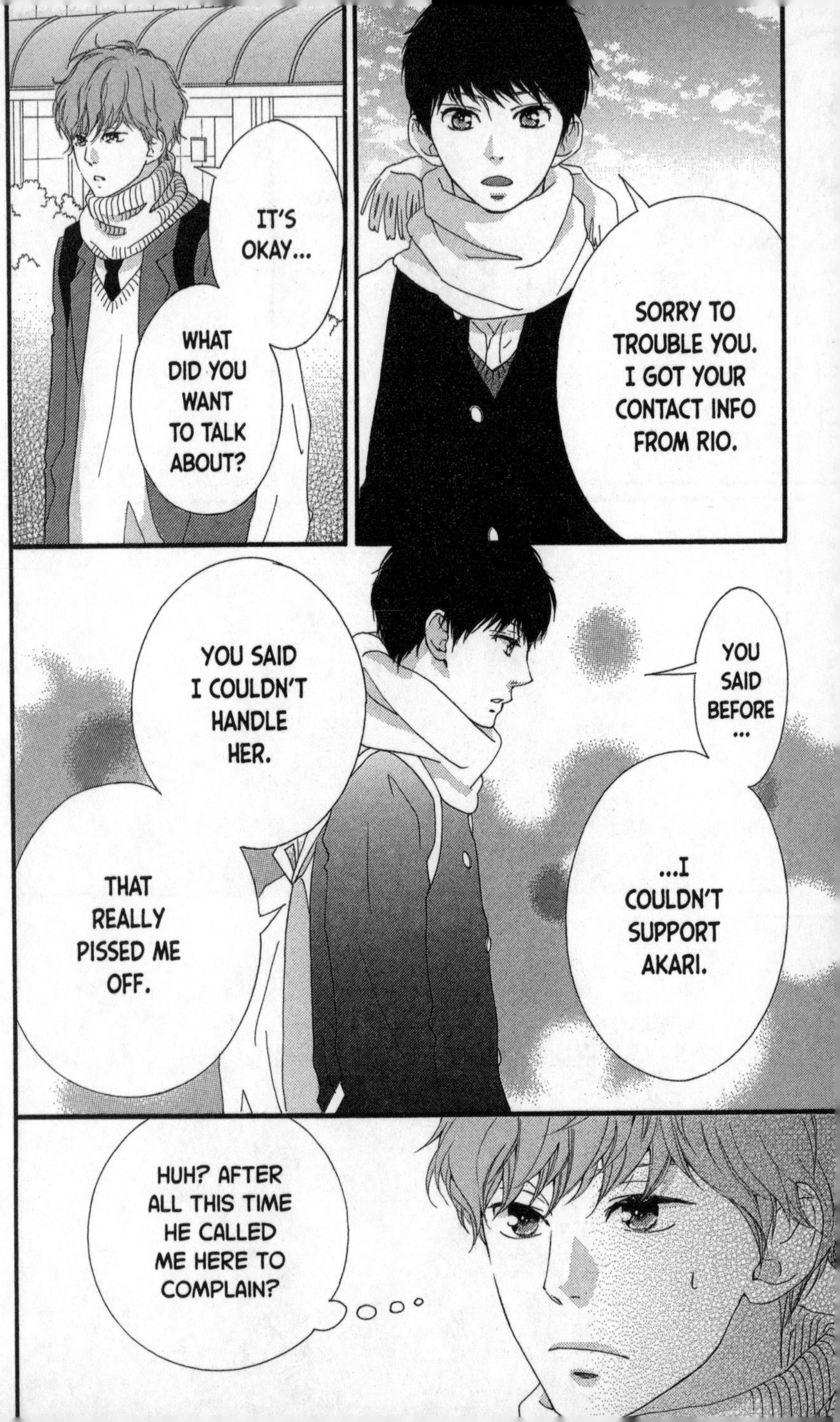
SORRY TO TROUBLE YOU. I GOT YOUR CONTACT INFO FROM RIO.
IT'S OKAY...
WHAT DID YOU WANT TO TALK ABOUT?
YOU SAID BEFORE ...
...I COULDN'T SUPPORT AKARI.
YOU SAID I COULDN'T HANDLE HER.
THAT REALLY PISSED ME OFF.
HUH? AFTER ALL THIS TIME HE CALLED ME HERE TO COMPLAIN?

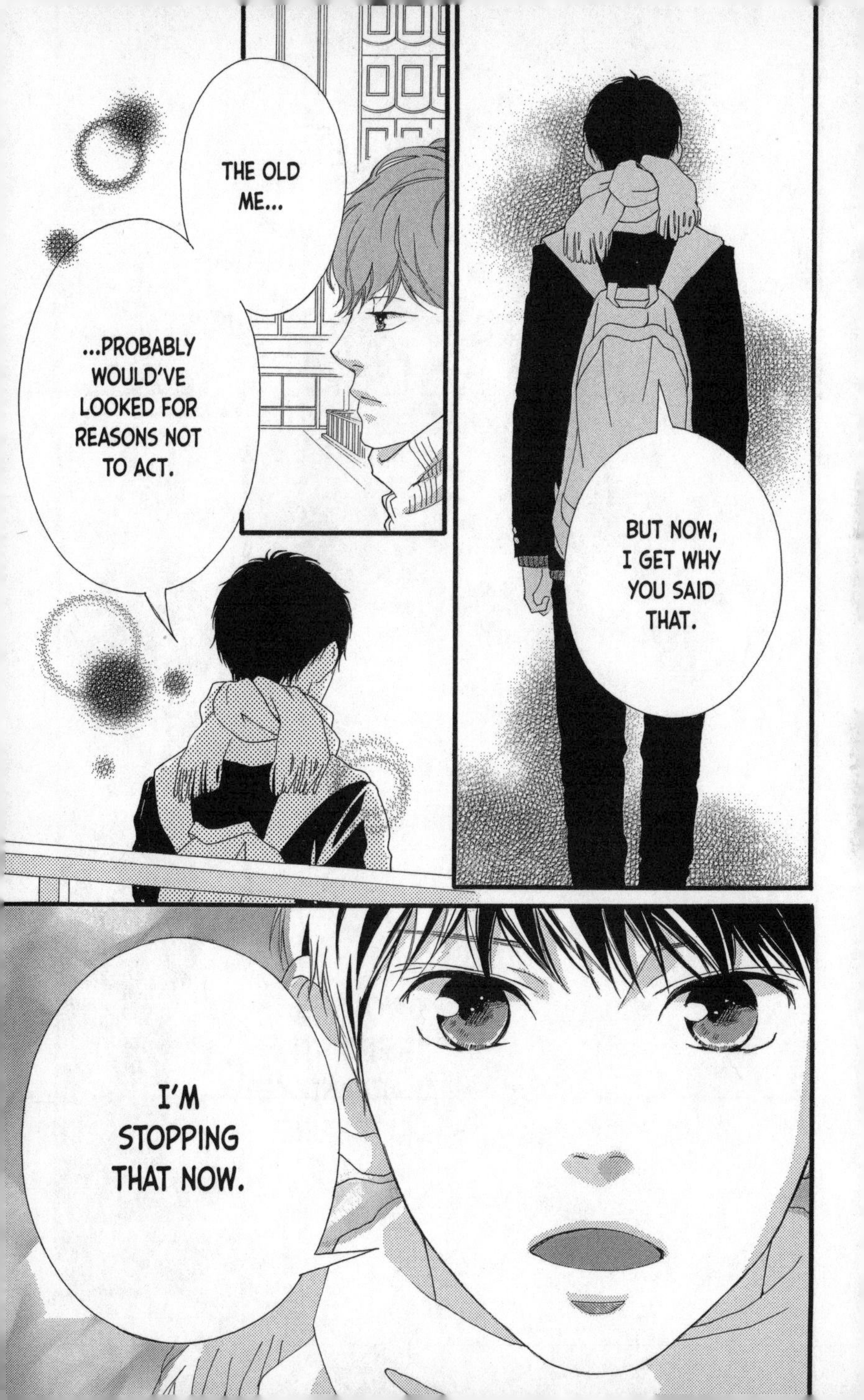
BUT NOW, I GET WHY YOU SAID THAT.
THE OLD ME...
...PROBABLY WOULD'VE LOOKED FOR REASONS NOT TO ACT.
I'M STOPPING THAT NOW.

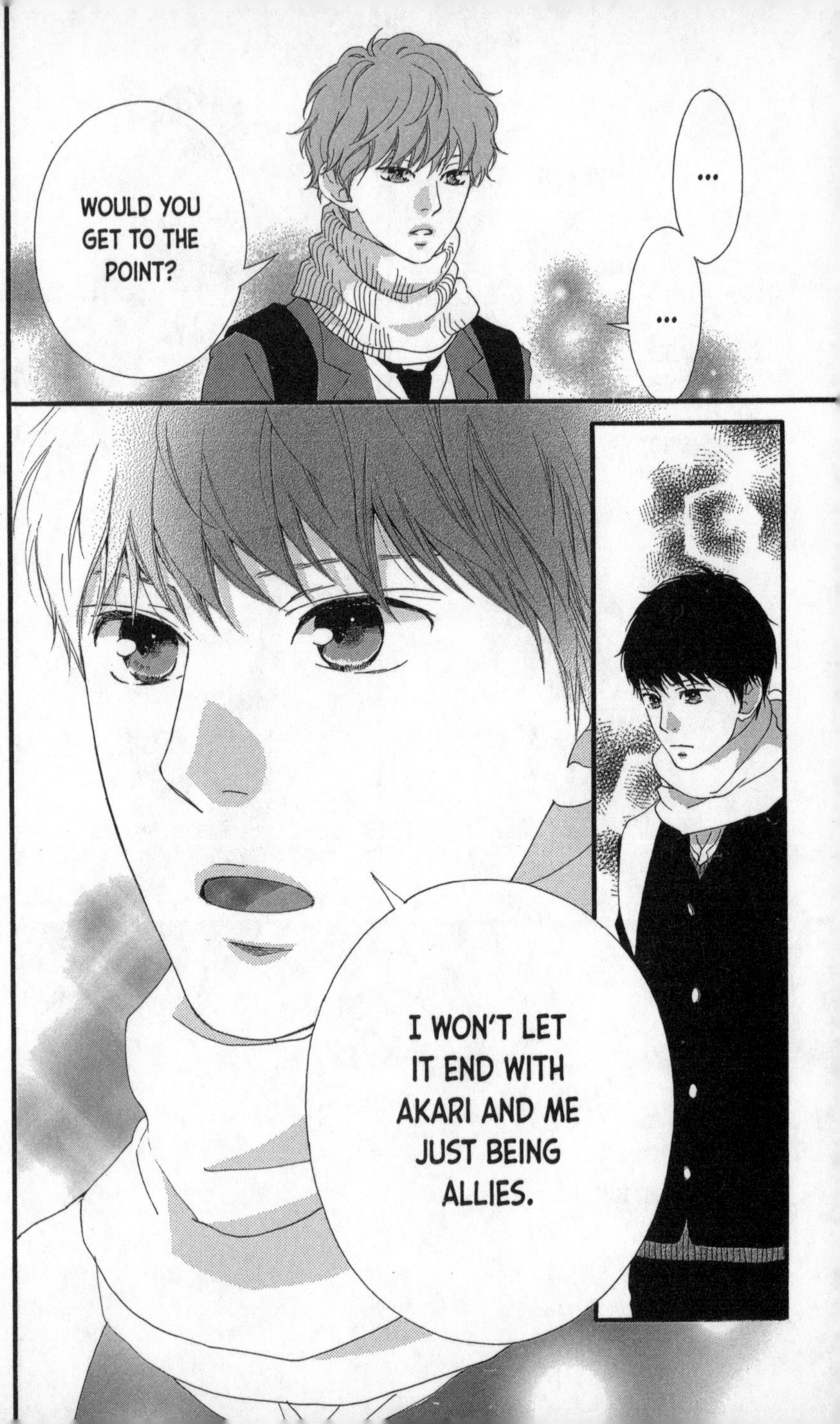
...
...
WOULD YOU GET TO THE POINT?
I WON'T LET IT END WITH AKARI AND ME JUST BEING ALLIES.

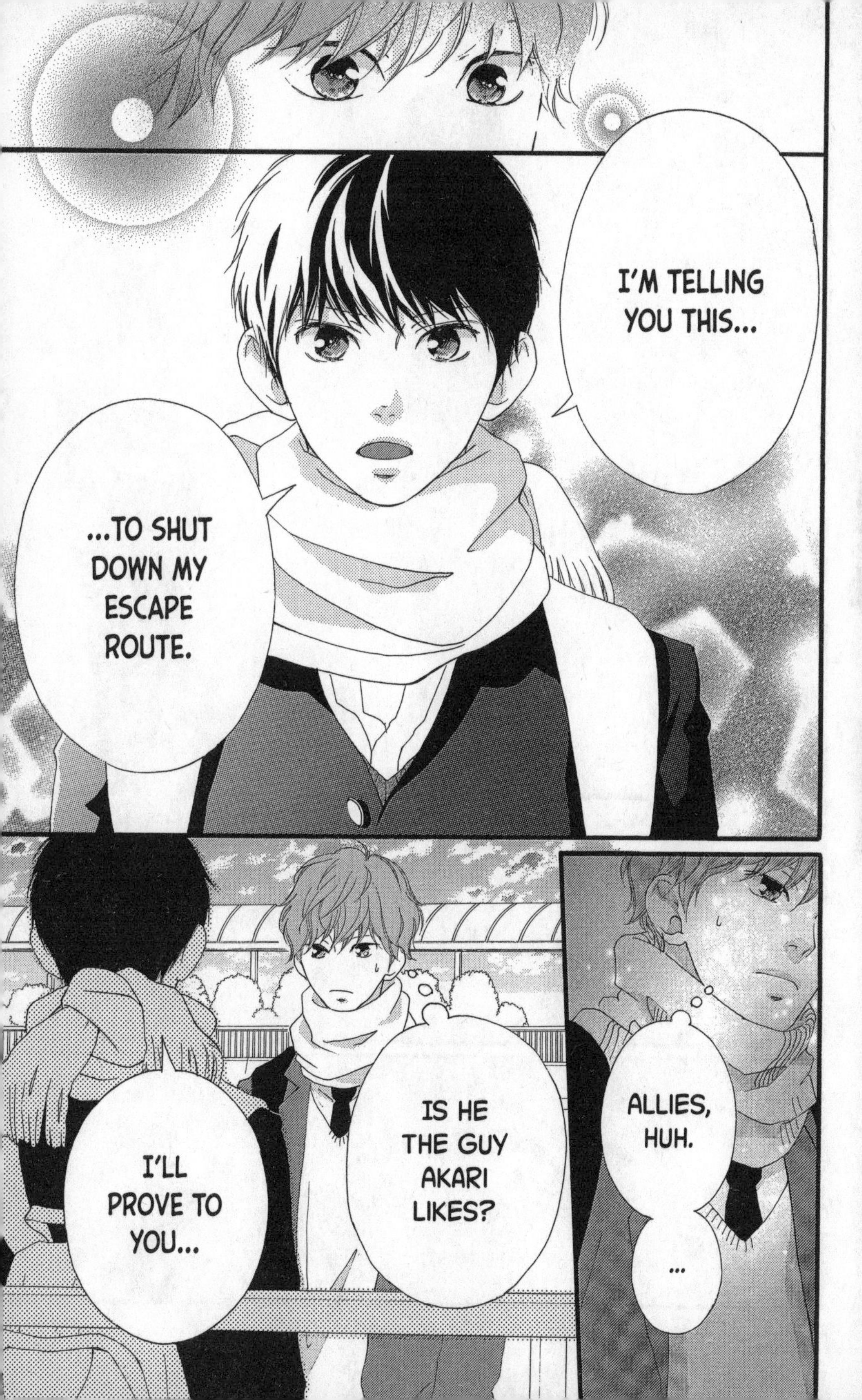
I'M TELLING YOU THIS...
...TO SHUT DOWN MY ESCAPE ROUTE.
ALLIES, HUH.
...
IS HE THE GUY AKARI LIKES?
I'LL PROVE TO YOU...

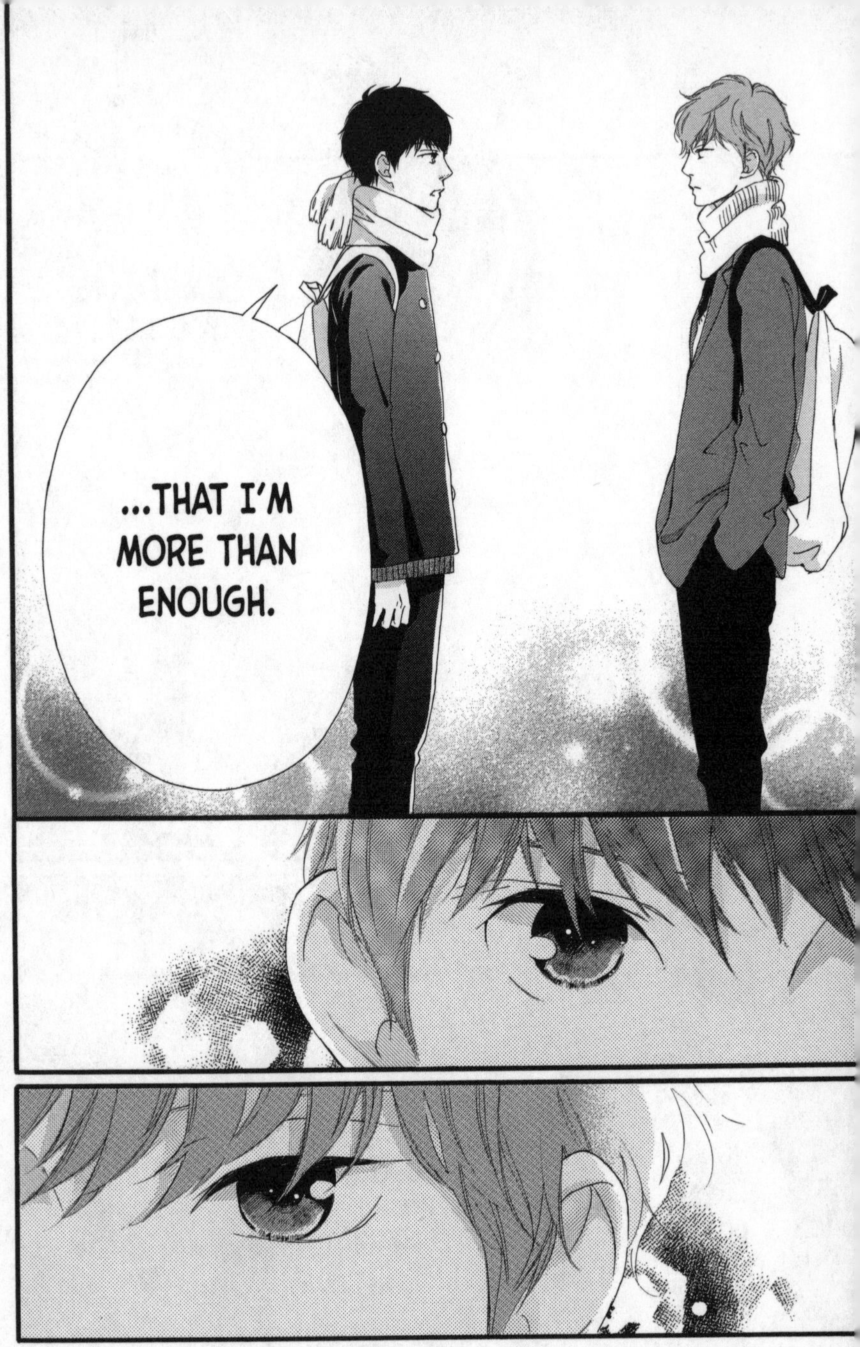
...THAT I'M MORE THAN ENOUGH.

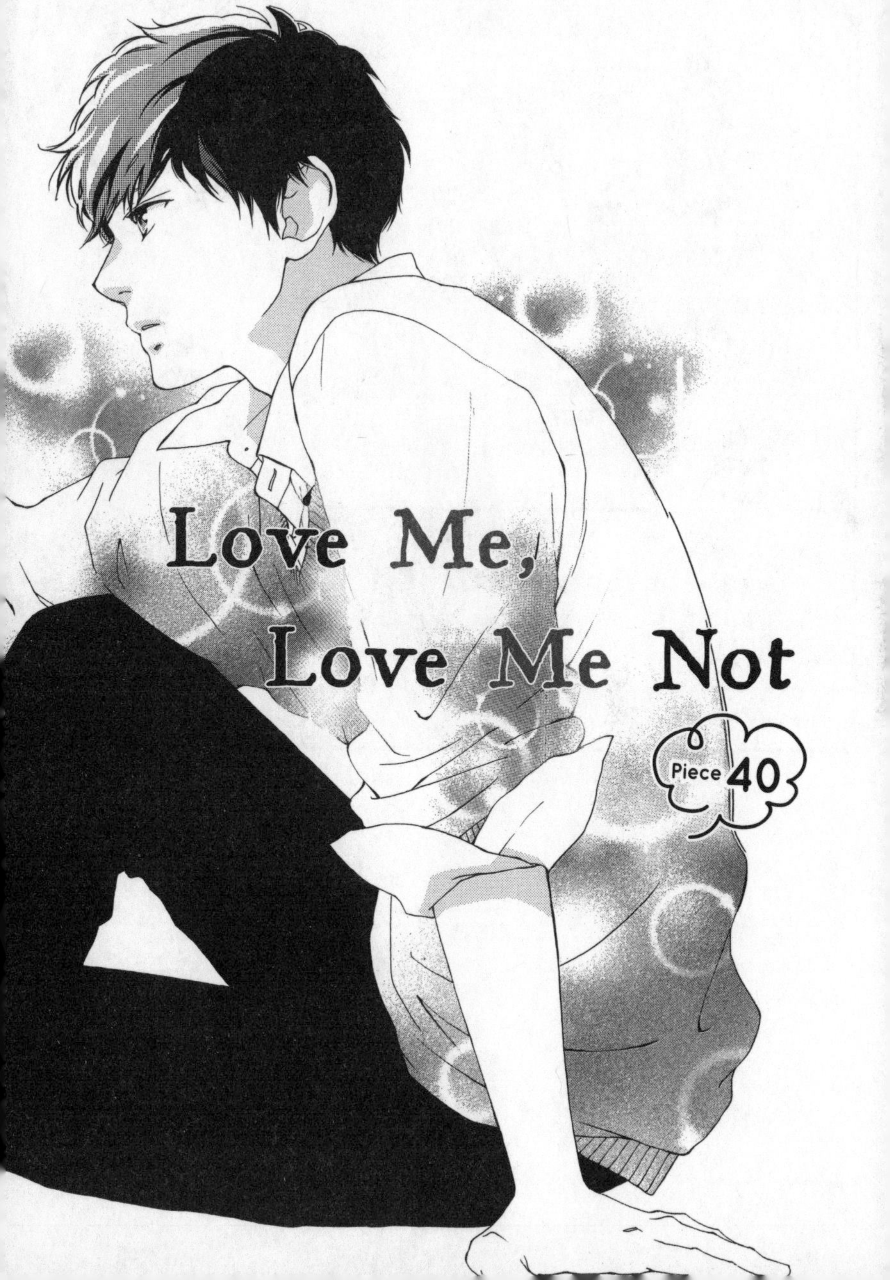
Love Me,
Love Me Not
Piece 40

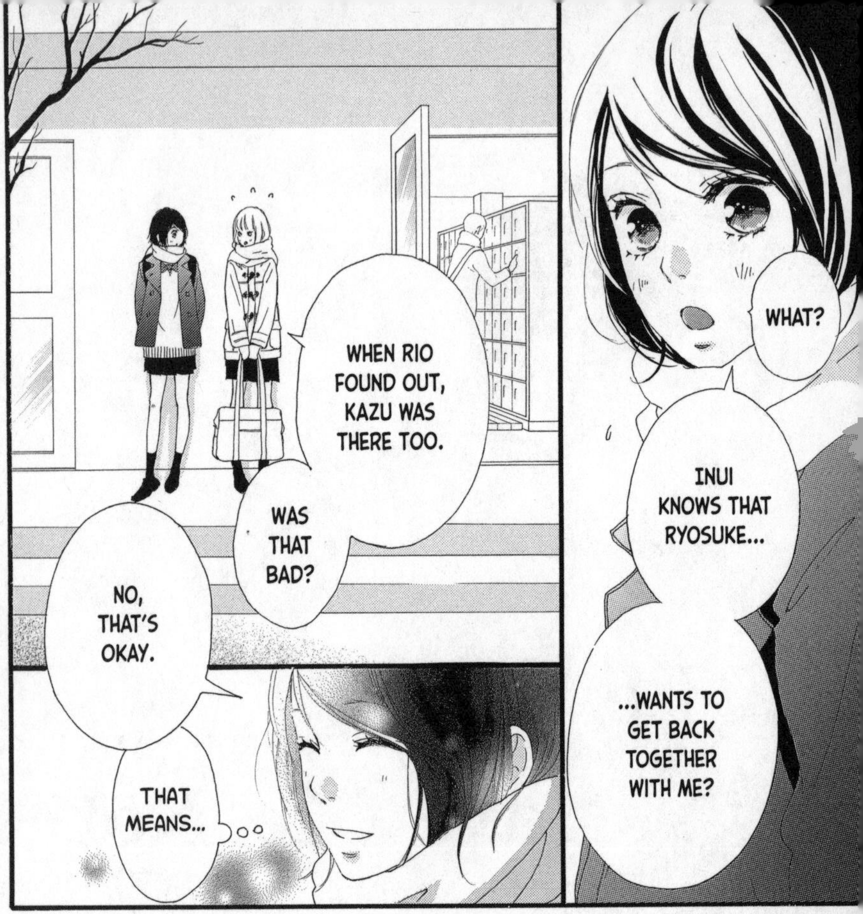
WHAT?
INUI KNOWS THAT RYOSUKE...
...WANTS TO GET BACK TOGETHER WITH ME?
WHEN RIO FOUND OUT, KAZU WAS THERE TOO.
WAS THAT BAD?
NO, THAT'S OKAY.
THAT MEANS...

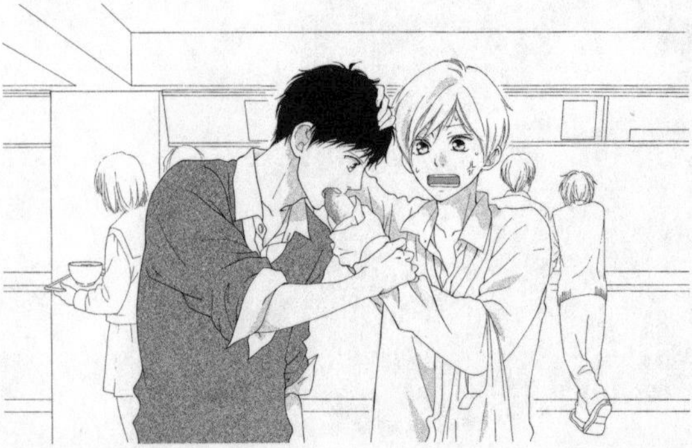

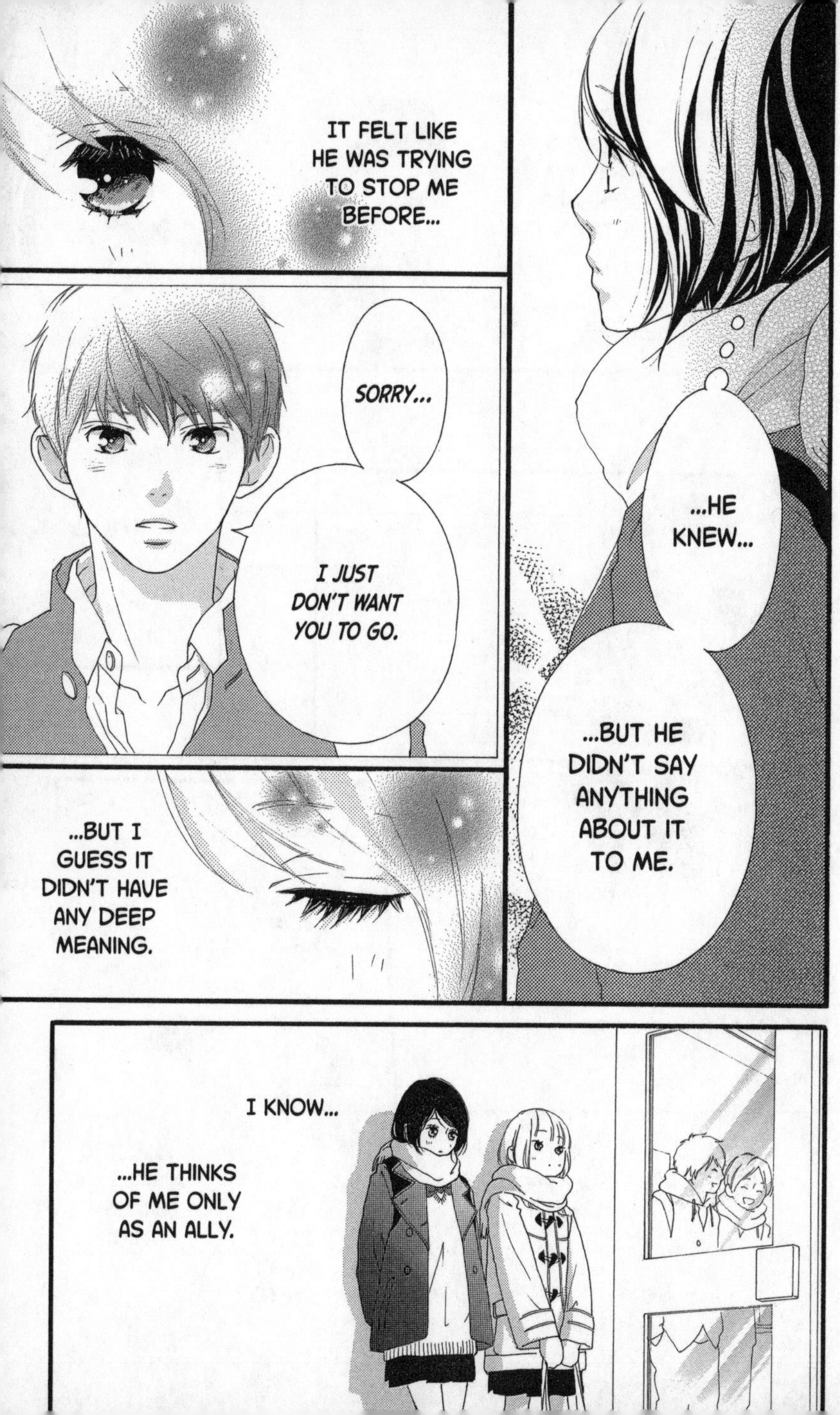
...HE KNEW...
...BUT HE DIDN'T SAY ANYTHING ABOUT IT TO ME.
IT FELT LIKE HE WAS TRYING TO STOP ME BEFORE...
SORRY...
I JUST DON'T WANT YOU TO GO.
...BUT I GUESS IT DIDN'T HAVE ANY DEEP MEANING.
I KNOW...
...HE THINKS OF ME ONLY AS AN ALLY.

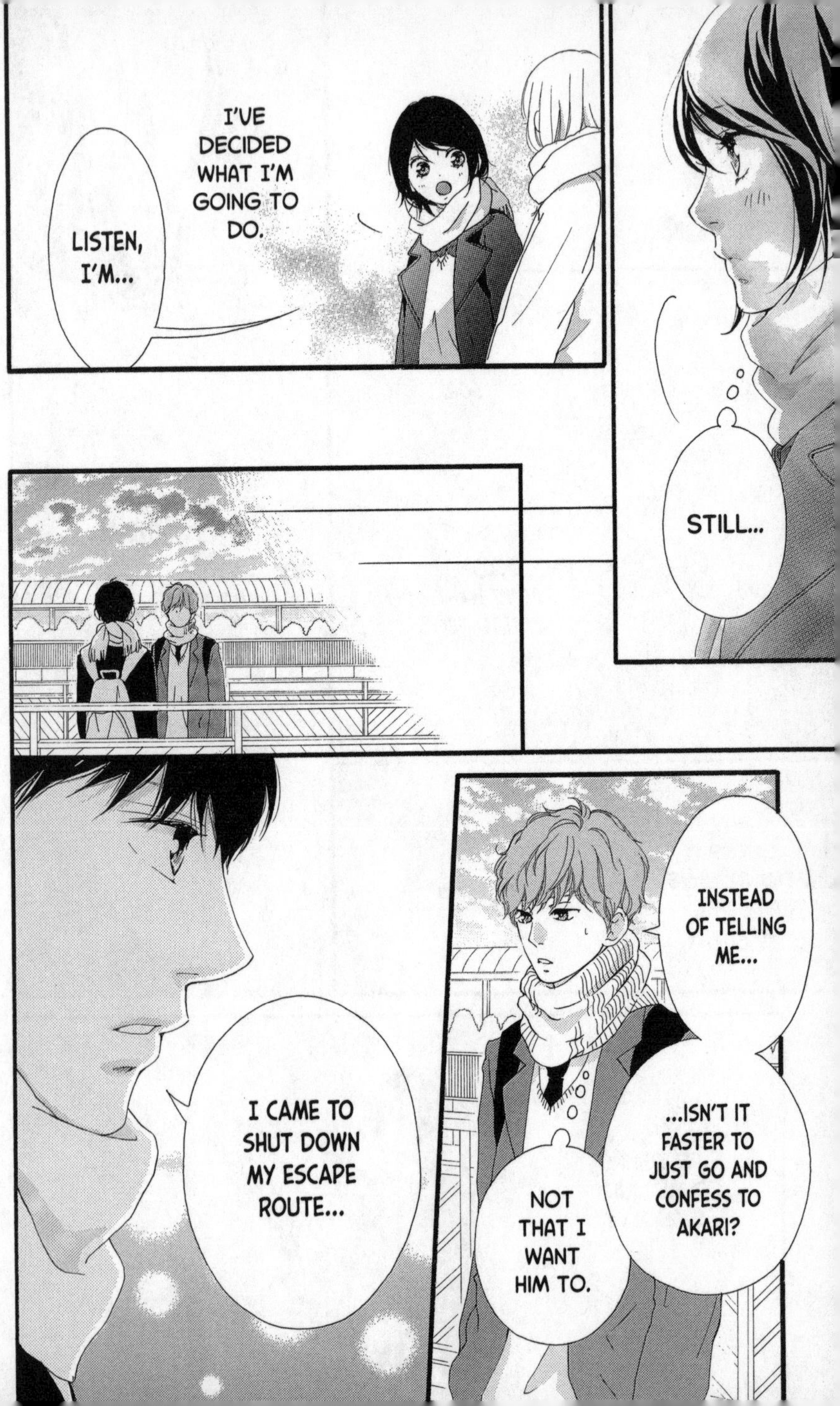
STILL...
I'VE DECIDED WHAT I'M GOING TO DO.
LISTEN, I'M...
INSTEAD OF TELLING ME...
...ISN'T IT FASTER TO JUST GO AND CONFESS TO AKARI?
NOT THAT I WANT HIM TO.
I CAME TO SHUT DOWN MY ESCAPE ROUTE...

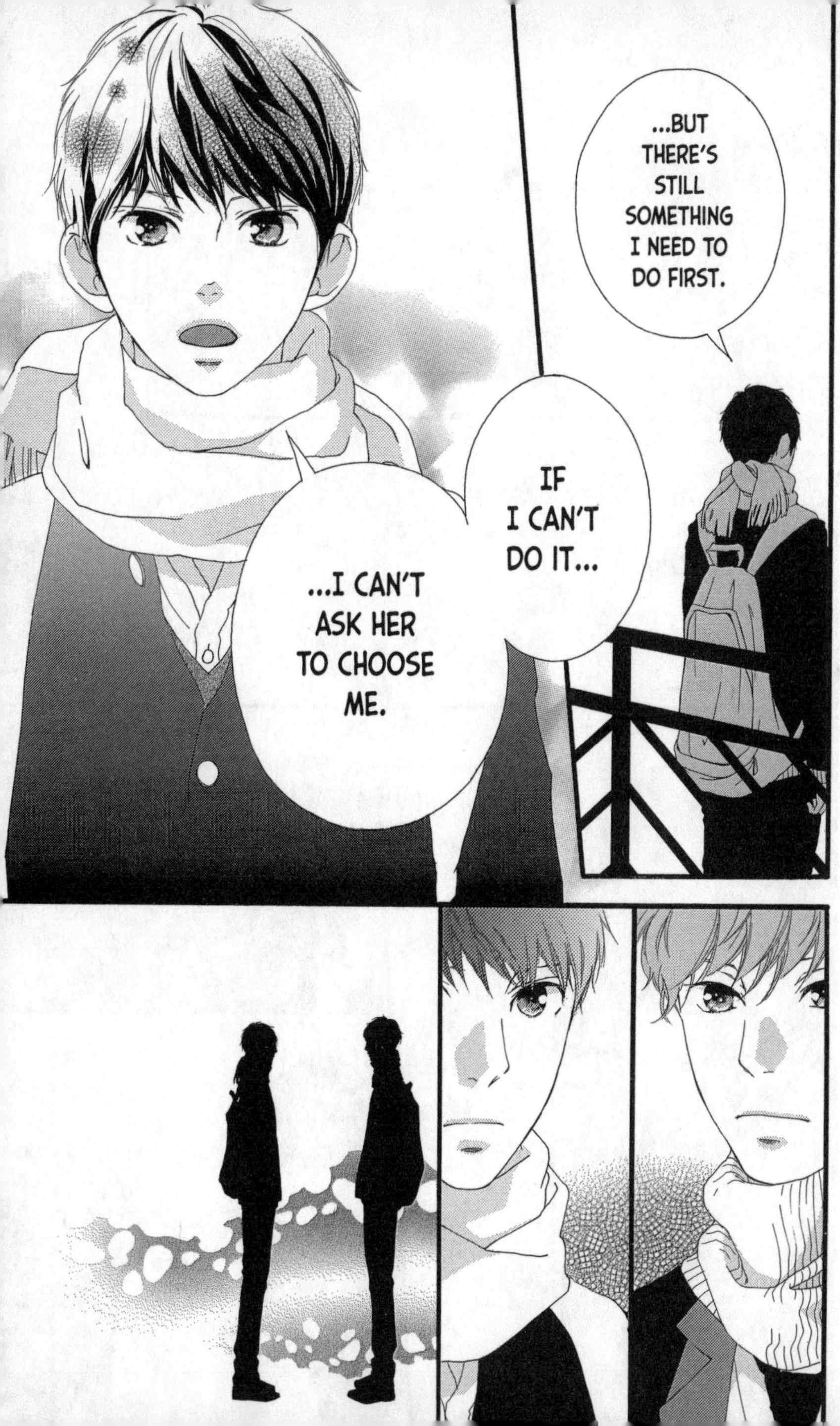
...BUT THERE'S STILL SOMETHING I NEED TO DO FIRST.
IF I CAN'T DO IT...
...I CAN'T ASK HER TO CHOOSE ME.

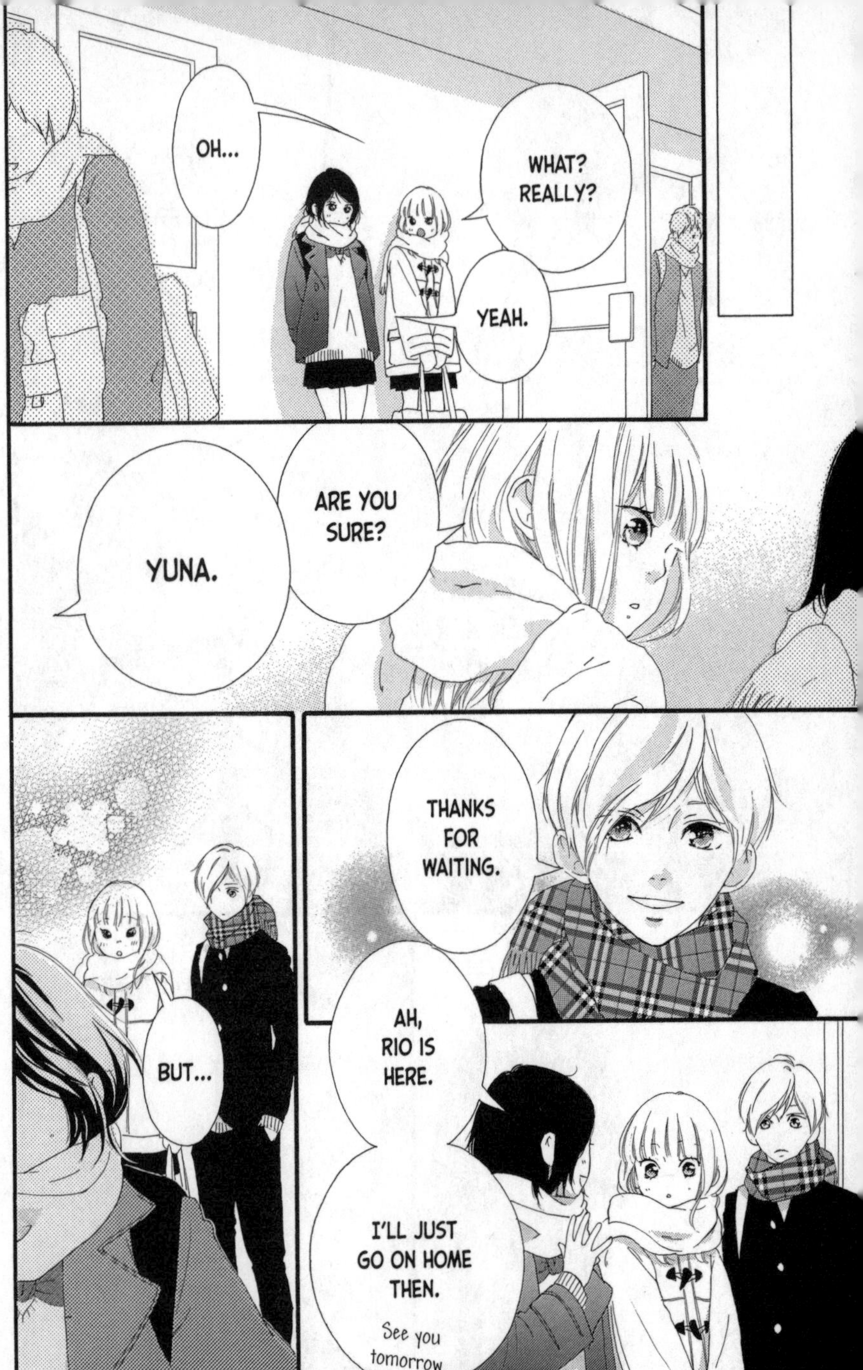
WHAT? REALLY?
YEAH.
OH...
ARE YOU SURE?
YUNA.
THANKS FOR WAITING.
AH, RIO IS HERE.
I'LL JUST GO ON HOME THEN.
See you tomorrow.
BUT...

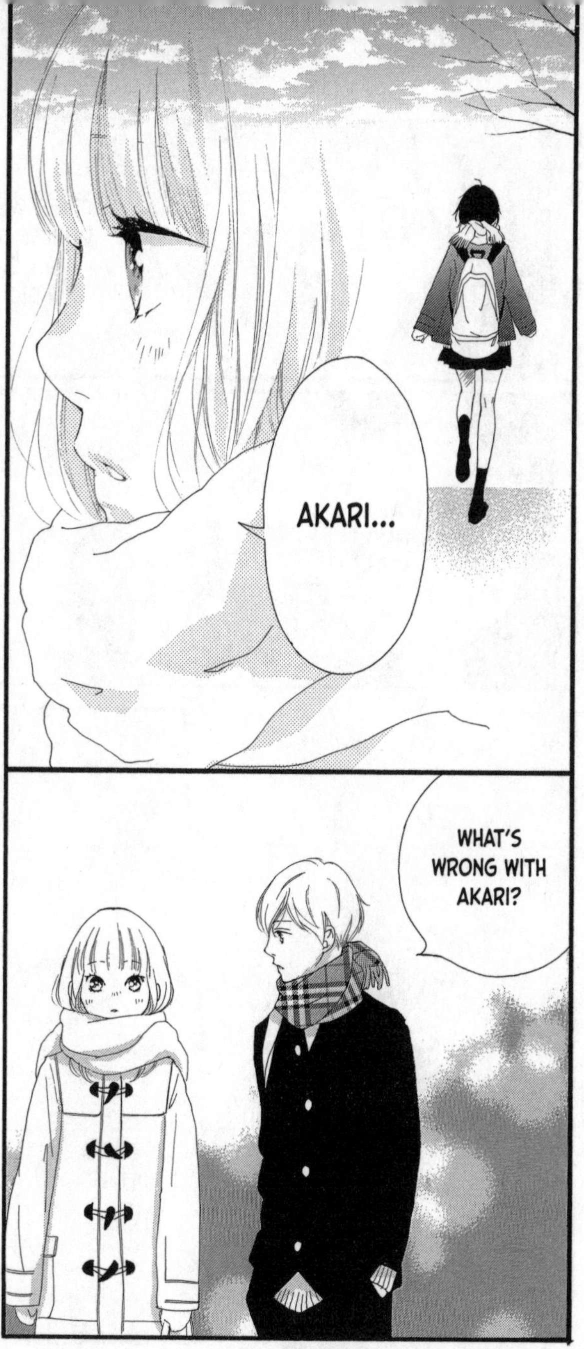
AKARI...
WHAT'S WRONG WITH AKARI?

I went to Fuji-Q Highland the other day. We'd been saying we should go for a couple of years now, but our schedules never worked out. I went with Hanemi Ayase and Yuri Nakagawa. We went on every single thrill ride that was operating that day. It was the first time we went on so many of them. We rode Fujiyama, my favorite, four times. It's such an amazing roller coaster that if I was sentenced to ride Fujiyama all day for one day, I would be okay with that. I had such a good time. Yuri's screaming was so much fun too. She kept saying, "Stop it!" I thought, "She's the best customer." (By the way, all three of us love thrill rides.)

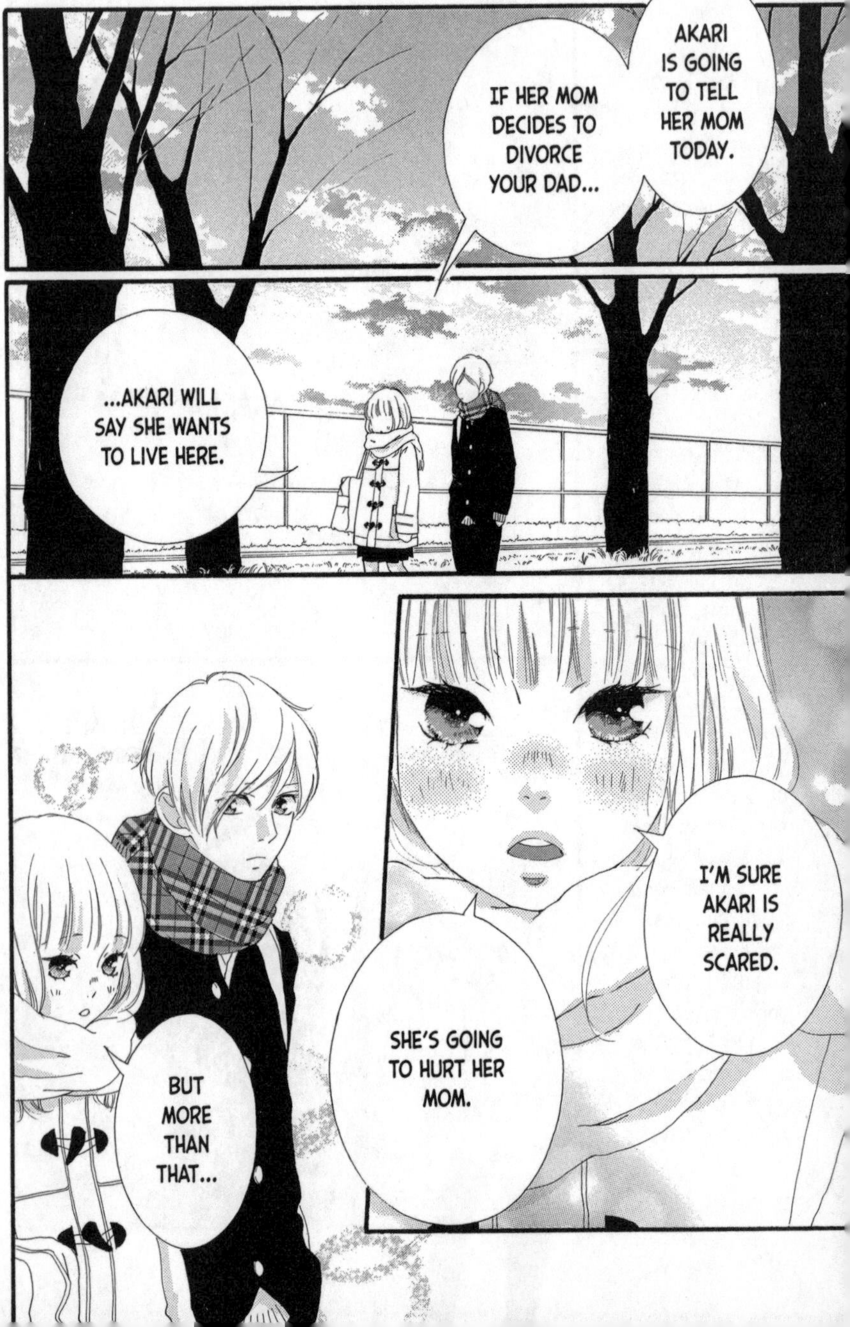
AKARI IS GOING TO TELL HER MOM TODAY.
IF HER MOM DECIDES TO DIVORCE YOUR DAD...
...AKARI WILL SAY SHE WANTS TO LIVE HERE.
I'M SURE AKARI IS REALLY SCARED.
SHE'S GOING TO HURT HER MOM.
BUT MORE THAN THAT...

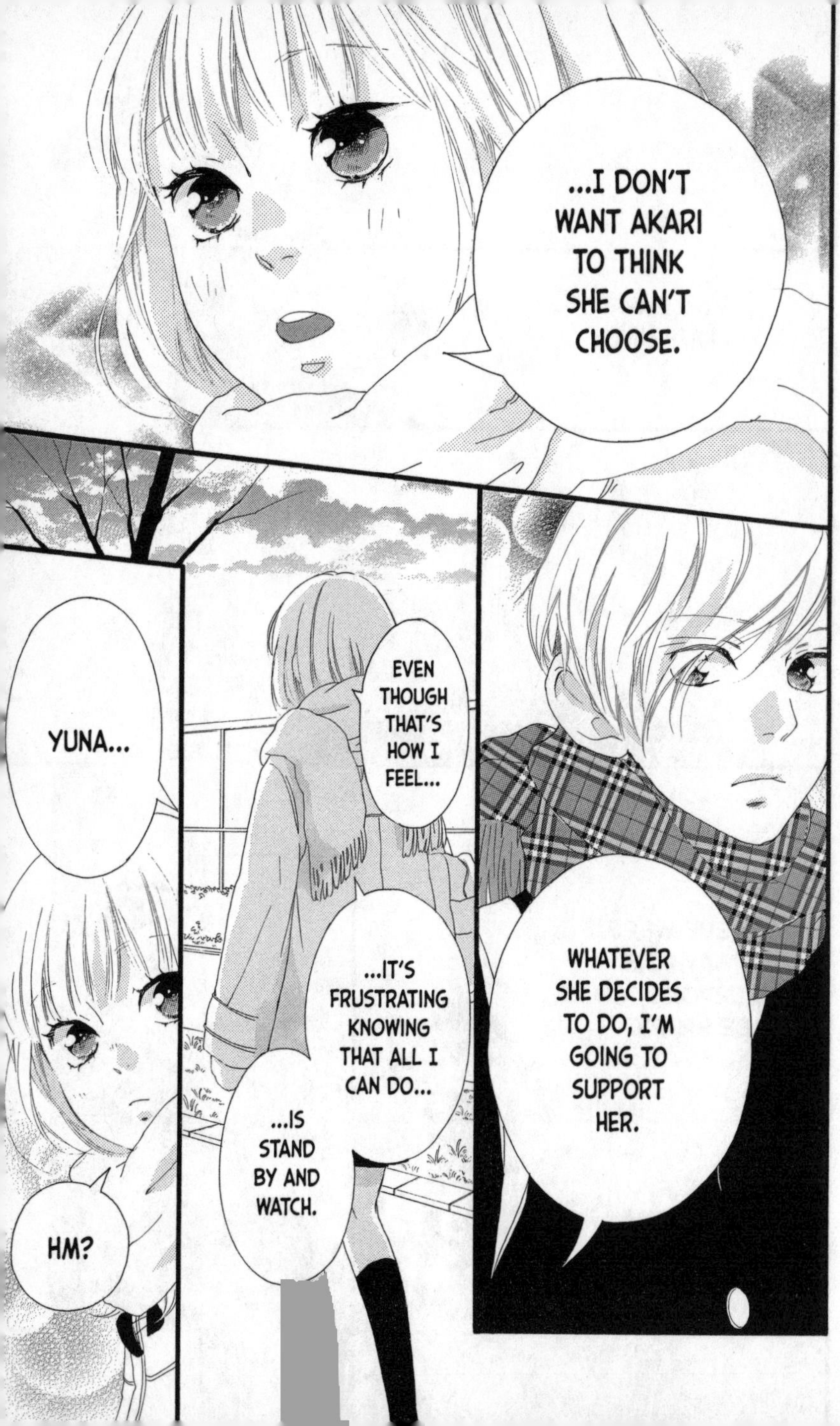
...I DON'T WANT AKARI TO THINK SHE CAN'T CHOOSE.
WHATEVER SHE DECIDES TO DO, I'M GOING TO SUPPORT HER.
EVEN THOUGH THAT'S HOW I FEEL...
...IT'S FRUSTRATING KNOWING THAT ALL I CAN DO...
...IS STAND BY AND WATCH.
YUNA...
HM?

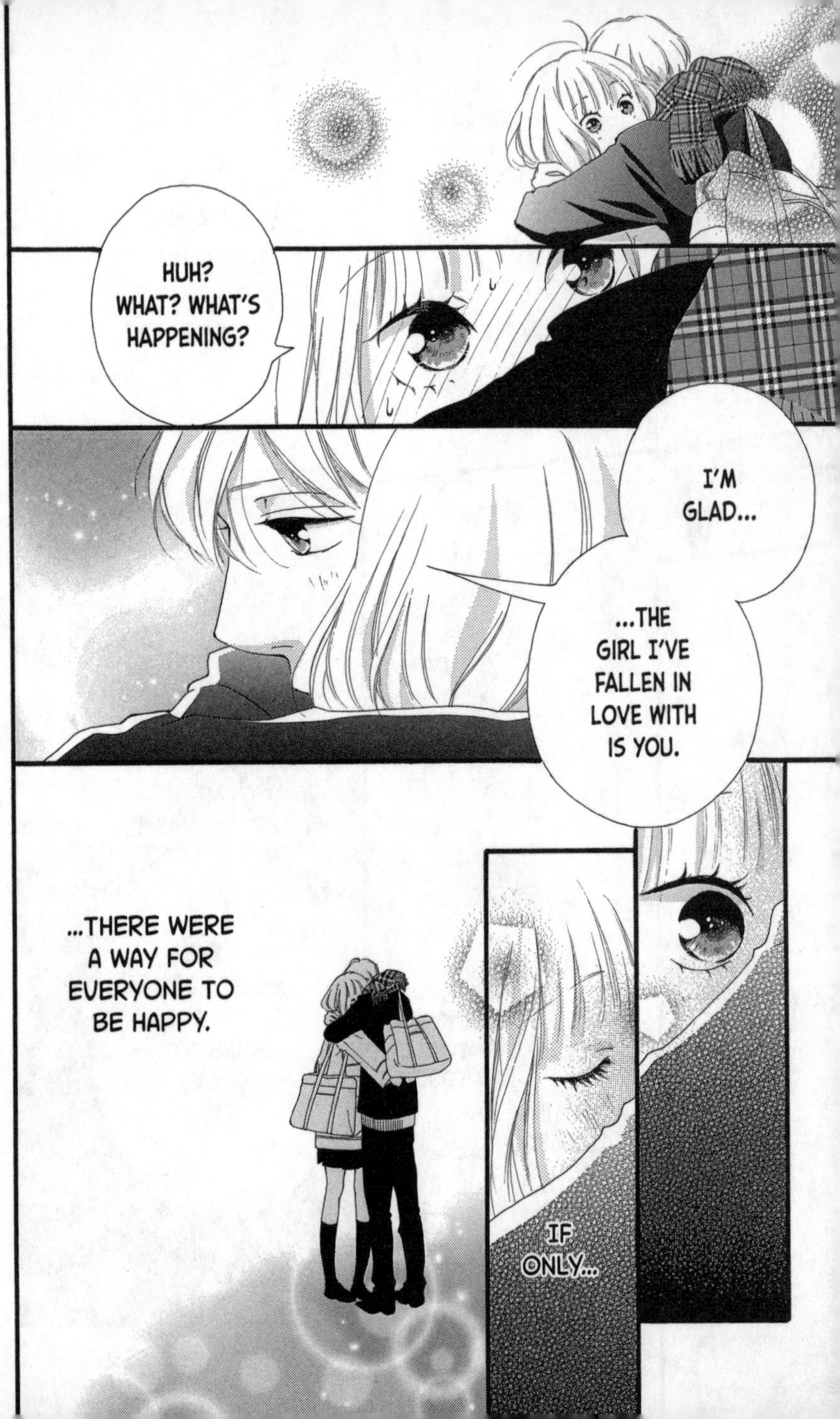
HUH? WHAT? WHAT'S HAPPENING?
I'M GLAD...
...THE GIRL I'VE FALLEN IN LOVE WITH IS YOU.
IF ONLY...
...THERE WERE A WAY FOR EVERYONE TO BE HAPPY.

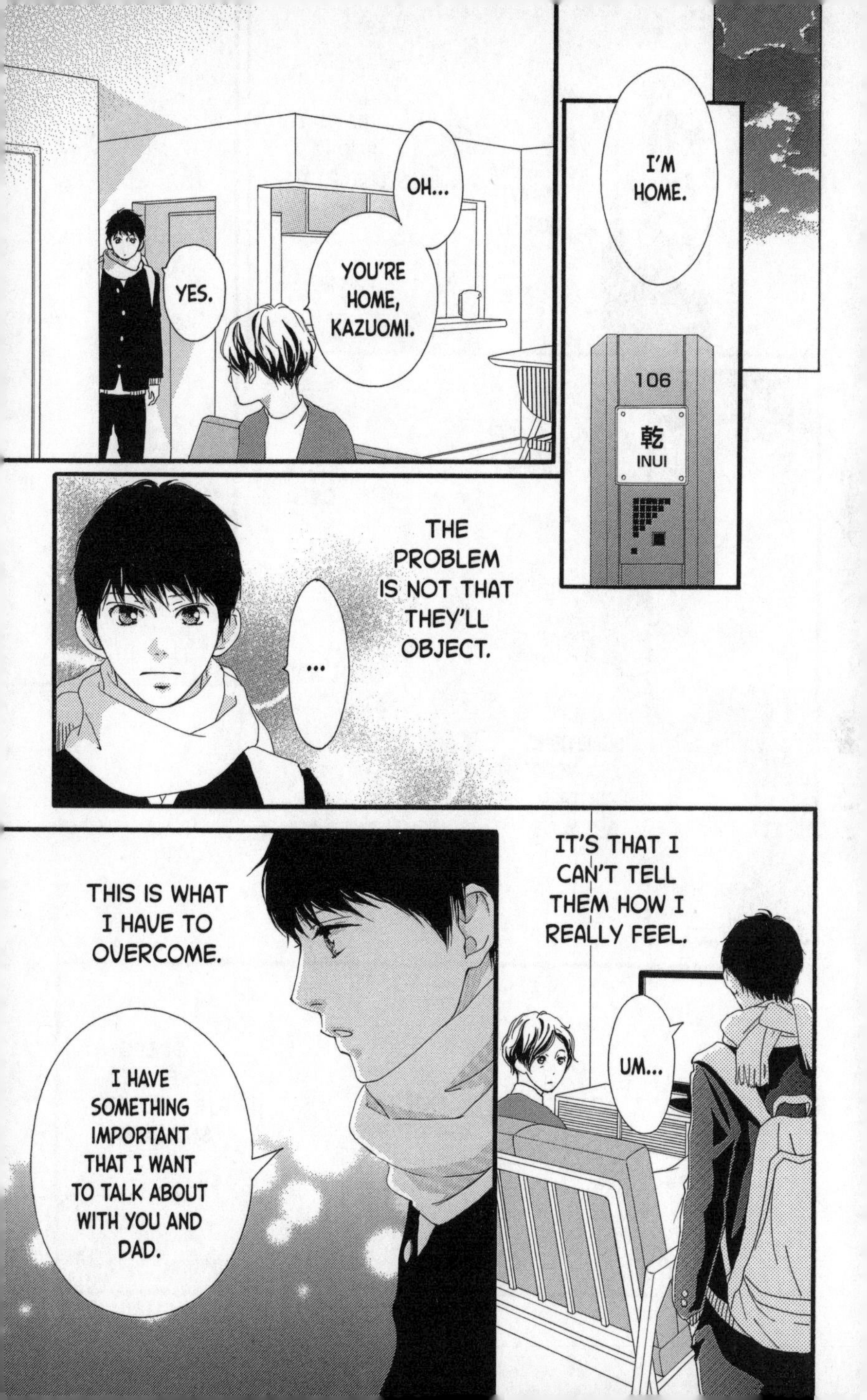
I'M HOME.
106
乾
INUI
OH...
YOU'RE HOME, KAZUOMI.
YES.
THE PROBLEM IS NOT THAT THEY'LL OBJECT.
...
IT'S THAT I CAN'T TELL THEM HOW I REALLY FEEL.
UM...
THIS IS WHAT I HAVE TO OVERCOME.
I HAVE SOMETHING IMPORTANT THAT I WANT TO TALK ABOUT WITH YOU AND DAD.

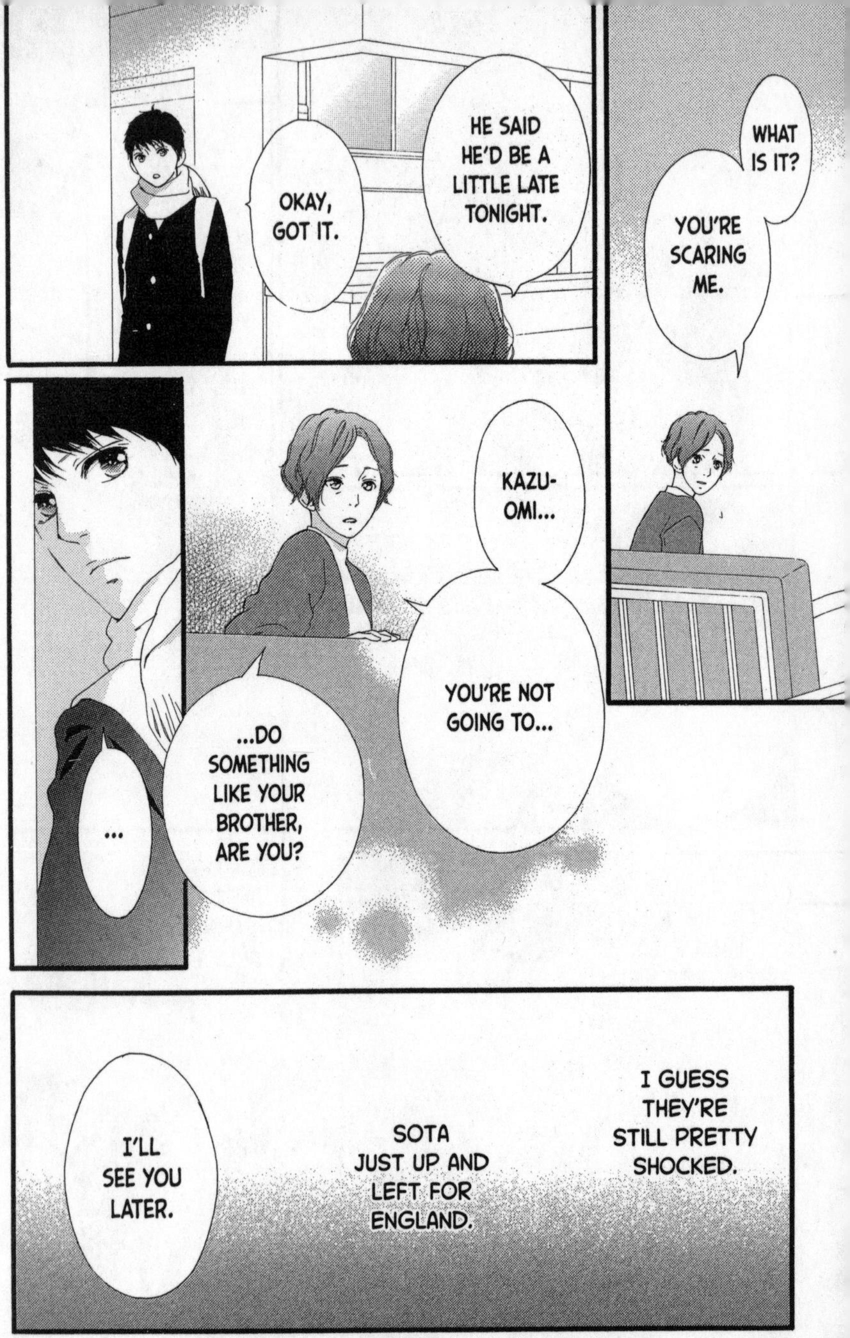
WHAT IS IT?
YOU'RE SCARING ME.
HE SAID HE'D BE A LITTLE LATE TONIGHT.
OKAY, GOT IT.
KAZU-OMI...
YOU'RE NOT GOING TO...
...DO SOMETHING LIKE YOUR BROTHER, ARE YOU?
...
I GUESS THEY'RE STILL PRETTY SHOCKED.
SOTA JUST UP AND LEFT FOR ENGLAND.
I'LL SEE YOU LATER.

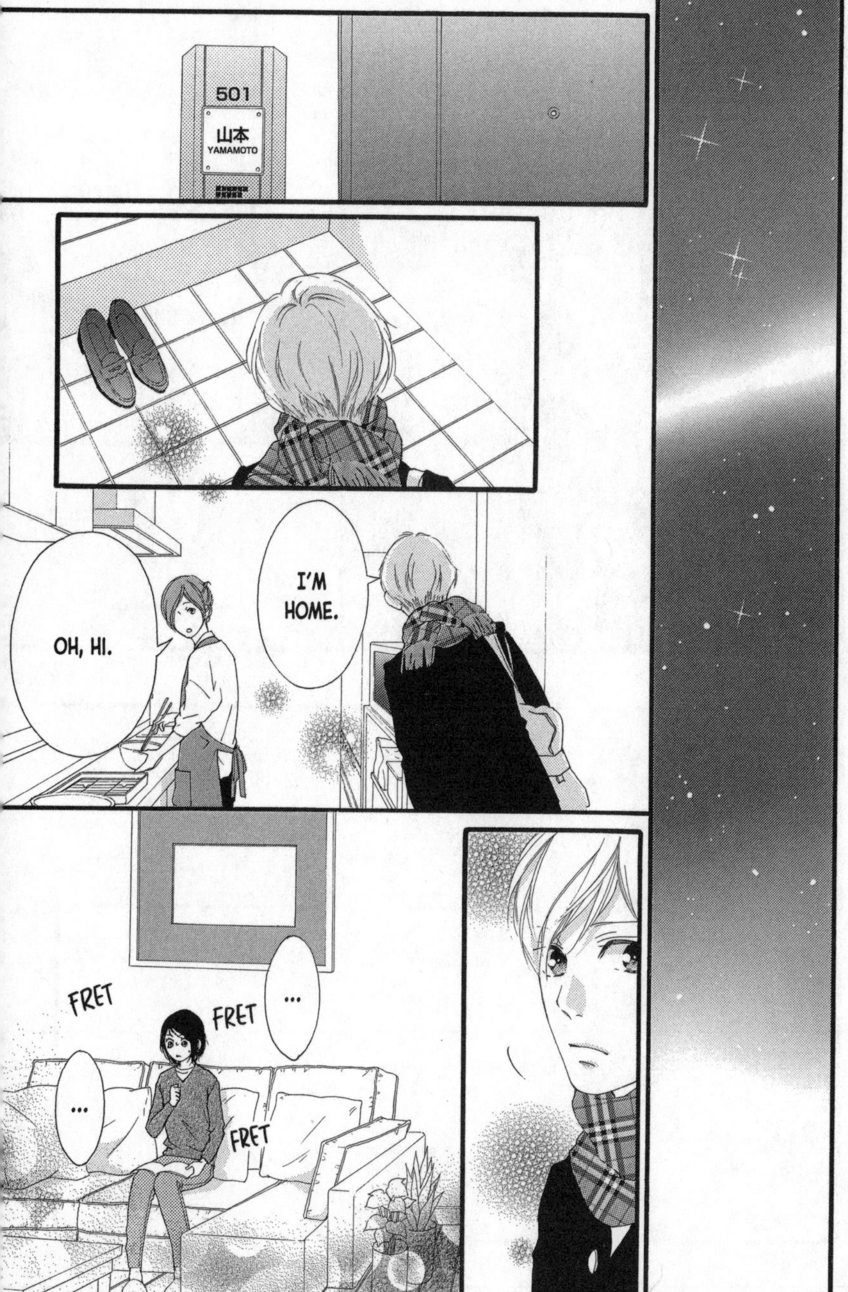
501
山本
YAMAMOTO
I'M HOME.
OH, HI.
...
FRET
FRET
...
FRET

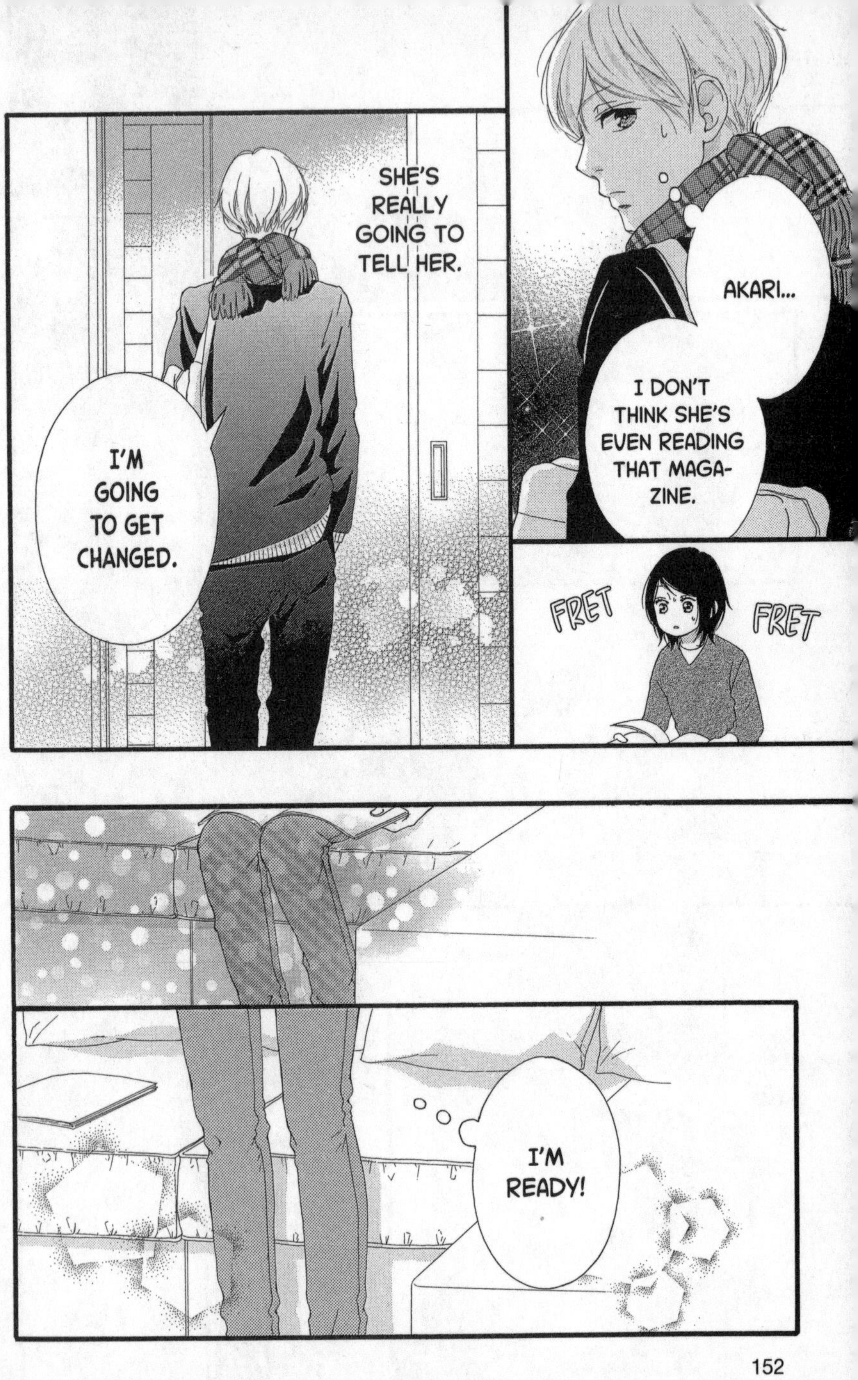
AKARI...
I DON'T THINK SHE'S EVEN READING THAT MAGA-ZINE.
FRET
FRET
SHE'S REALLY GOING TO TELL HER.
I'M GOING TO GET CHANGED.
I'M READY!

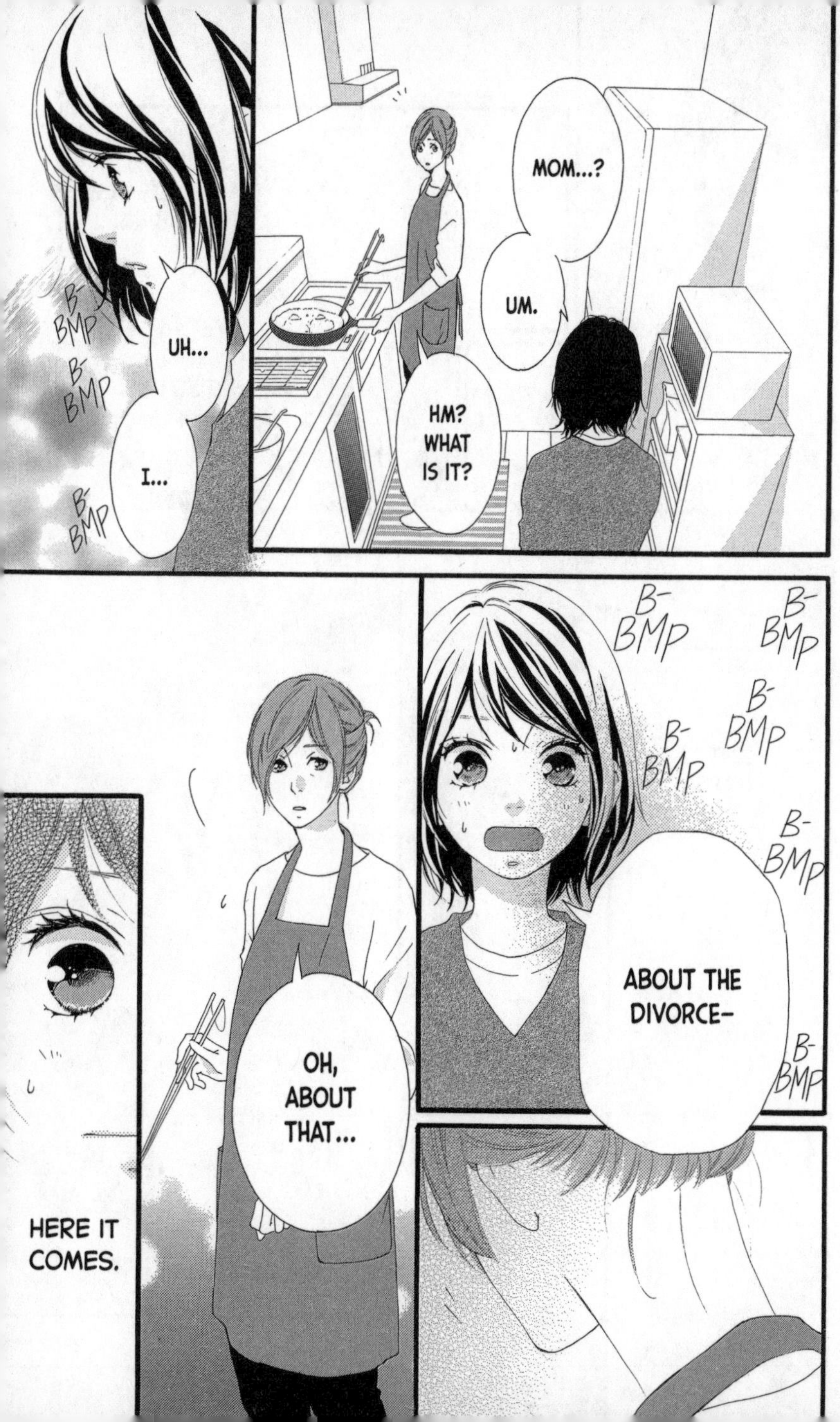
MOM...?
UM.
HM? WHAT IS IT?
B-BMP
UH...
B-BMP
I...
B-BMP
B-BMP
B-BMP
B-BMP
B-BMP
B-BMP
ABOUT THE DIVORCE–
B-BMP
OH, ABOUT THAT...
HERE IT COMES.

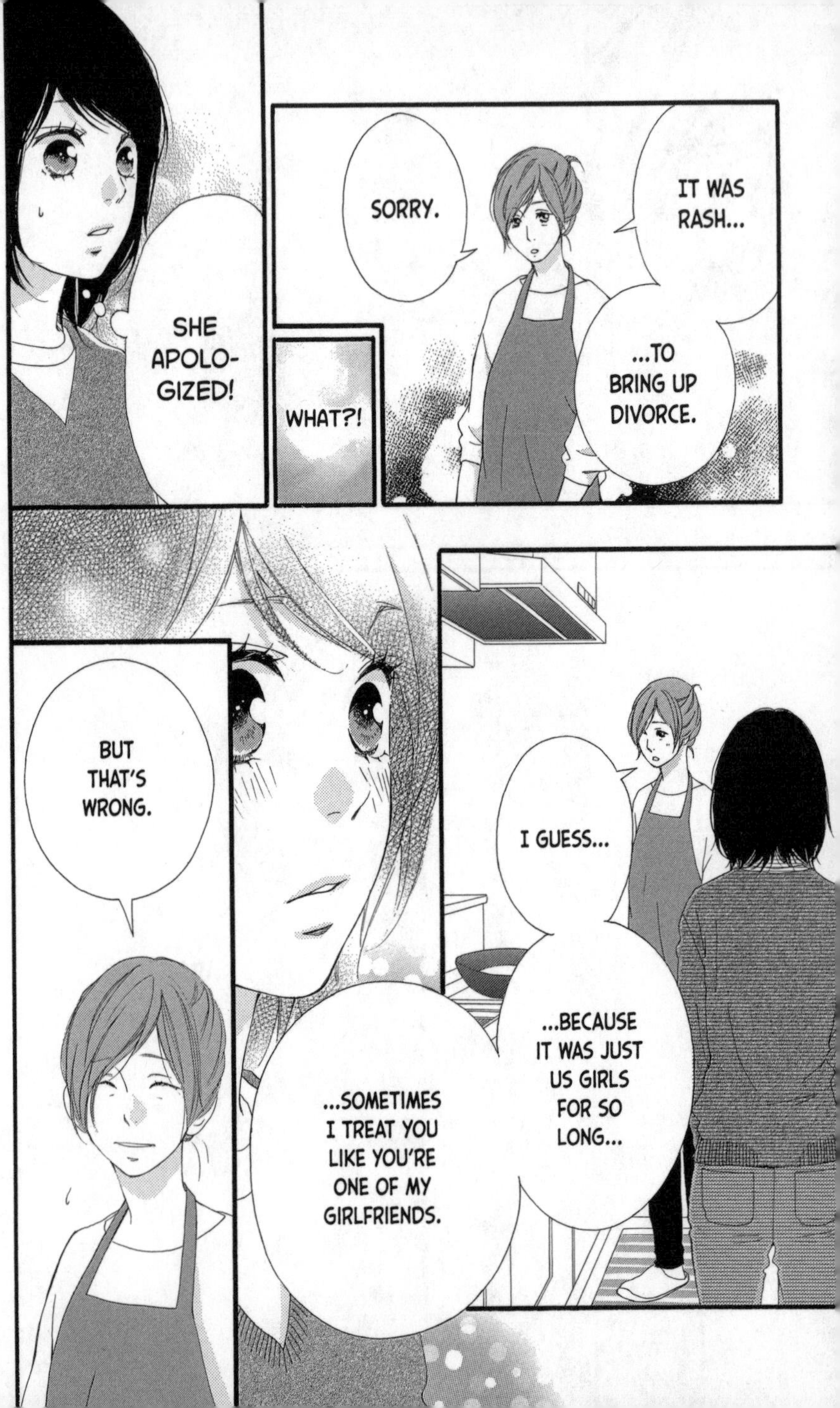
SORRY.
IT WAS RASH...
...TO BRING UP DIVORCE.
WHAT?!
SHE APOLOGIZED!
I GUESS...
...BECAUSE IT WAS JUST US GIRLS FOR SO LONG...
...SOMETIMES I TREAT YOU LIKE YOU'RE ONE OF MY GIRLFRIENDS.
BUT THAT'S WRONG.

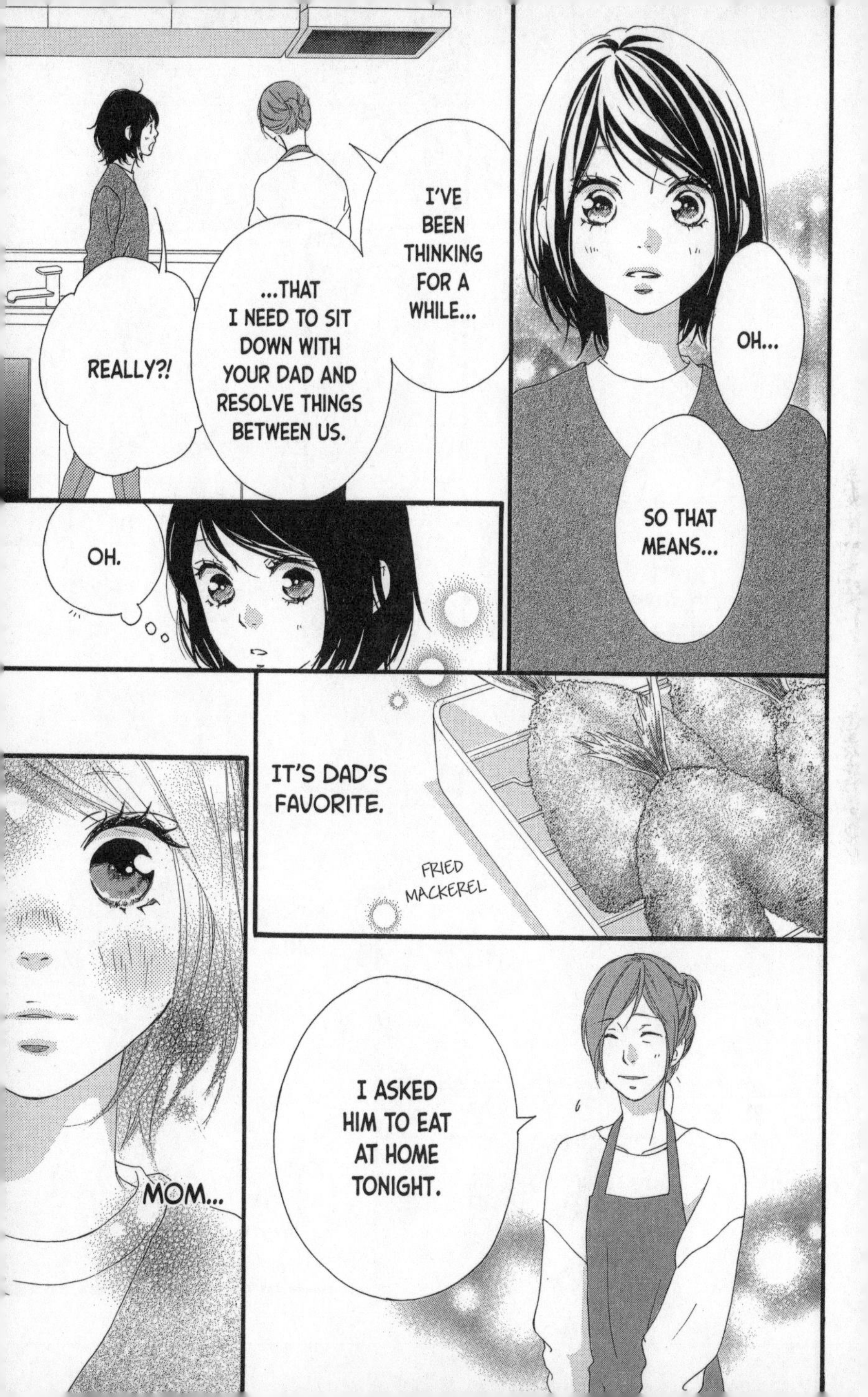
OH...
SO THAT MEANS...
I'VE BEEN THINKING FOR A WHILE...
...THAT I NEED TO SIT DOWN WITH YOUR DAD AND RESOLVE THINGS BETWEEN US.
REALLY?!
OH.
IT'S DAD'S FAVORITE.
FRIED MACKEREL
I ASKED HIM TO EAT AT HOME TONIGHT.
MOM...

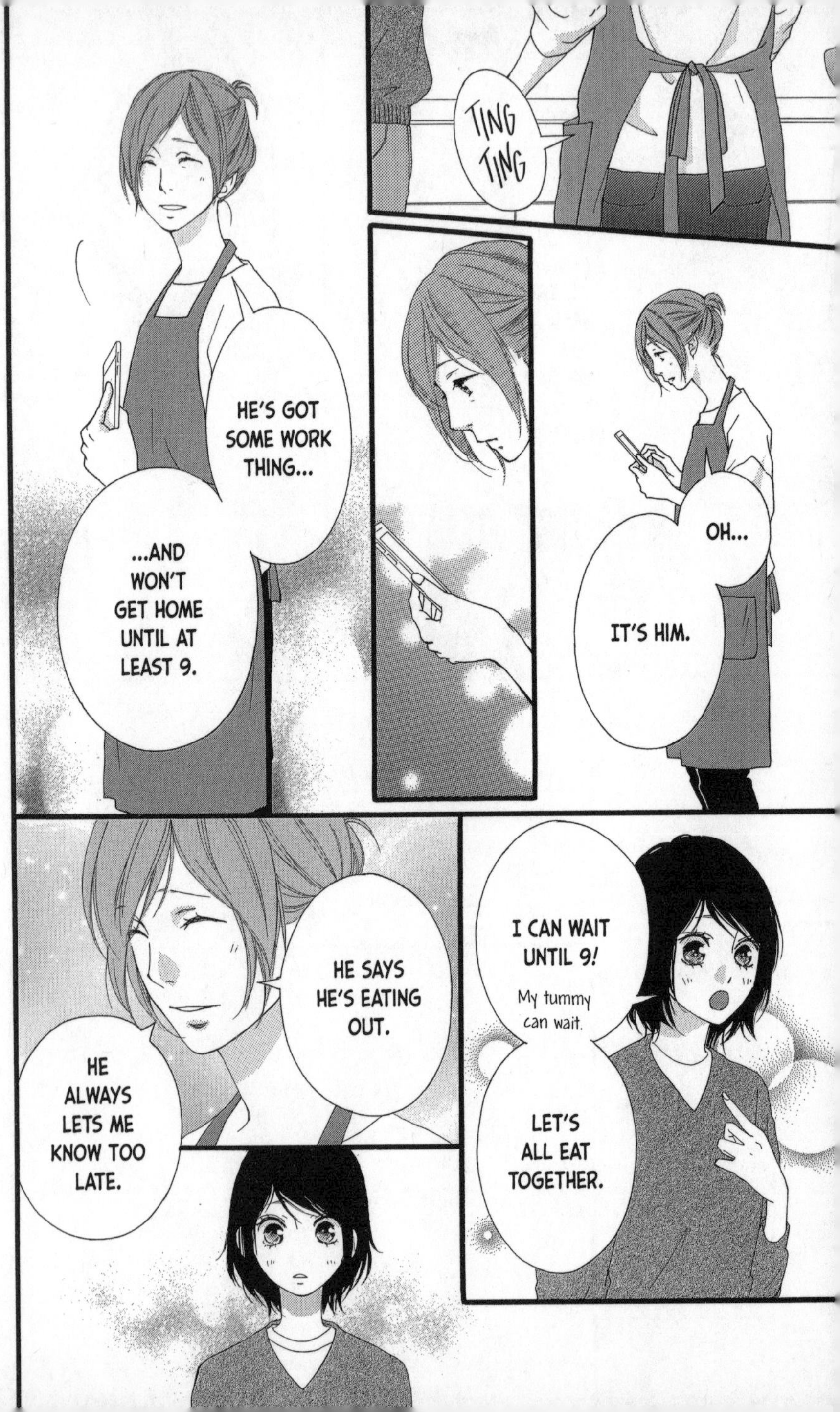
TING TING
OH...
IT'S HIM.
HE'S GOT SOME WORK THING...
...AND WON'T GET HOME UNTIL AT LEAST 9.
I CAN WAIT UNTIL 9!
My tummy can wait.
LET'S ALL EAT TOGETHER.
HE SAYS HE'S EATING OUT.
HE ALWAYS LETS ME KNOW TOO LATE.

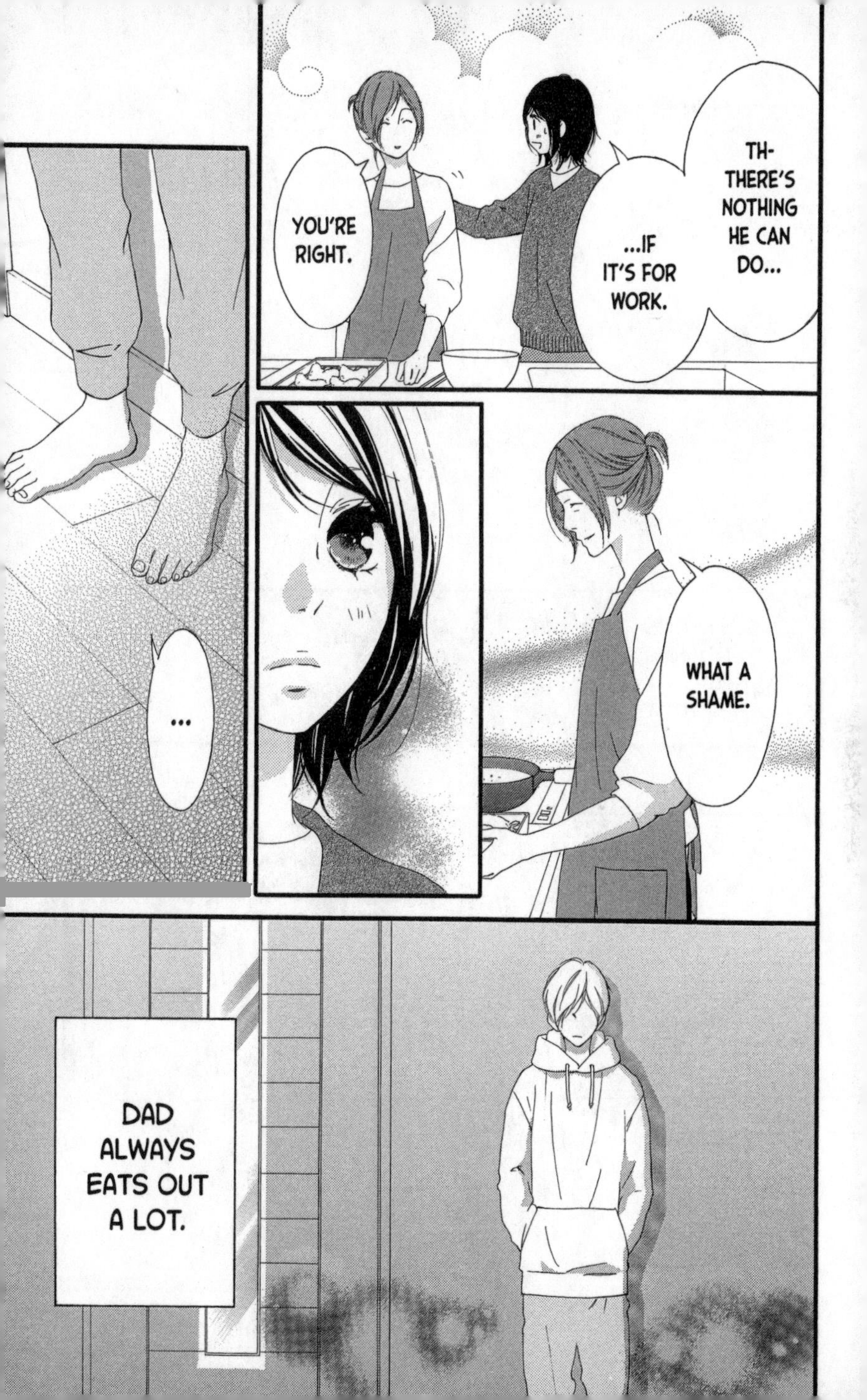
TH- THERE'S NOTHING HE CAN DO...
...IF IT'S FOR WORK.
YOU'RE RIGHT.
WHAT A SHAME.
...
DAD ALWAYS EATS OUT A LOT.

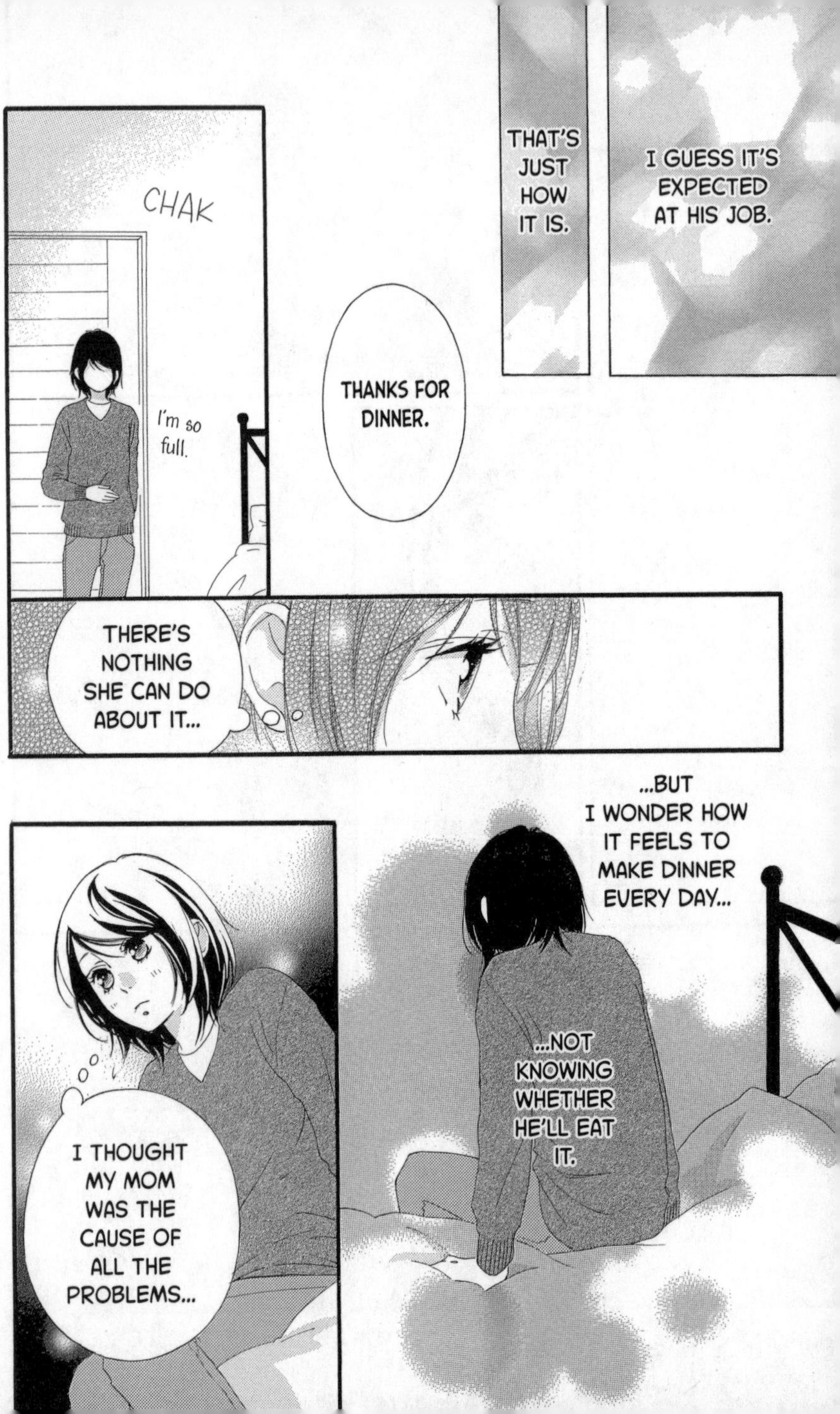

I GUESS IT'S EXPECTED AT HIS JOB.
THAT'S JUST HOW IT IS.
THANKS FOR DINNER.
CHAK
I'm so full.
THERE'S NOTHING SHE CAN DO ABOUT IT...
...BUT I WONDER HOW IT FEELS TO MAKE DINNER EVERY DAY...
...NOT KNOWING WHETHER HE'LL EAT IT.
I THOUGHT MY MOM WAS THE CAUSE OF ALL THE PROBLEMS...

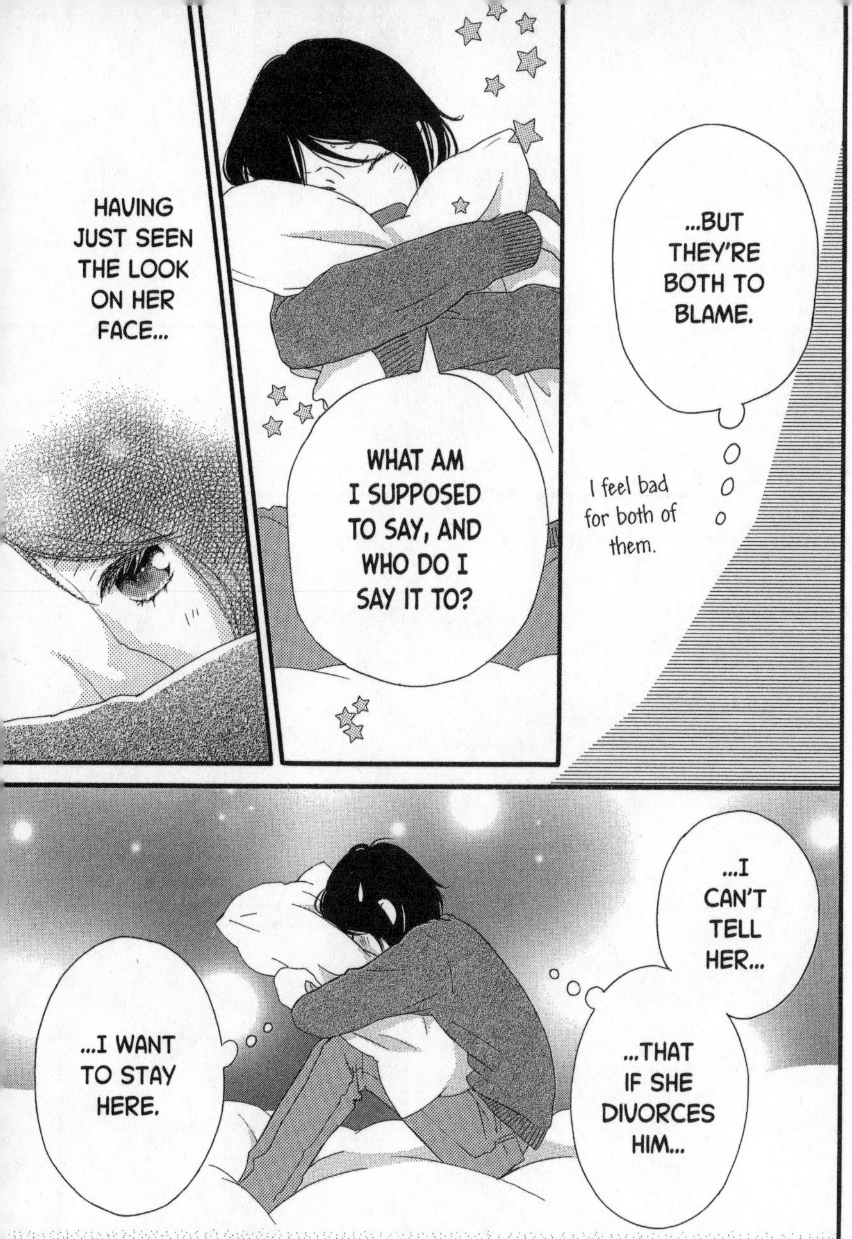
...BUT THEY'RE BOTH TO BLAME.
I feel bad for both of them.
WHAT AM I SUPPOSED TO SAY, AND WHO DO I SAY IT TO?
HAVING JUST SEEN THE LOOK ON HER FACE...
...I CAN'T TELL HER...
...THAT IF SHE DIVORCES HIM...
...I WANT TO STAY HERE.

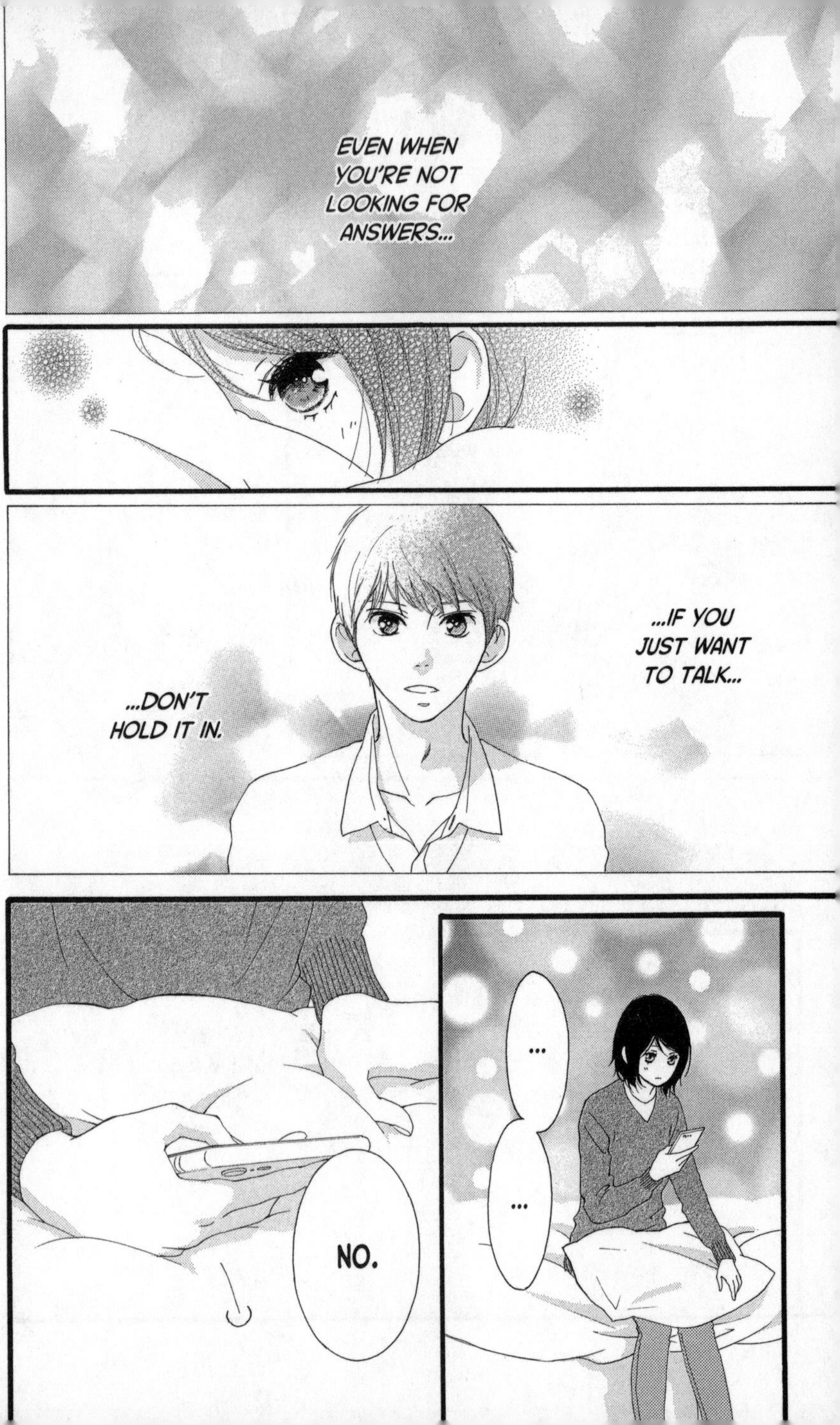
EVEN WHEN YOU'RE NOT LOOKING FOR ANSWERS...
...IF YOU JUST WANT TO TALK...
...DON'T HOLD IT IN.
...
...
NO.

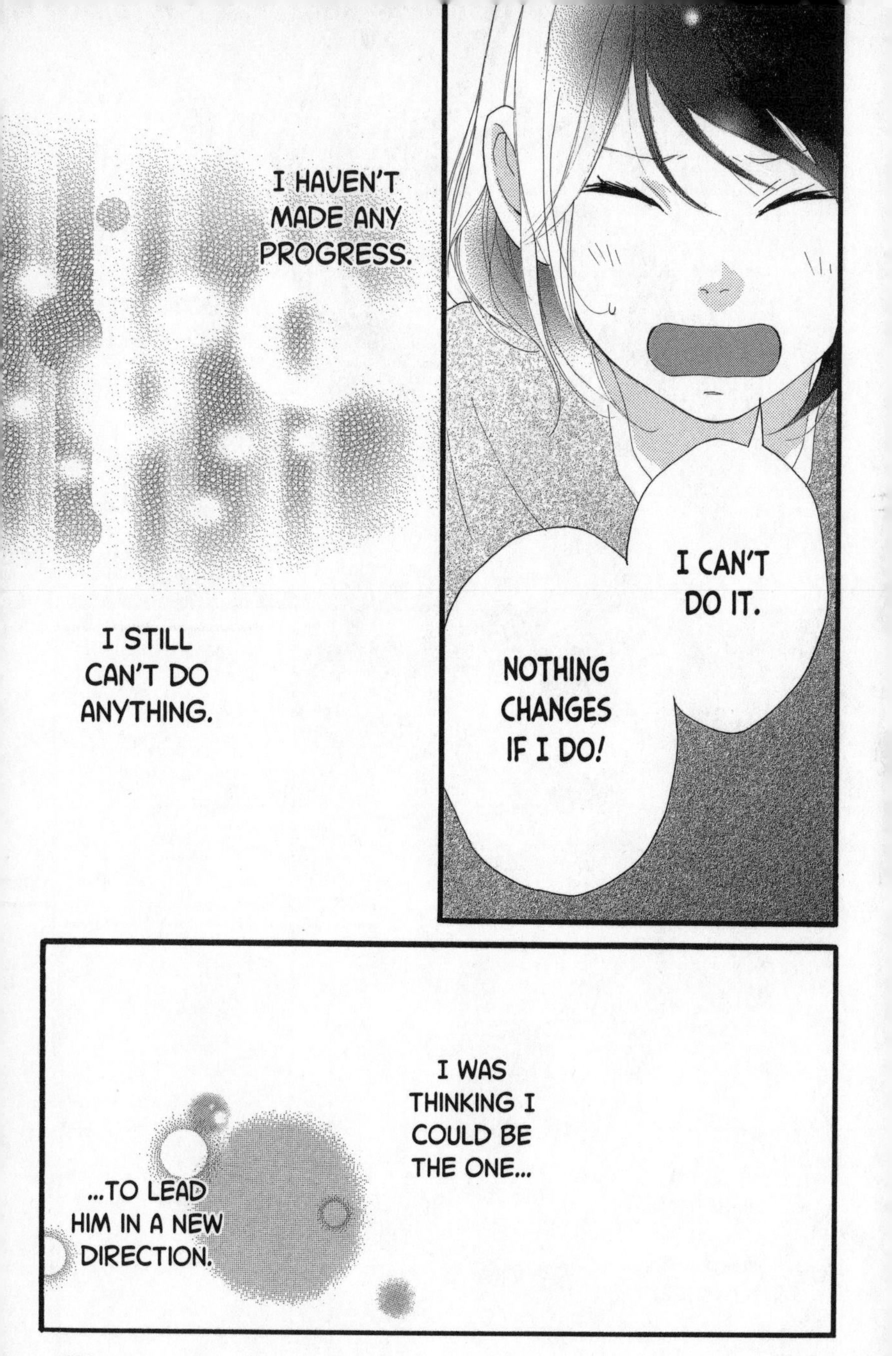
I CAN'T DO IT.
NOTHING CHANGES IF I DO!
I HAVEN'T MADE ANY PROGRESS.
I STILL CAN'T DO ANYTHING.
I WAS THINKING I COULD BE THE ONE...
...TO LEAD HIM IN A NEW DIRECTION.

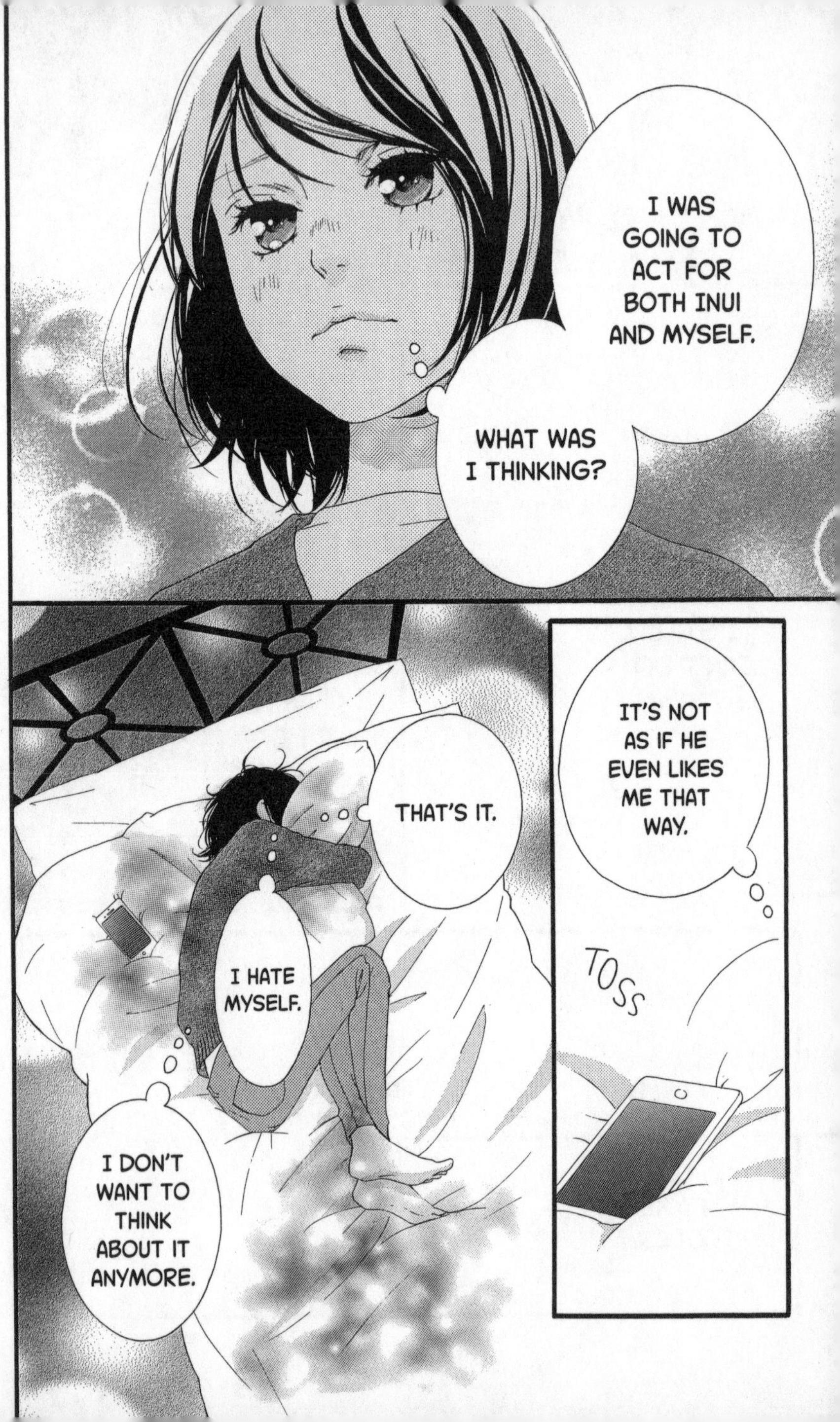
I WAS GOING TO ACT FOR BOTH INUI AND MYSELF.
WHAT WAS I THINKING?
IT'S NOT AS IF HE EVEN LIKES ME THAT WAY.
TOSS
THAT'S IT.
I HATE MYSELF.
I DON'T WANT TO THINK ABOUT IT ANYMORE.

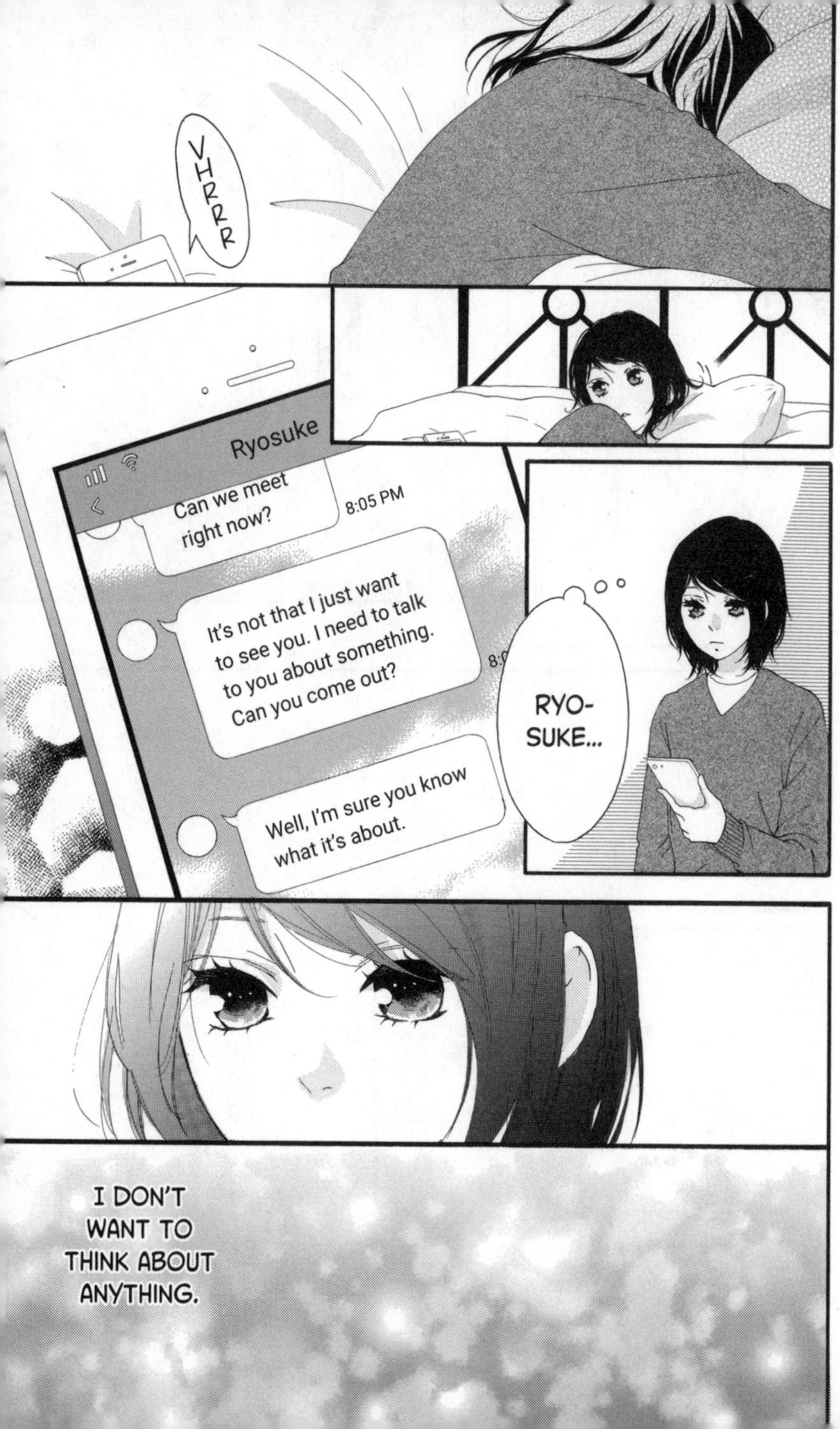
VHRRR
RYO-SUKE...
Ryosuke
Can we meet right now?
8:05 PM
It's not that I just want to see you. I need to talk to you about something. Can you come out?
Well, I'm sure you know what it's about.
I DON'T WANT TO THINK ABOUT ANYTHING.

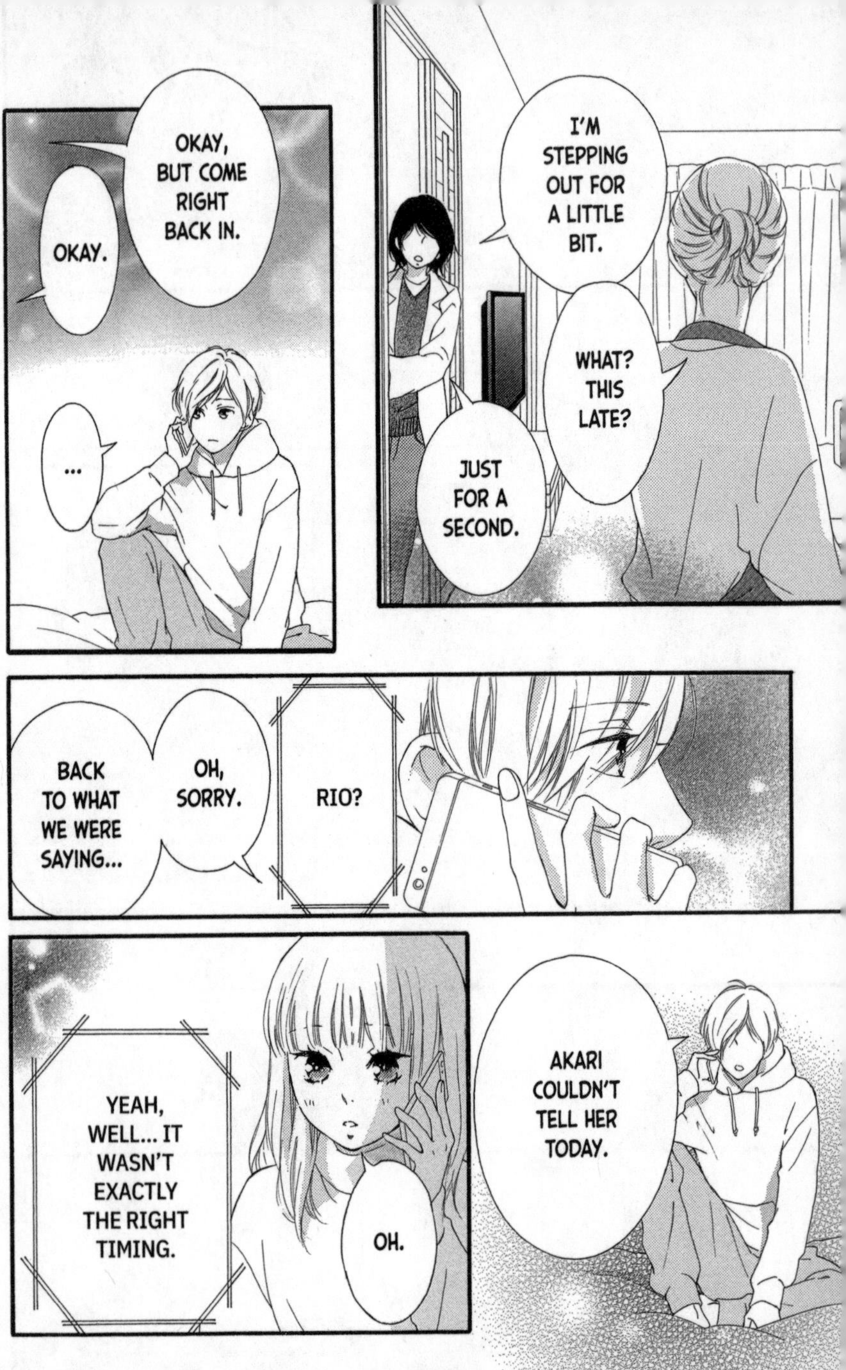
I'M STEPPING OUT FOR A LITTLE BIT.
WHAT? THIS LATE?
JUST FOR A SECOND.
OKAY, BUT COME RIGHT BACK IN.
OKAY.
...
RIO?
OH, SORRY.
BACK TO WHAT WE WERE SAYING...
AKARI COULDN'T TELL HER TODAY.
OH.
YEAH, WELL... IT WASN'T EXACTLY THE RIGHT TIMING.

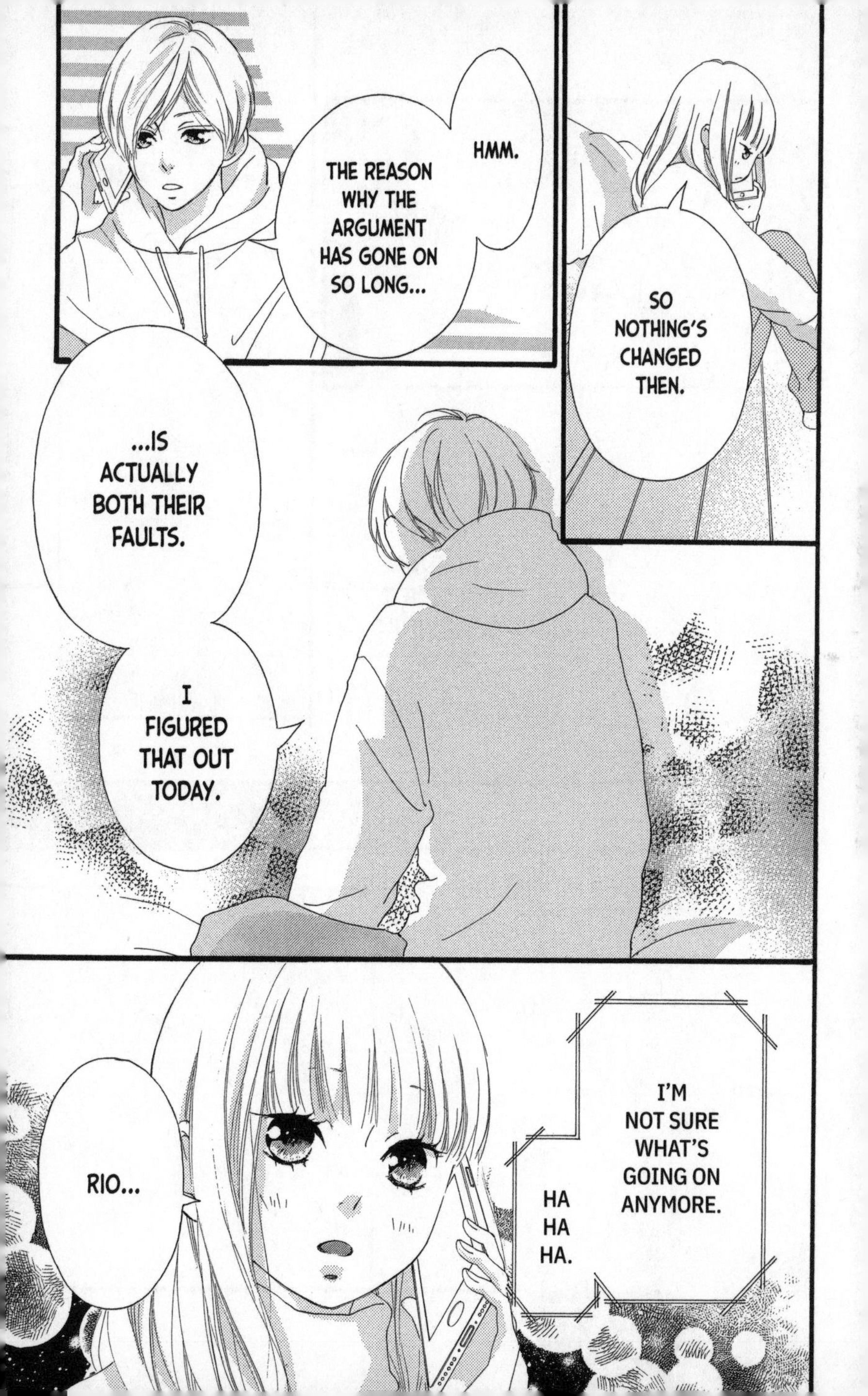
SO NOTHING'S CHANGED THEN.
HMM.
THE REASON WHY THE ARGUMENT HAS GONE ON SO LONG...
...IS ACTUALLY BOTH THEIR FAULTS.
I FIGURED THAT OUT TODAY.
I'M NOT SURE WHAT'S GOING ON ANYMORE.
HA HA HA.
RIO...

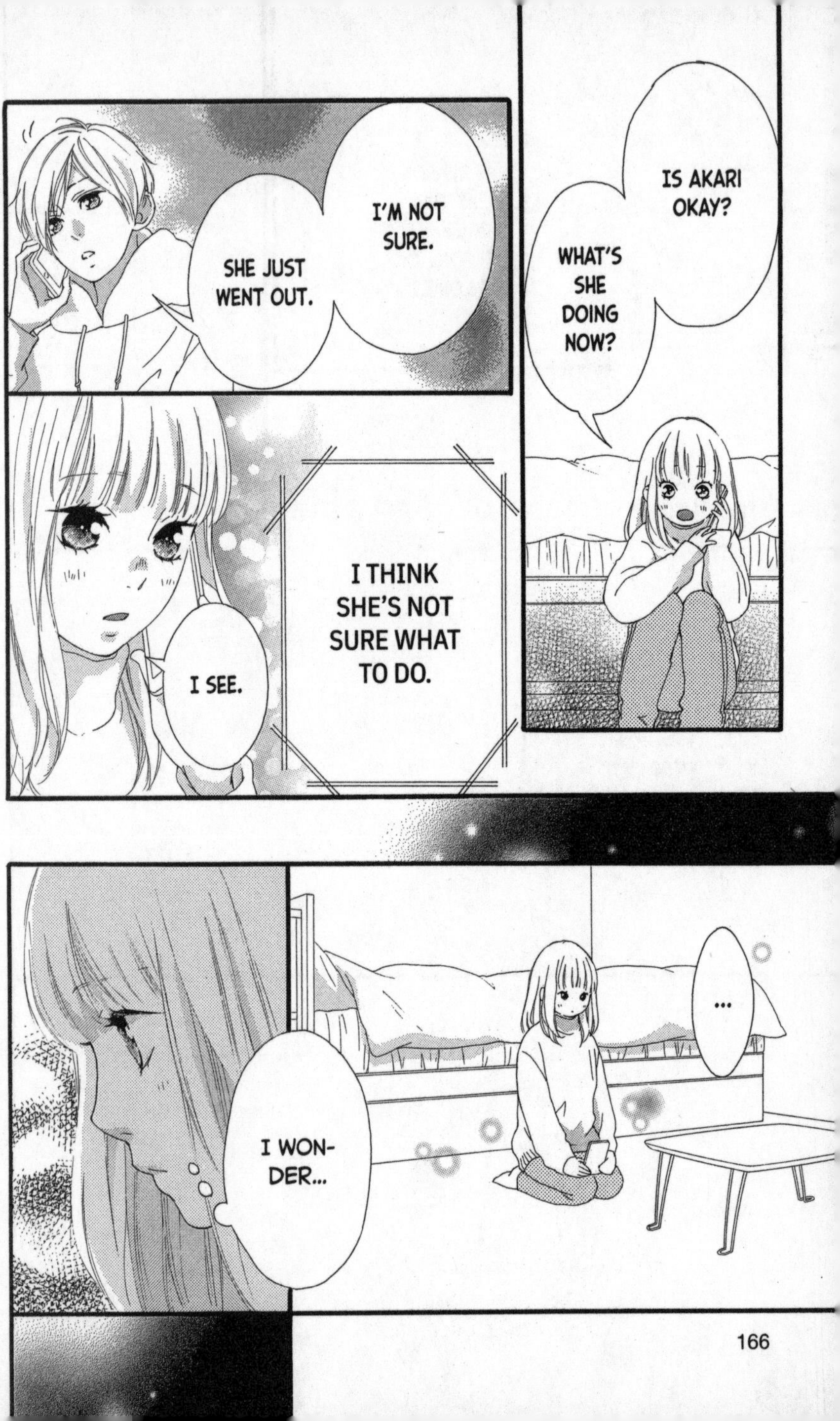
IS AKARI OKAY?
WHAT'S SHE DOING NOW?
I'M NOT SURE.
SHE JUST WENT OUT.
I THINK SHE'S NOT SURE WHAT TO DO.
I SEE.
...
I WON-DER...

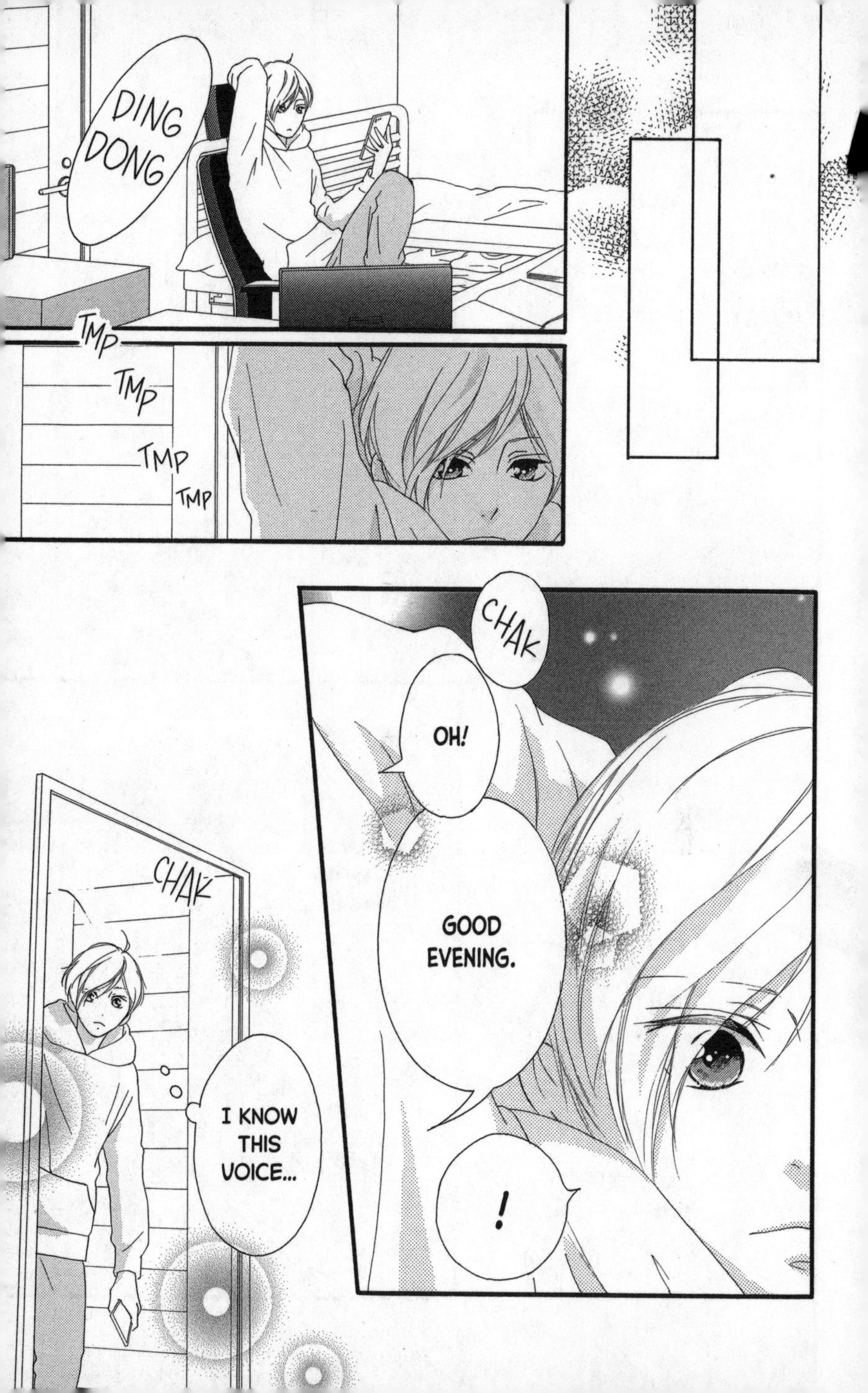

DING DONG
TMP
TMP
TMP
TMP
CHAK
OH!
GOOD EVENING.
!
CHAK
I KNOW THIS VOICE...

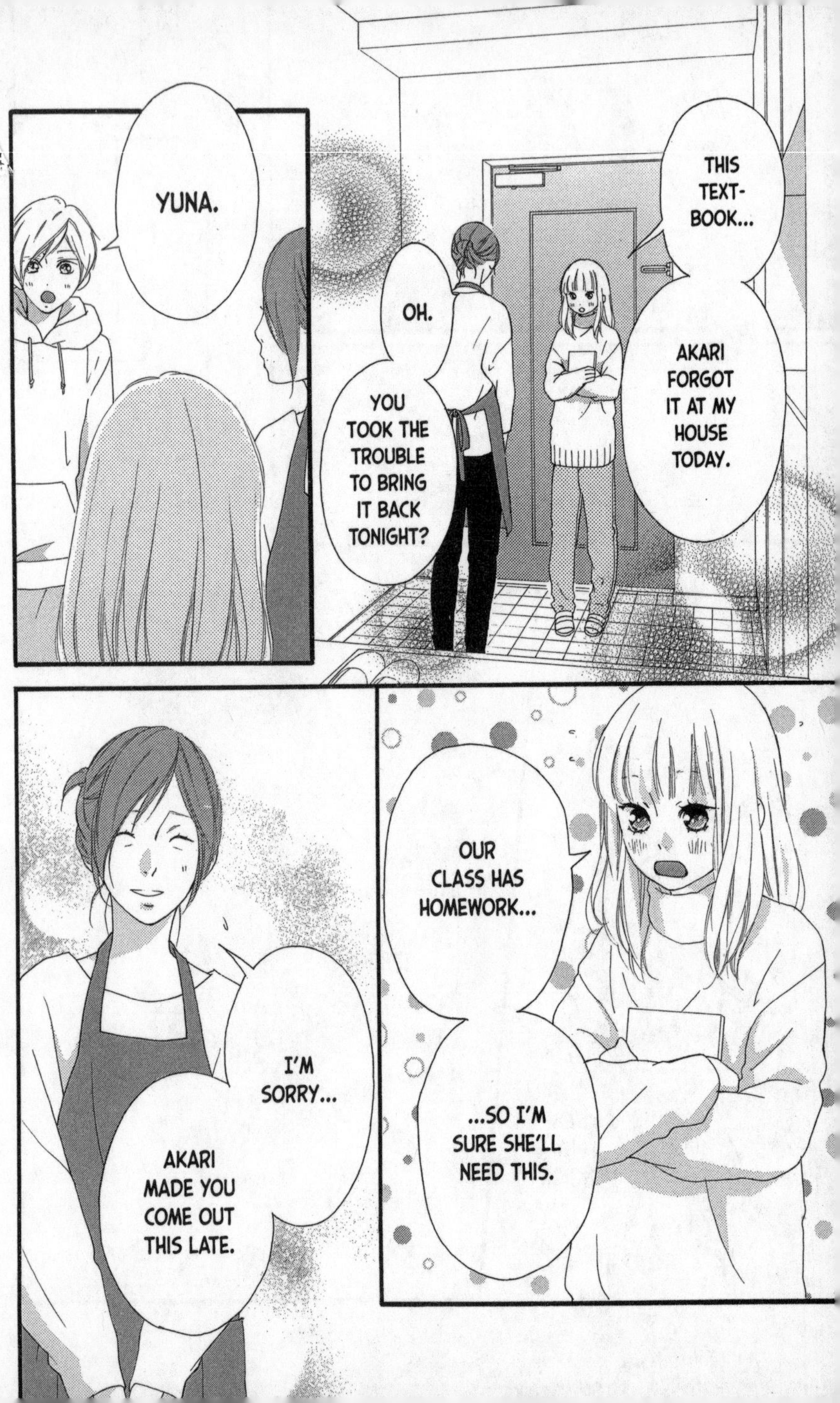
THIS TEXT-BOOK...
AKARI FORGOT IT AT MY HOUSE TODAY.
OH.
YOU TOOK THE TROUBLE TO BRING IT BACK TONIGHT?
YUNA.
OUR CLASS HAS HOMEWORK...
...SO I'M SURE SHE'LL NEED THIS.
I'M SORRY...
AKARI MADE YOU COME OUT THIS LATE.

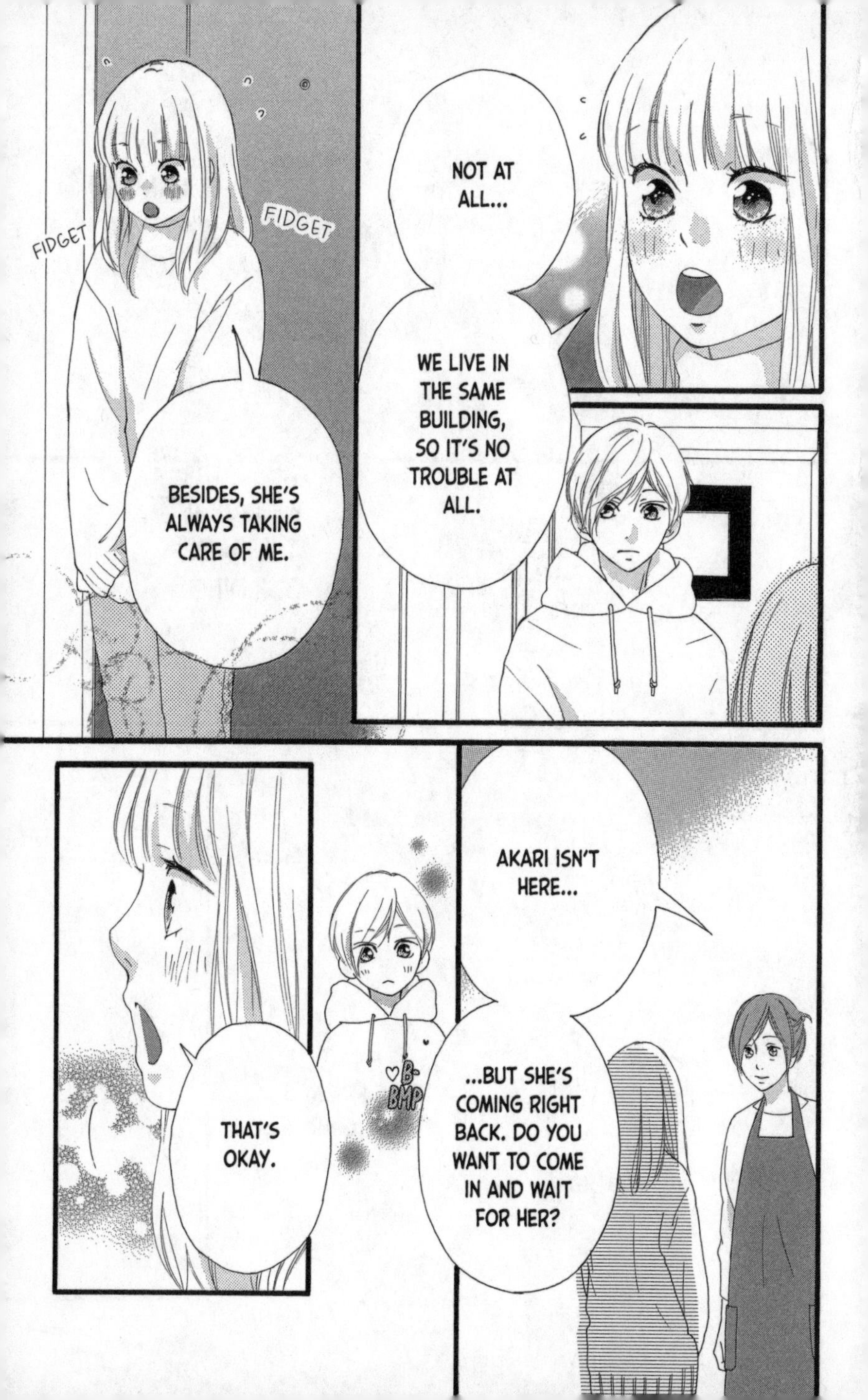
NOT AT ALL...
WE LIVE IN THE SAME BUILDING, SO IT'S NO TROUBLE AT ALL.
FIDGET
FIDGET
BESIDES, SHE'S ALWAYS TAKING CARE OF ME.
AKARI ISN'T HERE...
...BUT SHE'S COMING RIGHT BACK. DO YOU WANT TO COME IN AND WAIT FOR HER?
♡B-BMP
THAT'S OKAY.

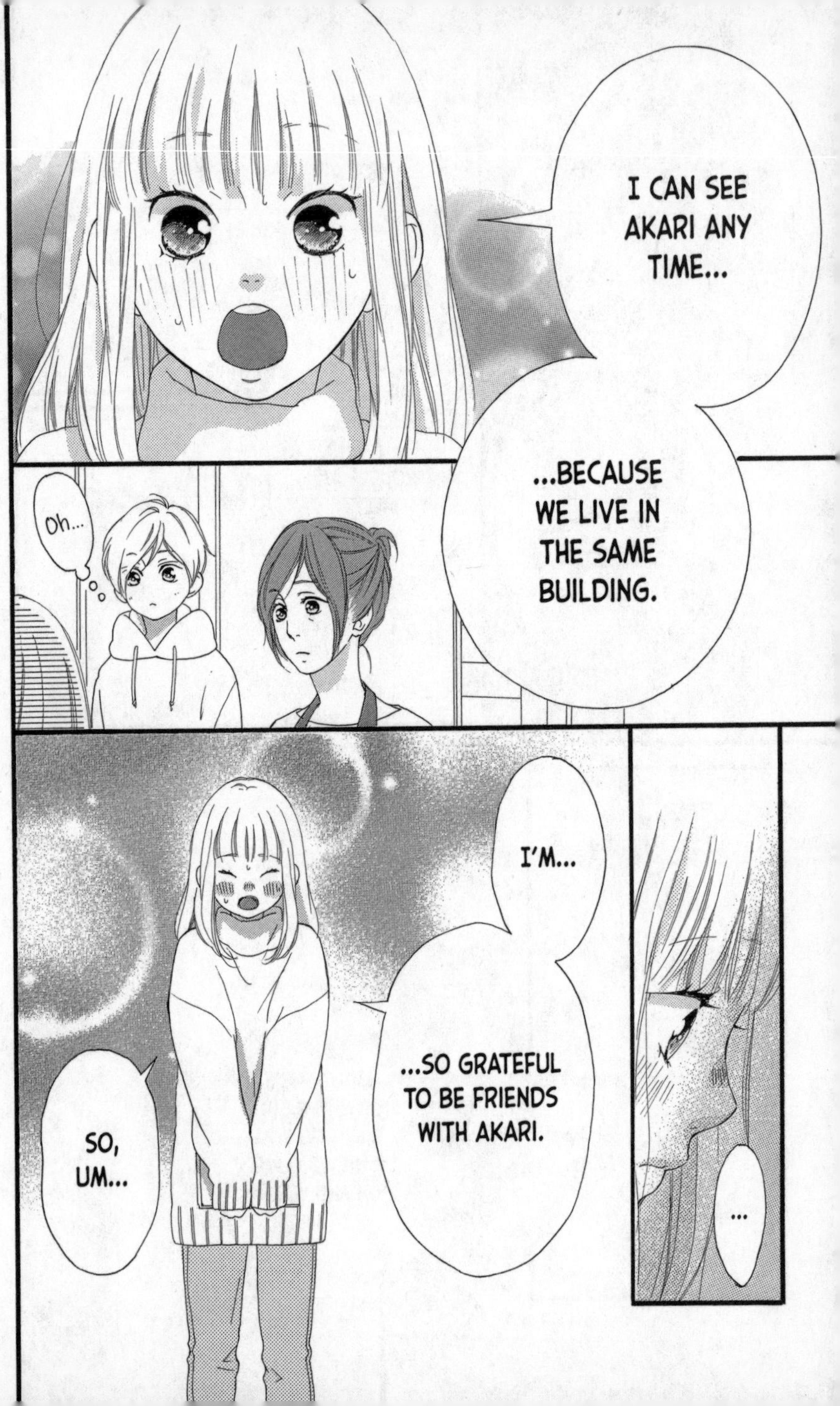
I CAN SEE AKARI ANY TIME...
...BECAUSE WE LIVE IN THE SAME BUILDING.
Oh...
...
I'M...
...SO GRATEFUL TO BE FRIENDS WITH AKARI.
SO, UM...

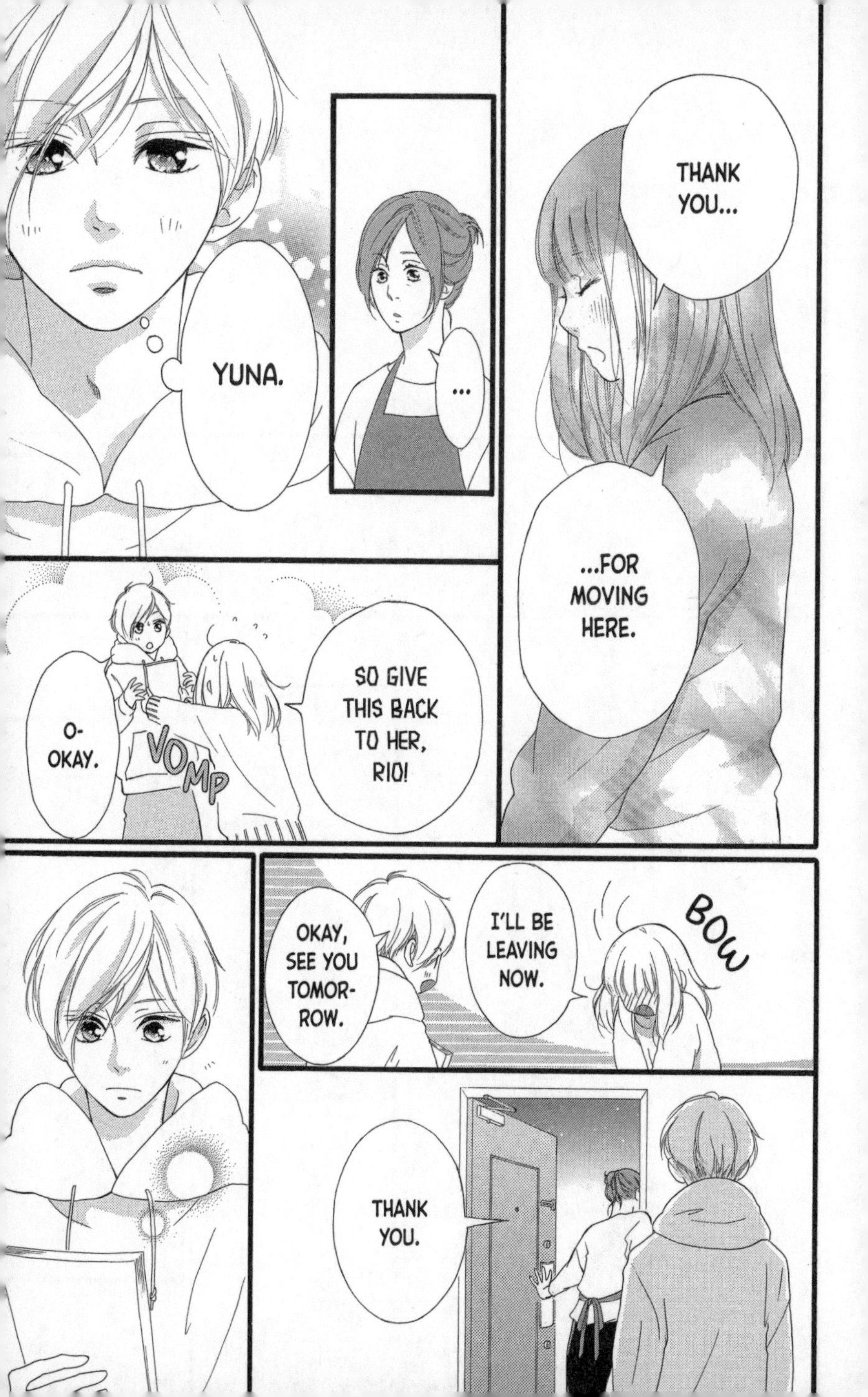
THANK YOU...
...FOR MOVING HERE.
...
YUNA.
SO GIVE THIS BACK TO HER, RIO!
VOMP
O- OKAY.
BOW
I'LL BE LEAVING NOW.
OKAY, SEE YOU TOMOR- ROW.
THANK YOU.

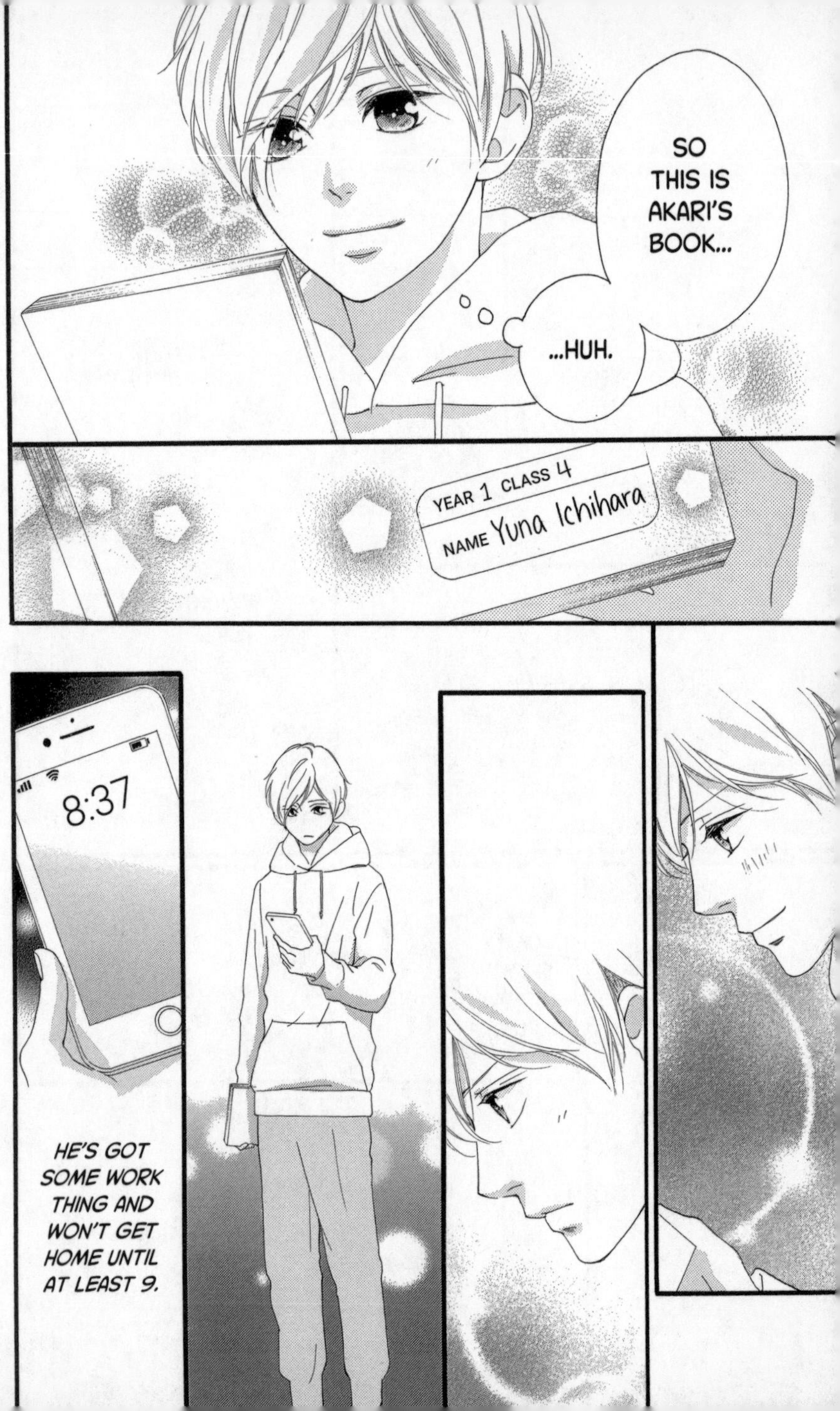
SO THIS IS AKARI'S BOOK...
...HUH.
YEAR 1 CLASS 4
NAME Yuna Ichihara
8:37
HE'S GOT SOME WORK THING AND WON'T GET HOME UNTIL AT LEAST 9.

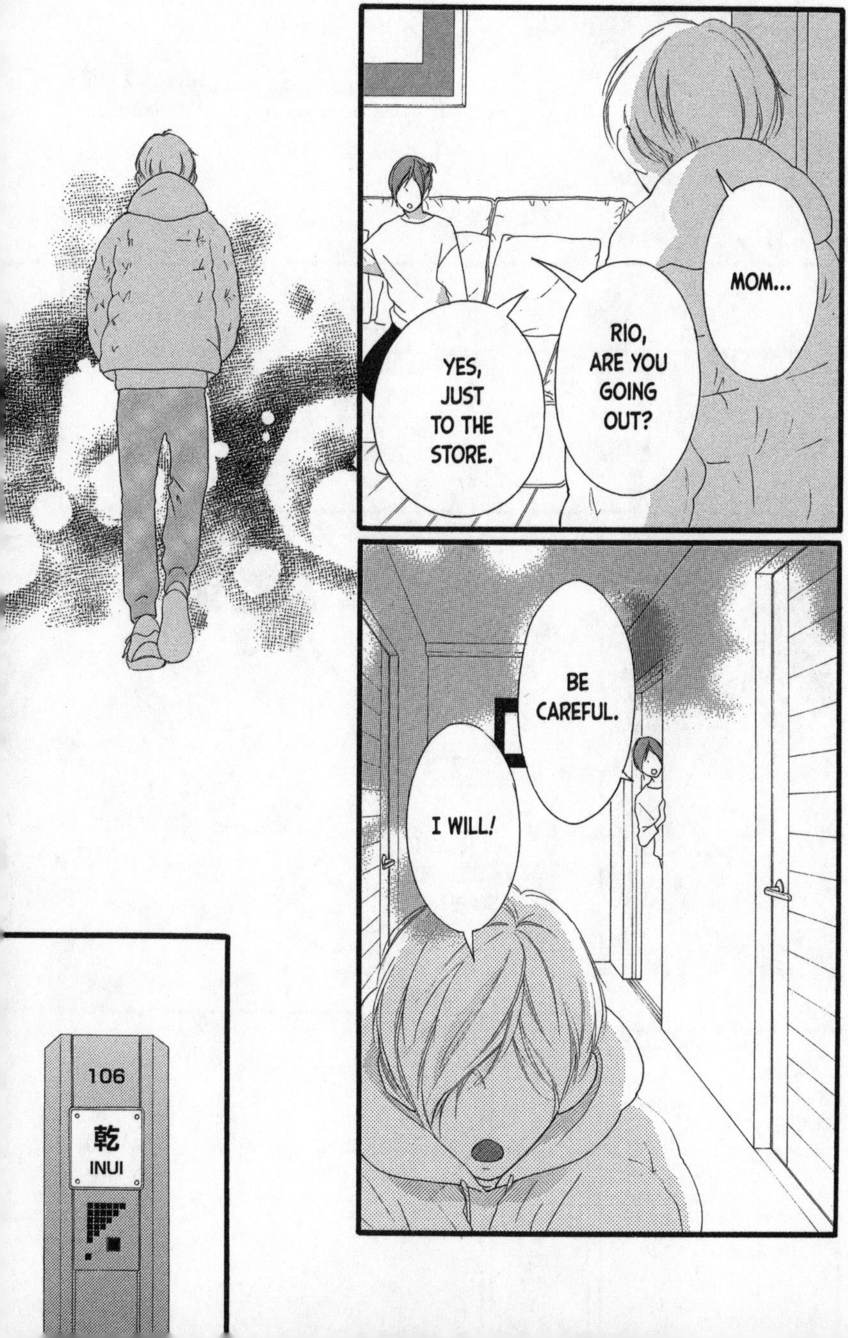
MOM...
RIO, ARE YOU GOING OUT?
YES, JUST TO THE STORE.
BE CAREFUL.
I WILL!
106
乾
INUI

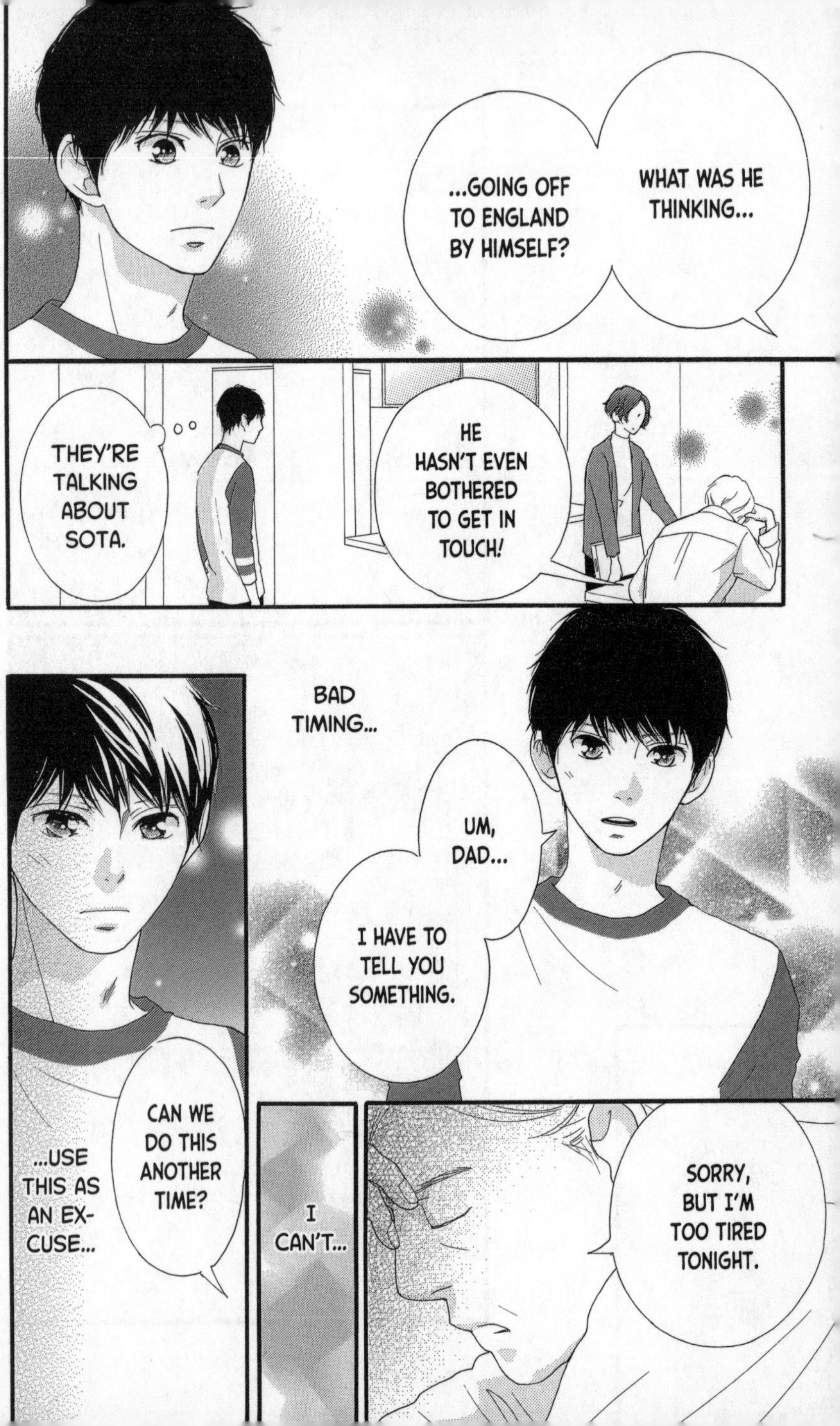
WHAT WAS HE THINKING...
...GOING OFF TO ENGLAND BY HIMSELF?
HE HASN'T EVEN BOTHERED TO GET IN TOUCH!
THEY'RE TALKING ABOUT SOTA.
BAD TIMING...
UM, DAD...
I HAVE TO TELL YOU SOMETHING.
SORRY, BUT I'M TOO TIRED TONIGHT.
I CAN'T...
CAN WE DO THIS ANOTHER TIME?
...USE THIS AS AN EX-CUSE...

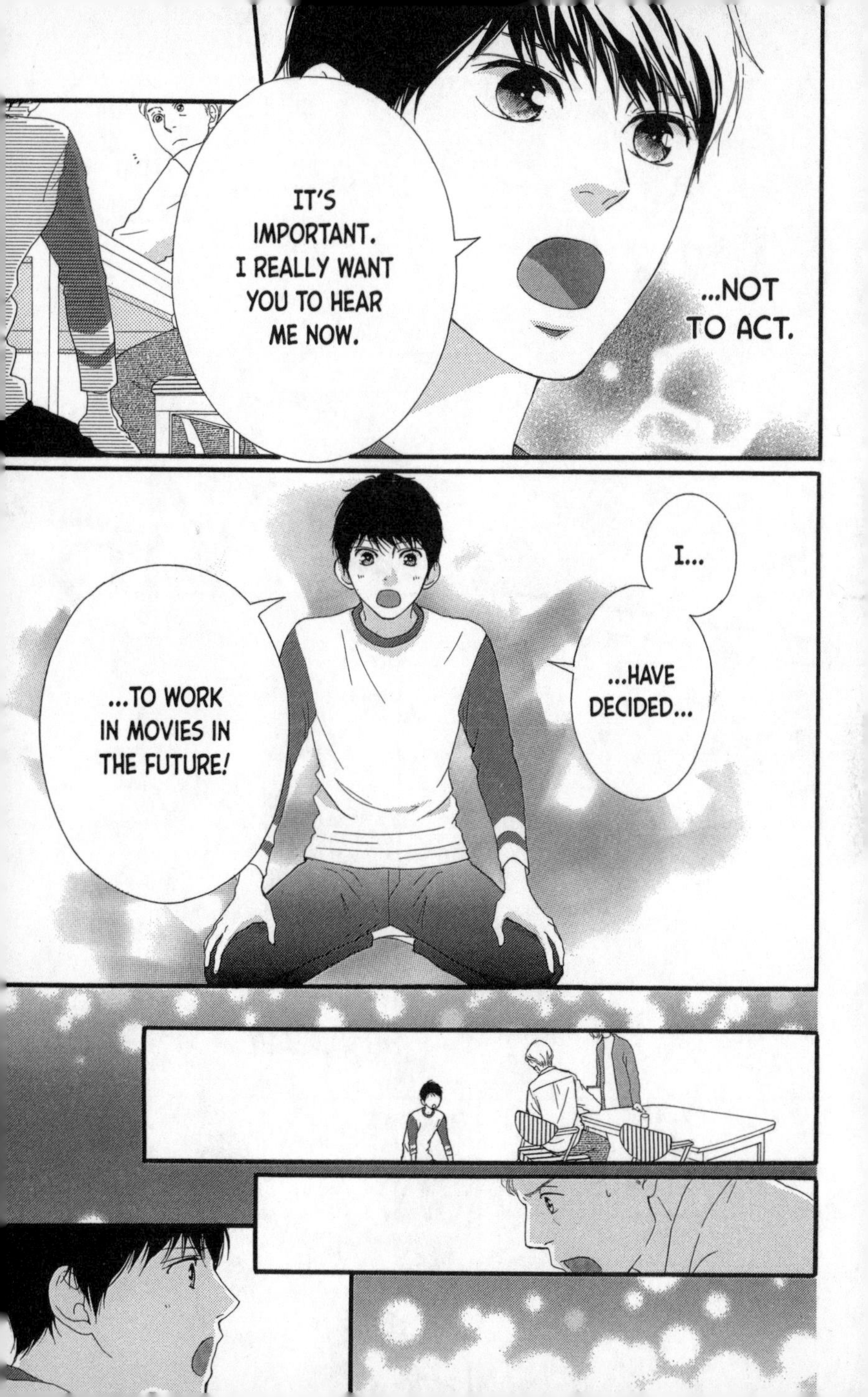
...NOT TO ACT.
IT'S IMPORTANT. I REALLY WANT YOU TO HEAR ME NOW.
I...
...HAVE DECIDED...
...TO WORK IN MOVIES IN THE FUTURE!

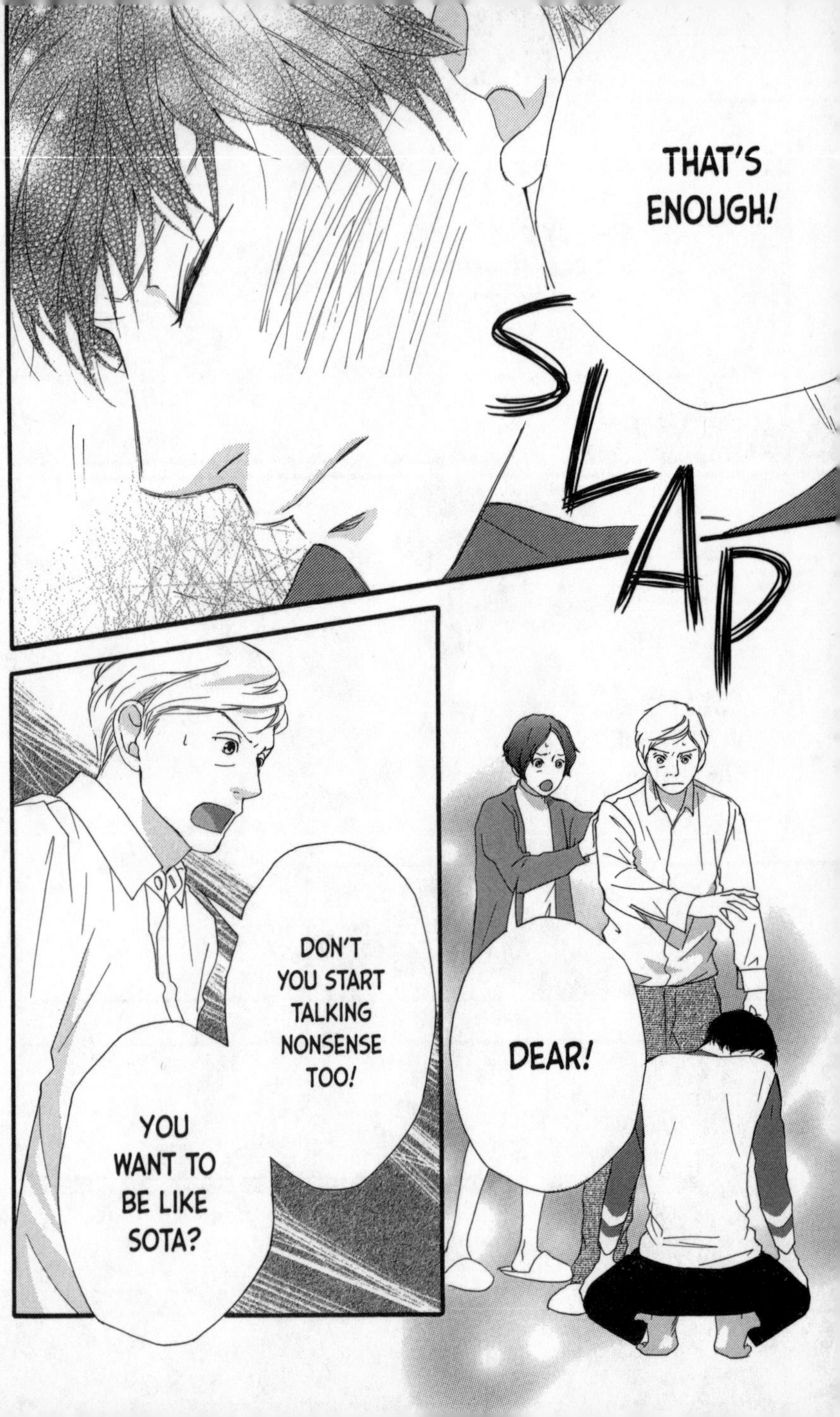
THAT'S ENOUGH!
SLAP
DEAR!
DON'T YOU START TALKING NONSENSE TOO!
YOU WANT TO BE LIKE SOTA?

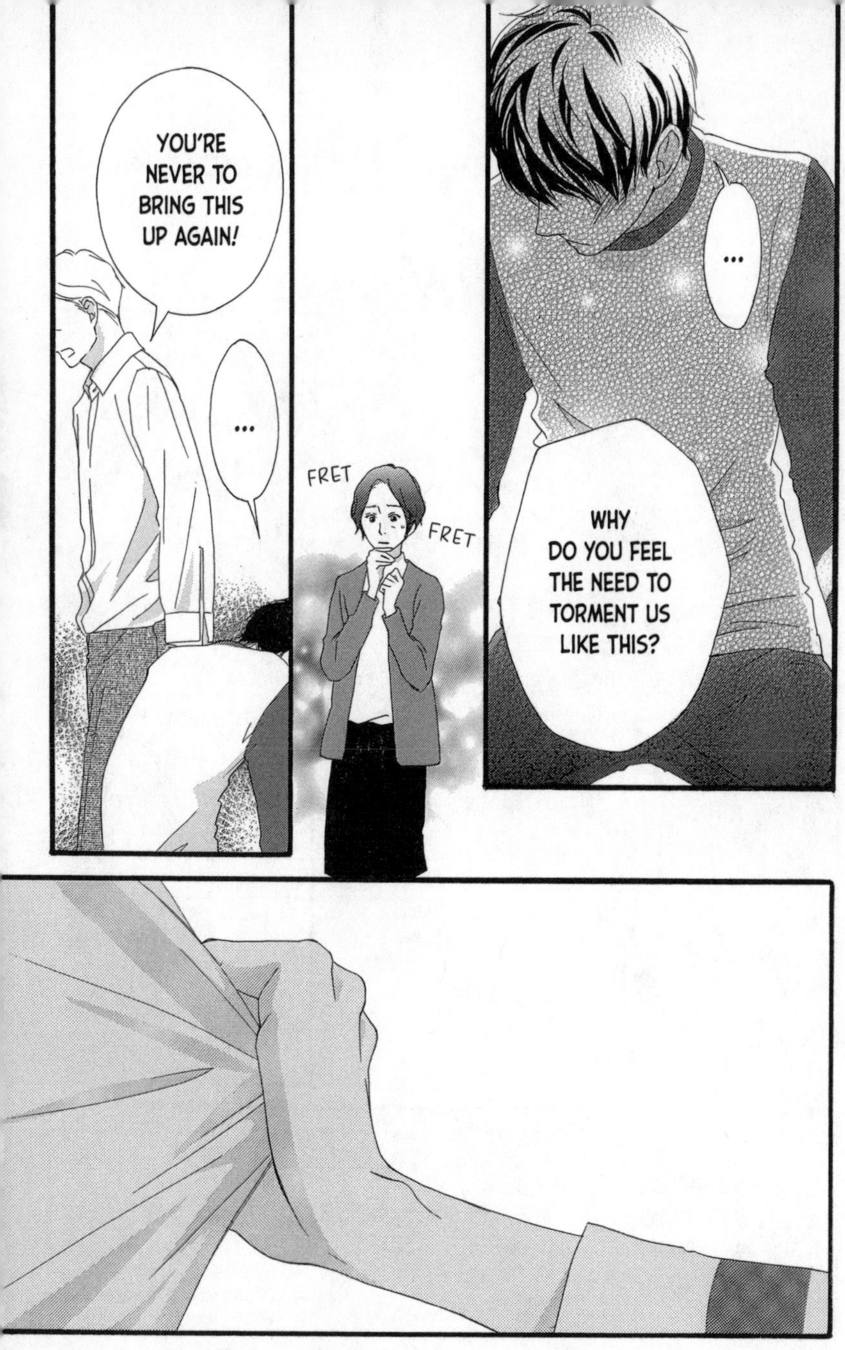
...
WHY DO YOU FEEL THE NEED TO TORMENT US LIKE THIS?
FRET
FRET
YOU'RE NEVER TO BRING THIS UP AGAIN!
...

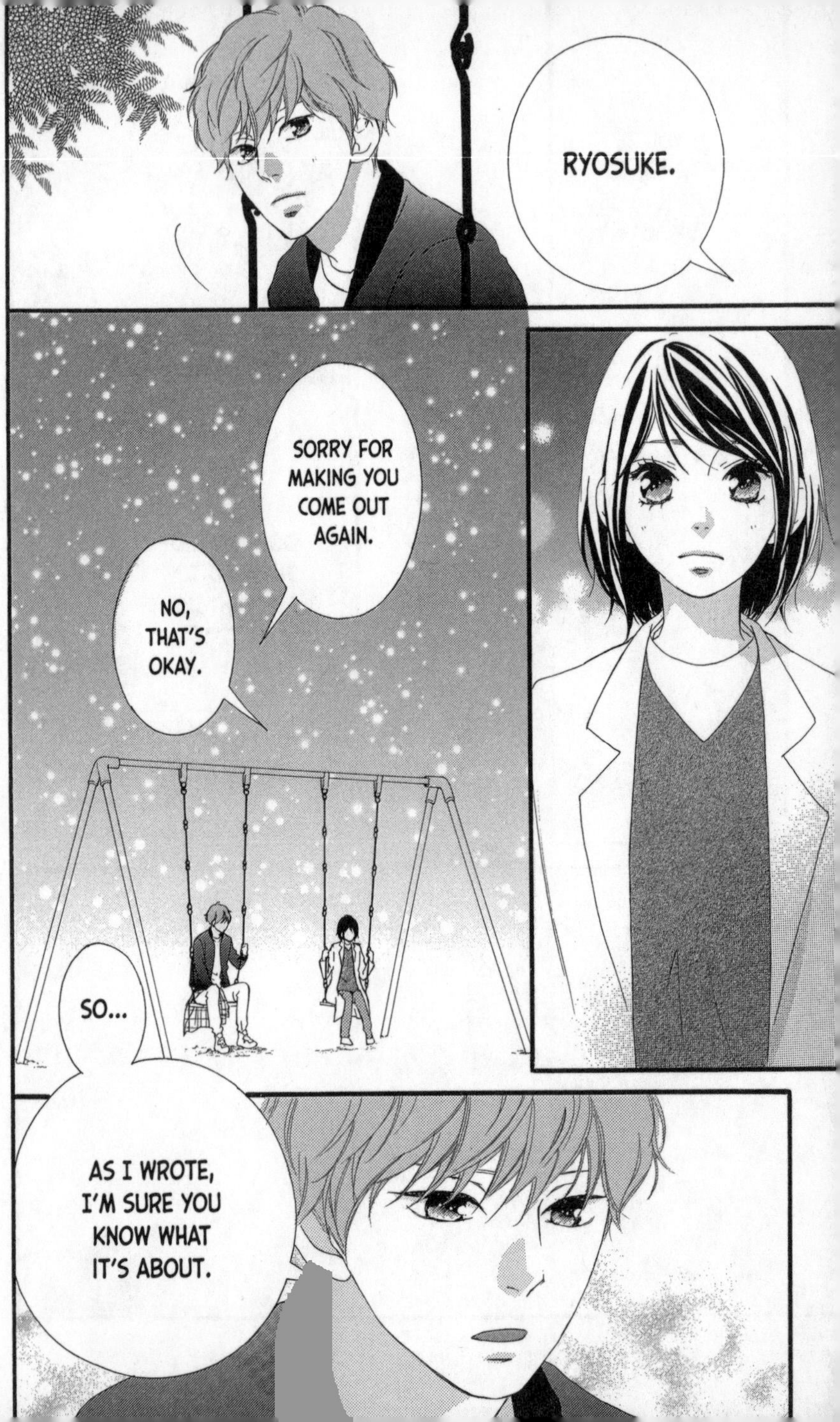
RYOSUKE.
SORRY FOR MAKING YOU COME OUT AGAIN.
NO, THAT'S OKAY.
SO...
AS I WROTE, I'M SURE YOU KNOW WHAT IT'S ABOUT.

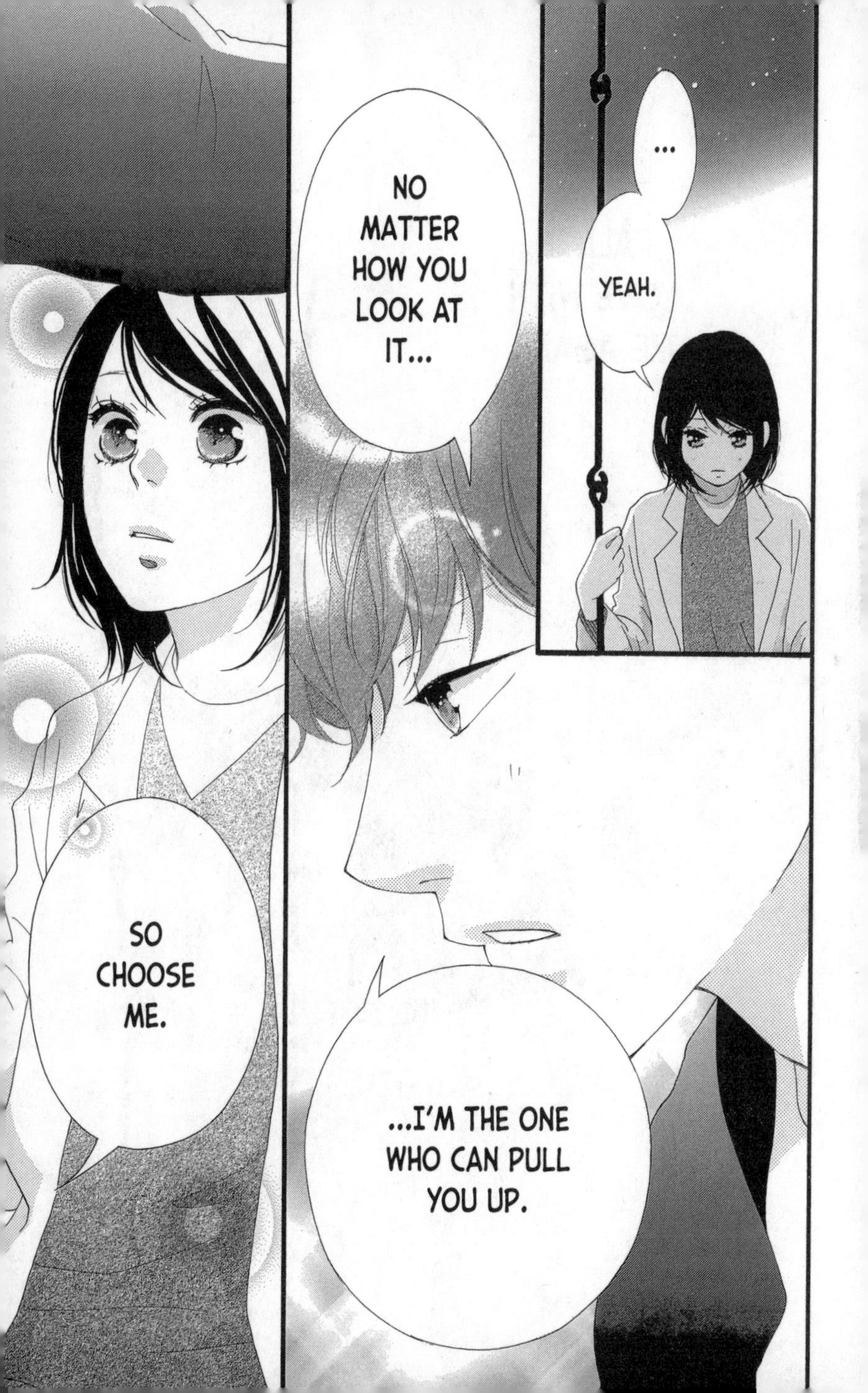
...
YEAH.
NO MATTER HOW YOU LOOK AT IT...
...I'M THE ONE WHO CAN PULL YOU UP.
SO CHOOSE ME.

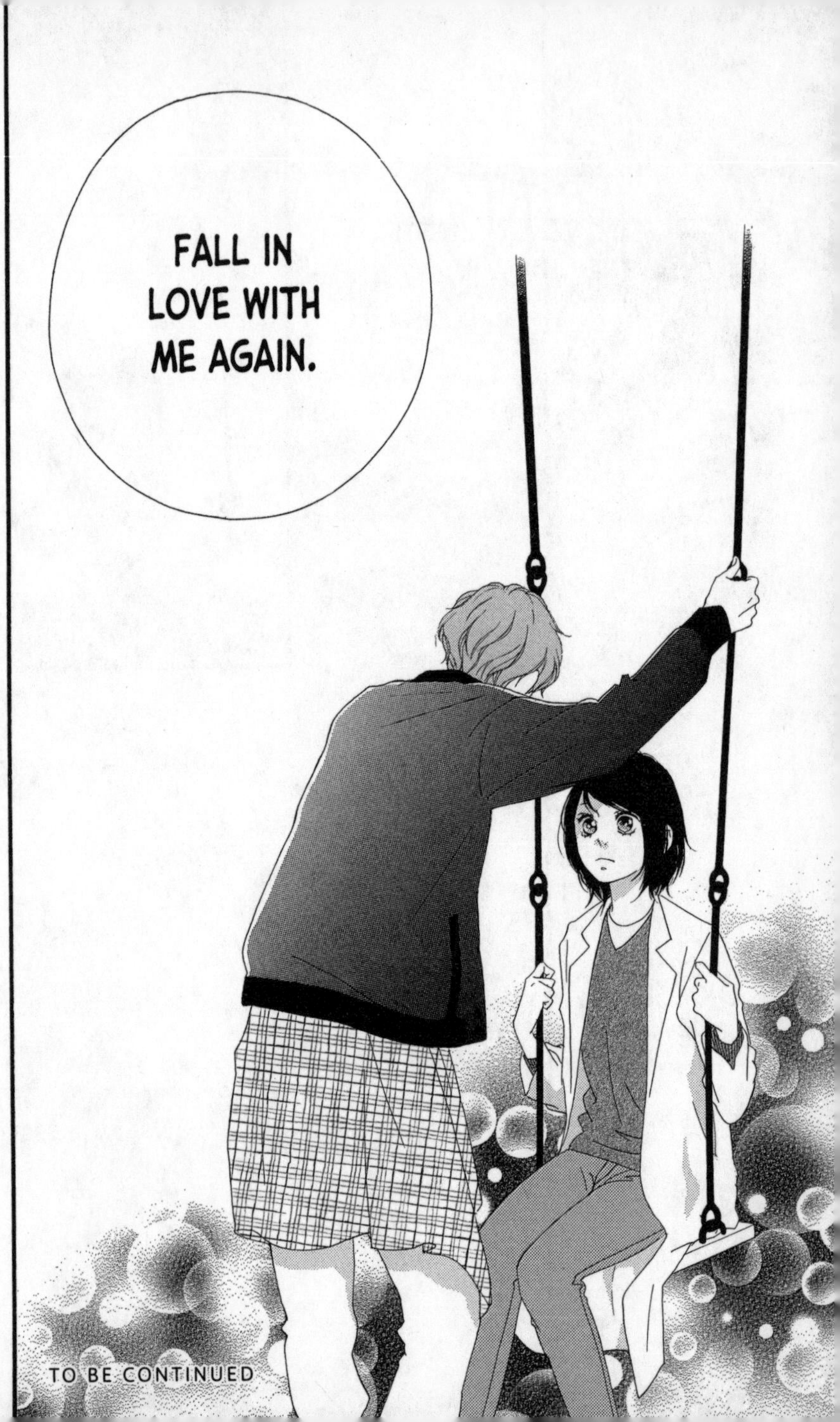
FALL IN LOVE WITH ME AGAIN.
TO BE CONTINUED

AFTERWORD

Thank you for reading this to the end.

I like to sleep. Falling asleep right after I turn in my work is something that brings me pure joy. On a rare occasion, I actually get so excited I've finished my work that I feel wide awake. But usually I'm asleep in about three seconds after hitting my bed. Well, that's an exaggeration, but I think I'm asleep within a minute. Of course I never set an alarm and sleep as much as I want. Looking at the clock when I wake up is another perk. Because when I wake up, I get that nice feeling of having slept so much. I even enjoy that heavy feeling I get when I've slept too much. So it's a little sad when I gradually move back into my usual cycle. It's not that I want to stay sluggish forever, but I feel like someone's telling me that my fun is over. I just realized that I always work up until the very last second for this blissful sleep.

I'll see you in the next volume!

Io Sakisaka

The other day, I found a notebook in my desk drawer labeled "Notes for Stories." I opened it, wondering what it contained. It was completely blank. Not a single word. But the "Notes for Stories" on the cover was written with conviction. It made me laugh.

I found two of them.

I really hope a third doesn't turn up.

Io Sakisaka

Born on June 8, Io Sakisaka made her debut as a manga creator with *Sakura, Chiru*. Her series *Strobe Edge* and *Ao Haru Ride* are published by VIZ Media's Shojo Beat imprint. *Ao Haru Ride* was adapted into an anime series, and *Love Me, Love Me Not* was made into an animated feature film. In her spare time, Sakisaka likes to paint things and sleep.